Campaigns for peace

*This book is dedicated to all those,
in Britain and throughout the world,
who have campaigned for peace
in the twentieth century*

Campaigns for peace:
British peace movements in the twentieth century

EDITED BY RICHARD TAYLOR
AND NIGEL YOUNG

Manchester University Press

Published by Manchester University Press
Oxford Road, Manchester M13 9PL, UK

Distributed exclusively in the USA and Canada
by St. Martin's Press, Inc.
Room 400, 175 Fifth Avenue, New York, NY 10010, USA

British Library cataloguing in publication data
Campaigns for peace: British peace movements in the twentieth century.
1. Peace—Societies, etc—History
2. Antinuclear movement—Great Britain
—History
I. Taylor, R.K.S. II. Young, Nigel
327.1'72'0941   JX1908.G7

Library of Congress cataloging in publication data applied for

ISBN 0 7190 1829 7 *hardback*

Photoset in Linotron Sabon with Syntax
by Northern Phototypesetting Co., Bolton
Printed in Great Britain
by Billings & Son, Worcester

Contents

Preface and acknowledgements

The idea for this book was first suggested by John Banks of Manchester University Press and we are grateful to him both for this and for his continued support, and forbearance, during the preparation of the text.

We would also like to thank all contributors for their co-operation and valuable comments; and all those numerous individuals and organisations who provided material and information for the book.

Several people have had to cope with the typescripts, but particular thanks are due to Liz Dawson for her efficient and quick work in the final stages.

This has not been an easy book to write and edit, not least because one of us – Nigel Young – has been mainly based in the USA since 1985 and many of the consultations have had to be in rushed meetings in airports or over the transatlantic telephone. We are more than usually indebted, therefore, to Jenny Taylor and Antonia Young for their support and forbearance.

Richard Taylor
Nigel Young
1986

Notes on contributors

Richard Taylor, b. 1945 (MA Oxford, PhD Leeds), is Director of Extramural Courses and Senior Lecturer in the Department of Adult and Continuing Education, University of Leeds. After reading PPE at Oxford he worked at the University of Lancaster before moving to Leeds in 1970. From 1973 to 1983 he was warden of the Adult Education Centre in Bradford, and from 1982 to 1985 co-ordinator of the Pioneer Work programme of community-based adult education. He has been involved in the Peace Movement since 1959 and has researched and published widely in the field. His five co-authored books include *The Protest Makers: the British Nuclear Disarmament Movement of 1958 to 1965, Twenty years on* (Pergamon, 1980, with Colin Pritchard), and his doctoral thesis analysed the politics of the Peace Movement of the late 1950s and early 1960s. His other publications include books and articles on adult and continuing education, social work, the contemporary British Peace Movement, peace education, and various aspects of radical politics in modern Britain. He is married with two daughters and a son.

Nigel Young, b. 1938 (MA Oxford, PhD California, Berkeley), is Director of the Peace Studies program and Professor of Peace Studies at Colgate University, Hamilton, New York. He has been involved in studying and participating in peace movements since the 1950s, both in Britain and in other parts of Europe and North America. Since 1970 he has been active in developing peace studies in Higher Education and was a founder member of Bradford University's School of Peace Studies, where he was Reader. After studying modern history at Oxford (1956–60), he worked full time for CND before returning to research and teaching. He completed his doctoral thesis, 'War resistance and the nation state', at the University of California, Berkeley (1963–68). This was accompanied by activity against the Vietnam War. He has taught at the Universities of Birmingham, Bradford, California, Munster, Oslo, at Earlham College and now at Colgate. His extensive writing in the field includes books and articles on the New Left (*An Infantile Disorder? The crisis and decline of the New Left*, Routledge and Kegan Paul, 1976), war resistance, peace movements, peace strategy and peace education. Recent research on peace movements has been conducted as Senior Research Fellow at the International Peace Research Institute in Oslo, Norway. He was active in END and travels widely from his home bases in the Yorkshire Dales and central New York. He is married with three daughters.

Martin Ceadel (b. 1948) is Fellow and Tutor in Politics at New College, Oxford. He is author of *Pacifism in Britain 1914–1945: the defining of a faith* (Oxford University Press, 1980), and of various articles on the twentieth-century British Peace Movement, on which he is also writing a general history. His latest book is a theoretical work, *Thinking about Peace and War* (Oxford University Press, 1987).

Peter van den Dungen (b. 1948) is Lecturer in the School of Peace Studies at the University of Bradford and is a graduate of Johns Hopkins University. His doctoral thesis, in war studies, was from the University of London in 1975. He is the author of a number of short monographs such as *Foundations of Peace Research* and *The Making of Peace: Jean de Bloch and the First Hague Peace Conference*. He is also editor of *West European Pacifism and the Strategy for Peace*, (Macmillan, 1985).

Josephine Eglin (b. 1951) is a graduate of the LSE and Durham University. She has researched the history of the Women's Peace Movement, at the School of Peace Studies, Bradford University, and has published articles and reviews in various journals. She is a member of CND and of the Women's Peace Alliance. She currently teaches in a secondary school but is making her escape plans.

David Ormrod (b. 1945) lectures in Economic and Social History at the University of Kent at Canterbury. He is author of *English Grain Exports and the Structure of Agrarian Capitalism* (Hull University Press, 1985) and of various essays and articles on commercial history in the early modern period and on the social history of religion. He has participated in several peace actions co-ordinated by Christian CND at American nuclear bases in Britain.

Michael Randle (b. 1933) was a member of the Direct Action Committee Against Nuclear War and Secretary of the Committee of 100 from 1960 to 1961. He was sentenced to eighteen months' imprisonment for his part in organising the 'sit-down' at Wethersfield USAF base. He is a council member of the War Resisters International and, since 1980, has been co-ordinator of the Alternative Defence Commission.

Martin Shaw (b. 1947) lectures in Sociology at Hull University. His books include *Marxism and Social Science* (Pluto, 1975) and *The Dialectics of War: An Essay in the Social Theory of War and Peace* (Pluto, 1987) and he has edited *War, State and Society* (Macmillan, 1984), *Marxist Sociology Revisited* (Macmillan, 1985), and (with Colin Creighton) *The Sociology of*

War and Peace (Macmillan, 1987). He has been active in END and CND since 1980.

1

Introduction

MARY KALDOR

The biggest demonstration against Cruise and Pershing II missiles took place in the autumn of 1983. There were demonstrations in Bonn, Rome, The Hague, London, Oslo, Helsinki, Copenhagen, Paris, and Brussels. Altogether, some five million people took to the streets. In Finland and Holland, the demonstrators represented some five per cent of the total population.

This remarkable outburst of transnational public sentiment could be said to have marked the beginning of a new kind of movement. Peace groups emerged all over Europe in 1980–83 and spread to North America, Australia and New Zealand. Although the Peace Movement has had less public impact since the deployment of Cruise and Pershing missiles, at any rate in Western Europe, its numbers have continued to grow. Peace camps, various forms of non-violent direct actions, courses and discussions about peace issues, new books and magazines, films, plays and concerts have all contributed to the creation of what might be described as an emerging peace culture in our society. In Britain, for example, there have been over 7,000 arrests of peace activists for symbolic actions like wire-cutting or daubing paint on missiles over the last two years. Local councils, accounting for over half the population of Britain, have declared themselves nuclear-free zones; to implement the nuclear-free zone policy, they refuse to participate in civil defence exercises and they undertake programmes of public education about the effects of nuclear war and related questions.

This book describes the historic roots of the new Peace Movement in Britain. While, undoubtedly, the new peace activists were able to rediscover and learn from some important peace traditions in British history, they faced an entirely novel historical context. The context was one, as the editors point out, of threatened species destruction, or exterminism, as E. P. Thompson has called it.[1] The danger has been with us since 1945. And yet it was only as the first post-atomic generation approached middle age that the new Peace Movement came into being. It seems, therefore, that it was not so much fear of nuclear war as such that mobilised so many people. Rather, it could be attributed to a growing sense of disillusionment with the conventional political process. Peace activists became increasingly aware that political institutions are inadequate for the task of nuclear decision-making and this seemed to reflect a deeper malaise in current forms of social organisation. These concerns were especially important in Europe, where decisions about nuclear war, about life and death, would not be taken by European leaders, let alone on the basis of public or parliamentary discussion.

Miroslav Pecujlic has used the term 'social exterminism', by which he means that the danger of the arms race is species destruction, not just through nuclear war itself, but equally through a slow process of what he calls social involution, the reversal of civilisational progress.[2] Nuclear weapons were the consequence of the application of science and technology to destruction. Since the Second World War, nearly half the world's scientific and technological resources have been devoted to military purposes. New conventional and chemical weapons have been developed that are nearly as destructive in both human and environmental terms as nuclear weapons. The new American binary nerve gas programme is likely to lead to the militarisation of new areas of biochemistry, especially genetics, with unthinkable results.

And while the art of destruction is perfected, the art of living, it can be argued, is gradually lost. The fear of species destruction, the permanent wartime atmosphere generated by the arms race, can be said to interfere with the normal functioning of democracy: freezing politics, entrenching institutions and narrowing the space for human and social creativity.

Hence the problem is not simply the abolition of nuclear weapons. The problem is one of social relationships. How are we to restructure our institutions, our ways of organising ourselves, so that the fruits of civilisational progress are enjoyed by 'the last man', to quote Gandhi? Peace activists put considerable emphasis on participation. Terms like 'empowerment' or 'control over life and our lives', some of which were drawn from the Women's Movement, are fundamental to the new discourse. Self-determination, in both a personal and political sense, seems to be a central tenet of the New Peace Movement, especially in Europe.

The interest in democracy is not, of course, new. As this book shows, many of these ideas were present in earlier movements, especially the war resistance movement. Clifford Allen, quoted in one of Nigel Young's chapters, objected to the 'claim of the state to dispose of a man's life against his will'. Many peace activists identified the link between war and militarisation and political authoritarianism. The totality of the First World War and the invention of the bomber, which so influenced the inter-war Peace Movement, were intimations of what was to come.

What is new, however, in the early 1980s is the fusion of these other traditions – feminist, socialist, libertarian, Christian, conservationist – so that the peace issue is coming to displace other issues in the way we perceive the world and its problems. In the eighteenth and nineteenth centuries, a class perspective came to dominate both social theory and political institutions, and class was defined in relation to material production. Political parties were class parties and both past and present were interpreted, not just by Marxists, in class terms. Social relationships that were formed outside the production process – the state, households, nature – were viewed as dependent upon or subsidiary to class politics. New social movements have emerged in the 1960s and 1970s, in an *ad hoc* fashion, aimed at transforming and restoring the centrality of these other relationships – women (households), Greens (nature), peace and human rights (the state).

The Peace Movement is fundamentally about the social relationships that constitute the state. The peace issue encompasses the balance of institutions that comprise the state (warfare versus welfare), how the state relates to other states (peace and war), and how the state relates to society (democracy, accountability, and empowerment). It is about finding new political ways of relating to each other, in contrast to the earlier emphasis on economic relationships. Peace activists share with human rights activists in Eastern Europe, especially Solidarity in Poland, the view that their task is not to capture state power but to transform it. The Peace Movement will succeed when peace demands are put into practice, not when peace leaders achieve political office.

It is this new way of seeing global problems that is coming to displace the earlier economistic definitions. This is not to suggest that problems like starvation or unemployment are not important. On the contrary, they are intrinsic to the concept of social exterminism. Even if not a single nuclear shot is fired, millions will die by the end of the century from economic or ecological disaster. The point is that what is required is not so much an adjustment to economic relationships, either the market or the central plan, as a radical transformation of political structures. Therefore the poor, the dispossessed, the powerless, share a common platform. Peace activists are also struggling against global poverty.

What this means in practice, how to articulate a philosophy and appropriate organisational forms around the wide-ranging, specific and random demands of the peace movements, is something we are only beginning dimly to learn. This book explores the various strands, historically and politically, that have constituted the twentieth-century Peace Movement in Britain and analyses the nature of this movement. It will thus be of relevance and importance for all those who, whether they are Peace Movement supporters or not, are concerned about the Movement in Britain that evolved to campaign for a radical change in political strategies and cultural attitudes towards the achievement of peace – the most central issue of our time. And, more specifically, the book will also help those of us actively engaged in the Peace Movement to stand back and look at ourselves and our past and will, therefore, make an important contribution to this learning process.

References

1 E. P. Thompson *et al.*, *Exterminism and the Cold War*, New Left Books, London, 1982.
2 Miroslav Pecujlic, 'The Other Europe', paper presented at the UNU Conference on East–West Relations and Europe, Amsterdam, October 11–13, 1985.

2

Tradition and innovation in the British Peace Movement: towards an analytical framework

NIGEL YOUNG

Introduction

As the author of one of the chapters in this book remarks, it is difficult to talk of the British Peace Movement because of the range of definitions of the term 'peace', and the range of organisations and ideologies associated with the word, with a widely divergent set of objectives and traditions. One must go further than this and add that the idea of a single continuous Peace Movement in Britain is difficult to sustain because of the major discontinuities over the past 200 years. There have been periods when not only was public activity on peace issues reduced to a minimal level, but when some of the organisations and even intellectual traditions faded away. It is also the case that even in the periods of mass activity, such as those associated with the Campaign for Nuclear Disarmament between 1958 and 1963, and 1980 and 1985, no one organisation ever captured or totally 'represented' the Peace Movement. There were always large segments of the Peace Movement – for example the Committee of 100 in the 1960s (see Chapter 7) and the Women's Peace Movement in the 1980s (see Chapter 10) – which operated largely autonomously, despite some overlap of support.

This study represents a sampling of different dimensions of the Peace Movement (even, to some extent, different peace movements) at different periods. The themes, traditions and periods analysed and discussed are, in the editors' opinion, of central importance to an understanding of the development of the Peace Movement as a whole. By analysing critically and in detail both crucial periods (the inter-war years, for example, as in Chapter 5), *and* crucial ideological interrelationships (the Labour Party/Socialist/Marxist/Peace Movement relationships in all their complexity, for example, as in Chapters 4, 6 and 8), the study attempts to provide a solid core of sociological, political, and historical understanding of the British Peace Movement. Particular periods and themes *are* omitted: this does not purport to be an exhaustive chronological *history* of the Peace Movement. (Thus, for example, there is no sustained discussion of Welsh and Scottish anti-militarism, or of the pre-twentieth century religious and secular pacifist intellectual origins of the Peace Movement.)

The focus is, generally, on the more contemporary period, and upon analysis and critical discussion of the Movement and its problems, as opposed to detailed narrative description. Overall, the book delineates the main aspects of an extraordinarily diverse, deep-rooted and complex social and political phenomenon, and attempts to examine critically its successes and failures, its ideologies and politics, its problems and divisions, and, perhaps most important of all, its potential for the future.

This chapter attempts to place the study in context and create a set of classifications or typologies – as well as periodisations – into which the later chapters can be set.

Since the rest of the book is thematic rather than chronological and is concerned mainly with the post-1914 period, any kind of definition and analysis of the British Peace Movement needs to deal with the issue of classification and typologies of what would otherwise seem an amorphous, unmanageable and discontinuous phenomenon. I have tried to solve this methodological problem by looking at periodicity, and taking a 'one-shot photograph' of the movements as they had emerged in 1914 – and later deal with the range of intellectual approaches that had emerged in six major traditions by that period. And later in the chapter I illustrate some of the later traditions to emerge since 1914.

As a final footnote to the above it must be stressed that some groups and organisations which employ the term 'peace' are arguably not part of the Peace Movement at all, whilst a number of groups (feminists, ecologists, religious groups, civil libertarians, anti-nuclear power campaigners, humanists, and communitarians – as well as war-resistant groups outside the peace organisations) which do not directly associate with the term 'peace', perhaps *should* be included because of their participation in peace coalitions and recruitment into the Peace Movement.

To exclude 'peace through strength' groups or earlier German sympathisers, who each claimed to be 'for peace', are arbitrary exclusions. Indeed, some analysts have excluded pro-Soviet groups for the same reason. In the end, this issue cannot be other than subjective. I have suggested that, despite all the variety, one can see a core mainstream in the Peace Movement in Britain since 1820 (even when fundamentally divided as in 1833, 1914, 1939 and 1968). Moreover, all the groups and traditions mentioned (including the pro-Soviet groups) have collaborated in one of the broad coalitions at some stage or another. The same cannot of course be said of the Fascist appeasement groups or the pro-military lobbies.

Typologies and traditions

To some extent we deal here with three *main* time periods: the movement up and including the 1914–18 war; the inter-war period; and the post-nuclear period, especially after 1957. The Peace Movement must also be examined according to a classification of *traditions* or through a typology of *goals* and *objectives* (an approach deployed usefully by Bob Overy in his recent introductory survey 'How effective are peace movements?' London, 1984). The present book implicitly classifies according to traditions rather than objectives, in so far as it has chapters on the war resistance tradition (3), the Marxist– Socialist tradition (4), the liberal internationalist and pacifist traditions in the inter-war period (5), the Labourist tradition in the 1960s and beyond (6), the direct actionist tradition in approximately the same period (7), and the Feminist Peace Movement, both in its earlier 1900–20 and later post-1980 phases (10). The religious peace tradition, focused upon the later period, is dealt with in Chapter 9.

In Chapter 8 the role of the Marxist peace tradition in both its pro-Soviet and Trotskyist variants is examined in the period since 1945. In Chapter 3 I have dealt in part with the absolute pacifist and socialist anti-militarist traditions, and touch also on the anti-conscriptionist movement. One tradition *not* included here is the radical secular pacifism concerned with alternatives to Marxian models of change and influenced by Gandhi, although this is alluded to in Chapter 7 and others. Except for some reference in the chapter on the inter-war period, there is a relative neglect of the 'abolition of war' movement (the absolute pacifist and 'no more war' groups). In terms of periodisation there is a heavy emphasis on the movements of the late 1950s and early 1960s, in Chapters 6, 8, 7 and, to a lesser degree, 9 and 10. Chapter 11 takes a broader thematic concern and analyses critical perspectives on the Peace Movement and its activities from those *outside* its political culture. In the final chapter the editors raise the issue of a new emergent tradition: the issue of whether, in the 1980s, a new model is emerging that draws together most or all of these traditions in a synthesis influenced by the New Left of the 1960s and the revival of socialist anti-militarism and internationalism in END, reminiscent of the pre-1918 years.

The book includes analyses of movements against specific weapons (nuclear) and, implicitly, certain weapons systems; and a movement against military service (the No Conscription Fellowship or NCF in the First World War). There is relatively little on peace movements organised to oppose specific wars or on movements aiming at the abolition of war as such, though these are referred to in the chapters on the First World War and its aftermath.

The following typology of goals helps to clarify these distinctions within the Movement:

Goals and objectives in the Peace Movement

Opposition to specific weapons or weapon types	(Opposition to bombing civilians)	Anti-nuclear, poison gas
Opposition to weapons systems or foreign bases		Polaris, Trident, Cruise, US bases
Opposition to arms races		Pre-1914, the 1930s, the 1960s, the 1980s
Opposition to war as such		Pacifist, socialist anti-militarist, liberal 'abolition of war through international law arbitration'
Opposition to types of war		Nuclear, aggressive, 'imperialist'
Opposition to military service		Religious (conscientious objectors), socialist (capitalist wars), civil libertarian (liberal)

Opposition to specific wars	Boer, Algerian, Spanish, Vietnamese, Falklands (Malvinas)
Support for transformation of militarist structures	Socialist, anarchist, Gandhian movements, revolutionary and alternativist (Utopian)
Non-violent social change	Positive, programmatic peace scenarios

Since most peace movements have been coalitions they have included both single-issue and multi-issue or programmatic elements or groups: in other words they have rarely been restricted to any one element in the left-hand column above, and have contained individuals and organisations with differing priorities, goals and objectives usually reflecting different peace traditions.

Periodisation

It is hard to date the beginning of the British Peace Movement as a permanent presence in society as a secular political force. But the foundation of the Peace Societies in 1815, the conferences of the 1840s associated with Cobden, Bright, Cremer and Burritt are an appropriate indication of organisational continuity. Liberal free-trade and working-class internationalism (including the strike against war) go hand-in-hand in this period, reaching a new peak in the 1860s. This was not yet a mass peace movement. Nonetheless, public support for a wide range of peace-related organisations was already steadily growing by the 1880s – though whether one can yet talk of a *single* 'Peace Movement' at this stage is doubtful, since the groups and activities lacked inter-communication and were so diverse in character and aims, and in their widespread sources of social support.

After 1900 the Peace Movement moved through a series of at least six major cycles of peaks and troughs, both in terms of public support and in the numerical membership of peace organisations. There have been moments of mass activity on issues related to war and peace in which various strands and traditions, immensely diverse in character and often contradictory in their stances, have joined, or been precipitated into, broad coalitions with the politically mobilised from the mainstream of public life, to oppose war in general or, more typically, particular wars, weapons or arms races. At other times – in the 1860s,

1890s, 1915, the 1920s and 1930s – these divergent fragments have had little or no contact either with society at large or with one another and have all but disappeared from the historical scene.

Two major waves of mass involvement occurred in the decades immediately preceding and following the First World War, and again a third wave during the 1930s as fear of a further war grew. There were then three significant waves of support after 1945: on nuclear issues from 1957 to 1963, during the years of the Vietnam War (especially 1966–70), and again on nuclear issues from 1979 to 1984. There were other shorter periods of significant but less widespread activity (e.g. in the 1860s, 1880s and in the early 1950s).

In other words, the history of peace movements, as with so many other radical social and political movements in Britain and elsewhere, is one of discontinuities and divisions. Moments of great social significance and political leverage are followed by moments of paralysis, impotence and near terminal despair. The prophetic minorities remained even after war mobilisation (1915, 1940), and political sects and religious groups have sustained anti-war or anti-militarist positions even when these have lacked popular support; but certain traditions, such as the Feminist Peace Movement of the early twentieth century, or the libertarian–socialist, anti-militarist tradition of the same period, have appeared to be at times on the point of extinction. But as any historian of the Peace Movement knows, it is a great mistake to write off such traditions. The revival of the peace issue within the churches in Britain after 1980, for example, indicates the way in which the ethic of Christian pacifism (which underwent such grievous testing in the early 1940s, and was indeed abandoned by many of its staunchest adherents) may reappear on the political stage in revitalised forms in new situations.

The peace traditions

Detailed description of events and organisations after 1914, as well as peace ideas, will be left to later chapters. What will be suggested here, however, is the way in which the various *traditions* relate to the periodic waves or cycles of activism. This can be summarised as follows: from the seventeenth century onwards religious pacifism found a particular home in certain Nonconformist sects, particularly the Quakers (the Society of Friends). In the 1840s (and even more in the 1860s) such

Figure 1 – The mass peace movements in Britain, 1815–1981

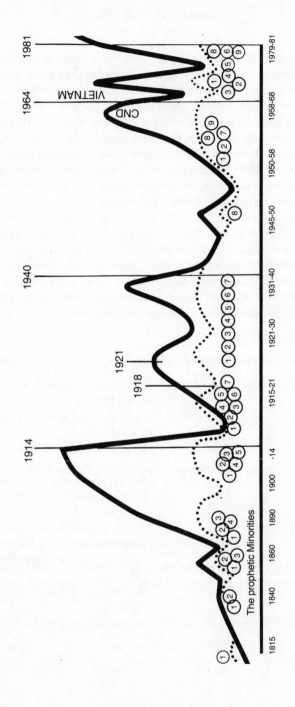

Notes: The numbers refer to the peace traditions (pp. 12–14).
The dotted line suggests their strength as a whole in the given periods.

groups became involved in liberal (and to a lesser extent, socialist) internationalist activity. At the grass-roots level, the Labour Movement and socialist intellectuals were becoming involved in anti-militarist agitation, which overlapped with the growing liberal–radical lobby, to prevent the introduction of conscription – already occurring elsewhere in Europe – in Britain. During the 1880s and 1890s this led to a marked proliferation of groups pursuing peace and internationalism – or opposing war and militarism – in different ways and for different reasons. There was, for example, agitation against imperialism, including the Boer War; and support for the liberal international conferences at the Hague, and for ideas of international law and arbitration. Socialists (especially non-Marxist Socialists) saw a hope of creating proletarian strategies based on cross-boundary solidarity through the Second International which, it was argued, could prevent a major European war. There was also a peace wing within the Women's Suffrage Movement which developed its own identity. Many Liberals identified with the cause of internationalism, civil liberties and anti-militarism.

The peace traditions: some examples/organisations

1. Religious peace traditions	Religious Pacifism, Society of Friends (Quakers), International Fellowship of Reconciliation, Pax Christi
2. Liberal internationalism	League of Nations Association, National Peace Council, Peace Society, Disarmament Campaigns, Union of Democratic Control
3. Anti-conscriptionism	(Single Issue lobbies) No Conscription Fellowship, War Resisters' International, NCCL, PPU
4. Socialist war resistance	War Resisters' International (END?)
5. Socialist internationalism	Second International, END

6. Feminist anti-militarism	WILPF, Women's Peace Party, Women Strike for Peace, Women for Peace, Women Oppose the Nuclear Threat, WFLOE
7. Radical (secular) pacifism	War Resisters' International, No More War Movement, Gandhian groups (DAC)
8. 'Cominternationalism'	Branches of the World Peace Council; peace committees
9. Nuclear disarmament	Campaign for Nuclear Disarmament, DAC, Committee of 100, END
10. The 'new Peace Movement'?	New Left, The Greens, END, 'Greenham women'

A Peace Movement encompassing the five or six most important traditions had emerged before August 1914. Moreover, as will be seen, there are continuities, both ideological and organisational, with these traditions into the current period. After 1915, a number of newer traditions accumulated, responding in part to the failure of the peace efforts to prevent the war of 1914–18 – and by the mid-century to the developments of new weapons (e.g. civilian mass bombing) and new political systems.

By 1918 new forms of internationalism had emerged which were reflected in the International Fellowship of Reconciliation (religious), the secular pacifist War Resisters' International (WRI – radical pacifists and conscientious objectors), the Women's International League for Peace and Freedom (formed in 1915 at The Hague) and the Third International (Comintern) founded in 1919 – the Soviet-controlled successor to the Second Socialist International. The International Peace Bureau in Geneva, formed before the war, attempted to co-ordinate the more liberal peace organisations. Support for the League of Nations was mobilised through the League of Nations Unions (liberal internationalist). A coalition of pacifist and socialist anti-militarists was involved in the 'No More War movement' during the 1918–30 period (see Chapter 5).

In the 1930s the pacifists formed their own separate organisation, the Peace Pledge Union (PPU), affiliated to the WRI and the older National Peace Council. The PPU was based on a formal pledge of renunciation of war as an institution, and was founded on individualistic, moralistic assumptions.

Yet another ingredient in the development of the various peace traditions was the systematisation of non-violent thought and action. By 1919 news of Gandhi's first major campaigns in India was being published in the British Peace Movement and identification with his philosophy of civil disobedience and alternative life-style began to influence parts of the Peace Movement, particularly its Utopian and Communitarian wing (represented by figures like Wilfred Wellock). In effect, this represented a pacifist alternative to orthodox Marxist views on the necessity for class conflict and thus violence to achieve social change, and provided a counter-example to the Leninist/Bolshevik experiences with which radical pacifists could identify. Even within Marxism there was a strong anti-militarist undercurrent: but there were in Britain no equivalents of Luxemburg and Liebknecht, and this tradition was thus largely overwhelmed by the influence of the Stalinist Comintern. (However, John MacLean's activities on Clydeside provide a significant, though small-scale, exception to this generalisation.)

The Peace Movement in 1914

By 1914, therefore, a series of maturing peace strands or traditions can be discerned: religious peace or pacifist ideas and groups (like the Friends), liberal internationalists, anti-conscriptionists, socialist internationalists, socialist anti-militarists and an embryonic Women's Peace Movement.

It may well be that, proportionate to the population and given the difficulties of communication, the range and intensity of peace and anti-war activity in the decade before the First World War was relatively greater than at any other period in British history. The reason for this was the great range of constituencies mobilised: women, trade unionists, educators and the professional middle class (Liberals), members of churches and religious groups, as well as anarchists, and socialist groups like the Independent Labour Party (ILP). This was not a single movement with a single goal, however, and 1914 had a traumatic impact on the Peace Movement, creating divisions throughout all sections of Peace Movement opinion.

The Women's Suffrage Movement divided between a pro-war majority, and an anti-war minority which included Socialists, Liberals and feminist pacifists. The Labour Movement was similarly divided: the ILP provided a strong base for opposition led by Keir Hardie, but even here there was a significant minority supporting the war. In the rest of the Labour Party, and the trade unions, the large *majority* supported the war. The anti-conscriptionists continued to oppose conscription (though even they became weakened and divided by 1915) but were not necessarily opposed to a voluntary war effort (indeed many encouraged voluntarism as an alternative). Liberals were divided between those who remained sceptical and critical of the war effort, and those (a large majority) who saw it as a struggle for liberal democracy and justice. The minority retained their concern with military influence in government (through the Union of Democratic Control), worried about the allied war aims, and opposed conscription. The churches, too, divided, with the large majority supporting or acquiescing in the war and even members of peace churches (e.g. Quakers) serving in some cases. The numbers of conscientious objectors, which ran into thousands (about 6,000 took an 'absolute resistance' stand against military service), were a tiny proportion of those who had opposed the idea of war before August 1914. Even the revolutionary Socialists were divided over tactics, whether to support partially this 'semi-progressive' war, to use it as a means to revolution, or to resist it altogether – inside or outside the army. The anarchists were dismayed when one of their international mentors, Kropotkin, announced in London his support for the allied cause.

Soon after the war started Keir Hardie died, after almost superhuman efforts to prevent the war; and with him the most significant anti-war leader amongst the Socialists in Britain was lost.

Thus, by 1915, the mass Peace Movement had shattered, leaving a series of prophetic fragments. But, rapidly, new cohesive groupings of those with a more dedicated anti-militarism emerged. The 'No Conscription Fellowship', bringing together Liberals like Russell, pacifists like Allen, and Socialists like Brockway, was formed to oppose both conscription and, by implication, the war (supporting conscientious objectors – COs). Many Quakers were COs or dedicated to oppose the continuance of the war and conscription. A minority of the Women's Movement supported the NCF or the ILP in its anti-war position and also included the idea of the international peace conference of women, organised across the warring frontiers in 1915 in The Hague. Internationalist Socialists and anti-militarists continued to preach an anti-war position inside and outside the ILP; and a significant number of Liberals continued to support the NCF or the UDC.

Given the atmosphere of 1914–16, outright denunciation of the war was difficult. Only as the casualties and war weariness grew, could further opposition emerge, though still with real risk. The campaign for conscientious objection as a right gathered strength once military service became compulsory in 1915, and forged a coalition of great significance for the future Peace Movement. Out of it a new radical pacifism emerged, involving a number of religious, ethical and political standpoints which characterised the COs themselves.

Nineteen-fourteen clearly demarcated those who were prepared to oppose war even after war mobilisation had occurred, from those who had tried to prevent the war, but did not refuse to support it.

The peace traditions: goals and objectives

It is now necessary to look a little deeper into the traditions that had emerged by the twentieth century as a prelude to looking at their contemporary counterparts in the nuclear era – since 1945.

Clearly, the religious peace tradition is the oldest of the major peace traditions and predates the growth of the concept of a peace movement as a secular and political force independent of churches or the representatives of states. Peace ideas in British Christianity certainly predate the Reformation, though they can be found in the less orthodox social undercurrents of the church and monastic movements which in some sense prefigure both the Anabaptist revolt and the cosmopolitan humanism of Erasmus, both of which had English counterparts. It was out of that crucible, and the civil war of the seventeenth century, that one group emerged which has played a virtually continuous role on peace questions in England, including a witness against war since the 1650s: the Society of Friends, or Quakers. The Quakers have had an influence on the sustenance and growth of the Peace Movement through more than 300 years in Britain that is truly remarkable and quite out of proportion to their size. Indeed, their activity is worth analysis, since it has combined a number of elements which were to remain part of the broader span of the Movement as it grew in the nineteenth century. There was, in the first place, the desire to resist war, or at least distance the religious community and the individual from the institution of war and the performance of military service. It thus laid one of the moral and political foundations for the 'civic right' of conscientious objection, a claim which secular liberal individualists, socialist war resisters, and members of other churches (including other peace sects) came to support in different ways, at different times, and to different degrees. The second dimension to Quaker activity was the search for the means of preventing war, through the reformed behaviour of states – peace plans, treaties and proposals, negotiations, international law and arbitration between all groups and peoples. This was to develop first in the concepts of civil disobedience, mediation, conflict resolution, and then non-violence.

This search was closely linked to a third dimension that remained general in peace movement activity and thought – a universalism, whether religious or humanistic, a cosmopolitan ethic that sprang from both the Enlightenment and religious ideals and a universal or transnational church. With the growth of socialism, a new form of this internationalist ethic joined these first two elements, to complete a peace view based on the relativity of national boundaries and frontiers, and the limitation of sovereignty of states. Whilst this lent unity neither on strategy nor ideology to the Peace Movement, it did lay the foundations for a simple lowest common denominator of action and aims – the survival of the species, the eventual elimination of war, and the ultimate unity of human society. It was this that spurred the long-delayed but deeply-rooted reaction to the nuclear arms race in the later twentieth century.

It was socialism also which coincided with a fourth element in the inspirational roots of the British Peace Movement – the necessity for social and human change, the view that the problem of war was linked to problems of economic injustice and political repression, to the selfishness of the narrow elites of powerful ruling groups, and national and imperial, as well as racial, chauvinism. This surfaced in the struggle against the causes of war as well as the opposition to expansionist national capitalism, slavery and serfdom – including compulsory military service. And for some – as for the more Utopian or radical Quakers and Utopian or libertarian Socialists – it involved centrally the struggle against the modern state (or nation state), which was seen as the embodiment of legitimised, centralised and territorialised violence.

All four of these elements were to remain after the mid-nineteenth century as part of the broad peace movement tradition, but also as controversial and contested elements in theory and practice. For example, to take the last element first; the legacy of the Enlightenment was acutely ambiguous as far as the vehicle of liberation and universalism was concerned. On the one hand it preached a globalism and internationalism that transcended the petty interests of given kings and territories. On the other, it suggested that the democratised republic (a people's state) might be a means of human progress. Liberal internationalists and socialist internationalists often differed only on the economic character or class character of the units that would make up the new peace order. For liberal internationalists peace would emerge with the abolition of tyranny and the spread of world trade. For Socialists war would disappear only when capitalism, imperialism, and the arms trade were overthrown by class struggle and social revolution. The workers would join hands across national boundaries, and socialist states would establish fraternal co-operative relations with one another, and eventually 'wither away'.

In the wake of the butchery of the Napoleonic Wars, these ideas jostled each other in a somewhat unresolved and kaleidoscopic scatter of peace societies and pressure groups. Whilst many of them remained religious in character, the secular development of modern ideological formulae began to play a more dominant role. The idea of a workers' strike against war was heard for the first time. With the French Revolution and the *levée en masse*, the reality both of the 'people's army' and the ambiguities of France's wars of liberation in Europe became apparent. The latent dilemmas of violent social change were answered in part by Utopian and communitarian views of social change without violence, or at least without resort to arms. From now on the Peace Movement would be divided over the ethics and issues of 'just wars', whether by progressive states or progressive oppositional groups – just as in the 1860s the Peace Movement, and indeed pacifists such as the Quakers, found themselves divided over a war that would emancipate black slaves in 1863.

Time and again in the nineteenth and twentieth centuries this pattern would be repeated. On each occasion (including 1914, 1936, 1940 and the late 1960s – over the Vietnam War) the Peace Movement would divide over whether a war was 'just' or 'progressive'; whether the evil to be overcome was any greater than the injustice and violence of the war; and whether military service – the 'democratisation of the means of violence' (by conscription) – might itself be a progressive phenomenon or lead to radical change.

Having analysed the core traditions of the Peace Movement and their historical genesis, attention can now be turned to the more contemporary period. Subsequent chapters in this study examine in some detail many of the central aspects of the contemporary (post-1945) Peace Movement. Here, attention is focused upon a profile of the British Peace Movement in the contemporary period – in the 1950s to the 1980s.

The contemporary Movement: fusion and fission

How far does the British Peace Movement of the latter half of the twentieth century represent a continuity with the past traditions, and how far does it represent an innovatory new model? How far is it unified as a movement – how far amorphous and fragmented?

Clearly, certain strands of the minority sects – the religious and secular pacifists, those in groups like the PPU, Pax Christi and FOR, the liberal internationalists in the UN associations, the socialist internationalists inside and outside the Labour Party, and the Communist internationalists of the World Peace Council – all remain clearly visible in the post-1945 period. Indeed, the Comintern-backed peace committees were a major force behind the short-lived but widespread Stockholm appeal movement of the 1950s.

Pacifism, both religious and secular, had been dealt a severe blow by the rise of Fascism and the failure to arrest the drift to war in the 1930s. After 1945, however, the implications of mass civilian bombing produced the beginnings of a new mood that absolutely rejected the use of atomic weapons, and interested itself in non-violence.

Agitation against conscription continued up to and during the Suez invasion of 1956, but conscription proper was phased out shortly afterwards. Anti-conscriptionists turned their attention to the plight of COs elsewhere and opposed various aspects of military training and recruitment and the role of troops in Ireland or the old colonies.

Socialist anti-militarism at the grass-roots had been largely subdued with the rise of the internationalist versions of social democracy, liberalism and Communism – though some echoes remained in the Labour Party and the New Left of the late 1950s. The legacy of Labourism and social democracy on the one hand and Soviet-oriented Marxism on the other, remained a deadening political burden on parts of the Peace Movement for nearly fifty years and have been part of the Cold War freeze.

The Women's Peace Movement had little more than organisational continuities with the movement of the early years of the century, and was not to reappear as a serious force in peace politics until the new Women's Peace Movement of the Greenham Common encampment and the feminist anti-militarist sentiment of the 1980s, expressed in groups like Women Oppose Nuclear Threat (WONT) and Women for Life on Earth (WFLOE), though women were active in the 1960s.

Another strand of importance was the social change-oriented wing of the pacifist movement which had identified with Gandhian ideas, communitarianism and alternative life-styles, and sometimes anarchism. In the 1960s this was closely allied to the direct action wing of the nuclear disarmament movement and led into the counter-cultural and alternative society dimensions of the Peace Movement and the later New Left and anti-nuclear power movements. The continuities with the ecology, feminist and anti-nuclear power movement of the 1970s are unmistakable and represent key dimensions in the revival of the mass Peace Movement after 1979. Gandhian ideas of civil disobedience, together with ideas of civilian resistance, flourished particularly in the Committee of 100, the radical wing of the Peace Movement in the early 1960s.

To talk of a new Peace Movement is thus to talk of a coalition of new and old elements.

The organisational forms of the Peace Movement in the mid-1980s express a reactivation of almost all the accumulation of older traditions and prophetic minorities. Religious peace groups active within the churches, and outside, helped produce the Church of England's shift. Liberal internationalists are active in UNA and the World Disarmament Campaign; independent Marxists, socialist internationalists and anti-militarists are prominent in the European Nuclear Disarmament campaign. And parts of CND are still dominated by unilateralists (nuclear pacifists). The radical secular pacifists grouped around *Peace News* and the peace camps, and the Feminist Peace Movement represented above all by the Greenham protest, have both a more prominent *and* a more integrated role in the contemporary Peace Movement. As before, the Communist internationalists have focused on the American alliance, the US bases and Euro-missiles, *but* with a Eurocommunist wing leaning towards a radically critical attitude to the USSR and its policies.

The one tradition that remains largely latent is the anti-conscriptionist wing – for obvious reasons – but even here the continuation of the PPU and other war resistant and absolutist groups represents a potential obstacle to any reintroduction of compulsory military service (even though favoured by some Socialists and others as an alternative to nuclear deterrence).

A striking innovation in the contemporary Peace Movement has been the formation of local coalitions of these elements around local issues but with an internationalist perspective. This represents a deepening and strengthening of the Movement's potential to unite different social constituencies and synthesise differing ideological emphases into a form of social programme. Certainly, some of the liberal and Communist internationalists would draw back from any idea of the peace movement taking on a social programme: they have their own. Equally, some religious and nuclear pacifists are not committed to the idea of the necessity of social change. At the core of the Movement, however, there is a belief in social transformation towards a juster and more 'globalist' society through local steps. And there is a belief that, at least in Britain, this change should and must be largely non-violent and unilateralist.

Within this very general consensus, the coalition of the Peace Movement masks considerable differences (as the Greens in Germany have shown). Attitudes to conventional defence, socialism, the Labour or other parliamentary parties, nuclear energy, radical separatist feminism, strategies for transnational change (including the issue of membership of NATO) – all these are contentious and unresolved issues and matters of tactics as well as principle. But to some extent one can talk of these as debates within a *single* international Peace Movement: a movement that is not exclusively British (or English), but both European and global, and both local and regional in a way that the Peace Movement has never been before.

One key problem, and not only in Britain, has been the tendency to narrow down the campaign to a purely national and single issue movement – focusing on one party (usually the Labour, or Communist Party), one weapon system (e.g. Cruise, the Neutron Bomb, or Trident), and one national political arena (i.e. 'little Englandism'). It is here that the new consciousness-raising and peace educational work of END has been most critical in sustaining a transnational and indeed global consciousness, a sense of the larger Europe – not just NATO or the EEC, but including the neutral and non-aligned nations, and Eastern Europe.

In different ways, and on different themes, the chapters that follow reveal part of the density and texture of this diverse and plural movement – the potential of its evolving and renewed traditions and the obstacles of its frozen and sectarian ones. For a peace movement that can look at and know its sociology and history more fully and more critically such an exercise helps it to be a more mature and sophisticated movement, and potentially a more successful one. Indeed, the ability to understand itself is a key to further advance.

Moreover, the Peace Movement in Britain has been a key part of the social and political fabric of twentieth-century society. And at certain critical periods, not least the 1980s, peace issues and the moral and political campaigning of the Peace Movement have been of central importance. To understand British society and politics in the twentieth century, therefore, an analysis of the Peace Movement, in all its complexity, is essential.

This chapter has attempted to set the scene for that recovery of peace movement history and sense of long-term strategy and context that it has often lacked. The other chapters in this book may aid that critical understanding and lead to a fuller appreciation of the multi-dimensional nature of the Movement, both past and present.

3

War resistance and the British Peace Movement since 1914

NIGEL YOUNG

Introduction

War resistance in Britain first became a public political act with the first refusal of compulsory military service in 1916. It was certainly not, however, the first such refusal, since various forms of military duty and militia service had been imposed over many centuries, in feudalism, during the Civil War, and impressment and militia duty after that. Until the emergence of explicitly war-refusing religious sects (e.g. the Quakers in the 1650s – including many ex-soldiers) the documentation of such resistance is scattered. The basis of refusal was often religious (the claim to exemption on religious grounds was a basis for conscientious objection) but could also be ethnic – the refusal of minorities to serve an English (London-based) military order. It could be economic or humanitarian: the loss of a son to impressment or feudal levy could mean depletion of a family labour force. Thus the history of war refusal before and except for the Quakers, remains sketchy until the introduction of conscription in 1915. In other countries, war resistance, not explicitly linked to the Peace Movement, has a much older history reaching back many centuries, and indeed to early Christianity.

The other explicitly war-resistant movement was socialist anti-militarism, that wing of the socialist and Labour movements (usually part of the non-Marxist, or anarchist-influenced wing) which opposed conscription, a militia or other forms of socialised military service. This expressed itself in such acts as leafleting army barracks (or the Woolwich arsenal) in the later nineteenth century, urging soldiers to desert, and no longer serve the ruling group of the day.

This other wing of war resistance was not entirely separate from the pacifist and religious wing. Quakers often combined a libertarian and spiritual detachment from secular power, with a social and political involvement – fusing 'witness' and activism. In so far as Quakers, and some other Protestant groups, overlapped with early socialist ideas or later the 'social gospel', the dividing line between 'religious' and 'political' objection to war became more and more difficult to draw.[1] By the twentieth century the emergence of socialist secular objection on a larger scale meant that such claims as rights of political exemption *did* directly impinge on state power.

Moreover, war resistance in many of its phases was closely linked to notions of egalitarian communal democratism. Since the seventeenth century, those groups most involved in anti-war activity were those also most closely linked to experiments in small-scale democracy of a participatory kind. The abolition of established political relations in favour of a non-violent commonwealth, potentially to be constructed here and now – the radical and democratic (if millennial) dream of such groups for over three centuries – is formally expressed in communitarian experiments, in libertarian ideologies of mutual aid, and in the acts of 'holy disobedience' that link such figures as George Fox, the early Quaker, with the thousands of individual 'non-co-operators' who followed.

Such experiments can be seen as continuous with other (e.g. nineteenth-century) alternative institutions; or later communitarian impulses and experiences (such as the Bruderhof) amongst war resisters in Britain during the Second World War.[2] They were conceived of as voluntarist bases for emerging values and action; and occasionally overlapped with previous religiously inspired and migrant communitarianisms.[3]

As a pacifist, Aldous Huxley argued in the 1930s, 'religion can have no politics except the creation of small-scale societies of chosen individuals outside and on the margin of the essentially unviable large-scale societies whose nature dooms them to self-frustration and suicide'.

Like their medieval counterparts, latter-day Christian anti-militarists tended to refer back to the early pre-Constantinian church's distanced relationship with both the state and idolatrous military service, as exemplifying an approach more clearly commensurate with the Gospel's teaching.[4] By the sixteenth and seventeenth centuries the new marginal middle classes in Europe, who in places came to constitute a civilian militia, and in others were still inspired by the Sermon on the

Mount, followed early Christian precepts of 'non-resistance' to evil. It was from here that such millennial and Nonconformist sects as the Quakers emerged.

As one Quaker put it, 'war destroys that which is God's, and invades things that have not been committed to Caesar'.[5] But unlike other sects, deriving their spiritual dynamic from Anabaptism, the Quakers did not see the state necessarily as an evil. Until the nineteenth century, Quakers were excluded by law from public office in England, and this civic exclusion encouraged a retreatist rather than rebellious attitude to politics once toleration had been established (1689).

But war resistance in the early decades brought persecution. 'Sufferings' was the term used by Friends to denote persecution; for conscientious witness (e.g. against militia or army service). Even the emergence of the concept of 'conscience', or the Quakers' 'inner light', was a notion that Dr Johnson pronounced 'entirely incompatible with religious and political security'.[6] Moreover, in seventeenth-century Protestantism, the prevalent idea of 'the priesthood of all believers'[7] was seen to encourage both ideas of participatory democracy and a 'fetish of conscience'.

Most of the problems to be faced by religious nonconformity with the new states (emerging partly *through* the impact of Protestantism) are prefigured in seventeenth-century England. Backed by a new army, English Puritanism in the 1650s forcibly contained its left wing and, for a while, appeared to be politically successful. But as it split further and suffered reverses, it introduced in the process a predictable recession in individual liberties, and a by now familiar pattern of authoritarian response to the multiplying demands for the rights of groups and consciences, at least of those who had helped make the revolution.[8]

However, the Interregnum and Caroline Restoration do not mark an end to these connections. For two more centuries, free churches 'influenced British political life' both by 'the genius of their inner spirit and by the challenge which they steadily offered to all policies of conformity'.[9] This is evidenced by their continuing role in dissent and civil libertarianism.

The politicisation of religious dissent that matches the spiritualisation of political radicalism finds an end point in secular ideology. In Britain there are accounts of Redcoats being jeered at in the streets – even late in the nineteenth century – not least as symbols of ruling-class tyranny, agents of oppression and state injustice, or of an alien

(English) elite.

The major military campaigns of the Peninsular War under Welling-ton were conducted whilst similar operations at home were prepared to deal with political agitation amongst working people. Indeed, the deployment of troops at home was even more extensive[10] and, later, during the Chartist upsurge in Britain, artillery displays were given to radical gatherings; almost everywhere, service as soldiers taught workers the 'hopelessness of armed resistance':[11] more troops were often needed for domestic policing deterrence, or in order to prevent working-class insurrection, or strike-breaking, than for external action.

Conscription and resistance

It was the nineteenth-century spread of the concept of *compulsory military service* which persuaded many pacifists to make conscription their prime political target.[12] Confrontation with the state also pro-vided repressive conditions in which pacifism rediscovered its sectarian roots. 'Conscription was the occasion for this confrontation and redis-covery'.[13] Yet significantly, it was also where universal conscription had *not* yet been introduced (as in Britain) that such peace and war resistance groups were able to gain and sustain the strongest foo-tholds.[14] In the Protestant democracies liberal freedoms aided anti-war minorities, and allowed pacifism to survive with some continuing statutory concessions to conscience.

Even before 1915, one can distinguish between the uniformity of response to conscription of peace churches of 'collectivist' type, and the variety of those of a more 'individualist' kind, like the Quakers. Based on conscience, such positions, taken up by Quakers and others in England, had earlier opposed the militia acts of the eighteenth and nineteenth centuries.[15] Despite such sentiments, there were other lob-bies at work. Following earlier conscriptionist campaigns the British National Service League (1902) was influential on the new organs of mass communication,[16] and prepared the way for war. Indeed, the pro-conscriptionist lobby was a high-level coalition (including news-papermen) of Conservative politicians and military men who cam-paigned, in the two decades before 1914, for compulsory service. One by-product of this was a media silence on alternative options to con-scription (and later on that of 'conscientious objection') which was long to remain a key factor. This lobby gained a degree of popular support, especially through its use of press stories, but never sustained a broad base. Yet after 1914, with an ill-informed wartime population, it was possible for the media to gain substantial influence.

This interpretation appears to be confirmed by the dramatic events in Britain during 1914–15. In the first twenty-two months of the war, nearly 2,700,000 men 'freely' volunteered for the army (i.e. joined-up before compulsory service was introduced).[17] Yet this view would over-emphasise both the degree of voluntarism and exaggerate the stability of such allegiances generally. As will be shown, the introduction of universal conscription in Britain (clearly foreshadowed in the national registration of 1915) was extensively opposed. Asquith[18] showed himself well aware of the 'objection to compulsion which now so widely exists'. This objection, a substantially libertarian opposition to conscription, represented a response to major political change in Britain. The crisis of 1915, resulting in the introduction of universal manhood service, signified 'the abandonment not only of familiar military tactics, but also of cherished beliefs in the extent of individual freedom and the limits of government control'.[19]

The state, ultimately trusting compulsion as against voluntarism, increasingly abandoned classic liberalism and as a result reinforced the connection between those who opposed the war and wartime libertarians (for example, groups such as the British Union of Democratic Control, or UDC).[20] In the first decades of the twentieth century, most of the opposition to conscription by alliances of Liberals, Socialists and pacifist reformers and libertarians – as well as organised labour – was based on the belief that conscription represented a nationalist, anti-progressive reaction to change. Before the First World War, most trade unions, as much as civil liberties groups, feared the loss of rights presaged by compulsory military service: to pacifists like Keir Hardie 'militarism and democracy' could not be blended: conscription was the 'badge of the slave'.[21] Many Socialists who opposed conscription argued that militarism and democracy were incompatible: 'compulsory military service', Hardie insisted, 'is the negation of democracy'.[22]

In Britain, the consistent opposition of the Independent Labour Party (ILP) was also based on the view that such compulsory service could 'only be for the purpose of obtaining a powerful reactionary weapon which would continually menace the future industrial and political developments of democratic institutions': conscription was the 'thin end of the wedge of Tsarism',[23] it would 'gravely imperil the foundations of British civil and political liberty' which constituted 'the main difference between the British and continental nations'.[24]

There is evidence that the pressure for conscription was indeed linked to a social reaction which opposed the expansion of the number of voters, liberal reform and the advance of organised labour.[25] Certainly the political orientation of the National Service League had been, and remained, overwhelmingly conservative.[26] Hardie's remark that 'no liberty-loving people would tolerate having old forms of servitude like compulsory service forced upon them',[27] confirms the alternative libertarian synthesis represented by 'socialist opposition to militarism, to restrictions on personal freedom', and to freedom to 'engage in undemocratic diplomacy'.[28] The UDC's argument against conscription, on the other hand, stressed that it was 'not in the nation's best interest', and unnecessary for its needs.

War resistance in Britain: 1914–18

A study of opposition to conscription in Britain in this period initially identifies four major categories of resistance: the Liberal Party in parliament; organised labour (the unions); the left wing of the new Labour Party (especially the ILP); and religious pacifists and peace sects. Of these, only the latter two categories sustained their opposition in any systematic or committed fashion after the introduction of conscription.

A fifth group, which, whilst it was not mobilised on the issue as a political force of opposition in England, nevertheless represented a significant and hostile constituency – as well as an unpredictable one – was the Irish community, both in Ireland and in England. Together, these five elements, had they been united in early 1915, might well have effectively prevented conscription. Had the measure been introduced at this stage, at the very least they would have disastrously disunited the country at a crucial juncture in the war.

Britain only endorsed the introduction of conscription when these major sources of opposition had each been separately defused, assuring a solid parliamentary majority.[29] During the war the various anti-war traditions had overlapped, coexisted and fused, or been renewed. War resisters in prison included religious pacifists and anti-conscriptionists. (In Britain, where conscription was introduced in 1915–16, they were organised into the No Conscription Fellowship (NCF), an organisation headed by Fenner Brockway, Bertrand Russell and Clifford Allen, and socialist anti-militarists of various hues.) But despite their attempt to co-ordinate actions against conscription, Liberals and libertarians alike were politically outmanoeuvred, lacking the ruthless and manipulative approach to politics and public propaganda of the conscriptionists; as a result, voluntarism and pacifism were continually driven on to the defensive.[30]

From January 1916, the NCF in Britain campaigned to obtain the repeal of the Military Service Act, and up until the actual introduction of conscription, it acted mainly as a pressure group on government, shifting only gradually towards more radical and extra-parliamentarist tactics as the end of voluntarism came nearer.

But for many, including Liberals in Britain, a conscript army was conceived of as being a basically civilian body organised for emergency purposes in wartime under military discipline – but for a limited period; there was still strong suspicion of continuing service after the end of hostilities.[31] But as early as 1914, it became obvious even to many British Liberals that military victory would depend on 'the efficient mobilisation and control of the nation's resources; once this truth was accepted, a system of voluntary recruiting would become an anachronism'.[32] It was in this period that the notion of using military modes of manpower control first gained importance.

A particular problem in England arose for the First World War authorities with an Irish immigrant population of about one million, amongst whom Sinn Fein's ideas were prevalent. The conscription of 1916, during a period of growing tension in Southern Ireland, did not extend to Ireland; anti-English feeling would have made such an imposition a hazardous undertaking.[33] The attempt in 1918 to include Ireland in the provisions of the National Service Act was faced by total non-co-operation, and abandoned. In Britain itself it was the uneven course of *prosecutions* for conscientious objection that tended to limit the legitimacy of legal compulsion after 1915.[34] Welsh conscription was a noticeable variant. Subsequently, Northern Ireland too was exempted, as a whole, from British conscription during the Second World War.[35]

Conscription was relatively unfamiliar; and mass involvement was new enough for governments still to be uncertain as to how 'subjects would react to a declaration of war'.[36] It has been argued that Asquith's policy in the years 1914–16 was determined by a belief in the formidable character of opposition to conscription at that time.[37] Britain had no previous experience of mass conscript armies, and merely an influx of new recruits presented an enormous problem of discipline and control that many modern armies have only partially solved.

It came as a shock to many Liberals that it was a coalition government with Liberal leadership that introduced conscription (and that, prior to the formation of this coalition, the Liberal Government had conducted the war mobilisation at the expense of ordinary freedoms). The Editor of the *Economist,* Francis Hirst, expressed the fear that conscription would bring with it 'the substitution of martial law for trial by judge and jury' and destroy 'self-government'; indeed, he criticised Morel and the UDC for failing to make this connection.[38] The leader of the more radical and militant NCF, Clifford Allen, called 'the claim of the state to dispose of a man's life against his will . . . the most insidious danger that can confront a free people', and attacked the Government for fighting a war 'which you can only win by the compulsion of unwilling men and the persecution of those who are genuine'.[39]

In England, unlike continental Europe, few now defended conscription on libertarian grounds (i.e. that there was less danger of a conscript army being deployed to uphold domestic tyranny than a permanent professional force).[40] Rather, libertarian, Liberal and Social Democrat alike insisted that military organisation *per se* implied authoritarianism and hierarchy, and a latent negation of all democratic values. The introduction of military modes of obedience into civil life provided an added basis for liberal war opposition, and converted most pacifists into civil libertarians. Wartime situations revealed a tendency to abandon trappings of legality and democracy, suspension of the 'rules of the game', the use of martial power and the suspension of liberties (as well as growing jingoistic appeals); in these moments of potential national solidarity, governments seem to fear most the sovereignty of the people.[41] Despite mass support for war in Britain in 1914, the Government combined secret diplomacy and decision-making with domestic repression. The new libertarian mood, which linked war to political authoritarianism, was reflected in the political stance of many ordinary war resisters.

Official secrecy in Britain, as well as wartime economic controls, with the whole fabric of government centred on the War Cabinet, was 'brought into existence without the political participation of the public or the endorsement of the parliamentary parties'.[42]

The syntheses of segments of pre-1914 pacifism with dissenting libertarian attitudes forged by the war, were accompanied by a growing concern with the 'general militarisation of civil life, along authoritarian Prussian' lines.[43] Trevelyan referred to the centralising wartime state of the Liberal Government as a 'Prussian system', and in opposing conscription, libertarian oppositionists were quick to point out that it had earlier developed in partnership with serfdom in Eastern Europe and Prussia.

The UDC (1914), which was the principal opponent of these encroachments of 'Prussianism' on British life, noted in particular the degree to which the methods of the enemy were being copied in the conflict: censorship, compulsion, and regimentation. Snowden of the ILP observed that it was the state's intention to 'suppress every opinion which is disagreeable to them', 'putting the intellect of the citizen in chains' (Morel).[44] *Habeas corpus* was suspended; in Britain, under Regulation 18b, indefinite imprisonment without trial was made legal and war resisters were confined under its provisions.[45] Pacifists within the established churches in the First World War were dissenting minorities.[46] Refusal emerged once more. But within the Quaker 'sub-culture' during the First World War in Britain there was a tremendous variation in response, from absolutist resisters to early Quaker volunteers for front-line service in August 1914.[47]

Conscientious objection in Britain in the First World War, although described as a 'minor but intractable problem', was one which was said to exercise 'the mind of the Prime Minister' (Asquith), even at the height of crisis.[48]

Fewer than one in five British conscientious objectors in the First World War would accept military control. Of about 16,500 'official' COs, 3,000 carried out non-combatant duties,[49] about 7,000 finally accepted alternative service, and over 4,000 were released under the Home Office scheme. There were more British absolutists than elsewhere, and of these, at least 1,700 remained intransigent throughout (not all had applied for CO status), with between 350 and 600 absolute exemptions, and most of the rest remaining in prison because they were unwilling to accept their official status. Even amongst those who did accept it, there was increasing resistance. As the war continued, non-co-operation amongst all types of objectors intensified, including refusal to work, sit-down strikes and hunger strikes.[50]

An increasingly acceptable solution for most religious COs was civilian service. But in Britain after 1916, the NCF politically opposed alternative service as a compromise with a war-making state. 'I should be false to my own belief', its leader wrote, 'if I avoided the dangers of military service only to accept some safe civil work as a condition of exemption from such service'.[51] Under the Home Office scheme, nearly 4,000 COs were released from prison once they agreed to do 'work of national importance' under civilian control; failure to abide by this condition meant a return to prison, but the majority continued in such work.

During the war, partly working underground, the NCF built up a local network of groups that could act independently and thus hope to escape the effects of repression of the central organisation, or arrest of the leaders, which was envisaged. Beatrice Webb (reacting to the extra-parliamentary actions of the NCF) accused them of being 'a militant minority of elects, intent on thwarting the will of the majority'. The experiences formed here and in the prisons sustained a group feeling beyond the war itself.[52]

Whilst it would be wrong to describe feminists as a war-resistant sub-culture, a noticeable component in many anti-war organisations was the new role for women. Although at first entering male-dominated organisations as individuals after 1914, as the males were imprisoned or conscripted, they tended to take increasingly dominant and essential roles. Women were already emerging as a social constituency in the period before the war and many were active in the Peace Movement, as will be shown.[53] But by and large, even Suffragists, or eventual pacifists like Vera Brittain, were swept into the war effort – as nurses, workers, wives and recruiters – and the major women's organisation in Britain supported the mobilisation, though a significant minority split with this position.

After 1914, those Liberals who remained pacifists and interna-tionalists held that opposition to war mobilisation itself sustained the liberal values, as well as that of human life. The segment of this liberal and pacifist internationalism surviving into the war maintained that the state system of Europe had itself helped bring about the war. With their growing recognition of the power of nationalism, whether in economic, political, cultural or military terms, those who continued to oppose the war tended to become at least implicitly anti-statist or anti-nationalist. The Socialist Hardie and the Liberal Russell saw *militarism* as a base problem: one that had produced German autocracy and was now undermining English democracy.[54]

In Britain, the UDC represented a Left–Liberal, Labourist organisation, not officially opposed to conscription; the more radical NCF, however, was formed specifically to oppose compulsion. From the outset, its direction was towards libertarian defiance of the Government's right to introduce compulsory service. Its main aim became the 'removal of conscription from the life of this country of free tradition',[55] and only secondarily opposition to the war as such. Nevertheless, Allen's leadership, distinctly libertarian in its emphasis on individual propaganda of the deed, also rejected war. He stated at one of his courts martial: 'I resist war because I love liberty. Conscription is the denial of liberty.'[56]

Despite pacifist and socialist opposition to the war, the civil libertarian component was as significant as the anti-war one. To some it bordered on anarchism, by generating less compromising stances than pacifism and giving a political justification for absolutist objection to service. Webb, with some justification, accused the 'professional rebels' of the NCF of being 'out to smash the military service act because it was the latest and biggest embodiment of authority hostile to the conduct of their own lives'.[57]

Many COs saw their resistance as a political strategy and the Government feared that their influence could spread. Child accused the absolutists of not only refusing to 'undertake any service for the state', but also of endeavouring to 'induce their fellow citizens to defy the government'. 'Unconditional exemption' would, an imprisoned absolutist claimed, 'carry with it the seeds of ultimate, even if not immediate, destruction of conscription'.

Libertarian opposition to conscription amongst pacifists, on both sides of the Atlantic, also at times took the form of 'non-registration', though this was discouraged by the NCF. As a result of this stance, Lloyd George began to perceive the absolute objectors as a dangerous challenge to the state and in 1916, when he was Secretary of State for War, promised that he would deal with them in a more repressive fashion.[58]

In Britain only a very few First World War objectors were prepared to describe themselves to tribunals as 'anarchists'. Clearly, many or most of the leaders of war resistance shared or were *influenced* by some anarchist ideas; but, equally, anarchists who shared a general socialist anti-militarist position (or the pacifism of Tolstoy) would not necessarily choose openly to identify themselves as such before a wartime tribunal. Indeed, some anarchists then in Britain even supported the war, including Kropotkin.

Much of the opposition derived from the classic *laissez-faire* principle of individual rights against the state: 'to the militant individualist conscription epitomised the authoritarian invasion of freedom'.[59] Much objection had as a result an erratic and existential quality: it was 'wrong to delegate one's private judgment by agreeing to obey orders without question'.[60] Even the more collectivist and socialist ILP 'recognised the right of every individual member to act as his or her conscience dictates'. Many of the protections sought through civil rights were relevant to the war resister and the conscientious objector, and were closely intertwined with the achievement of religious toleration on a pluralist basis. Bertrand Russell, at his trial for war resistance in 1916, emphasised respect 'for the individual conscience' and warned against forgetting ancient traditions of liberty.[61]

As the war progressed, however, many Liberals active in such organisations as the UDC (and even in the more radical NCF) often actively supported the position of COs. Between 1914 and 1918, absolutists included both those bearing personal witness against conscription, and those engaged in civil disobedience as a political tactic to end it. Refusal to apply to tribunals (discouraged in Britain by the otherwise militant NCF) was based on an unwillingness to recognise the legality of conscription or the legitimacy of the process of selection. Whilst the number of those in prison for refusal to go before tribunals was relatively small, they remained a significant minority.

Non-registrants, who refused to co-operate with the legal preliminary to conscription or selective service, have been sent to jail, as in most Western countries (whether or not CO provisions exist). Many anarchist and socialist objectors have taken absolutist, though not always non-registrant, stances. As a result there were only a few of such persuasion at the outset; however, there was a tendency for many other non-political COs to move towards a more anarcho–socialist standpoint during the course of the war. The loss of status and personal security for objectors, especially 'absolutists', was such that many would not risk the social isolation, opprobrium and 'criminal' label that resistance entailed, as well as the economic costs of objection, which left dependents unsupported whilst serving sentences or doing unpaid work. These sanctions were too great for many who remained ideologically opposed to conscription.

Such penalties were not of course new: there had for a long time been other informal barriers to objection. Both before and after the First World War COs were often manhandled, in and out of jail, sometimes brutally. Even in 'liberal' Britain, as a direct result of their objections,[62] or their experiences in prison, an estimated seventy-three died, forty were driven insane, and over thirty were sentenced to death. In sending some COs to the front, the state's monopoly of coercion over those it selected as agents of its violence was affirmed with relentless insistence in the First World War.

Not only outright war resistance, or evasion of service, had to be placed on the scales. There was also within the services the substantial evidence of desertion, mutiny, inertia and disorganisation – evidence often suppressed by the state for security or propaganda reasons. For example, the scale of upheaval in both the French and British armies in the 1917–20 period has only recently been recognised.[63] Significant study of trench warfare in the First World War shows how even the ephemeral sub-cultures developed in combat were able to activate and sustain *opposition* to, rather than necessarily reinforcing, the status of the war and the hierarchy of its command structure.

In the stalemate situation after 1914, a reciprocity and a 'live-and-let-live' attitude decisively increased between troops on the Western front. As a result, the 'norms' of respect for human life reasserted themselves and reduced combat effectiveness, whilst disorientation both from self and the officer class occurred on a large scale.[64] The 1917–18 mutinies, in particular, exemplify the informal organisation and patterns of interdependence between the armies at this stage of the war. The degree of alienation of troops from the war itself reflected these developments, as well as a revival, at the face-to-face level, of principles of transnational solidarity between primary groups, which had been apparently abandoned in 1914 by most of their supposedly socialist leaders.

Asquith insisted in 1915 that 'Compulsion, to be effective, must be adopted with substantial general assent'.[65] The main tactic was to show that all possible non-compulsory means of troop-raising had been exhausted, (for example, by encouraging volunteer recruitment, which at first showed great effectiveness, but which by January 1916 appeared insufficient). This in itself reveals the fact that the idea of limitless or total 'voluntary' participation was an illusion.[66]

Conscription was not necessarily linked to increasing the numbers of

recruits but rather to their occupational character and their distribution.[67] 'A conscription act', in 1915–16 in Britain, 'would check rather
than stimulate the flow of men.'[68] Its main function would be to 'bring
indiscrimate recruiting under control and be a first step towards the
rational use of manpower without which victory in a long war would
prove elusive'.[69]

It was this aspect of labour control (and, implicitly, *direction*) that the
trade union movement most feared. Before more systematic co-ordi-
nation was experimented with, a system of 'badging' was introduced to
avoid the recruitment of men in essential work (i.e. before conscription
proper was introduced). The inadequacy of this system led to the
register of total work-force resources in the summer of 1915, before the
onset of universal conscription itself.[70] The quotas for each industry
and service had to be precisely estimated: only then could new labour
power be introduced to release others for war (for example, the new
role of women's labour in armaments industries in Britain). Demobilisation after both world wars was intentionally slowed down to enable
reabsorption of labour, and for other reasons, both social and political.
This led to massive discontent, especially in 1918–19.

At the end of the war, many refused to apply for pardons. In their
view, a pardon would be taken to legitimate, retrospectively, the actions
of the state. Meanwhile, a campaign for amnesty, endorsed by the
various civil liberties groups after the signing of the armistice,
demanded 'the release of all political prisoners'.

It is true that part of the failure of war resistance can be ascribed to
the state's monopoly of repression: whilst organised war resistance
eventually became a prerogative of other groups, the NCF was nevertheless so harassed and persecuted under the Defence of the Realm Acts
that Russell argued that 'the whole condition of English liberty' was on
trial. He concluded in 1919, however, that 'the will to resistance had
been stronger than the community's will to persecution'.[71] In particular, he referred to those who had maintained the absolutist stance
throughout the war. 'The whole power of the state has not been able to
compel the members of the NCF to kill or help in killing.' The NCF had
been 'victorious in its stand for freedom'.[72]

The recognition of the rights of objectors to humane treatment in a
number of Western societies after 1939 was generally acknowledged to
have been conceded as a result of the organised *political* resistance to
the previous Anglo-American war mobilisations, especially that of

absolutist objectors from 1915 onwards: these 'rights now accorded to conscience were gratefully acknowledged (as a) significant achievement in the struggle for preserving individual liberties', despite persecution.[73]

Although the civil liberties groups of 1914–18 in Britain and America generally confined their attacks to their own states, and although they included Socialists, amongst whom there was much sympathy for the Russian Revolution of 1917, their critique of the restricted rights of war resisters was extended to 'socialist' governments as well in the 1920s.

War resistance, 1939–45

By the mid-twentieth century, universal compulsory military service appeared to be becoming accepted as a norm throughout the world, including Britain. Differences amongst pacifists became particularly clear during the Second World War, when a 'silent majority' of Quakers seemed ready to endorse the war effort.[74] Although in Britain no equivalents to the NCF emerged during the Second World War and conscription seems to have been accepted as almost a foregone conclusion, nevertheless, reimpositions of service of themselves *can* provoke opposition, as they did in 1939.

In order to understand the numbers of resisters and CO applicants after 1940, it is necessary to appreciate the substantial size of the mass pacifist movements of the 1930s: there were far more conscientious objectors and non-co-operators than might have been predicted from simply assessing the ideological character or justification of the Second World War. Moreover, the official figures reveal only the tip of the iceberg, of dissociation, evasion and non-compliance.

In Britain, the official figure of 67,000 males is of those who *officially* registered in the Second World War as conscientious objectors; it may be taken as an approximate indication of the size of this particular minority (i.e. under one per cent of those actually registering).[75] Of these, only eighty per cent were finally upheld as official COs.[76] However, in addition there were those who became COs *after* military registration, most of whom were sent to prison. Altogether about 6,500 people were imprisoned in Britain in the Second World War for war resistance (not including those for home guard offences), and this number included many of the nearly twenty per cent of provisional

COs who failed to gain official recognition. Besides these, there were about 400 openly absolutist objectors who refused even to register as provisional COs and were arrested.[77] Judging by these figures, there is no evidence that increasingly liberal legislation led to a decrease of war resistance, but rather, that it changed its character.

Whilst in Britain exemptions and civilian service options may have decreased the absolutists' appeal, absolute resistance actually tended to gain support. Harassment and internment of COs still occurred (especially in Britain during the height of the *blitzkrieg*), but generally speaking the appeal to values of choice, dissent, individualism, the sanctity of the person, and democratic control – all affirming the rights of conscientious objection – won considerable sympathy from Liberals. In Britain, after 1939, even Chamberlain, the Prime Minister, was ready to tolerate the absolutist stand, and non-registration for alternative service was also overlooked. Given such extensive liberalisation of the CO position, including complete exemptions, 'to attempt to withdraw from society to the extent that the absolutist position required, appeared now to many pacifists unrealistic'.[78] Yet during the Second World War, it is arguable there were more 'absolutists' in Britain than there had been in the First World War. Whilst there is some uncertainty about total numbers of those who applied for CO status or who were accepted in the Second World War in Britain, the 10,000 absolutists still represent a significant proportion.[79]

The experience of sectarian withdrawal from the reality of the Second World War[80] was especially marked in the absolutist wing of the conscientious objector movement which was concentrated in prisons or work camps; this developed, in Britain, a solidarity and fellow-feeling, including a press of its own,[81] often distributed in an underground fashion. The absolutists became something of a sect within the ranks of pacifists and COs, even more than between 1916 and 1918.[82]

During this period the religiously inspired Fellowship of Reconciliation (FOR) reproduced the character of the older Protestant dissenting and sectarian tradition – a 'kind of Quaker conventicle inside the traditional church' (Niebuhr) – but with greater ambitions for society as a whole, and increasingly *secular* programmes.[83]

There were several thousand Anarchists during the Second World War in Britain who called themselves 'political resisters'. Many of them took the position that they objected to 'conscription' rather than to war in general, or the particular war against Germany: however only a fraction of these were of military age or suitability, and fewer still actually faced tribunals. The majority of Britain's conscientious objectors were still, in 1939, church members, though this affiliation might have been largely formal. But churches not by tradition pacifist now took a more helpful and sympathetic attitude to COs.[84]

In the Second World War, the cases of absolutist objectors and 'cat-and-mouse' treatment of COs – or ill-treatment in military prisons – were taken up with sympathetic MPs. Like the NCF in the First World War, organisations such as the Central Board for Conscientious Objection (CBCO), from 1940, lobbied MPs and acted as a pressure group on parliament on behalf of COs, disseminating information on prison conditions and the nature of their cases.

Many pacifists devoted their wartime energies to giving such legal help and advice to COs in Britain, through the CBCO. However, in Britain, 'conspiracy' to persuade people to avoid military service (which may be construed as including offers of information on CO status as later cases indicated) had, after 1915, been a major form of legal attack on peace advocates.[85] Official interpretation was that it could be used to penalise *any* opposition. Governmental silence on alternative options to military service was seen in particular as an attempt to make conscientious objection still illegitimate and inaccessible, if no longer illegal. Literature which caused 'insubordination, disloyalty or mutiny' in the military or which discouraged enlistment, or which might 'embarrass or hamper the government in conducting the war', could be confiscated, and many magazines were in fact suppressed (including *Peace News*).[86] Even the issue of providing help and information to COs thus proved extremely divisive, even though it was clear in Britain, after the call-up for the Second World War, that no mention was made of the laws or provisions for conscientious objectors.[87] Thus the pacifist response was mainly geared to the advice and legal defence of COs rather than to 'resistance' of any kind.[88]

Moreover, there was a range of other 'nationalist' objectors to military service during the Second World War (Scottish and Welsh, as well as the Irish who were living in England, Scotland or Wales). As in other states, in Britain the peripheral rural areas were also often areas of religious nonconformity; in Scotland and Wales, where nonconformity had deep roots, overlapping nationalism also ran strong. Moreover, during the nineteenth century, the Welsh had become more self-consciously pacifist in their national cultural orientation.[89] In the 1930s

Welsh groups engaged in direct action, including sabotage against English military sites. However, subsequent claims by COs based on grounds of Welsh Nationalism were consistently dismissed. Although political objection and war resistance has been associated usually with groups on the Left, there were a number of examples of 'right-wing' COs. In Britain, a few Italian Fascists resident in Britain and some British Fascists claimed political exemption during the Second World War; others went underground to evade service.

But in general there continued to be a close association between ethical pacifism and Protestant groups. Western peace organisations and pacifist sentiments continued to flourish mostly among white, middle-class Anglo-Saxons, whether or not part of the 'peace church' traditions.[90] Whilst amongst the Second World War objectors there was a preponderance of 'white collar' and relatively few manual workers, a high proportion of objectors from lower income groups were members of fundamentalist sects (four per cent were Jehovah's Witnesses). Studies of non-military resistance in the Second World War have shown the degree to which, elsewhere, occupational and professional groups (especially teachers and ministers) also provided the bases for communal resistance to Fascism.[91]

Hans Speier has detailed the kinds of strains involved in balancing the needs of supply (the industrial sector) and those of combat (the military sector) in a modern total war.[92]

Even from a social democratic standpoint, planners stressed the effects of the 'needs of the war machine' in Britain during the Second World War, 'for more men and more work', on both social policy and political structure. One effect was the degree to which socialist planning and levelling reforms were accelerated by war,[93] and were linked to the issue of manpower control and the acceptance of 'the direction of labour', so feared by trade unions. 'Industrial conscription' was introduced in Britain in 1940, and it is significant of the close interlocking of conscription with such control that the functions of the Ministry of Labour and National Service were combined in 1939, as a prelude to 'call-up'.

Nobody could leave a job without permission; both workers and employers were under the direction of the Ministry, before hiring or firing could take place. Labour controls under the Emergency Powers (Defence) Act (1940) were rigorously enforced, and substantial resistance to this led to about 1,000 convictions for non-compliance.

No conscientious exemptions were granted from direction to civilian employment, although legal COs were never sent to armaments work. Yet industrial conscription represented to many as authoritative a control of the life and work of citizens as military service. As in the First World War, the British Labour Movement, worried about the impact of compulsory direction on its rights, stressed that such wartime conscription of workers – for whatever purpose – inevitably abridged any union's freedom of action, but the TUC did little actively to prevent it. During the Second World War, opposition to industrial conscription also related to both civil defence and the Home Guard, objecting to the coercive nature of the state and the degree to which it was an aspect of the war effort, and an encroachment on the freedoms of labour organising.

When resisters to manpower control were imprisoned, the ILP's paper *New Leader* argued in 1941: 'human beings are, because of their convictions, fighting alone against the power of the state'.

War resistance in a nuclear age

Conscription, reintroduced in Britain in May 1939 before war was declared, established a precedent for peacetime conscription. It survived into peacetime and did not formally end until the 1950s. (The decision to phase it out in 1953 was implemented in 1958 when the last conscripts were enlisted.)

Like the NSBRO, the British Central Committee for Conscientious Objectors (CCCO), founded in 1948, involved pacifists in the legal aid and information aspects of conscientious objection. The CCCO particularly concerned itself with absolutist 'civil disobeyers' or those unable to meet the 'supreme being' criterion of religious belief: it kept a close watch on Parliament for anything relevant to the objectors' situation.[94]

Since 1945 peacetime conscription has been overwhelmingly unpopular in Western countries; but this was not as true for Britain, where the main pacifist group, the Peace Pledge Union, was split after 1947 on the issue of whether to refuse to co-operate with it. The use of British national servicemen in various 'peace-keeping' operations abroad – the Palestinian settlement before 1948, Kenya, Cyprus, Malaysia, Aden and Egypt – continued without militant opposition until 1953, when discontent erupted from within the services. And not until the Suez adventure in 1956 was there substantial *public* resistance, either.

Since the use of conscripts overseas cannot be justified as defending domestic boundaries, the sudden imposition of unpopular service abroad often undermines the legitimacy of conscription. Rumours of the reintroduction of conscription in 1964 led to an immediate campaign springing into existence to pre-empt such a move.

One of the indirect effects of the reawakening of the Peace Movement on the nuclear issue generally, and of pacifist ideas in particular, at the end of the 1950s, was that the legitimacy of conscription was again called into question in a number of Western countries. With the increasing role of nuclear deterrence, it was predicted that conscription might be widely replaced by smaller professional armies. However, only in Britain – and here with reluctance – did this occur.

In the same period, the spread of nuclear weapons itself posed the issue of war resistance in a new way; the act of individual conscientious objection, particularly where, as in Britain, conscription had been removed, no longer seemed a relevant form of non-co-operation with modern war-making. Only for those working within the defence hierarchy or in arms manufacture, research and development, could such conscientious dissociation be a relevant act. On the other hand, the principle of collective resistance could be extended to the whole nuclear state. The whole population was complicit in some sense in nuclear preparations (civil defence or tax payments, for example), and would fall victim to nuclear attack. Thus the CO principle moved towards a logic of mass political non-co-operation with the state (a form of radical absolutism).

Yet some 'nuclear pacifists' argued that as an alternative to nuclear weapons an expanded conventional force might be needed and thus conscription become necessary, particularly if linked to territorial defence. Thus there was certainly no sudden or widespread abandonment of the idea of conscription in Britain.

Between 1915 and 1945, conscientious objection had significantly widened from its initially narrowly religious basis. Following the example of US draft resisters against the Vietnam War, after 1969, pacifists encouraged those in the army to employ Selective objection to the war in Northern Ireland and seek discharge. The British withdrawal campaign, like its nineteenth-century counterparts, leafleted barracks to this effect.

Conclusion

The orientation of the British state to the war resisters was typically pragmatic and was thus not considered to involve a concession of principle; it was both a useless and exasperating waste of time and effort for the state to attempt to force the absolutists to act in a manner which was contrary to their principles.

Nevertheless, once conscription was introduced, even when exemption was granted, the CO was not freed from his reponsibilities. This situation reflects the preponderantly 'liberal' and middle-class background of many English COs,[95] where 'it was probably easier to challenge the authority of the state and get away with it . . . than in any other European country'. It is significant that Britain became the first and only country with complete exemptions for absolutist objectors, even though these were unevenly granted.[96]

The pluralist dimension of Anglo-Saxon democracy, and the delayed introduction of compulsory military service, enabled a diversity of voluntary associations and religious sub-cultures to sustain tolerated centres of political opposition to war and conscription, even in wartime. At the same time, the cell division and voluntarism of the Peace Movement created a multiplicity of such associations and groups, revealing both middle-class and sectarian dimensions. These have proved both a weakness and a strength in the Movement's relations with the state: the emphasis on conscience may clearly reflect and reinforce individualist rather than collectivist aspects of resistance.

War resistance has always been a militant minority wing of the British Peace Movement, often shunned by the larger legalistic and more respectable movements and peace organisations. But through it individuals of significance like Russell, Brockway, and Hardie have emerged to play leading roles – in some cases over many decades. The direct action movement of the 1950s emerged directly out of the activities of those like Brock, Byng and Skinner, who had been COs or war resisters in the Second World War. The journal *Peace News* linked the war resisters of 1940 with the direct actions of the 1980s, over a fifty-year span. War resistance has shown the resilience of the prophetic minorities which have included Anarchists and anti-war Socialists, pacifists and Quakers; and it has often thrived when the larger Movement has collapsed – as in 1915, 1940 and the 1950s. It has maintained, by its presence within the Peace Movement, an indomitable

Utopian witness and reservoir of obstinacy, courage and vision which casts doubts on the easy acceptance of service in even the most 'just' of wars, and maintains the view that a 'progressive war' or army may be a contradiction in terms. What it has lacked in ideological prescience or analytical sophistication, it has made up for by dogged example and willingness to make sacrifices that give it a historic significance larger than its level of support might indicate.

References

1 See David Boulton, *Objection Overruled,* p. 129, McGibbon and Kee, London, 1967.

2 See Andrew Rigby's work on communes (e.g. *Communes in Britain,* Routledge and Kegan Paul, London, 1974; *Alternative Realities,* Routledge and Kegan Paul, London, 1974); and B. Zablocki, *The Joyful Community,* Penguin, Baltimore, 1971 (on the Bruderhof).

3 See Chapter 9 of my *War Resistance and the Nation State,* Xerox Microfilms, Ann Arbor, Michigan, 1977.

4 See G. Nuttall, *Christian Pacifism in History,* World Without War Council, Berkeley, 1971.

5 For George Fox's statement to Oliver Cromwell, see P. Mayer, *The Pacifist Conscience,* Penguin, London, 1966.

6 See A. D. Lindsay, *The Modern Democratic State,* Oxford University Press, 1962, p. 85.

7 In the twentieth century, at least one Protestant sect (Jehovah's Witnesses) invoked this principle as a basis for comprehensive exemption of all 'ministers of the gospel'.

8 This pattern that emerges in the Civil War recurs in all modern revolutions and their aftermath, not least the Bolshevik.

9 See. E. Barker, *The Development of Public Services in Western Europe,* Oxford University Press, New York, 1944, p. 29.

10 See G. Rudé, *The Crowd in History,* Lawrence and Wishart, London, 1981, and E. P. Thompson, *The Making of the English Working Class,* Penguin, 1963.

11 V. Kiernan, 'Conscription', in M. R. D. Foot (ed.), *War and Society,* London, 1973.

12 See M. Ceadel, *Pacifism in Britain,* Oxford University Press, 1980, p. 60.

13 P. Brock, *Pacifism in the twentieth century,* Ch. 1, Van Nostrand, New York, 1970.

14 See J. Rae, *Conscience and Politics,* Oxford University Press, 1970.

15 The Friends convened 'Meetings for Sufferings' to denote persecution for conscience-based resistance to militia or military service.

16 See Rae, *Conscience and Politics,* p. 8 and Boulton, *Objection Overruled.*

17 There were strong financial and other inducements to volunteer rather than wait for conscription.

18 The British Prime Minister introducing plans for military service in 1915. Quoted in Rae, *Conscience and Politics,* p. 15.

19 *Ibid.,* p. 2.

20 See Blanche Wiesen Cooke, 'Democracy in Wartime: Anti-Militarism in England and the US, 1914–18', in C. Chatfield (ed.), *Peace Movements in America,* Schocken, New York, 1973.

21 K. Hardie, 'The Case Against Conscription', April, 1913, ILP pamphlet.

22 Quoted in Boulton, *Objection Overruled*, pp. 99–100.

23 Hardie's remark is quoted in Rae, *Conscience and Politics*, p. 83.

24 ILP resolution of 1915, quoted in Rae, *ibid.*, p. 83.

25 See Denis Hayes in his study *Conscription Conflict*, London, 1949.

26 As was the later Citizen Service League of the thirties; and also its counterparts in Australia and the USA.

27 Boulton, *Objection Overruled*, p. 100. Quotation from Hardie's pamphlet, 'The Case Against Conscription'.

28 Rae, *Conscience and Politics*, p. 82.

29 See G. Dangerfield, *The Strange Death of Liberal England*, New York, 1961, and Rae, *Conscience and Politics*, Chs. 1 and 3.

30 See especially Boulton, *Objection Overruled*, pp. 76. *et seq.*

31 See A. Vagts, *History of Militarism*, Greenwood, London, 1981, p. 77. It was argued in 1916 (and again in 1939) that temporary conscription was necessitated by a clear and present danger.

32 See Rae, *Conscience and Politics*, p. 3. Opposition to manpower control continued and a broad Liberal anti-militarist coalition urged limitations.

33 The sixty Irish Nationalist MPs voted against the 1916 Military Service Bill.

34 See C. Braithwaite, 'Legal problems of conscientious objection', *Journal of Friends Historical Society*, No. 68, London, 1952. Also D. Prasad and T. Smythe, *Conscription, a World Survey*, War Resisters International, p. 104. (See also J. Rae, *Conscience and Politics*, and D. Boulton, *Objection Overruled*.)

35 See R. Barker, 'Conscientious Objection in Britain, 1939–45', unpublished PhD thesis, Cambridge University, 1979.

36 Kiernan, 'Conscription', p. 143.

37 See Rae, *Conscience and Politics*, Ch. 1 *passim*.

38 See Cooke, 'Democracy in Wartime', p. 50.

39 *Ibid.*, p. 51.

40 Some Socialists maintained this position, however.

41 Cooke, 'Democracy in Wartime'.

42 Fraser, in Foot, *War and Society*: 'With the shock of war, the state comes into its own again'. But Fraser notes that 'the new system was regarded as a permanent reform which would survive the peace'.

43 The comparison with Tsarism and use of the term Prussianism was widespread. See B. Russell, *Autobiography, 1914–44*, Allen and Unwin, 1968. An NCF pamphlet on 'The Scandal of the Tribunals' was entitled *British Prussianism* (see Boulton, *Objection Overruled*, p. 136).

44 Indeed the mail and publications were seized and censored; and offices raided and ransacked. Quoted in Cooke, 'Democracy in Wartime', pp. 52–3.

45 This suspension also occurred in the Second World War.

46 They were far more vulnerable than members of the Peace Churches and Sects (see Rae, *Conscience and Politics*).

47 *Ibid.*

48 *Ibid.*, p. 1.

49 It is remarkable that in both world wars, figures on conscientious objection, even in liberal democracies with apparently developed systems of official statistics, have been notoriously difficult to arrive at; most secondary sources differ both with each other

and with the official figures. Often figures given are amalgamations of incomplete local ones which vary in both accuracy and the criteria used for classification (some categories also overlap). The figures for Britain in the First World War are of 16,500 'known' COs (i.e. including all who went before formal tribunals) including non-combatants; civilian-service (including ambulance work); and those who were sent to prison. There are also the separate military figures which are of the 5,944 who were court-martialled for conscientious objection and were sent to prison. However, in addition to these were all those who evaded official notice, and a few who were granted *locally* complete exemptions, but do not appear in these figures (see Prasad and Smythe, *Conscription, a World Survey*, p. 56; and Brock, *Pacifism in the twentieth century*, p. 47). By 1918, nearly a third of all the *court-martialled* objectors had *not* been before a tribunal, which suggests the limitations of these figures if taken alone (Rae, *Conscience and Politics*). Like the figures for those court-martialled (above), Rae's figures, although official, may be underestimates: another estimate of complete *exemptions* from military service on grounds of conscience in the First World War is 6,511, including a special category of 1,400 certified Christadelphians who did *not* have to face tribunals.

50 Non-combatants did not usually object to being part of a military organisation if this did not involve implications in killing; most would, however, refuse to handle ammunition. This selectivity caused acute administrative problems for each group; see Rae, *Conscience and Politics*, Ch. 4. This continued into 1919, both in prisons and camps: see Boulton, *Objection Overruled*, pp. 211–31 and Ch. X; also Rae, pp. 228–31.

51 Clifford Allen (quoted in Chatfield, *Peace Movements in America*). On the opposition to the scheme, see Boulton, *Objection Overruled*.

52 Vera Brittain, who became part of this milieu just after the war, defended the functions of such a minority in wartime at the outbreak of the Second World War.

53 See Ch. 10 in this volume.

54 Russell, quoted in Boulton, *Objection Overruled*, pp. 183–4.

55 Rae, *Conscience and Politics*, p. 292. Figures such as Allen in Britain invoked radical libertarian traditions more than pacifist ones.

56 Quoted in Cooke, 'Democracy in Wartime'. For Allen, libertarianism – 'the infringement to human liberty' – came before all other reasons for opposing the draft.

57 Quoted in Rae, *Conscience and Politics*, p. 85. Allen expressed his 'uncompromising opposition to the principle of conscription of life by the state for any purpose whatever, in time of war or peace'.

58 See Brock, *Pacifism in the twentieth century*, p. 41, and Boulton, *Objection Overruled*, pp. 164–75. And this was despite his earlier opposition in the Boer War. It was about this time, though without the knowledge of the Prime Minister, that some absolutists were shipped to the front and thirty-four of them condemned to death.

59 Rae, *Conscience and Politics*, p. 85.

60 David Garnett, quoted in *ibid.*, p. 82. Note also D. H. Lawrence's remark, 'I will not be compelled to anything'; and Russell, too, stressed *individual* conscience.

61 Quoted in Boulton, *Objection Overruled*, pp. 183–4.

62 See *ibid.*, pp. 10–11, Introduction, and Ch. 10. In the summer of 1916, thirty-four COs were sentenced to death by British courtmartial; sentences were at the last minute commuted to ten years' penal servitude. Some COs were shipped to the front under military discipline and repression, and harassment in Britain also included CID

investigations, and 'cat-and-mouse' treatment of war resisters.

63 See for example, D. Gill and G. Dallas, 'Mutiny at Étaples', *Past and Present*, 69, November 1975. This whole episode received very wide and controversial publicity in 1986, following Alan Bleasdale's television documentary drama, 'The Monocled Mutineer'. See also the survey by *Solidarity*, 'Mutinies 1917–20', D. Lamb, Oxford, 1977. Resistance to continuing conscription after the armistice was a major motivation for the later upheavals.

64 K. Ashworth, 'The sociology of trench warfare', *British Journal of Sociology*, 1968, p. 407 *et seq.*

65 Quoted in Rae, *Conscience and Politics*, p. 15.

66 See Everett Hughes, Introduction to M. Useem, *Conscription, Protest, and Social Conflict*, New York, 1973.

67 Hans Speier, *Social Order and the Risks of War*, Cambridge, 1969.

68 Rae, *Conscience and Politics*, Ch. 1.

69 *Ibid.*, p. 4 (my emphasis).

70 Census resistance by anarchists was linked to its usage for military registration.

71 Quoted in Brock, *Pacifism in the twentieth century*, p. 43.

72 Quoted in Boulton, *Objection Overruled*, p. 291.

73 Brock, *Pacifism in the twentieth century*, p. 167.

74 *Ibid.*, p. 184. The Quakers remained ambivalent about resisting the state.

75 On conscientious objection in Britain in the Second World War, see Denis Hayes, *Challenge of Conscience*, London, 1949 (from the COs perspective). From the government standpoint, see Barker, unpublished PhD thesis.

76 Thus there was a higher percentage of 'official' COs accepted (62,000 out of 8½ million) in Britain, than in the First World War, but this is balanced by proportionately fewer imprisonments (6,500). The combined total of absolutist 'non-registrants', and those who became COs after military registration, was under 1,000; but these were of course additional to the 67,000 applicants. Unconditional exemptions of registered absolutists declined during the Second World War, to 3,100.

77 Of the 67,000 applicants (62,000 granted), 4·7% (6·1%) were initially given unconditional exemption, 37·0% (48·5%) alternative (civilian) service, and 27·4% (22·8%) non-combatant duties under military supervision. Appeals were subsequently made against a third of these decisions: 3,600 (over half) of those imprisoned had refused their status as COs (3,500 were refused absolutist exemption).

78 Brock, *Pacifism in the twentieth century*, p. 168.

79 Although there were far more unconditional exemptions in the Second World War, it is arguable that the overall number taking an absolutist stance was less.

80 Expressed in Donald Soper's interview with John Freeman, 1963.

81 For example, *Peace News*, the main organ of pacifists' resistance in the Second World War, circulated widely.

82 See Mayer, *The Pacifist Conscience*, p. 283 ff.

83 Niebuhr, quoted in Brock, *Pacifism in the twentieth century*, p. 149 (see also p. 144).

84 See *ibid.*, pp. 165–6; and E. Cain, 'Conscientious objection in France, Britain and the United States', *Comparative Politics*, 1970, p. 286.

85 There were twenty-eight prosecutions during the Second World War for counselling or abetting war resisters. In 1974, proceedings against fourteen pacifists were instituted in Britain under the 'Incitement to Disaffection Act'; most of them (and one

other) were also charged with conspiracy. They had all been charged with giving information on conscientious objection, and other alternatives to military service in Northern Ireland: they were acquitted.

86 See Cooke, 'Democracy in Wartime', p. 45. The NCF paper was suppressed towards the end of the war.
87 The Military Training Act of 1939. Up until the end of conscription the BBC carried no information on CO status.
88 The voluntary Central Board for Conscientious Objectors (CBCO) did this whilst the PPU advised and represented pacifists in general.
89 See Gwynfor Evans (Plaid Cymru), *Nonviolent Nationalism,* Fellowship of Reconciliation, 1973. And see Hayes, *Conscription Conflict.*
90 See Brock, *Pacifism in the twentieth century,* pp. 144–65, on these social backgrounds.
91 See A. Roberts, *The Strategy of Civilian Resistance,* Faber, 1967.
92 Speier, 'Class Structure and Totalism', Ch. 20 in *Social Order and the Risks of War.*
93 A. Marwick, *The Deluge: British Society After the First World War,* London, 1965.
94 For accounts of this activity, see the PPU's paper *The Pacifist,* FOR's *Reconciliation; Peace News* and the Quaker reports, between 1945 and 1975.
95 See discussion in Cain, 'Conscientious objection in France, Britain and the United States', p. 287.
96 Braithwaite, 'Legal problems of conscientious objection', pp. 3–18.

4

War, peace and
British Marxism, 1895–1945

MARTIN SHAW

The first half of the twentieth century saw an immense change in society's experience of warfare. As it opened – albeit with an unprecedented naval arms race between Britain and Germany – the general perception of war, tied as ever to yesterday's battles, was that of the limited wars of the nineteenth century. Yet less than fifty years later, the world had entered the atomic age, and the danger of total human annihilation was upon us.

This half-century which saw such a change in war was also the most crucial period of advance for all kinds of socialism. 'Socialism' apparently prospered in the period of total war. The First World War, which saw the rise of 'state socialism' in the belligerent countries, brought in its wake a revolutionary disintegration of the old order. The Second World War completed the advance of the state in the West, launching a period of 'social–democratic' political consensus, while in the East it created the space in which Red Armies, whether Russian or indigenous, assured the triumph of new 'socialist' regimes.

The connection of socialism and world war presents a deep paradox, in the light of the claims of Socialists to insight into the workings of society. It was almost wholly unforeseen, since classical socialist theories of all descriptions had given remarkably little weight to war as a social process.[1] Socialist ideas, inherited from the nineteenth-century era of peace and economic growth, had far more to say about 'class war' than about real military struggle. But however bitter class struggle might grow, it was dwarfed both in its violence and destructiveness and in its significance for social change by the 'progress' of war.

This innocence of socialist consciousness, faced with the rapid advance of warfare, boded poorly for the integrity of the socialist project. A political doctrine which had not really begun in any of its varieties to grasp the enormity of the problem which war posed, was hardly likely to provide the basis of consistent political response. Issues of war and peace, then, provided repeated occasions for division of the socialist movement (as indeed they do to this day, since the deficiency has hardly been remedied).

The success of certain varieties of socialism was achieved largely by riding the tiger of war; but the character of 'socialism' changed just as fundamentally as the character of war itself. The forms of socialism which defied militarism were almost invariably condemned to maintaining and resuming the oppositional stance of the early socialist movement, often in even greater marginality than before.

There was, however, no clear and continuing intellectual division between pro- and anti-war socialisms. Even the most anti-militarist Socialists rarely saw war as such as the problem; indeed it was almost invariably a particular war or kind of war to which they objected. An anti-war stance in one context became a military stance in another, as in the classical case of the Russian Bolsheviks, whose anti-militarism in the First World War gave way to the revolutionary militarism of the Civil War.[2]

These shifts were not always indices of betrayal. To a large extent they reflected real and difficult choices, in an era in which war did not yet equal total extermination. Short of absolute pacifism, such choices were unavoidable; what can generally be said of socialism is that it lacked a coherent basis for making them, and that the consequences of embracing various military–political options were rarely fully anticipated. That these generalisations can be made about socialism internationally is important to stress, since in Britain the adherents of any sort of consistent socialism (as opposed to Labourism) were always very much a minority in the working class and in society at large. There is a danger of seeing the vicissitudes of the British Left, in its relationship to issues of war and peace, as a series of local quirks. They were in reality the national expressions of very fundamental dilemmas in the socialist tradition.

Enough has been said to indicate the difficulties even of defining the area of discussion of this chapter. If there was a single coherent socialist

tradition in 1895 (in itself a large assumption), there most certainly was
not in 1945. If the issues of war and peace presented themselves in one
form at the turn of the century, they were vastly transformed in each of
the subsequent decades. If peace activism meant certain things in the
1900s, it meant others in the First World War, others in the 1920s and
early 1930s, yet others in the later 1930s and during the Second World
War. In the early part of the century, Socialists tended to propagate
their own attitudes towards peace independently; later there were
organised peace movements to which Socialists might relate, although
these too took varied and often conflicting forms.

The opening date of our period is in a sense more arbitrary than the
close. The intention, however, is to cover the period of pre-atomic
world wars: the build-up to the First World War and the beginnings of
socialist response; the war itself; the 'post-war' period of 'peace' and the
build-up to the Second World War; and the war itself. Nineteen-forty-
five, with the dropping of the atomic bombs and the end of the Second
World War, marks a more fundamental turning-point: not just the end
of a war, but clearly the beginning of the end of the period in which
world wars could be fought to resolve the conflicting interests of great
powers. By the late 1950s, the prospect opened up in 1945 had been
brought to fruition: it was unlikely that a major war could take place
without what the strategic planners later called 'mutually assured
destruction'.

This chapter will concern itself with the attitudes to war and peace of
the Marxist groups in Britain: primarily the Social Democratic Federation, the sects which split off from it in the early 1900s, its successor
the British Socialist Party, and finally the Communist Party, in its
various phases, and the Trotskyists, whom it in turn spawned. Just as
the self-definition of these groups as Marxist hardened, so their attitudes to internationalism and war changed. The Marxist tradition was
clearly originally one of socialist internationalism, but what this meant
in questions of war and peace was less than clear in the thought of Marx
and Engels themselves and muddled still further among the early British
Marxists. If the formation of the British Communist Party, affiliated to
a revolutionary International, appeared to settle the question, it did so
only by identifying internationalism with loyalty to the USSR, which in
turn quickly exacerbated the contradictions of the British comrades'
positions. This chapter is less about the pursuit of a clearly defined
internationalist position than about the interaction of changing forms

of socialist internationalism, with the conflicting commitments of British Marxists and their responses to war and peace.

Indeed, it is arguable that more consistent internationalist positions and activity against war can be found on the non-Marxist left, especially the Independent Labour Party. From about 1895, when he started to campaign against colonial wars, until the outbreak of war in 1914, Keir Hardie's was often the most effective socialist voice against imperialist militarism. This is not to say that the ILP necessarily had a full understanding of what might be needed to prevent the war – arguably no-one on the British left did – but the ILP knew which side it was on rather better than the British Marxists, as we shall see. During the war, and in the 1920s, the ILP (unlike the main Marxist organisations) provided the main political base for active war resistance. Fenner Brockway stands out as a central figure; only the independent revolutionary, John Maclean, compares in stature among anti-war activists.

Ideally, this chapter would have done full justice to the ILP tradition as well as the Marxist Left. Unfortunately, my own expertise is restricted to the Marxist movement, and the ILP has been much less exhaustively studied, perhaps because of the fascination of Marxist historians with their own antecedents. Douglas Newton's seminal study, *British Labour, European Socialism and the Struggle for Peace 1889–1914*, which focuses on the ILP, appeared only as this chapter was undergoing final revision.[3] A comparable study for the period after 1914 is still lacking.

A related problem in writing about this subject is that attitudes to war were not always, or even normally, expressed as such, but were bound up with other issues – not just with ideas about international affairs generally, but also, especially in wartime, with economic, social and domestic political issues. Left-wing Socialists could be active in fomenting militancy about such problems, which both reflected and indirectly affected the war, without directly opposing the war as such. Historians, moreover, have often deepened this difficulty since they have frequently been more interested in the socio-economic and political effects of war in a general sense, than with attitudes to and activities about war itself. Historians sympathetic to the socialist movement, not least those who are in some sense Marxists, often share its characteristic limitations and reproduce them in their work.[4]

These facts are all the more significant because this chapter is not based on primary historical research – much of which remains to be done – but relies on the existing secondary literature. In trying to present an overview of the ways in which Marxists responded to war in such a full and complex period, we shall limit ourselves to defining and explaining the changing course of political attitudes. Although we shall refer to major practical activities of the Left, it will be beyond our scope to represent a full historical account of organisations, movements and individuals reflecting socialist attitudes to war and peace over this time.

Marxism and militarism before 1914

For nineteenth-century Socialists, war was not a major problem. The great upheaval of the Napoleonic Wars at the beginning of the century had aroused radical and working-class agitation in Britain, even if it had driven it underground. Superimposed on the rapid changes of the Industrial Revolution, war helped to produce, in its aftermath, the most tumultuous phase of early working-class revolt. But this connection was largely missed when Marx came to frame the theoretical basis for a revolutionary working-class movement, as it has been in later radical historiography.[5] The mode of production and the new productive class of wage-labourers seemed the essential things; the state was a secondary institution, derivative of class conflict, and war, the conflict between states, an accidental intrusion not seriously theorised in the scheme. The wars of the second half of the century saw important applications of industrial technology, in which Engels especially was interested – the telegraph in the Crimea, the railroad in the American Civil War, the breach-loading gun in the Austro-Prussian war of 1866.[6] But for Marx the most important consideration was how each war affected the balance of power, and hence the prospects of democratic and socialist advance. The human suffering of war was real, but seemed of significance to Socialists only when clearly linked to the political cause of the workers, as in the bloody repression of the Paris Commune at the conclusion of the Franco–Prussian War. Even the crucial fact that it was military defeat, not economic crisis, which had provoked this first practical demonstration of working-class power, was missed as a lesson for Socialists: although its importance was to be demonstrated again in Russia in 1905.[7]

The prevention of particular wars was certainly a legitimate cause for radicals and Socialists. William Morris, perhaps the greatest British

Marxist, entered politics (at a time when organised socialism in Britain was still to come) via the 'Eastern Question': the cause of opposition to any British intervention on behalf of the Ottoman Empire against Tsarist Russia.[8] This experience helped push Morris past the established liberal variety of radicalism towards his ultimate alignment with independent, working-class socialist politics. Indeed he had already expressed a view typical of such Socialists, when at the time of the Commune he had written: 'The *Real* war in Europe, of which this fighting is the Inauguration, is between (the Capitalists) and the workmen . . .'.[9]

By the mid-1880s, however, this essentialist commitment to class 'war' was being brought into question by the all too tangible preparations for what was ultimately to prove appallingly 'real' war. Morris (with Belfort Bax) had already laid out a Marxist account of imperialism, some years before comparable – if more sophisticated – analyses appeared in Germany and elsewhere on the Continent.[10] Within the Social Democratic Federation, or SDF (with the demise of the Socialist League, the sole British Marxist organisation), the political battle-lines were already anticipated in the first half of 1896. On one side, H. M. Hyndman, the organisation's founder and leader for thirty years until 1914 – whose sympathies for British imperial designs had long been apparent – succeeded in January 1896 in committing its Executive to a policy of naval expansion. On the other side, William Morris, in his last May Day article – intended without doubt, says Thompson, 'as a final testament to the movement' – attacked the imperialist scramble which was enslaving colonial peoples in the search for markets.[11]

Although the naval build-up was well under way by the turn of the century, and the socialist division on the issue had certainly been foreshadowed, it was some years before the danger of European war hardened into a clear issue. In the meantime the nascent British socialist movement had to face its first major taste of militarism in the Boer War. According to Kendall, even Hyndman at first acquitted himself well: his 'advocacy of the rights of small nations led him to support wholeheartedly the SDF's courageous stand against the jingo hysteria generated'.[12] The SDF also advocated a militia-based 'citizen army', as opposed to a standing army, and the success of the Boers in resisting superior British forces was held to vindicate this approach. The SDF stood alongside the ILP and some Liberals (including Lloyd George) in its opposition; but before long Hyndman's chauvinism led to doubts about the anti-war stand, and the SDF's Executive called off its anti-war campaign.

In 1904, the Russo-Japanese war provided new evidence of the global drift towards Armageddon. The Socialist press was united in denouncing an 'imperialist war', and yet, Newton argues, there was an 'important difference in tone' in the SDF's response. There 'was not that same sense of moral revulsion against the horror and inhumanity of war' which was evident in the ILP. Indeed, 'Hyndman insisted that the war was beneficial to the socialists' cause' and 'appeared to excuse entirely the Japanese resort to war' on the grounds of defeating Tsarist imperialism in Asia. 'The horrors of peace are often worse than the horrors of war', he wrote. 'Following in Marx's footsteps', Newton points out, 'Hyndman was judging war solely from the standpoint of the political advancement of socialism.'[13]

Already, Hyndman was starting to identify German militarism as a threat to politically advanced Western Europe. In the Moroccan crisis of 1905, Hyndman clearly identified the 'German menace' which was to be the fixed reference point of his subsequent politics.[14] By 1906, Kendall recounts, his consequent advocacy of British rearmament was provoking a major division in the Social Democratic Federation. The SDF had already split twice, spawning in 1903 the Socialist Labour Party, based mainly in Scotland and subscribing to the ideas of the American Marxist Daniel De Leon, and in 1904 the Socialist Party of Great Britain, largely London-based and still today, after eight decades, a standard-bearer of pure propagandist socialism. Both of these groups were (albeit in different ways) sectarian Left offshoots, revolting against Hyndman's opportunism, but not yet posing his national chauvinism as a main issue. This was left to a new opposition within the SDF, as the militarism of the leadership jarred increasingly with the rising tide of anti-war sentiment in the international socialist movement. The 1906 SDF Conference had asked the International to provide a statement of general principles and policies to be followed in the event of a war crisis: the 1907 Stuttgart Congress of the International passed a resolution, amended at the instigation of Rosa Luxemburg and V. I. Lenin, which called for co-ordinated action by the workers of different countries to prevent the outbreak of war. As Kendall comments, the debate at the Congress, and its outcome, was not without its ambiguity – the betrayal of 1914 was anticipated as well as the anti-war resistance of the minority – but the obvious implication in Britain was to lend the authority of the International to the critics of the SDF leadership's pro-armaments policy.[15]

In 1909–10, Hyndman's ever more open advocacy of militarism, backed by other leading members, was reinforced by a series of scare-mongering articles by Robert Blatchford, editor of the *Clarion,* in the Conservative *Daily Mail.* But this in turn increased support for the internationalist opposition, which broke the Hyndmanites' control of the Social Democratic Party (as the SDF had renamed itself) when the latter merged with a section of the ILP and the Clarion Cycling Clubs to form the British Socialist Party (BSP) in 1911–12. By the end of 1912 the BSP Executive had adopted an internationalist, anti-war stance on clear class lines proposed by Zelda Kahan. This was quickly compromised, but Kendall's conclusion is that by 1914 the internationalist minority was set to become a majority in the major Marxist organisation.[16]

While the SDF/BSP's history can certainly be seen as a slow polarisation in favour of the internationalist, anti-war forces, it is nevertheless striking that for three decades, and almost twenty years after the division over imperialism had first appeared in the Movement, it should have been dominated by leaders sympathetic to British rearmament. However much this can be explained by the personality, money and manipulative skills of Hyndman and his associates, it is also a testimony to how unclear was the contradiction between class and nation even to supposed Marxian Socialists. And this is not to mention how little the character of the coming war was understood by them (this was largely true even of the anti-war internationalists, who tended to argue their case on the class character of the state rather than the death and destruction which was to come).

The SDF/BSP never represented a clear anti-militarist position of any kind; its main proposal, Hyndman's consistent support for naval expansion apart, was the idea of a 'citizen army' to replace the regular army. This concept, borrowed from European socialism, implied support for national defence (and indeed the Socialist International had acknowledged its legitimacy). In the context of Hyndman's views on the German threat, on the impossibility of German socialists defeating it from within, and on the need for British preparedness, it was at best highly ambiguous. The dangers came out in the debate over Haldane's army reforms, first broached in 1906, and attacked by the Left as a thinly veiled form of conscription. 'Unfortunately for the SDP', as

Newton comments, 'it strained credibility to attack the Haldane scheme as the thin edge of the conscriptionist wedge while arguing for compulsory military training in its place.'[17]

These contradictions were pointed out both by the pacifists of the ILP and the revolutionaries of the SLP, each of whom were, in their different ways, to manifest more meaningful opposition to war when it came. The SLP, although very modest in influence, adopted a clear position in favour of anti-militarist agitation, and for extra-parliamentary action – the general strike to defeat war.[18] Partly because of this, it was to assume an importance out of proportion to its numbers in the later regrouping of British Marxists.

The revolutionary Left in the First World War

The outbreak of war plunged Socialists into turmoil and confusion. All sections of the Labour Movement and the Left were divided: the parliamentary Labour Party between its leader, Ramsay MacDonald, who resigned at the outbreak of war, and his successor, Arthur Henderson, who took Labour into the wartime coalition; the Independent Labour Party, which was overwhelmingly anti-war, between varying pacifist and revolutionary positions; and the BSP itself, between the Hyndmanite support for the war and various strands of anti-war politics. It might be said, as G. D. H. Cole put it, that

> in Great Britain, as in other countries, there were really two anti-war oppositions, the one, headed internationally by Lenin, revolutionary and entirely unconcerned with the merits of the case advanced by any capitalist Government, and the other either out-and-out pacifist or working for peace by negotiation, but opposed to any attempt to invoke revolutionary violence as a means of ending the war by international working-class revolution.

But it is barely true to suggest, as he goes on to do, that 'The ILP, though it had revolutionaries in its ranks, belonged essentially to the second of these groups; the British Socialist Party, having shed its pro-war section, was moving rapidly towards the first.'[19]

Certainly, a major result of the war was the final departure of Hyndman and his jingoistic followers from the British Socialist Party. Nevertheless, it was not until April 1916, after more than eighteen months during which the BSP paper *Justice* had actively supported the war, that the split finally occurred. During 1915, the revolutionary anti-war standard had been raised in Glasgow by John Maclean, who published a new paper, *Vanguard,* to propagate this position – and was imprisoned for his views. In September came the internationalist Zimmerwald conference, which both BSP and ILP delegates were prevented from attending by the Government's refusal to grant them passports. The Zimmerwald declaration, which fell short of the revolutionary defeatism advocated by Lenin, nevertheless represented a major statement of internationalist opposition to the war, and helped bring about the final 'purification' of the BSP from the Hyndmanites, which Maclean and others called for.[20]

Kendall presents a more critical judgement than Cole's on the politics of the BSP:

> In December 1914 Lenin classified socialists into the three following groups, according to their attitude to the war. They were open chauvinists; those 'capable of leading revolutionary work in the direction of civil war' and 'the confused and vacillating elements' in between. By the terms of Lenin's division, Hyndman and his allies represented the open chauvinists, John Maclean and his followers the revolutionaries, leaving the 'confused and vacillating elements' as the majority of the BSP.[21]

The BSP majority did not even endorse the Zimmerwald declaration: they remained advocates of peace by negotiations, opponents of direct working-class action as advocated by the International before the war broke out, and supporters of the largely defunct International Socialist Bureau rather than any regrouping of anti-war Socialists.

The BSP, then, did not differ greatly in its real orientation from the majority of the ILP, whose opposition to the war was more on pacifist than revolutionary grounds. The difference seems to have been that whereas the ILP was a political base for both the middle-class peace campaigners in the Union of Democratic Control and the war-resisters of the No Conscription Fellowship,[22] the BSP was largely uninvolved in such activities. A decision, early in 1917, to affiliate to the Peace Negotiations Committee, was quickly slapped down by the Party's conference.[23] The main British Marxist organisation thus appears to have fallen between two stools, committed neither to the 'peace movement', nor to revolutionary anti-war activity, but carrying on its own rather indecisive anti-war propaganda.

The revolutionary position was left therefore to the tiny Socialist Labour Party – although its highly sympathetic historian acknowledges that it, too, had its 'national defencists' at the outbreak of war[24] – and most strikingly, to John Maclean and his followers, primarily in the BSP but with support in the working-class Left which went far beyond that relatively small party.[25] Both the SLP and Maclean responded to the example of Karl Liebknecht's revolutionary opposition to the war, and to Lenin's ideas of utilising the ferment of war to bring about the revolutionary overthrow of capitalism. Both were based in Scotland, and especially Glasgow, and played their part in the wartime upheavals which earned the label 'Red Clydeside'.

The heroic propaganda of Maclean – the power of whose speeches and articles still attracts Socialists today, as it then convinced Lenin that he was Britain's most impressive revolutionary leader[26] – and the systematic industrial organisation of the SLP, succeeded in gaining revolutionary Socialists a mass working-class audience on the Clyde, and to a lesser extent elsewhere. The intensification of exploitation, the oppressive increase in the state's powers, the arrest and deportation of working-class militants – all combined to sharpen the class struggle. With the official trade union leadership, along with Labour's parliamentary leaders, incorporated into the Government, unofficial shop-floor organisation developed rapidly, as well as political radicalisation. To the revolutionary Left, these were the ingredients for a major political upheaval. Like the pacifist war-resisters, many such Socialists were imprisoned for their propaganda, and shop stewards for their attempts at industrial resistance, in the period from 1915 to 1918.

Socialist historiography in the late 1960s and early 1970s paid a good deal of attention to the shop stewards' movement, seeing in it a model of working-class self-organisation relevant to the then hoped-for revolutionary revival.[27] What emerges from their accounts, however, is that despite the fact that the leaders of working-class resistance were often members of or influenced by the socialist Left (the SLP providing most of the members of the Clyde Workers' Committee, for example), their politics had little direct expression in the mass struggles of workers. The Clyde workers' movement, and the shop stewards' movement in England even more so, were about resistance to the effects of war (dilution, wages, rents), not to the war itself. Even allowing for the fact that some socialist historians have been more interested in the forms of working-class struggle and organisation than their political content, there is little evidence that even Maclean managed to overcome this fundamental weakness. There is no reason to doubt

Kendall's conclusion, that the Clydeside industrial militants and the revolutionary wing headed by Maclean were 'two movements which ran side by side, each influencing and conditioning the other but never, in fact uniting'.[28]

The Communist Party and peace, 1918–39

If, despite the far-reaching effects of total war, there was no effective revolutionary opposition to it, this period did have one major legacy: the unification of almost all the serious revolutionary forces in the Communist Party. If the continuing weakness of revolutionary socialism in Britain encouraged it to look for external inspiration, this was readily available from Russia after 1917. Whatever the local processes of political maturation, stressed by Kendall, the Russian Revolution was undoubtedly the catalyst of the particular form of regrouping which occurred between 1918 and 1921. And the Soviet Union, both indirectly by example and directly through the Comintern, had a major and generally decisive influence on the Communist Party.[29] This was to become increasingly apparent in the decade after the war.

The 1920s are perhaps the period covered by this chapter for which there is least documentation and discussion of Marxist attitudes to war and peace. The period as a whole was, of course, one of great disillusionment with war in the aftermath of the 1914–18 slaughter, and there were active socialist–pacifist movements. The successor to the wartime No Conscription Fellowship, wound up in 1919, was the No More War Movement, founded in 1921, and the British section of the War Resisters' International. Its leaders were the same absolute pacifists and ILP Socialists (such as Brockway) who had resisted wartime conscription. Its membership pledge committed its members not to take part in any war, 'international or civil', directly or indirectly, while at the same time striving for a socialist society and international order. As Ceadel points out, 'The problem which was to dog the NMWM throughout its history was, in effect, whether the two halves of this pledge were compatible.'[30]

Revolutionaries, in the Marxian sense, were not likely to be absolute pacifists, and were therefore able to resolve this contradiction by a particular version of what Ceadel calls 'pacificism' rather than pacifism – support for measures to prevent the outbreak of war, but falling short of an outright refusal of war.[31] Marxist support for 'peace' had of course always been implicitly of this kind; as we noted earlier, before and during the First World War, most Marxists objected more to the imperialist character of the war than to the fact that it was war. But in that period, it had been less clear which wars revolutionaries would actually support, and so the difference between them and other war-resisters or pacifists had seemed to be, as we have largely presented it above, one of means. Now that a socialist state actually existed in Russia, the differences of principle were much clearer. 'Class-war' had been shown to be more than just the sharpening of a political or economic class struggle. The civil war in Russia from 1918–21, ferocious and destructive as civil wars invariably are, called forth a revolutionary militarism which Marxists in Britain, as elsewhere, were bound to embrace. To the extent that the civil war was seen as a heroic and radicalising episode, as it tended to be among the Bolsheviks themselves, Marxists positively identified with military struggle as a means of spreading the international revolution.[32]

What then was the role of 'peace' in Marxist politics? While a Bukharinist enthusiasm for armed confrontation between proletarian and capitalist states held sway, it had of course little meaning. But the Soviet Union was weak compared to its capitalist enemies, as the enforced peace of Brest-Litovsk had shown. In reality there was little prospect of a major extension of Communism through military struggle; on the contrary, the Soviet state, although it had fought off the interventionist armies in the civil war, had much to fear from a major war with any major Western state, especially Germany. The chief substantive basis of the Communist concern with 'peace' was, as it remains among 'Stalinists' in the Peace Movement even today, the national defence of the Soviet Union. Since the main concern of the Communists in any future war was the defence of the USSR, the slogan of 'peace' was invariably linked with that of 'friendship with the USSR' in the propaganda of the Western CPs.

Since the Soviet Union was politically, and, with the 'Bolshevisation' of the CP in the mid-1920s, organisationally, the centre of the Communists' universe, the line of the British party on war and peace varied in accordance with Soviet domestic and foreign policy.[33] In the period of stabilisation following the Russian Civil War (domestically in Russia the period of the New Economic Policy or NEP), the Soviet Government sought closer economic and diplomatic relations with the West. This period is the origin of the 'peace and friendship' line, and the committees and organisations which went with it, although this sort of campaigning was not such a major part of the Party's activity as it was to become in the 1930s. This line was superseded in the ultra-Left 'Third Period' at the end of the 1920s, in which the Soviet Union opted for international isolation and repudiation of Labour Movement leaders in the West as 'social Fascists'. Durable peace between the Soviet Union and capitalist states was not seen as possible; wars were inevitable; all sorts of 'pacifist swindlers' were to be 'relentlessly exposed and combated'.[34] By 1934–5, however, as the party and the Comintern belatedly recognised the disaster of the Nazi seizure of power, the line altered again, the tactic of the united front was developed, and finally the fully-blown 'Popular Front' policy was adopted.

The Popular Front involved a drastic change in the international line of the Soviet Union, which joined the League of Nations in 1934 and henceforth sought an alliance with the Western democracies against fascism. The political consequences of this were that the Communist Party moved from being to the left of everyone else on the Left, to a position well to the right not only of the ILP but also of much of the Labour Left, which was then organised in the Socialist League led by Stafford Cripps. The CP was now completely converted to 'collective security' and the broadest of alliances (the idea of a 'Peace Bloc' of states was matched by the call for a 'peace alliance' of all 'progressive' forces at home). Their allies on the left were dismayed as the party lurched towards new links on the right.[35] By 1938 the CP was seeking a 'United Peace Alliance' of 'democratic peoples of all political parties', and clashed with the Labour Left over its demand that Labour should stand down in favour of pro-Peace Alliance Liberal candidates in a series of by-elections.[36] In many localities the party was busy in Peace Councils, campaigning in support of the League of Nations and collective security.

By the mid-1930s, therefore, both socialist pacifism (of the ILP kind) and revolutionary anti-militarism (as advocated by many of the BSP and SLP founders of the Communist Party) were declining and very marginal traditions. Ceadel described how the events of 1935–36 (Abyssinia, the Spanish Civil War) 'had achieved the destruction of the long-standing compatibility between pacifism and the needs of the socialist movement'.[37] Most Socialists now accepted the need to use violence to defeat Fascism. Brockway's conversion from the absolute pacifism of his No Conscription Fellowship days, and the decline of the No More War Movement, were typical.[38] Although there was much suspicion of the Chamberlain Goverment's rearmament programme,[39] few still made the classical Marxist distinction between the class violence of the revolutionary proletariat and the war preparations of the bourgeois–democratic state in the struggle against Fascism. As Ceadel again points out, 'Only a rump, mostly to be found in the ILP, was prepared to fight in Spain but felt that to prepare for a general war against Nazism would be merely to favour, in the words of George Orwell who took this view, "British Fascism (prospective) as against German Fascism".'[40] (Orwell was to reverse his position at the onset of war.)

Only the Trotskyists maintained, in principle, the classical Leninist position of revolutionary defeatism. The British Trotskyist groups were so small, however, and immersed in the ILP and the Labour Party, that there was little public expression of their position; although Trotsky himself, and his more numerous American followers, were attempting to deal with the severe practical problems of applying Lenin's line at a time when the politically aware working class in the West was moving increasingly towards support for the coming war against Fascism. Already in 1935–36, the British Trotskyists were beginning to disagree among themselves about whether to support the ILP policy of advocating 'workers' sanctions' against Fascist Italy, at the time of its Abyssinian war.[41]

By the late 1930s, it was the case that virtually the only remaining viable inspirations of war resistance were those of religious and humanitarian orientations. From Spain onwards, the Left had been moving – if in a confused manner – in the direction of supporting war; it was increasingly remote from the rebirth of absolute pacifism in the Peace Pledge Union, a growth whose only political allies were 'right-wing isolationists and pro-Germans'.[42] The mainstream of the Marxist Left had moved, irrevocably it seemed, away from revolutionary anti-militarism towards a policy of 'peace' through collective security and, if need be, towards supporting total war.

The Communist Party in the Second World War

The story of the Communist Party's policy in the Second World War is, at first sight, so appalling, that it has not surprisingly been told very effectively by historians opposed to the party.[43] The bare facts are therefore well known: that in September 1939 the Party supported the war, but in October, on instructions from Moscow, it moved into opposition which it maintained until June 1941, when the German attack on the USSR led the CP back into fervent patriotic support of the war effort. The 'war against Fascism' suddenly became an 'imperialist war' and then equally suddenly turned back into a 'war for democracy'. The contradictions are so glaring that the Party itself has now acknowledged them: a paper by one of its leading intellectuals, Monty Johnstone, argues that the policy of opposition to the war between October 1939 and 1941 was fundamentally wrong.[44]

Against all the trends of the 1930s, therefore, the 1939–41 period saw the revival of the revolutionary anti-militarism which Lenin and the more radical British Marxists had advocated in the First World War. It is difficult to take this seriously as an example of war resistance, since the line was dictated from Moscow against the better judgement of the Party's main leaders. Nevertheless, the experience of the CP in carrying out the policy, and the critique of it which is offered today, tell us something about the problems of such a policy in the Second World War.

The difficulties of a 'revolutionary opposition' to the war became acute with the end of the 'phoney war', the replacement of the Chamberlain Government by the Churchill coalition, and the Battle of Britain. With France fallen, and Britain itself directly threatened with invasion, Nazism seemed a real and direct danger. Johnstone suggests that, in private, the CP's leaders realised this and were looking for a change of line from Moscow; publicly, they were building the 'People's Convention' held in January 1941, which avoided open denunciation of the war as imperialist. It concentrated largely on demands for the defence of living standards, democratic rights, air-raid precautions, etc., as well as, of course, 'friendship with the Soviet Union'. The Convention's main demand was for 'a People's Government' to make 'a People's Peace'. The argument was that a genuine 'People's Government' in Britain would stimulate the German workers to overthrow Hitler and create their own German People's Government to negotiate peace with Britain.[45] As Johnstone says, this was an utterly unrealistic perspective: 'there was a failure to make a crucial distinction between the situation in the First World War (on which Lenin based his concept of revolutionary defeatism), when the main working class organisations continued to function on both sides, and the position in the Second World War, when this was so only on the British side.'[46]

Because the CP's policy in 1939–41 faithfully reflected the foreign policy of the USSR, it was not regarded as a genuinely Leninist policy by Britain's small Trotskyist groups, the only Marxists formally to adopt a policy of revolutionary opposition to the war throughout its duration. The Trotskyists saw themselves (as the CP never did explicitly even in 1939–41) as working to turn the 'imperialist war' into a 'civil war'. Trotsky's own perspectives at the beginning of the war (he was assassinated in 1940) were for revolutionary upheavals in the wake of war, such as had occurred in Russia and elsewhere as a result of the First World War. Used as they were to working as a tiny minority 'against the stream', the Trotskyists nevertheless found themselves under great pressure to adapt to the pro-war sentiment of the mass of workers. As Upham suggests, the Trotskyists 'found it difficult to move beyond an abstract anti-war line'.[47] Attempts to give practical substance to their policy inevitably meant taking the threat of Nazi militarism seriously, and led to a search for a 'military policy' which would advance 'positive proletarian tactics for winning an anti-fascist war'. This naturally led to a debate on whether the movement was replacing 'revolutionary defeatism' by 'revolutionary defencism'.[48]

In the event, the Trotskyists' influence remained negligible until 1941. Then the CP's full-blooded support for the war left them (along with the ILP, which had never had significant industrial influence) as the only political group to advocate protecting working-class interests in industry. Even more than the SLP members in the First World War, the Trotskyist groups, united for the first and last time in the Revolutionary Communist Party founded in 1944, won industrial influence without convincing more than a tiny number of workers of their political ideas. They were prominent in the Barrow shipyard strike of 1943, the Tyneside apprentices' dispute of 1944 (which led to the arrest of their leaders and hence momentary fame), and the dock strike of 1945. But this was a transitory influence, which unlike the revolutionary anti-war movement in 1914–18 achieved no significant change in the nature of the post-war left: the RCP disintegrated in 1949. All the immense hopes of the Trotskyists came to naught: a sympathetic historian concludes, in terms reminiscent of Johnstone's verdict on the CP's anti-war phase, quoted above, that 'Where Trotsky erred was in analysing the Second World War through the prism of the first imperialist war.'[49]

Arguably, a more relevant Marxist contribution in this period was that of Tom Wintringham, an ex-Communist Party member who made himself a major advocate, organiser and theorist of the Home Guard.[50] Wintringham's strategy was one of territorial defence based on guerrilla struggle: an application of the lessons of the Spanish Civil War (in which he had fought) to the defence of the British mainland against Nazism. The Home Guard itself was likened to the militia of Republican Spain: a people's army, based on democratic methods of organisation and mass military struggle. It is of more than passing interest that Wintringham's model (which of course was never realised in the Home Guard, which was in turn a very subordinate element in the British forces in the Second World War) is now held up as a basis for a non-nuclear defence strategy;[51] and that real guerrilla struggles elsewhere in 1939–45 are celebrated by E. P. Thompson as a major element in a justifiable anti-Fascist war.[52] (It is not clear, however, that these experiences are really relevant as 'alternative defence' in the nuclear age.)

Certainly, there was little political basis, from a Marxist point of view, for war resistance in 1939–45. Whatever conflicts of interest between British and German capitalists might be held to underlie the war (and Marxists have generally been better at asserting than explaining these),[53] there was undoubtedly an overriding interest of the working class in defeating Nazi expansionism. To this extent Johnstone is right in saying that the CP line in September 1939 and after June 1941 was more in tune with realities – and with working-class opinion, as the rapid increase in CP membership in 1941–42 showed. But the existence of this overriding interest in Allied victory did not abolish class conflict – including the debate over the way in which the war was being organised and fought. For all the levelling effects of war, Britain at war was still very much a class society;[54] the economic mobilisation for arms production stimulated industrial unrest, particularly in the later stages of the war; the support of the working class for the war had to be won with far-reaching proposals for economic and social reform.[55] Equally, however unavoidable an enormous amount of killing and suffering, the exigencies of total war did not necessarily justify the deliberate, wholesale slaughter of civilians which the Allies carried out at Hamburg and Dresden, Hiroshima and Nagasaki.

The Communist campaign from 1939 to 1941 had tied an awareness of some of these issues (particularly the socio-economic contradictions), wrongly into a policy of opposition to the war. The Communist campaign from 1941 to 1945 seemed to lose sight of all these issues in a blind and uncritical drive to victory. Nevertheless, these campaigns created an impressive base in these years: Hinton's study of Coventry shows that this was the result not just of popular support for the war or admiration for the Soviet Union, but also of the way in which the CP built an element of class politics into its 'productionism' at factory level.[57] But this base was not to survive: the excesses of the Party's coalitionism meant that it was outflanked to the left even by Labour's right-wing leaders in 1945, and then finally marginalised by the onset of the new 'Cold War'.

Conclusion

If one wanted to be cruel, one could summarise the history of Marxist attitudes to war in this half-century by pointing out that what began with Hyndman's advocacy of naval rearmament in the 1890s, concluded with the Communist Party's support for the atomic bomb on Hiroshima in 1945. Certainly the strand of national defence and support for armaments and war is a real one; but against that has to be seen the long tradition of opposition to imperialism and militarism, from William Morris to John Maclean and the Trotskyists in the Second World War. Although to portray the history of Marxists' involvement with these issues in terms of a conflict of these two traditions is better than to suggest that one or other of them is 'the' Marxist tradition, it may still oversimplify a complex set of issues.

For while Hyndman, in the period before 1914 and even more during the First World War, and the CP in the late 1930s and even more from 1941 to 1945, both represent cases of support for rearmament and war, and both clearly went 'overboard' in their nationalism and patriotism, there are important differences in the meaning of their positions in each period. Similarly, while there is a clear continuity from the anti-war internationalists before and during the First World War to the Trotskyists in the Second World War (and in a more doubtful sense the CP itself during 1939–41), there is a major difference in the significance of the anti-war position in the two cases. This is not just that the anti-war position was very much a majority position among left-wing Socialists and Marxists in 1914–18, while the pro-war position was greatly more influential in the Second World War, especially after the CP's adoption of it in 1941. Nor is it just that the present writer believes, broadly, that anti-militarist internationalism was a justifiable and viable position in the First World War, while critical support for the war was unavoidable in the Second.

A more adequate way of understanding the shifting pattern of pro- and anti-war positions in the half-century under review is to see them as responses by Socialists to the development of total war and its effects on society. The problem of the Marxist tradition was that it provided a mode of politics which was in a sense over-theorised – so that it could provide instant explanations for any political twist or turn – but which, in relation to war, was *under*-theorised. War, as a problem for Marxism, was always subordinate to economics and politics, and never really tackled as an intellectual and practical issue in its own right. So that Hyndman's chauvinism, if it was a betrayal of socialist internationalism, could nevertheless be wrapped up in the same pragmatic political language that Marx had used to judge the wars of the nineteenth century. Or the Communist Party's support for Hiroshima could be justified in the general political terms of the rationale of the war. In neither case was what was actually happening in the war, to whole societies and the individuals who made them up, of real concern. But the same could equally be said at times of 'anti-war' Marxism: the Trotskyist case in the Second World War, and the CP's in 1939–41, both had an abstract character which did not connect with the fundamental experiences and aspirations of the working class for whom they claimed to speak.

In broad terms, it can be argued that the 'simpler' intellectual basis of non-Marxist socialism, in the ILP tradition for example, often allowed a more direct response to the human and political problems of total war. The ILP never produced a Hyndman, with sophisticated Marxist arguments for imperialist militarism, even if it had its share of malleable and politically corrupt parliamentarians. The non-Marxist left never got itself into quite the contortions over Fascism and war that the CP managed, however difficult it was to square revulsion against war with the growing recognition that war might be necessary to defeat Fascism. (Similarly, the loose non-Marxist Left in today's peace movements generally avoids the peculiar double standards of many Stalinists and Trotskyists over Soviet nuclear weapons.)

The frequent superiority of less theorised 'moral' and 'practical' responses to total war should not, however, lead us to conclude that war is really a simple business. Pacifism led to heroic war resistance in

1914–18, as did the revolutionary anti-militarism of John Maclean and others, but it generated no strategy for preventing or ending the war. The alliance of pacifism and ethical socialism fell part, as we have noted, under the pressures of the 1930s. Clearly the problems posed by twentieth-century total war have changed so rapidly that no *a priori* moral stance, any more than a nineteenth-century economic theory or politics, is likely to be sufficient for a response. It may be argued that whatever the failings of Marxism, its aim of a historically informed political approach to war is valid and necessary. What is important, however, is that war should be seen as a central and constitutive process of modern society, not as something marginal or derivative. We cannot develop adequate political responses to war without understanding the inner dynamics of total war, and the social, technical and political relationships which it involves. The 'mode of warfare', to use Mary Kaldor's unorthox Marxist concept, and its relationship to society, are constantly changing.[58] This is what explains the rapidly shifting issues of war and peace which have challenged and confused all political traditions, Marxist and non-Marxist alike.

The First World War might therefore appear as a conflict of states, differing only in degree of repressiveness and in the precise form of nationalism which they employed, and acting on behalf of their respective national capitalists. The war was based on unprecedented mass mobilisation which generated, as the left-wing Marxists saw, radical and even revolutionary contradictions. But the very success of European revolutionary movements in the aftermath of the war, and the depth of the counter-revolutionary reaction which they provoked, ensured a profound politicisation of the next phase of total war. So the Second World War appeared as a conflict of political systems – Fascism, Stalinist state socialism, parliamentary democracy – which entailed different models of war-mobilisation. And yet by the end of the war, the strategic and technical dynamics of total war had generated such indiscriminate mass slaughter as to threaten to nullify the political meanings which had seemed so strong. In the nuclear age, while international conflict remains ideologically charged, the means of war are such as to render them self-defeating.[59]

The way in which particular issues of war and peace are embedded within these dynamics of total war means that it is inappropriate to carry over political positions from one phase to the next. This is not to say that there are no meanings, let alone lessons, in these earlier struggles. Resistance to a threatening exterminist climax will surely draw on the varied traditions of war resistance in 1914–18, and maybe even, as E. P. Thompson has recently suggested, on the democratic impulses of military resistance in 1939–45.[60] But we need a politics of war resistance which is based on understanding the realities of war in our time. This is the real lesson of the divided and often inadequate socialist responses to war in the first half of the century.

References

1 For a discussion of this problem, see my Introduction, 'War and Social Theory', to *War, State and Society,* Macmillan, London, 1984.

2 For further discussion see my *Socialism and Militarism,* Spokesman, Nottingham, 1981.

3 Oxford, Clarendon Press, 1985.

4 A symptomatic case is that of James Hinton, author of a fine study, *The First Shop Stewards' Movement,* Allen and Unwin, London, 1973, which discusses workers' organisation in the First World War, and more recently of a general history, *Labour and Socialism,* Wheatsheaf, Brighton, 1983. Although at the time of writing James is National Projects Convenor of the CND, his main historical works do not make war resistance – or even the lack of it – a central concern in his discussion of the world wars.

5 It is interesting that the most famous of all English Marxist historical works, E. P. Thompson's *The Making of the English Working Class,* Gollancz, London, 1963 – whose author was then involved in the first phase of CND, as he was later to initiate its second – falls almost completely under the above general strictures. There are plenty of references to the way in which the Napoleonic Wars affected working-class radicalism in particular, but no *general* consideration of the relationship.

6 See Bernard Semmel (ed.), *Marxism and the Science of War,* Oxford University Press, 1981, pp. 3–12.

7 Theda Skocpol, *States and Social Revolutions,* Cambridge University Press, 1979, pp. 94–5.

8 E. P. Thompson, *William Morris: From Romantic to Revolutionary,* Merlin, London, 1977, pp. 192, 202–25.

9 *Ibid.,* p. 197.

10 William Morris and Belfort Bax, *Socialism, Its Growth and Outcome,* London, 1893.

11 Thompson, *William Morris,* pp. 631–2.

12 Walter Kendall, *The Revolutionary Movement in Britain,* Weidenfeld and Nicholson, London, 1969, p. 48.

13 Newton, *British Labour,* pp. 137–8.

14 *Ibid.,* pp. 146–56.

15 Kendall, pp. 49–51, 137–8; for documentation on the International see also Olga Hess Gankin and H. H. Fisher (eds.), *The Bolsheviks and the World War: The Origins of the Third International,* Stanford University Press, 1940.

16 Kendall, *The Revolutionary Movement,* pp. 52–62.

17 Newton, *British Labour*, p. 164.
18 Kendall, *The Revolutionary Movement*, pp. 75–6.
19 G. D. H. Cole, 'Labour at War', extract from *A History of the Labour Party from 1914*, in Peter Stansky (ed.), *The Left and the War: The British Labour Party and World War I*, Oxford University Press, 1969, p. 139.
20 Kendall, *The Revolutionary Movement*, Ch. 6, 'War and the BSP', pp. 84–104.
21 *Ibid.*, p. 97.
22 See Keith Robbins, *The Abolition of War: The 'Peace Movement' in Britain, 1914–1919*, University of Wales Press, Cardiff, 1976; Martin Ceadel, *Pacifism in Britain 1914–1945*, Clarendon Press, Oxford, 1980; F. L. Carsten, *War Against War: British and German Radical Movements in the First World War*, Batsford, London, 1982.
23 Kendall, *The Revolutionary Movement*, p. 172.
24 Raymond Challinor, *The Origins of British Bolshevism*, Croom Helm, London, 1977, p. 155.
25 The SPGB, the other turn-of-the-century split-off from the SDF, also opposed the war, but its sectarian passivism prevented it from making any impact; indeed its propaganda and membership, uniquely for a socialist organisation in these years, actually declined. See Robert Barltrop, *The Monument: The Story of the Socialist Party of Great Britain*, Pluto, London, 1975, Ch. 6, 'A World Gone Mad'.
26 John Maclean, *In the Rapids of Revolution: Essays, Articles and Letters, 1902–23*, ed. Nan Milton, Allison and Busby, London, 1978; Nan Milton, *John Maclean*, Pluto, London, 1973.
27 See especially, Hinton, *The First Shop Stewards' Movement*, and reprints of J. T. Murphy, *The Workers' Committee* (1917) and *Preparing for Power* (1934), both Pluto, London, 1973 and 1972 respectively.
28 Kendall, *The Revolutionary Movement*, p. 141.
29 See Part 2 of *ibid.*; also Hugo Dewar, *Communist Politics in Britain from Its Origins to the Second World War*, Pluto, London, 1976.
30 Ceadel, *Pacifism in Britain*, p. 74.
31 For definitions see *ibid.*, pp. 2–6.
32 For further discussion, see my *Socialism and Militarism*.
33 For an account, see Dewar, *Communist Politics*, Chs. 2–5.
34 Theses of the Sixth Congress of the Comintern (1928), published by the CPGB, 1932, cited by Dewar, *Communist Politics*, pp. 127–8.
35 Sam Bornstein and Al Richardson, *Two Steps Back: Communists and the Wider Labour Movement 1935–1945*, Socialist Platform, Ilford, 1983, pp. 30–3.
36 *Ibid.*, pp. 36–44.
37 Ceadel, *Pacifism in Britain*, p. 194.
38 *Ibid.*, pp. 198–201.
39 See the interesting discussion of the confused attitudes of the Left in John Saville, 'May Day 1937', in Asa Briggs and John Saville (eds.), *Essays in Labour History 1918–1939*, Croom Helm, London, 1977, esp. pp. 249–59.
40 Ceadel, *Pacifism in Britain*, p. 195.
41 Martin Upham, *The History of British Trotskyism up to 1949*, unpublished PhD thesis, University of Hull, 1976, Vol. 1, pp. 99–101.
42 Ceadel, *Pacifism in Britain*, p. 195.

43 Dewar, *Communist Politics,* Ch. 10; Bornstein and Richardson, *Two Steps Back.*
44 Monty Johnstone's contribution in John Attfield and Stephen Williams (eds.), *1939: The Communist Party of Great Britain and the War,* Lawrence and Wishart, London, 1984, pp. 21–43. This book is based on the proceedings of a conference organised by the CP Historians Group in 1979, and the comments on Johnstone's presentation reflect the reluctance of many older Party members to believe that the Party could have been so wrong. Disappointingly, but not surprisingly, therefore, Johnstone makes his own concessions to Stalinist apology, chiefly in continuing to justify the Nazi–Soviet Pact which was the reason for the Comintern's instructions to Western parties on the outbreak of war. 'The justified support on the diplomatic plane for the Soviet–German Non-Aggression pact had led to unwarranted conclusions on the plane of the political tasks of the Communist Parties', writes Johnstone (p. 41). He also makes a scandalous apology for the USSR's role in Poland in 1939: 'The Eastern part (of Poland) was saved from Nazi occupation by the Soviet entry (sic) on 17 September' (p. 28). Here we see some of the limits of the emancipation from Stalinism which Eurocommunists claim to have achieved.
45 Convention pamphlet by D. N. Pritt, quoted by Johnstone, *ibid.,* p. 37.
46 *Ibid.,* pp. 38–9.
47 Upham, PhD thesis, Vol. 2, p. 274.
48 *Ibid.,* pp. 272–93.
49 John Callaghan, *British Trotskyism: Theory and Practice,* Blackwell, Oxford, 1984, p. 15.
50 The fullest account of Wintringham's ideas is given by Peter Tatchell, *Democratic Defence: A Non-Nuclear Alternative,* GMP/Heretic Books, London, 1985, Ch. 6, pp. 129–56.
51 *Ibid.,* Ch. 8, pp. 177–204.
52 E. P. Thompson, 'VE Day', *Sanity,* May 1985, pp. 18–24, esp. pp. 18–22.
53 See, for example, the conclusion to Dewar, *Communist Politics,* p. 142.
54 For subjective accounts of this, see Pete Grafton, *You, You and You! The People Out of Step with World War II,* Pluto, London, 1981.
55 For the social history of the war, see Angus Calder, *The People's War,* Panther, London, 1971; for the political history, Paul Addison, *The Road to 1945,* Quartet, London, 1977.
56 James Hinton, 'Coventry Communism', *History Workshop,* 10, Autumn 1980, p. 92.
57 *Ibid.,* esp. pp. 112–13.
58 Mary Kaldor, 'Capitalism and Warfare' in E. P. Thompson *et al., Exterminism and Cold War,* Verso, London, 1982.
59 The implications of these ideas are explored further in my book, *The Dialectics of Total War,* Pluto, London, 1988.
60 E. P. Thompson, 'The Liberation of Perugia', in *The Heavy Dancers,* Merlin, London, 1985. For a discussion, see my 'From Total War to Democratic Peace', in Harvey Kaye and Keith Clelland (eds.), *E. P. Thompson: Critical Debates,* Polity, Cambridge, 1987.

5

The Peace Movement between the wars: problems of definition

MARTIN CEADEL

What is a 'peace movement'? It is not clear, in particular, who can usefully be said to have 'peace' as a goal. Obviously not just those who merely prefer peace to war, since 'defencists' (i.e. supporters of ortho-dox defence policies) would be included and only militarists (i.e. glori-fiers of aggression) would be excluded. Nor, at the opposite extreme, only those who insist on peace at any price, since pacifists (i.e. those refraining from all war) would then be the sole members. Normal usage, though somewhat imprecise, seems to equate the Peace Movement with supporters of appeasement (to use the term in its laudatory, pre-Munich sense) and disarmament. But this definition would incorporate into the Peace Movement of the late 1930s and early 1940s isolationists (such as those in the United States), defeatists (such as those in France who welcomed the Vichy regime), and Nazi sympa-thisers (such as members of *The Link* in Britain). It would also exclude the largest peace societies of the time – for example, the League of Nations Union (LNU) – since these had come in the late 1930s to support armed resistance to Fascism.

Here it is argued that a peace movement should be defined with reference not to policies but to theories. Although rarely, if ever, seen in these terms, defence policy is itself the expression of a theory – indeed the most popular theory – about international relations.[1] Here called 'defencism', it is best summed up in the slogan 'if you want peace, prepare for war': it assumes, in other words, that 'true' peace can never be achieved, and all that can reasonably be hoped for is a stable truce between armed and watchful states. The Peace Movement consists of those putting forward alternative theories.

The most extreme and therefore the best known of these is pacifism; but since it makes the same assumptions about the international system as anarchism makes about domestic politics, it has always been a minority viewpoint, even in the Peace Movement. The most popular anti-defencist theories are not pacifist but 'pacificist': they give priority to the abolition of war, but do not deny that participation in certain defensive wars is justified in the meanwhile. There are in principle as many pacificist theories as there are political philosophies: the Peace Movement of the 1980s has seen the emergence of feminist and ecologist (or 'Green') varieties, for example. Between the wars, however, three pacificisms were predominant. The first, rooted in liberalism, assumed that states could co-operate if they were not blinded by irrational nationalism; the remedies it had formerly favoured were free trade and improved international law, but by the inter-war period it was supporting confederalism (support for the League of Nations – hereafter referred to simply as the League) and then, when that had failed, federalism. The second, inspired by socialism of a Marxist or syndicalist tinge, blamed capitalism for war and sought to overthrow it; it faced a choice between two contradictory interim policies: organising the working class for unconditional war resistance, and building up a 'peace front' of Socialists and progressives to resist Fascism. The third reflected the populism of the radical tradition: it blamed elites (aristocrats, diplomats) and vested interests (arms traders, overseas investors) for war scares; its basic remedy was democratic control of foreign policy, but its hostility to the errors made in the Treaty of Versailles led it into early advocacy of appeasement.

What all these theories have in common is an assumption that security is not primarily a matter of armaments, that the armed truce is inherently dangerous, and that the international system can be reformed in such a way as eventually to abolish war. It is this belief that 'true' or 'positive' peace, rather than a mere armed truce or absence of war, can be obtained, which justifies the claim of certain people to 'peace' as a defining goal.

But the political reforms which are required to bring true or positive peace may – as all except the pacifist minority accept – have to be defended by force against reactionary aggression. At times, therefore, members of the Peace Movement may have to pursue policies more normally identified with defencists. It must thus be recognised that, if this permissive definition is applied to Britain in September 1939, more members of the Peace Movement were supporting the Second World War than were opposing it.

This chapter will thus outline the main developments within the British Peace Movement between the wars, not merely because this has never been done before,[2] but because this period exposes the difficulties inherent in the term with a sharpness which could scarcely have been bettered in a controlled social–scientific experiment. That most futile of modern wars, the First World War, had done much to generate the broad yet harmonious Peace Movement which is discussed in the first part of this chapter. But, as the second part will show, its concealed fault-lines were to be exposed painfully by the approach of that most just of modern wars, the Second World War.

I

The pacificist feeling which reached a peak in Britain at the end of the 1920s reflected three main factors: an insular geographical location (together with naval strength); a liberal political culture; and the shock of the First World War (combined with the development of the bomber). The first two combined had, in the course of the nineteenth century, enabled Britain to develop both a marked aloofness from European entanglements, and an organised Peace Movement committed to the belief that international relations could and should be reformed. However, they had also enabled most of its citizens to ignore international affairs most of the time, since Britain did not have conscription and fought in relatively few and distant wars. Thus when a major European war broke out in 1914 a vocal campaign for British neutrality was mounted, though it collapsed tamely. There was also, among various pro-arbitration and anti-war groups, a well-established pacifist body, the Peace Society; but while not formally recanting its views this neither campaigned against the war nor maintained an active pacifist witness, lapsing instead into the moribund state in which it still supposedly survives to this day.

It took the First World War to supply the fear of war which ensured that international affairs became for the first time a highly salient issue in British politics. By developing into a war of attrition it showed modern warfare to have become qualitatively and quantitatively too serious an evil to be ignored. The trenches stripped most of the romance from war; and the pioneering air raids on London and other British targets made it clear that, whereas wars had formerly always been foreign ventures for Britain, its civilians had lost their traditional immunity. In 1918, moreover, those likely to suffer most in a future war acquired a measure of political power: in that year the electorate was almost trebled when most women and unskilled workers were given the vote.

Whereas all pre-1914 peace societies faded out under its impact (except for the National Peace Council, first set up in 1904, which was mainly a co-ordinating body), the First World War saw them replaced by bodies which, though careful not to mount stop-the-war campaigns, proved to be made of sterner stuff. A hard core of radical neutrality campaigners formed the Union of Democratic Control (UDC)[3] as early as August 1914; socialist pacifists led by Fenner Brockway founded a No Conscription Fellowship in November;[4] and Christian pacifists followed suit with a Fellowship of Reconciliation (FOR) in the very last days of 1914. In 1915 liberal pacificists and others founded a League of Nations Society in May; and a group of former Suffragists formed the Women's International League in October, following a women's international congress at The Hague in April.[5] And after 1916, when conscription was introduced for the first time, 16,500 men were to claim a conscientious objection.

For the first three years of the war all such activity was subjected to vilification. Not until 1917 did the tide start to turn in the Peace Movement's favour, which it did for two reasons. First, in that year signs of war-weariness began to appear among various sections of the population. Responding to it, the Labour Party's pro-war majority and anti-war minority in effect compromised and adopted a foreign policy programme that was very close to that of the UDC. Indeed, when in 1924 the first Labour Government was formed, fifteen UDC members were given office – nine of them in the Cabinet and one of these, Ramsay MacDonald, Prime Minister and Foreign Secretary. The second development of 1917 which favoured the Peace Movement was the entry of the United States into the war, which, thanks to President Wilson's personal enthusiasm, made the League a practical aspiration. A second, and self-consciously 'realistic', pro-League society was established in 1918, the League of Free Nations Association; the imminent ending of the war led it suddenly to merge with the League of Nations Society in October 1918 to form the LNU.

At the end of the war conditions were well suited to peace activity, which thrives best on a symbiosis of pessimism and optimism. The pessimism was induced by fear of war – an understandable response to four years of trench warfare and to a limited but alarming first taste of air attack on British cities. The optimism consisted of an expectation that international relations could be reformed and war prevented – a result of Britain's ingrained liberal values and a legacy of a time when insularity had provided it with a larger margin of security than was still available in an era of air power.

The post-war decade brought further contributions to this symbiosis. Economic difficulties and lack of progress towards the general disarmament promised in the Treaty of Versailles reinforced pessimism. And the establishment of the League in 1920, the belated start in the aftermath of the 1925 Locarno treaties of detailed preparations for a World Disarmament Conference (which eventually met in February 1932), and the signature in 1928 of the Kellogg-Briand pact, could all be taken as signs that structural reform in the international system might yet be achievable. There was evidence also of a change in public attitudes to war. From the autumn of 1928, the tenth anniversary of the armistice, books and plays about the First World War suddenly became popular and were for the next two years published (or republished) in considerable numbers. Although not all had a pacificist intent, a realistic account of the fighting from the individual soldier's standpoint could scarcely help conveying the impression of a tragic and futile struggle. In addition a scarifying 'next war' literature had started to appear, predicting the destruction of civilisation by bombers dropping canisters of lethal gas.[6]

In this climate of opinion it was not surprising that the new, post-1914 Peace Movement was able, during the 1920s, to consolidate its position. Most remarkable about the way it did this was its unity: few contemporaries seem to have noticed the underlying differences of approach between the four main schools of thought which were to become more apparent in the 1930s. The reasons for this were the growing ascendancy of one of these – liberal pacificism – and the policy consensus in support of multilateral disarmament.

Thanks mainly to the conscientious objectors of 1916–19, pacifism had made some progress towards establishing a separate identity for itself within a predominantly pacificist movement. But as long as pacifist – and therefore less arduous and more practical – approaches to war prevention (such as through the League) flourished, as they did in the 1920s, it could make little headway. Admittedly, the FOR had decided to continue its witness in peacetime and was growing at a modest pace; and a No More War Movement (NMWM) was formed in 1921 to replace the No Conscription Fellowship (wound up in 1919 when conscription ended). But the aggregate membership of pacifist societies remained small – well under 10,000, without allowing for overlaps. There was, it is true, some sign of untapped support: by December 1927 Labour MP Arthur Ponsonby had as a personal venture obtained 128,770 signatures for his (pacifist) Peace Letter even though it took him two-and-a-half years to do so. But in the 1920s most pacifists were content to work within the LNU.

Socialist pacificism has only exceptionally found favour even in the Labour Party. Before 1914 even the minority of enthusiasts for a general strike against war, such as Keir Hardie, accepted that their policy was 'bluff and bluster' (to quote a recent historian); at this time the party 'shared the views which were traditional in radical circles', as Clement Attlee, himself a UDC member, later acknowledged.[7] For a time, in the unstable international and domestic conditions of the early 1920s, it looked as though war resistance might catch on. There was a continuous current of criticism of the League as 'capitalist'; and war resistance enjoyed intermittent popularity: in 1920, upset at the Government's sympathy for Poland in its war with the Soviet Union, the Party and the TUC set up a Council of Action to threaten a general strike if Britain actually intervened; and an explicitly socialist war-resistance motion was passed by the Labour Conference in 1922, a year of intensifying Franco–German hostility. A similar resolution was passed by the 1926 Conference, in the embittered aftermath of the General Strike, although this success was to be repeated only once again (in 1933, as will be seen).

Radicalism, for the first quarter of the twentieth century the dominant strand in the Peace Movement's (as well as the Labour Party's) thinking, went into a sharp decline in the mid-1920s. The experience of the 1924 Labour Government was a crucial factor in its eclipse. The UDC never recovered from the departure into the MacDonald administration of its leading members, to which setback was soon added the death later that year of its driving force, E. D. Morel (to whom, significantly, MacDonald had not given office).

But the problem was less one of personnel than of policy. In applying their somewhat inchoate philosophy to international affairs in the first four decades of this century, radicals tended to favour two policies (neither of which was exclusive to them): isolationism, on which they had placed most emphasis before 1914; and appeasement – not yet a pejorative term – which took the form in the early 1920s of calls for the revision of the Treaty of Versailles. Though both were favoured by the UDC, its members soon discovered, once in government, that neither was suited to the prevailing European situation, which required a constructive initiative that would reassure France sufficiently to soften her policy towards Germany. Having earlier vetoed one such initiative, the draft Treaty of Mutual Assistance, on the grounds that it was too entangling, MacDonald felt unable, despite similar reservations, to dismiss out of hand a second, the Geneva Protocol (a proposal for strengthening the League's arbitration procedures), without appearing simply to be obstructive and endangering his politically crucial image as a peacemaker. Indeed, he was probably relieved to fall from office before having to make a final decision on the Protocol. According to the perverse logic of adversary politics, however, its rejection by the incoming Conservative Government helped Labour retrospectively to discover a positive enthusiasm both for that proposal and for the League in general. A further contributory factor was strong support from Arthur Henderson and young Labour intellectuals such as Philip Baker (later Noel-Baker) and Will Arnold-Forster. Left-wingers might complain, as one did at the Party's 1925 Conference, that the 'policy of the League of Nations was the policy of Liberalism';[8] but the sharp decline of the Liberal Party in the October 1924 election made this objection less embarrassing politically. In general, Labour's shift of emphasis from radical to liberal pacificism in the mid-1920s passed off without comment or controversy.

This shift by Labour was a symptom of the fact that by the mid-1920s liberal pacificism was by far the dominant ideology within the British Peace Movement – a position it was to sustain into the early 1950s. But a more obvious symptom was the rapid growth of the LNU into a peace society of unprecedented size and influence. The product, as already noted, of a somewhat hasty merger between two societies in order to present a united voice during the crucial discussions about setting up a League, it had only a relatively modest impact in its early years because even liberal pacificists found it hard to enthuse about the League actually set up in 1920. But the LNU decided to play down its own doubts and build up its organisation. With generous financial backers (David Davies and Lord Cowdray), a distinguished secretary (J. C. Maxwell Garnett), and a prominent, though maverick, Conservative politician as its acknowledged leader (Robert, Viscount Cecil of Chelwood), it was able to project itself as more 'respectable' than other peace societies – an educational body rather than a pressure group.

By 1925, in which year it received a Royal Charter, the LNU was already able to collect no fewer than 255,469 annual subscriptions. And, with the League gaining in prestige in the more optimistic international climate of the second half of the 1920s, this figure reached 406,868 in 1931. (For comparative purposes it may be noted that the equivalent national membership figure claimed by the Campaign for Nuclear Disarmament early in 1986 was just over 110,000.) Gross membership (which included all those who had in previous years paid a subscription but had since neither resigned nor died) was by 1931 over 950,000. Not only have these figures never been matched, nor has the LNU's capacity to intimidate defencist opinion: in the late 1920s and early 1930s Tory MPs found it prudent to give disingenuous answers to LNU questionnaires[9] and to play down their doubts concerning the World Disarmament Conference's prospects of success. When on 11 July 1931, for example, all three party leaders addressed a large and enthusiastic LNU disarmament rally in the Albert Hall, Stanley Baldwin revealed his true scepticism only in a muttered aside to a neighbour on the platform as the cheering reached its height: 'Rather pathetic, isn't it?'.[10]

But the LNU had achieved quantity at the expense of quality, having failed to warn its members that there were weaknesses in the League Covenant or that the League might not always be able to secure peace without resort to economic or even military sanctions. For example, even Cecil's *de facto* second-in-command in the LNU, Professor Gilbert Murray, could claim in 1928 that the League's 'normal sanction is the public opinion of the world; its most effective weapon publicity'; and Cecil himself later admitted privately that 'for ten years we practically evaded the problem of sanctions. I remember perfectly doing it myself . . . '.[11]

This evasiveness was not caused simply by the desire to woo or retain pacifists and radical isolationists as members so as to enhance the LNU's authority as a pressure group; it reflected the honest optimism of its leaders. In particular, they set great store by the long awaited World

Disarmament Conference, which in January 1931 was finally summoned to meet at Geneva in thirteen months' time. Indeed, the disarmament campaign, which the LNU had first mounted in 1927 when Cecil resigned from the Government, was given priority over everything, even over the duty to expound the case for collective security. This was made explicit in a letter from Cecil to Murray in January 1931: 'I believe that we shall be able to get all the Peace organisations into a campaign for making the Disarmament Conference a success, on the understanding that no part of the campaign will be to suggest any new commitments nor to emphasise Article 16.'[12] Such optimism received a severe dent in the 1930s, as will shortly be seen, with painful consequences for the LNU.

Nor was the general public's pacificist mood more soundly based. Major war was understood to involve far higher costs and lower benefits than had previously been realised; and it was politically riskier by the end of the 1920s to campaign for increased defence expenditure than for the League. But this was in part because of the unusually favourable strategic situation which then prevailed. Even defencists could not identify a short-term threat to the security of the British Isles in the late 1920s; and it seemed irresponsible not to give Geneva every chance of showing what it could do as an additional diplomatic mechanism to preserve a peace that was clearly in British interests.

Even such changes of attitudes which had occurred on the peace issue were, moreover, single-issue deviations from a prevailing conservatism (albeit conservatism of a fairly liberal variety), as a glance at domestic politics shows. Although Labour had emerged from the 1929 election as for the first time the largest party, it still lacked an overall majority and, confronted by the world slump, resigned after just over two years. It should not be forgotten that the Conservatives, who returned to power in August 1931 as the dominant force behind the National Government and soon secured an overwhelming electoral mandate, were in office (either on their own or as the major partner in a coalition) for all but three of the thirty years from 1915 to 1945.

As late as 10 September 1931, Viscount Cecil had told the League Assembly (which he was attending as a delegate – albeit a reluctant one – on behalf of the National Government): 'There has scarcely ever been a period in the world's history when war seems less likely than it does at present.'[13] With hindsight this demonstrates the extent to which the Peace Movement's position at the start of the 1930s was based on excessive hopes regarding the moral authority of the League and the achievability of disarmament, since only nine days later the Japanese conquest of Manchuria began.

II

This was, of course, the first of a series of aggressive acts which in the course of the 1930s brought about a strange transformation in British politics: much of the formerly anti-war Left came to support an assertive foreign policy; and much of the formerly jingoistic Right became appeasers. As a result the Peace Movement suffered a progressive loss of coherence. The process was, however, more gradual than is sometimes supposed, as is revealed by an examination of the impact of the successive crises of the decade.

Manchuria, September 1931

Although Japan's defiance of the League undoubtedly provided the first setback for the Peace Movement, it was only a modest one: LNU subscriptions fell in 1932 for the first time, for example, but by only 4·6 per cent. And although it also produced the first signs of polarisation between a new breed of 'sanctionists' who drew the lesson that aggression had to be deterred and a reviving alliance of pacifists and socialist war resisters, the vigour and clarity with which each side pressed its case should not be exaggerated.

A major reason for this was the LNU's failure to criticise either the League or the National Government for its failure even to consider sanctions against Japan. This omission, which distressed some of its keenest supporters,[14] was in large part attributable to its long-standing policy of respectability; but it also reflected a fear both of losing members and of distracting attention from, and damaging the chances of, the World Disarmament Conference.

The new body set up by the committed sanctionist David Davies in 1932, the New Commonwealth Society, failed to do the job either. For one thing it was too small even to offset the decline in LNU membership.[15] For another thing, instead of simply advocating rearmament and improved co-operation between League states, it called for the League to be equipped with an international police force (which would enforce the decisions of a new 'international equity tribunal') − a proposal which managed to be both obfuscating and divisive. It was obfuscating in that even some pacifists welcomed it on the assumption that it would take effect only after national armies had been abolished by the Disarmament Conference, and thus be truly comparable to a domestic police force. It was divisive because it alienated many of those who accepted that the provision of adequate security had in practice to precede disarmament: in particular, the Conservative members of the LNU's Executive Committee, such as Austen Chamberlain, felt that to equip the League with its own armed force would require the suspension of the Council's unanimity rule, and therefore amount to 'a complete change in the constitution of the League [from] an assembly of equal States [to] a super-State put above us all'.[16] So dangerous did this issue become to the unity of the LNU – it dominated all its discussions of international security until the Abyssinia crisis (and continued to be a troublesome issue thereafter) – that the leadership deliberately chose to emphasise instead 'the effectiveness of diplomatic, financial, and economic sanctions'.[17] Thus the New Commonwealth Society's Utopianism had the ironic effect of encouraging the LNU leadership to evade the issue of military sanctions altogether.

Nor was the other side of the argument presented much more effectively. The increase in support for pacifism and war resistance was not enough to compensate for the decline in the League Movement. The most conspicuous form pacifism took was the formation, albeit only on paper, of a Peace Army 'to put their bodies unarmed between the contending forces' in the Far East, as the preacher Dr Maude Royden suggested soon after the Japanese occupation of Manchuria began. When she and her fellow Christian pacifists, the Revd Herbert Gray and the Revd H. R. L. ('Dick') Sheppard, appealed for recruits, 800 pacifists volunteered. Although this gesture achieved more publicity for pacifism than it had received at any time since the gaoling of conscientious objectors in the First World War, not all of it was favourable.[18] It was not just because of the Manchuria crisis, it should be noted, that pacifists were starting at this time to consider techniques of non-violence as a way of making pacifism politically effective: another stimulus was the non-violent campaign against the salt tax which the Indian nationalist Mohandas K. Gandhi had begun in 1930. By coincidence it was just six days before the Japanese attack that Gandhi had arrived in London for talks on India and many leading members of the Peace Movement took the opportunity to meet him. But despite these new initiatives the major pacifist society, the NMWM, was going into a decline: like the ILP, with which it had a large overlap of membership, and which disaffiliated from the Labour Party in 1932, it was convinced that the slump and 1931 political crisis were harbingers of a British revolution. Many of its members came to accept the case for revolutionary violence, thereby clouding the pacifist message at a time when it might have been proclaimed with unprecedented clarity.

This increase in revolutionary sentiment helps to explain the revival of socialist pacifism, which caused the Left to become dissatisfied with the 'liberal' policies it had been pursuing. But it was also a result of the League's poor performance in the Manchuria crisis, which had not only reduced its prestige but had panicked the Soviet Union into believing that the capitalist states might connive at Japanese expansion into its own territory. On 27 April 1932 the Comintern launched a war-resistance campaign in order to forestall any such collusion.[19] A World Anti-War Congress held in Amsterdam from 27 to 29 August 1932 led to the formation in November of a British Anti-War Movement. But, since this gave the impression of being more anti-pacifist than anti-war,[20] it was slow to attract support and did little to clarify thinking on the justifiability or otherwise of the use of force.

The Nazi Revolution, 1933

'Hitler cured me of pacifism', G. D. H. Cole asserted in 1940.[21] The process was less instantaneous, however, than this and similar statements implied. Contrary to subsequent orthodoxy, the most noticeable short-term reaction to the new regime in Germany was an isolationist reaction, which expressed itself in various ways: most notably in upsurges of pacifism and war resistance.

The most famous – indeed overrated – expression of pacifism was the passing by the Oxford Union of the resolution 'That this house will in no circumstances fight for its King and Country' on 9 February, in response to a brilliant speech by the philosopher C. E. M. Joad arguing the case for reliance on Gandhi-style non-violence against an invader. During the debate, the motion was understood to imply absolute pacifism, the commonly expressed view that it had really endorsed a pro-League or a people's war being a subsequent rationalisation by those embarrassed by this evidence of pacifism.[22]

The upsurge of socialist pacifism was attributable also to further disillusion with the League as a result of Japan's continuing defiance of it, and a dispute between Britain and the Soviet Union which coincided with the increased tension in Europe in the early months of 1933. By March, for example, Sir Stafford Cripps had concluded: 'If the Disarmament Conference fails we can be no longer bound to any covenants of mutual assistance. . . . Our first duty is to try to prevent war breaking out, to counter the war hysteria by a general strike.'[23] During 1933, moreover, the British Anti-War Movement enjoyed a brief phase of relative success in attracting publicity and support. And the high tide of war resistance was reached early in October when the Labour Party Conference at Hastings unanimously – and, as it transpired, for the last time – committed itself 'to take no part in war'. The defeat for the party's pro-League leadership was slightly mitigated, however, by the passing of a long composite motion on disarmament which included an endorsement of the international police force, thereby enabling the National Executive Committee to pretend that support for the League had not thereby been ruled out.

Just eight days after the Hastings conference dispersed, Germany withdrew from both the Disarmament Conference and the League: the announcement came on 14 October 1933, 'one of the outstanding dates in European history'[24] (as John Wheeler-Bennett was soon presciently to describe it). Hitler's action prompted a few Socialists – A. L. Rowse conspicuous among them[25] – to adopt a robustly anti-Nazi position; but the more common initial response was again one of 'never again!' emotionalism. At a series of by-elections, starting with East Fulham which Labour won dramatically on 25 October, the Opposition blamed the National Government for the crisis at Geneva and accused it of being about to re-start the arms race.

Labour's 'peace' alternative was, however, unclear: Attlee was one of those privately admitting that the party 'has not really made up its mind as to whether it wants to take up extreme disarmament and an isolationist attitude or whether it will take the risks of standing for the enforcement of the decisions of a world organisation against the individual aggressor states'.[26] In most cases the party fudged the issue by putting forward what was in effect the radical critique, identifying profiteering arms traders and incompetent ministers and diplomats as the major threat to peace. The implications were implicitly appeasing and isolationist: Hitler's behaviour escaped criticism; and, although lip-service was often paid to the League, little reference was made to the security aspect of what tended euphemistically to be called 'the collective peace system'. The left's 'East Fulham' tactics were perceptively criticised by Guy Chapman: he wrote in December 1933 that 'the country has the wind up', but warned that 'negative fear' of the sort Labour was exploiting should not be confused with 'the true desire for peace for its own sake'.[27] Indeed, negative fear was also being exploited at this time by right-wing isolationists such as Lord Rothermere, whose motives for attacking Locarno and the League were not pacificist, let alone pacifist.

Only in 1934, when it became apparent that Hitler was likely neither to lose office nor to be tamed by it, did the British Government begin tentatively to rearm – a decision announced in July. The public then began to face up to the choice between two policies – containment or accommodation – for dealing with Germany; and, even so, many sought a middle course.

Evidence of growing support for containment was provided by both the Labour Party and the LNU. The former abandoned war resistance and reaffirmed its support for the League. The latter arrested the decline in its membership and successfully launched what became known as the Peace Ballot, a private area-by-area referendum designed to show that the League had far greater public support than the isolationist right-wing Press admitted. In reaction against these developments appeared the first signs of what came to be called a 'new pacifism', the most significant being Dick Sheppard's plea in a letter widely published in the Press on 16 October 1934 to be sent postcard pledges of unconditional pacifism.

But, despite receiving 50,000 such pledges, Sheppard was not to follow up his initiatives for a further nine months, and, despite his opposition to any form of sanctions, was prepared to support the LNU's Peace Ballot. This was a spectacular success, partly because it had been clumsily attacked by the Government, which caused the Peace Movement and the Opposition both to rally to it; indeed the Peace Ballot can be described as the greatest achievement by any British cause group. Between November 1934 and June 1935 half a million volunteers helped distribute the questionnaires; and thirty-eight per cent of the adult population filled them in, for the most part giving the pro-League answers for which the LNU hoped (although less resoundingly so on the controversial two-part fifth question, on sanctions).

Yet the LNU achieved this great feat by encouraging a roseate view of what by the spring of 1935 was starting commonly to be called 'collective security'. This was discussed mainly in the abstract: only in the last month of polling did Italy's intentions toward Abyssinia start to become a matter of public concern. The Ballot's organisers implied that collective security could be achieved mainly through the threat of economic sanctions, military sanctions being a last resort that would rarely, if ever, need to be invoked. Indeed, the LNU, which still (until 1936) opposed rearmament, implicitly regarded collective security as a middle way between pacifism and the traditional defencist policies of rearmament and alliances. The same, it should be noted, was true of the Labour Party. Although expressing support for the League, it opposed rearmament and continued at by-elections to attack the Government for creating an unnecessary arms race. Nor was the Communist position any more resolute at this time: although the British Anti-War Movement renamed itself the British Movement Against War and Fascism, in line with the change in Soviet foreign policy which led to entry into the League in September 1934, it too opposed rearmament and seemed to have shed little of its war-resistance mentality. As late as mid-1935, therefore, the Peace Movement still enjoyed both high morale and a fair degree of unity in support of economic sanctions.

The Abyssinian crisis, 1935

Mussolini's unprovoked aggression towards Abyssinia was a more significant watershed than either of those so far considered, and forced more people to admit that the choice for Britain lay between accommodation and containment.

Although the Italian invasion was not launched until 3 October, its evident imminence prompted a marked increase in support for the former during the summer of 1935. In July Dick Sheppard organised the signatories of his Peace Pledge into a new pacifist society, the Sheppard Peace Movement. Simultaneously, and with remarkable suddenness, was heard a chorus of demands for the grievances of 'have not' nations such as Italy to be taken seriously by 'have' nations such as Britain and France.[28] In a letter sent to the Pope and other religious leaders as well as to The Times on 19 August 1935, for example, Labour's leader George Lansbury called for a new peace conference to distribute the world's resources more fairly. Though in the first flush of hostility to the Treaty of Versailles there had been calls for appeasement, particularly from the UDC, the revival that ensured the policy lasting notoriety began as a response to Mussolini's propaganda rather than to Hitler's.

But while this was happening others were drawn – very reluctantly in many instances[29] – to accept the need for containment. At its 1935 conference, which was in session when Italy launched its attack, the Labour Party endorsed the case for (if necessary, military) sanctions; and, after a celebrated attack by Ernest Bevin, Lansbury resigned as leader. Stanley Baldwin, moreover, called a general election for 14 November 1935, not merely to exploit Labour's disarray, but on the assumption that to do so while the Government could be seen to be supporting the League (which had agreed to impose limited economic sanctions against Italy) was the best way to avoid attacks of the sort it had suffered at by-elections. And when, with the election safely out of the way, the insincerity of its stance was exposed in December by the leaking of the Hoare–Laval agreement for the appeasement of Italy, a public outcry forced Baldwin to dismiss his Foreign Secretary – perhaps the clearest instance, in peacetime anyway, of the sacrifice of a British minister wholly and exclusively in deference to public displeasure with the policy he was pursuing.

Yet though the Abyssinia crisis entered Labour mythology as the moment it ceased to oppose rearmament,[30] this was premature. G. D. H. Cole, for example, was still a pacifist, even though he was prepared to admit that support for the League was the next best policy.[31] For many Socialists the crucial experience was to be the Spanish Civil War; and it was not until 1937 that the PLP switched to a policy of abstention on arms estimates. Moreover, the public's support, like that of the LNU, for action against Italy largely reflected an assumption that, even if the worst came to the worst and economic sanctions failed, naval power would suffice; as Philip Noel-Baker privately acknowledged of the League supporters he found in Coventry when standing for Labour in the general election: 'There is no doubt that they are quite prepared for the Navy to have a fight.'[32] When the true risks of 'collective security' and 'anti-Fascism' became apparent, as they did in the early spring of 1936, the defiant mood of late 1935 rapidly subsided; and only a minority continued to press for them.

The 'triple crisis' of 1936

Three events in 1936 – the remilitarisation of the Rhineland in March, the final defeat of Abyssinia in May, and the civil war which broke out in Spain in July – together constituted the major watershed of the decade. They generated grass-roots activity of a type not matched until the 1980s: in the summer and autumn of 1936 local 'peace councils' sprang up in many cities and towns. Between them, the three crises appeared to show that Europe was moving towards a 'civil war' between two ideological camps. Since they also discredited the belief that a middle way between isolation and military intervention was possible, these crises stimulated a long overdue public debate on the question of whether or not Britain should commit itself to the maintenance of order in Europe. As a result, the polarisation of opinion between accommodation and containment began in earnest.

This was reflected in the local peace councils. Many, particularly those affiliated to the National Peace Council, were dominated by pacifists and appeasers. But an anti-Fascist line was taken by some, particularly those dominated either by those LNU members who remained convinced of the need for collective security or by left-wingers, many of whom had belatedly been convinced by the Spanish Government's resistance to Franco's insurrection that a just (i.e. non-capitalist) war was possible. (Especially active on peace councils were the Communists, who seem, in the interests of their popular-front strategy, finally to have abandoned the attempt to make a go of their British Movement Against War and Fascism.) By October 1936 the incoherence of the peace-council movement had driven the officers of the LNU's Finchley Youth to complain to Gilbert Murray and to attack the view

> that if the public can be made sufficiently keen on 'peace', there will be no difficulty about agreement on the policy by which it will be obtained; thus Peace Tableaux, Peace Pageants, Peace Exhibitions, Peace demonstrations, Peace Flags, Peace Bands, Peace Pennies. The fact that half of those who participate in these activities would want our Government to do one thing and the other half the exactly contrary thing is ignored as though the conflict did not matter.[33]

The reason that advocates of containment, such as the leaders of the LNU and New Commonwealth Society, used peace rhetoric was that of two options theirs was in the short term by far the less popular, both in the Peace Movement and – although such judgements are hard to prove in respect of a period in which opinion polls were still in their earliest infancy – among the public in general. The LNU's membership had already dropped slightly in 1935 because the Peace Ballot had distracted its members from the routine task of collecting subscriptions; but instead of recovering in 1936, membership began an uninterrupted decline so that by 1939 it was, at 193,266, down to less than half its 1931 total. A large part of the problem was that widespread talk of the 'reform' of the League in the light of the Abyssinian experience – a euphemism for the removal of the sanctions clause from its Covenant – discouraged the collection of subscriptions.[34]

Admittedly, the LNU and New Commonwealth Society did find some partially compensating support among defencists attracted to it for the very reasons that others were leaving. Most notably, Winston Churchill began to use League rhetoric ('Arms and the Covenant') in order to make containment politically more acceptable. He was invited to join the LNU executive committee in July 1936, and initially accepted, but later chose instead to become President of the British section of the New Commonwealth Society.[35]

But such recruits were rare, and added, moreover, to the diversity of a collective-security movement that was anyway suffering from embarrassing and unnecessary divisions. The most spectacular was the bitter dispute within the LNU, which brought Cecil to the brink of resignation several times, over the International Peace Campaign (IPC), a French-based international anti-Fascist grouping (*Rassemblement universel pour la paix*), to which Viscount Cecil wished in effect to subordinate the LNU. His argument was that the Abyssinian crisis had shown the urgent need for European governments (especially the French) to be placed under the sort of pressure which the LNU and the Peace Ballot had already placed on the British. But this was to admit that no new organisation was needed in Britain: what the IPC was designed to do was lend the prestige of the already adequate British League Movement to its weaker European brothers. Many LNU officials felt that to have another pro-League organisation was superfluous and confusing: what, they asked, was to be the relationship of local LNU branches to peace councils affiliated to the IPC? They were also suspicious of the close connections which the *Rassemblement universel pour la paix* enjoyed with the French Communist Party.[36]

But the basic problem for the collective-security movement was that containment was the policy blamed for the First World War. Since it was widely believed also that arms races caused wars – the concept of 'deterrence' being little understood – those advocating rearmament were accused of fatalistically accepting the inevitability of war. Only accommodation seemed to hold out any hope that peace could be preserved. Acknowledging this, the LNU and the New Commonwealth

Society tried to argue that their emphasis on containment did not rule out the possibility of peaceful change in Germany's favour. They were thus keen to retain the support of Lord Allen of Hurtwood even though he was emerging as a leading appeaser. In November 1936, for example, the LNU adopted as official policy a manifesto by Allen which urged the League to study territorial revision and economic co-operation – a move which its annual report for 1937 noted to have been 'an influential factor in preventing [further] defections'.[37] For its part, the New Commonwealth Society began to emphasise the opportunities for constructive change presented by its proposed international equity tribunal, instead of dwelling on the international police force. But by the end of 1937 this strategy had clearly failed. As Murray admitted privately to Cecil: 'We are no longer a peace party opposing a Jingo party, we are a "League and Collective Security" party, opposing pacifists, isolationists, pro-Germans, etc. We are actually for a "spirited foreign policy"!'[38]

Accommodation, on the other hand, was more obviously a peace policy. It took two forms: for a hard core, pacifism; for the majority, appeasement. The crucial step in the development of British pacifism came in May 1936 when the Sheppard Peace Movement was reborn as the Peace Pledge Union (PPU). Not only did it attract as its 'sponsors' a remarkable group of writers and thinkers (including Vera Brittain, Aldous Huxley, Rose Macaulay, Middleton Murry, Bertrand Russell and Donald Soper), it soon attracted more members than any other pacifist society in the world before or since. Indeed, during its euphoric first phase of expansion, there seemed a chance that the PPU might make pacifism a significant force in British politics.

Although a minority always took the view that pacifism was not 'a stop-the-war trick'[39] but a witness to eternal truths, most members of the PPU hoped at first that pacifism, the last untried strategy for preventing war, would prove to be practical politics. Either total disarmament would morally deter aggressors or, if this failed, an invading army would be disabled by Gandhian non-violence. But by the time of Sheppard's sudden death in October 1937, when its total of pledges stood at 120,000, it was clear that it would never be in a position to dictate national policy. It thus began to talk less of non-violence and more of appeasement, a policy which non-pacifists also supported.[40]

Indeed, in the form of calls for the revision of Versailles and for the creation of a new economic and colonial order so as to remove the causes of war, appeasement had been the most vocally supported peace policy since the Rhineland crisis in particular. One indication of its popularity was the revival of the National Peace Council. Never a particularly influential body, from 1933 to 1935 it had been almost completely paralysed by its inability to pronounce upon the question of sanctions in case one wing or other of the Peace Movement disaffiliated from it. By October 1936, however, it was convinced that 'circumstances are combining to give the [sanctions] controversy itself an air of increasing irrelevance and unreality' and that peaceful change was a policy on which the Peace Movement could unite.[41] Indeed, by 1937 'peaceful change' had clearly replaced collective security as the Peace Movement's major slogan.[42] With Neville Chamberlain becoming Prime Minister in that year, it was also about to become the Government's major policy.

The Prague crisis, March 1939

If it took the 'triple crisis' of 1936 to polarise opinion, it took Hitler's occupation of Prague on 15 March 1939 to alter the balance of opinion from supporting accommodation to supporting containment – or, more accurately, to complete a change which had been under way for some time. Already during 1938 Hitler's expansionist moves – the Anschluss with Austria in March and the taking back of the Sudetenland from the Czechs following the Munich agreement of September – had begun to raise doubts about whether Hitler could be accommodated, although sheer fear of war served to suppress them during crises such as that of September 1938. And various aspects of German behaviour since Munich had sharply increased those doubts, particularly for members of the Government. Yet it was Hitler's taking control of Czechoslovakia which constituted the first definitive proof that he was an imperialist rather than a nationalist wishing simply to incorporate all Germans into the Reich. All hope of accommodating Germany was thus destroyed; and war was widely seen to be inevitable. That psychological preparation for it was made at this time helps to explain why its actual outbreak in September 1939 was to be greeted with such calmness. A policy of rearmament and military alliances came widely to be seen as the only prudent course to follow.

That support for appeasement was severely and abruptly undermined is illustrated by the fate of a petition demanding a new peace conference which the National Peace Council had organised. By an unfortunate coincidence the Prague crisis occurred three days before the big public meeting intended to publicise the fact that the target of a million signatures – 1,062,000 in all – had just been reached. When this duly took place in the Queen's Hall on 18 March 1939, the Bishop of Chelmsford felt obliged to warn the German people that its government's breach of faith three days previously 'has almost universally destroyed confidence in its pledged word, has undermined the moral basis of its claims on other nations and has therefore made infinitely more difficult negotiations between the nations for the just and general peace which we and you desire and for which we shall continue to labour'.[43]

Those whose work for appeasement was unaffected by Prague were a hard core who for the most part were similarly unaffected by the outbreak of the Second World War and were thus prepared to urge peace negotiations with Hitler, at least until the summer of 1940. A few were socialist war resisters: the writer George Orwell was in this category until August 1939; while the party to which he belonged, the ILP, condemned the Second World War as imperialist, as did the Communists for the duration of the Molotov-Ribbentrop pact.

But an increasing proportion of appeasers and negotiated-peace advocates were from the far Right. A leading example was Sir Oswald Mosley: his British Union of Fascists and National Socialists was able to stage a minor revival during the summer of 1939 on the strength of a peace campaign; and at Britain's largest indoor political meeting, at Earls Court on 16 July, an audience of 20,000 heard him warn that 'a million Britons shall never die in your Jews' quarrel'; and in 1940 Mosley was interned. But although Fascists were not members of the Peace Movement, as here defined, but its fellow-travellers, a minor but significant connection between the pro-Nazi and pacifist movements developed in the aftermath of the Prague crisis. Not only did Sheppard's de facto successor in the PPU, its chairman, Canon Stuart Morris, imprudently join The Link, but a longstanding pacifist who became increasingly prominent in the PPU at this time, the Marquess of Tavistock (shortly to succeed to the Dukedom of Bedford), founded the anti-Semitic as well as pacifist British People's Party. By 1941 George Orwell was complaining of the 'moral collapse' of British pacifism since Sheppard's death, alleging that 'many of the surviving pacifists now spin a line of talk indistinguishable from that of the Blackshirts ("Stop this Jewish war" etc.) and the actual membership of the P.P.U. and the

British Union [of Fascists and National Socialists] overlap to some extent'.

That a minority of pacifists fell into bad company was because they were determined to remain politically relevant even in a context in which, as Orwell pointed out, the political implications of pacifism could not but be 'objectively pro-fascist'.[44] Political effectiveness was the initial aim of the PPU, as already noted; but the approach of war had converted many of its members to the alternative view that pacifism was a faith rather than a policy. Where the PPU's liveliest minds had once imbibed Gandhi's ideas, in 1939 they studied the communitarian ideal – as a way not only of maintaining their witness in a world they could no longer influence but, if the community was agricultural, also of satisfying a military-service tribunal.[45] When war broke out the PPU was balanced between a politically-minded 'Forward Movement' of young pacifists campaigning for immediate peace, and a distinguished 'Forethought Committee' taking a quietist view. Its spurt in membership during the phoney war, which took the total to 136,000 in April 1940, was due to its ability to attract recruits of both persuasions. When France fell and Britain faced invasion, it was mainly the 'practical' pacifists who recanted, giving the quietists the upper hand. They had always constituted a majority in the FOR, which, significantly, was able to expand steadily not only in the late 1930s (reaching nearly 10,000 members on the eve of the Second World War) but also throughout the Second World War. So, too, was the much smaller Anglican Pacifist Fellowship, which had been founded in 1937.[46] That so many pacifists had ceased to claim that their faith was a practical one was one of the reasons they were treated more tolerantly by British society in the Second World War.

Another reason, of course, was that they were too few to pose a threat to the war effort. Although signing a peace pledge required more courage than renewing a subscription to the LNU, it should be remembered that even at its peak the PPU was considerably smaller than a declining LNU, especially since its own figures referred to the accumulated total of pledges received over the previous four years, minus only those recantations of which it had been informed, rather than to current annual subscribers. The active membership of the PPU was tiny: although it still had 98,414 pledges in its 'live membership file' at the end of the war, less than 4,000 members had participated (by post) in any of the wartime elections for the PPU's national council, a discrepancy far too large to be blamed on administrative difficulties alone. A better impression of the strength of committed pacifism can be gained from the fact that *Peace News* had a circulation of 20,000, despite being boycotted by wholesalers. Conscientious objectors, numbering nearly 60,000, were nearly four times more numerous than in 1916–19, but made far less political impact. Denied martyrdom, they experienced 'sincere doubts and perplexities', as Fenner Brockway admitted in 1941, whereas the No Conscription Fellowship had 'gained in inner spiritual strength and in intensity of support from the persecution which it had to meet'.[47] Morale worsened, moreover, as the war went on: the percentage of conscripts registering as conscientious objectors began at 2·2 but fell sharply from the summer of 1940 to end the war at 0·2. It should be noted that nearly thirty per cent of these objectors had their claim for exemption dismissed outright by their tribunals; and the vast majority made no protest – only three per cent of objectors going to prison, a tenth of the proportion incarcerated for periods long or short in the First World War.

The Prague crisis thus reduced the accommodation wing of the Peace Movement to a rump: a small group of socialist war resisters, some pro-Nazi fellow travellers, and a pacifist movement of remarkable size by historical or comparative standards but nevertheless too small, subdued and quietist to have the political impact for which it had once hoped. In terms of numbers, they were a minority of the Peace Movement.

The latter's containment wing was, moreover, reviving its spirits. Admittedly the LNU found itself more than ever an ancillary of Churchillian defencism after the Munich crisis: in October 1938, for instance, its monthly journal *Headway* had been taken over by the 'Focus' group of anti-appeasers, although this arrangement did not succeed commercially and full control was restored to the LNU in August 1939.[48] But liberal pacificism was stimulated by a new campaign for federalism which was wholly independent of the LNU. The federalists' central proposition was that the League had been let down by its member states, which, in a confederal organisation, could decide for themselves whether or not to follow its recommendations and had chosen not to. They thus argued that the only way to ensure the success of collective security was to create a federation that would prevent states having any say in their foreign and defence policies by deciding these centrally.

With hindsight it seems surprising that federalism had previously received so little attention in Britain. The first peace society to campaign explicitly for it was Federal Union, set up in the immediate aftermath of the Munich crisis by four young unknowns without previous experience in the Peace Movement, who believed themselves to be breaking new intellectual ground. Their efforts passed unnoticed until March 1939, when two events suddenly created a climate of opinion which they were able to exploit. The first was the publication of the English edition of *Union Now,* by Clarence Streit, an American journalist whose experience as a Geneva correspondent had convinced him of the need for a federal union of the United States, the British Empire and Dominions, and democratic Western Europe. The second was the disillusionment with appeasement of which the Prague crisis was the culmination. Thus an enthusiastic former appeaser, Lord Lothian, was already looking for something new to believe in and was (according to his biographer) 'carried off his feet by Clarence Streit's book . . . making the most extravagant claims for it, speaking of it as perhaps destined to be epoch-making like *The Wealth of Nations* or *The Origin of Species*'.[49] After Prague, moreover, many supporters of collective security felt the need for a long-term goal to replace the tarnished League: even *Headway* thus welcomed *Union Now* in April 1939 as a 'book which may well influence world history'. When the Second World War broke out, federal proposals dominated public discussion of war aims: a notable example was the statement in November 1939 by Clement Attlee (like Ernest Bevin, a strong Federal Union supporter) that 'Europe must federate or perish'. As its Secretary, Charles Kimber, observed in December 1939: 'When war broke out . . . support for Federal Union changed abruptly from a merely polite interest into an active desire to help the movement.'[50] Membership had increased to 10,000 by early in 1940; and its quality was at least as impressive as its quantity: its Economic Committee, for example, comprised Evan Durbin, F. A. Hayek, James Meade, Lionel Robbins, and Barbara Wootton, as well as Beveridge. Its intellectual appeal at this time can be attributed both to the uncertain future of the nation–state in view of Hitler's aggression (with France on the brink of surrender in June 1940 even Churchill proposed an Anglo-French Union), and to the absence of other proposals for reforming the international system.

To sum up: Britain's experience between the wars clearly demonstrates the difficulties inherent in the notion of a Peace Movement. The conventional definition in terms of support for anti-war policies would by 1939 include a significant defeatist or pro-German element, as well as principled war resisters and pacifists. The definition suggested here in terms of support for theoretical alternatives to 'defencism' regards the LNU and Federal Union as part of the Peace Movement – and therefore as its largest element – since they believed that (in the words of the statement issued by the LNU executive committee in the immediate aftermath of the Munich settlement, of which it was critical) 'positive peace represents a spiritual ideal which, however paradoxical it may seem, men will defend, if need be, with their lives'.[51]

References

1 For an analysis of the ideological assumptions of the 'war and peace debate' see my *Thinking About Peace and War*, Oxford University Press, OPUS series, 1987.

2 Indeed there is no history of Britain's twentieth-century Peace Movement; this chapter is a by-product of one I am currently writing (for Oxford University Press).

3 See Marvin Swartz, *The Union of Democratic Control in British Politics during the First World War*, Oxford, 1971. The standard work on the Peace Movement as a whole during the war is Keith Robbins, *The Abolition of War*, Cardiff, 1976.

4 This organisation has been particularly well served by historians: Jo Vellacott, *Bertrand Russell and the Pacifists in the First World War*, Brighton, 1980, and Thomas C. Kennedy, *The Hound of Conscience*, Fayetteville, 1981.

5 It was founded at a meeting on 30 September and 1 October 1915, according to its 'First Yearly Report, October 1915–October 1916': see Women's International League Papers, British Library of Political and Economic Science. There is a lively account of the Hague congress in Anne Wiltsher, *Most Dangerous Women*, London, 1985.

6 For this literature see Martin Ceadel, 'Popular fiction and the next war, 1918–1939', in Frank Gloversmith (ed.), *Class, Culture and Social Change: a new view of the 1930s*, Brighton, 1980.

7 Douglas J. Newton, *British Labour, European Socialism and the Struggle for Peace 1889–1914*, Oxford, 1985, p. 293; C. R. Attlee, *The Labour Party in Perspective*, London, 1937, p. 200.

8 M. Jacobs: see *Labour Party Conference Report 1925*, London, p. 255.

9 See John Ramsden, *The Age of Balfour and Baldwin 1902–40*, London, 1978, p. 341; and also see L. A. Zimmern's remarks on 'Cynics and Pharisees', in her *Must The League Fail?*, London, 1932, p. 14.

10 Hugh Dalton, *Call Back Yesterday: Memoirs 1887–1931*, 1953, London, p. 255, citing his diary entry for 11 July 1931. For the speeches, see *We Want All Round Disarmament: The national demonstration of 11 July 1931 to promote the success of the World Disarmament Conference*, LNU pamphlet No. 302, July 1931.

11 Gilbert Murray, *The Ordeal of This Generation: the war, the League and the future* (the 1928 Halley Stewart Lectures), London, 1929, p. 131; Cecil to Murray, 14 November 1938, Gilbert Murray Papers, Bodleian Library.

12 Cecil to Murray, 23 January 1931, Box 16c, Murray Papers.

13 Cited in Christopher Thorne, *The Limits of Foreign Policy*, London, 1972, p. 4.

14 See the excellent account in Donald S. Birn, *The League of Nations Union 1918–1945*, Oxford, 1981, Ch. 5.

15 Its gross world-wide membership after five years was only 3,584. Its papers are in the David Davies collection at the National Library of Wales, Aberystwyth.

16 *Report, L.N.U. General Council Dec. 1934,* LNU 0304, February 1935, pp. 58–61.

17 Gilbert Murray to Philip Noel-Baker, 2 April 1933 (copy), Murray Papers.

18 For the pacifist upsurge of 1931–32, including the Peace Army, see Martin Ceadel, *Pacifism in Britain 1914–1945: the defining of a faith*, Oxford, 1980, Ch. 6.

19 Jonathan Haslam, *Soviet Foreign Policy, 1930–33: the impact of the depression*, London, 1983, pp. 89–91.

20 For the somewhat bemused Quaker reaction to the British Anti-War Movement see the Minutes, Friends Peace Committee, 2 February, 6 April, 8 June 1933, Friends House. At this time Communists such as T. H. Wintringham were prepared explicitly to claim: 'The struggle against war is first and foremost a struggle against pacifism' (*Labour Monthly,* May 1932, p. 290). For a similar assertion see R. D. Charques, *The Soviets and the Next War*, London, 1932, p. 13.

21 Cited in A. W. Wright, *G. D. H. Cole and Socialist Democracy*, Oxford, 1979, p. 244.

22 For a full account of the debate see Martin Ceadel, 'The "King and Country" debate, 1933: student politics, pacifism and the dictators', *Historical Journal*, 22, 1979.

23 *New Clarion*, 25 March 1933, pp. 301, 309.

24 John W. Wheeler-Bennett, *The Disarmament Deadlock*, London, 1934, p. 181.

25 See his article in the *New Clarion*, 4 November 1933.

26 C. Attlee to Thomas Attlee, 6 November 1933, cited in W. Golant, 'The emergence of C. R. Attlee as leader of the Parliamentary Labour Party in 1935', *Historical Journal*, 1970, p. 327. Golant comments: 'The Party's ambiguity became his own.' The same analysis had been put forward in Lord Ponsonby's letter of 22 October 1933, Lansbury Papers, British Library of Political and Economic Science.

27 *New Clarion*, 2 December 1933.

28 A prolific appeaser, H. Powys Greenwood noted in the *Spectator*, 27 December 1935, pp. 1061–2: 'Six months ago the title of this article ['The Claims of the Have Nots'] would have conveyed nothing to the reader except perhaps a vague form of socialism.'

29 For renunciations of their former 'pacifism' at this time, see Francis Meynell, *My Lives*, London, 1971, p. 250; Leah Manning, *A Life For Education*, London, 1971, p. 142; Lord Pethick Lawrence, *Fate Has Been Kind*, London, n.d. [1943], pp. 185–6; Ernest Thurtle, *Time's Winged Chariot*, London, 1945, pp. 132–4.

30 For the myth, see 'Cato', *Guilty Men*, London, 1940, p. 33.

31 G. D. H. Cole, *The Simple Case for Socialism*, London, 1935, p. 101.

32 Noel-Baker to Cecil, 11 November 1935, Cecil of Chelwood Papers, Add. MSS 51108, British Library.

33 Memorandum by Enid Cooper and Barbara Hayes, 27 October 1936, Murray Papers (Box 74); see their earlier memorandum enclosed with a letter to Murray, 12 October 1936.

34 One local branch resolved on 8 May 1936, for example, 'to postpone any recruiting on a large scale until the change in the League's constitution had taken place'. Minutes, Swinton and Pendlebury LNU Executive, 8 May 1936: I owe this source to Professor Daniel Waley.

35 Minutes, LNU Executive, 24 July, 17 September 1936, British Library of Political and Economic Science.

36 The best published accounts of this controversy so far are in Ernest Bramsted, 'Apostles of collective security: the L.N.U. and its functions', *Australian Journal of Politics and History*, XIII, 3, 1967, pp. 347–64, and Birn, *The League of Nations Union*, Ch. 10.

37 *L.N.U. Year Book (1938)*, p. 11.

38 Murray to Cecil, 27 December 1937 (copy), Murray Papers.

39 A phrase used in the Fellowship of Reconciliation's journal, *Reconciliation*, August 1935, pp. 145–7.

40 See Ceadel, *Pacifism in Britain*, Ch. 14, and David Lukowitz, 'British pacifists and appeasement: the Peace Pledge Union', *Journal of Contemporary History*, 9, i, 1974, pp. 115–27.

41 See the editorial in its journal, *Peace*, October 1936.

42 For a comment, see *Headway*, August 1937; for an early use see Arnold Toynbee, 'Peaceful change or war?', *International Affairs*, January–February 1936, esp. p. 26; see also C. A. W. Manning (ed.), *Peaceful Change*, London, 1937.

43 Cited in *Peace*, April 1939; see also Vera Brittain, *Testament of Experience*, London, 1939, pp. 196–7.

44 Cited in Sonia Orwell and Ian Angus (eds.), *The Collected Essays, Journalism and Letters of George Orwell*, Vol. 2, Penguin, Harmondsworth, 1970, pp. 69, 210.

45 See Ceadel, *Pacifism in Britain*, pp. 291–2.

46 Membership figures are taken from the General Committee Minutes, Fellowship of Reconciliation Papers, British Library of Political and Economic Science; and from the newsletters of the Anglican Pacifist Fellowship, consulted through the courtesy of the Revd Sidney Hinkes, its current Secretary.

47 Fenner Brockway, *The C.O. and the Community*, London, n.d., pp. 3, 4.

48 Minutes, LNU Executive, 28 August 1939.

49 J. R. M. Butler, *Lord Lothian*, London, 1969, p. 243.

50 'CDK Draft for *Federal Union News* (not used), 10 December 1939', Federal Union Papers, kindly shown to me by Mrs Sheila Barton. This account of Federal Union is based on these papers and those in the possession of Mr Ota Adler, and on an interview with Sir Charles Kimber, 28 July 1977. There is further material in the outstanding study by Walter Lipgens, *A History of European Integration 1945–1947: the formation of the European Unity Movement*, translated by P. S. Falla and A. J. Ryder, Oxford, 1982.

51 Minutes, LNU Executive, 6 October 1938.

6

The Labour Party
and CND: 1957 to 1984

RICHARD TAYLOR

'The battleground *was the Labour Party*. It was the only arena in which the campaign could ride'. (Ian Mikardo)[1]

Introduction

The close but ambiguous relationship between the Labour Party and CND has been centrally important to both organisations since the late 1950s. The intention here is to describe and analyse that relationship and to explore its political effects in the years since CND's creation.

From the outset of the campaign in 1958,[2] the CND leadership regarded the Labour Party as the natural vehicle for implementing CND policy. Although initially there had been antipathy within the campaign to politics *per se*, on the grounds that the issues were fundamentally moral (and to a lesser extent scientific) in nature, there was never any doubt that the leadership would opt for close alliance with Labour. As Jacquetta Hawkes has recalled, almost all the early CND leadership had been ' "Leftish", "Pinko", or whatever kind of term you like to use . . .'[3].

Whilst there were those in the Movement who rejected this CND/Labour alliance – notably the advocates of Gandhian Direct Action (in the Direct Action Committee and, later, the Committee of 100) – the position of the CND leadership was quite clear. As Canon Collins, Chairman of CND throughout these early years, stated in his biography:

. . . if CND were going to be at all successful, it would need to take into consideration political expediencies, and to gear itself to the realities of Britain's parliamentary democracy . . . one of our first aims should be to win a majority for CND policy within the Labour Party, and a second, so to put the case for British nuclear disarmament to the British public as a whole that, at a general election, a Labour Party committed to our policy would be returned to power.[4]

This remained CND's position, even after the reversals of 1961 which, as discussed below, rendered CND's strategy unworkable – at least in the short term. When the Movement 'reawakened' in the late 1970s, its alliance with the Labour Party became even closer, and with the adoption by the Party of an unequivocal commitment to the central aspects of CND's policy and the election to the leadership of Michael Foot (one of the founding fathers of CND), CND and the Labour Party entered the 1983 General Election in complete unity. (Although, of course, this was a unity to be shattered by the Right of the Party during the election campaign, as is discussed below.)

The commitment of CND's leadership in the early years to the Labour Party was the practical extension of a pre-existing attitude. The majority of CND's leaders had been involved previously in Labour Party pressure groups of varying types – usually in the peace or social fields – and they regarded the Movement as being of the same genre. The relationship was thus central for the leadership: it is no exaggeration to say that its whole campaign for unilateral nuclear disarmament stood or fell by the degree of success that it had in 'converting' the Labour Party. And, of course, after a sensational victory in 1960, it 'fell' rather than 'stood'. After 1961 CND entered a period of slow but sure disintegration and decline as the frustrations of the Labour Party failure exacerbated the tendency, already inherent, for the Movement to fragment into its incompatible and often mutually hostile component ideological parts. Not until 1979/80 was the Movement to grow again into a major force.

If the Labour Party were crucial for CND's strategy, the CND campaign has also been important for the Labour Party – both Left and Right.

In the 1957 to 1964 period the issue of nuclear diarmament was the focus of a bitter struggle within the Party between Left and Right. The issue itself was in the mainstream tradition of humanist, moral protest on defence and foreign policy affairs which had been strong on the Left for the whole of the Party's existence.[5] But, as the Movement gained momentum through 1958 and 1959, and as the Labour leadership became both more established and more explicitly revisionist in its attitudes (especially after Labour's third successive electoral defeat in 1959), so the nuclear disarmament debate became the focal point in the struggle to depose Hugh Gaitskell and the right-wing leadership, and to assert the control of Conference over the PLP.

In the changed circumstances of the 1980s, the issue no longer divided the Party in quite the same way. Labour's defence policy, in common with its overall policy stance, had shifted significantly to the Left by the time of the 1983 election. And the Party was unequivocally committed to the removal of Cruise Missile bases, the cancellation of the Trident programme, and the unilateral renunciation of nuclear weapons by Britain. Nevertheless, during the election campaign, latent divisions within the Party again erupted, and the public disagreements over defence policy were an important factor in Labour's humiliating defeat.

The analysis of the CND/Labour Party/Labour Movement relationship has thus been of central and continuing importance for all those concerned. The debate affected not only CND and the specific stance of the Labour Party on defence and foreign policy issues, but also the nature of the Labour Party itself.

Aneurin Bevan and the H-Bomb

Any consideration of the Labour Movement's[6] attitude to nuclear weapons and to the Peace Movement in the post-war period should take as a starting point the position of Aneurin Bevan. Following the Labour Party's defeat in 1951 there had been deep and bitter divisions between Left and Right, with Bevan the undisputed leader of the Left.[7] Essentially, the conflict was ideological in nature and consequently involved heated debate over the future orientation of the Party. But among other issues, those of defence and foreign policy played a major role. And, from 1951 to 1957, Bevan championed the cause of disarmament and campaigned for the Left perspective on a range of foreign policy issues.

Although Bevan had never questioned Britain's decision to manufacture nuclear weapons, there is no doubt that by the mid-1950s he was clearly in favour of unilateral action by Britain to end the arms race and begin the process of multilateral disarmament. 'If Britain had the moral stature she would say: "we can make the H-Bomb, but we are not going to make it, we believe that what the human race needs is leadership in the opposite direction, and we are going to give it".'[8]

Bevan's abrupt reversal of his stance at the 1957 Conference was unexpected and dramatic. At the first of two immediately pre-Conference meetings Bevan was the co-proposer (with Sydney Silverman and Barbara Castle) of a motion explicitly advocating unilateral cessation of Britain's manufacture of nuclear weapons.

By the second (Friday) meeting of the NEC Bevan had reversed his position. In response to the Mikardo/Silverman unilateralist resolution Bevan argued that to accept the resolution 'would mean the dismantling of international alliances and commitments, dismaying the Commonwealth and reducing Britain to complete negation in the councils of the world'.[9] This was the crucial dividing line: up until the second NEC meeting Bevan had held increasingly to the unilateralist line, albeit with a different emphasis at times from others on the Labour Left. What happened to change his mind between the two meetings? Ian Mikardo is certain that it was a discussion with Sam Watson, the miners' leader, that finally convinced Bevan to change tack. 'I had a very long talk with Nye', recalled Mikardo; '. . . and he'd talked with Sam Watson who'd said to him that only through Nye's becoming Foreign Secretary could détente be brought about, and there was no way he could become Foreign Secretary if he stuck to the unilateralist line. And that's what I think caused the change.'[10]

Bevan realised that Labour could only win with a united leadership, and that his own prospect of achieving high office rested on reaching some *modus vivendi* with Hugh Gaitskell. Bevan thus adopted an increasingly conciliatory attitude through 1955, 1956 and 1957. Moreover, the Suez débâcle achieved for the Labour Party the unity that had been eluding it since the late 1940s. For a short period the Labour Party was united on a political campaign appealing at both the moral and the political level to the whole Movement. The effect of this was to secure for the party a positive dynamism which Bevan was reluctant to relinquish once the Suez crisis had passed. Also, by 1957 there had been a shift away from Cold War politics as a result of Khrushchev's revelations about Stalin, and Bevan, as the probable future Foreign Secretary of a Labour government, was keen to exert his influence on the world stage to ensure that disarmament and coexistence could be brought about as soon as possible.

All these pressures served to bring Bevan to the 1957 Conference in very different mood, and in a very different political context. As Mikardo has pointed out, 'Nye really had a passionate desire to end the era of confrontation and he saw himself as a possible architect of a new international pact . . . and he swallowed some of his convictions in order to move forward to achieving that.'[11]

Whether or not such a perspective was justifiable or should be seen as a rationalisation for a self-interested 'sell-out', relates in part to the assessment made of Bevan's individual objectives and abilities. At a more fundamental level, however, such arguments involve the debate over whether unilateralism and its associated demands are necessarily linked to structural, socialist change. Further, this debate raises the wider question of whether the Labour Left was or is a viable agency for the achievement of these objectives. These are major themes and are returned to later in this chapter: they are also discussed, in a wider context, in the concluding chapter.

Here, however, attention must first be focused upon the 1957 Conference debate and its repercussions on the Labour Left, and, more generally, on the Peace Movement. The central resolution, which was opposed by the NEC, advocated an unequivocally unilateralist policy.

Bevan, speaking for the NEC, wound up the debate, following impassioned pleas for unilateral nuclear disarmament from, amongst others, Anthony Wedgwood Benn, Judith Hart and Frank Cousins. All made a strong *moral* case for unilateral nuclear disarmament, and Cousins in particular argued that Britain must 'take a moral lead', adding that 'there is no compromise with evil'.[12]

In his reply Bevan first emphasised the NEC's opposition to nuclear weapons and stressed that he himself had probably 'made more speeches to more people condemning the Hydrogen Bomb than anybody in this Conference'. He went on to emphasise the positive aspects of the Vienna declaration and laid great stress on his interpretation of the NEC policy that a commitment to the suspension of tests entailed a *de facto* suspension of manufacture. The crux of Bevan's argument, however, was that if Britain surrendered the Bomb, and thus severed her international connections and influence, she would lose the chance that Bevan believed she had of acting as the major bridge between East and West. And in his most notorious and emotive asides Bevan claimed that to surrender, unilaterally, the British nuclear deterrent would 'drive Great Britain into a diplomatic purdah', and 'send the Foreign Secretary naked into the Conference Chamber'. The resolution was rejected by 5,836,000 to 781,000, a resounding victory for the platform and the trade union leadership.

It was not only the *content* of the speech that dismayed Bevan's erstwhile colleagues, although this was shocking enough; even more galling and surprising was the vicious tone of the denunciation.

Why did he do it? And what were the effects? Bevan had turned against not only his previously held policy position, but also against almost all his former friends and supporters. All this could, conceivably, have been justified in Bevan's own terms if there had been an overriding moral imperative for his change of line. Yet no convincing case of this type has been, or could be, made out: Bevan never attempted to justify to the 'Bevanites' the reasons for his new position, save in the course of the speech itself. The only justification – and it was a strong justification, given the parameters of action available within the assumptions of the Labourist position – was *political*. Bevan's position demonstrated in microcosm, as Coates has pointed out: 'the perennial dilemma of the Labour Left MP, of needing a Labour government and a position within it if he was not to be totally impotent, but having to pay a high price . . . for his position of influence'.[13] In the specific case of Bevan subsequent events prevented his strategy being put to the test. Labour lost the 1959 election; and Bevan died, tragically early, in 1960. (By early 1963 Gaitskell too was dead, and the Party poised on the verge of the very different 'Wilson era'.)

Nevertheless, had these events not occurred, it seems reasonable to assume that the whole operation had badly misfired for Bevan: not only had he renounced unilateralism and sacrificed, effectively, his freedom to make any radical criticisms of domestic policy, he had also 'profoundly altered'[14] his relationship with the Left of the Party. 'For the first time, the Left in the Labour Party moved beyond him, leaving him behind.'[15]

Bevan was thus left without an effective power base, without a clear or coherent policy, and without the freedom of manoeuvre to present a challenge to the 'leadership of the man he disliked so bitterly'.[16]

One unforeseen consequence of the whole episode, however, was to bring into being the mass movement – CND – that had been promising to break through for some time. The Labour Left was incensed, upset, and bitter about Bevan's 'defection': nobody on the Left, not even his closest associates such as Michael Foot, followed Bevan's example.[17] For many, such as Peggy Duff and Olive Gibbs,[18] Bevan's *volte face* was a shattering blow, both personal and political. Frank Allaun's reaction was typical: 'I was absolutely downhearted – absolutely heartbroken. And there were many others who lost their faith in Aneurin Bevan from that time onwards. It didn't cause a split in the Labour Movement because those who were against the Bomb still went on being against the Bomb.'[19] The importance of the whole episode for future Labour/CND relations was profound: Bevan's 'defection' both precipitated the coming of the mass movement, and drastically weakened its power base within the Labour Movement.

The Labour Left and CND: 1958

The movement against nuclear weapons gathered momentum rapidly, following the 1957 Brighton Conference. The National Council for the Abolition of Nuclear Weapons Tests (NCANWT) and the Direct Action Committee (DAC) were growing, and *Tribune* intensified its already vigorous campaign for unilateralism in late 1957. Initially, following the 1957 Conference, the *New Statesman* did not support unilateralism.[20] Following Priestley's article on 2 November, however, events moved swiftly, and the *New Statesman* carried supporting letters from Russell, Trevor Huddleston, Stephen King-Hall, Frank Beswick and others.[21] By the end of December, the *New Statesman* had come out in full support of a unilateralist policy. Kingsley Martin, the *New Statesman*'s Editor, was instrumental with J. B. Priestley in bringing together the informal group which eventually gave birth to CND itself. Thus, by the time of the inaugural meeting of CND at the Central Hall on 17 February 1958, the Labour Left was fully involved in the Campaign.

Through 1958, as CND gathered strength, the Labour involvement grew, steadily rather than spectacularly. Labour CND activists were, however, concerned about the existence and growth of an anti-Labour Party, 'anti-politics' elements, centring in the DAC but also finding some response in the ranks of CND. Two distinct, indeed opposed, views must be distinguished. There were those, like Jacquetta Hawkes, Arthur Goss, and to some extent Collins himself, who, although in broad terms Labour Party supporters saw the Campaign as essentially a moral crusade and rejected and resented the intrusion of politics. And, at the other end of the spectrum, there were the 'militants' of the DAC who rejected conventional parliamentary politics, and saw working through the Labour Party as, at best, of secondary importance. The 'moral crusade' arguments were easier for Labour activists in CND to counter, not least because in their wider ideological assumptions people such as Collins and Jacquetta Hawkes were firmly in the Labourist tradition. As far as the CND leadership was concerned the issue thus tended to be one of emphasis and degree rather than a substantive difference of principle.

In practice, the CND leadership followed Collins's lead and realised that, even if the campaign were to remain a 'moral crusade', the need to work with and through the Labour Party was of paramount importance if any progress were to be made.

The same cannot be said of the DAC opponents of Labourism, whose prime objective was to mobilise the people through direct action. A central part of this philosophy was the 'Voters' Veto' campaign: and the whole notion of the Movement encouraging voters to abstain from voting for non-unilateralist Labour candidates struck at the heart of the Labour Party activists' view of politics and the purpose of CND. Apart from the risk of proscription, the very notion of attempting action outside the Labour Movement framework was, to both Labour left-wingers and the CND leadership, completely unacceptable.

Thus, by the time of the 1958 Conference, the CND/Labour Left relationship had grown firmer and stronger, and in late 1958 a Labour Advisory Committee was established to replace the H-Bomb National Campaign.

Given this firm CND/Labour left alliance the 1958 Conference was not as great a success for CND as might have been expected. In a major and lengthy debate on foreign affairs and disarmament, Bevan hedged on the issue of the Bomb. But the opposition to Bevan and the NEC – and the extent to which the Left had moved on past Bevan[22] – was evident from the support received for the straightforward unilateralist resolution proposed by John Horner of the Fire Brigades Union. Hugh Gaitskell, however, resolutely opposed unilateral nuclear disarmament in his speech, and the Conference gave overwhelming backing to NEC policy.

As always at Labour conferences the main element was the trade union block vote; and, in 1958, the major unions combined to back the Party leadership's policy on defence. Having established its position solidly on traditional left-wing territory, the crucial area in 1959–60 for those expounding unilateral nuclear disarmament lay in the trade unions.

The trade unions, CND and the lead-up to the 1960 decision

Through the early summer of 1959 trade union support for CND policy grew rapidly. The first major breakthrough was the adoption by the GMWU of a unilateralist resolution at its June Conference. The GMWU had been the most reactionary of the major trade unions and this decision was, as Peggy Duff later remarked, rather 'like the Daughters of the Revolution tearing up their draft cards'.[23] Significantly, the debate was concerned far more with the moral and environmental aspects of the issue than it was with the political. The vote reflected the trend of public opinion, as shown in the polls, in the growing concern in the media with the dangers of nuclear tests and radiation, and, of course, in the rapid growth of support for CND.

However, Conference was recalled on 24 August, on the pretext that the original conference had not had the chance of discussing the Labour/TUC joint policy statement, 'The Next Step'. The Union's decision was duly reversed[24] but the psychological damage had been done, and more trade unions were to adopt unilateralist policies during the summer.

The major blow to the leadership of the Party came when the TGWU rejected the 'official' policy of the Labour/TUC document and adopted instead a complicated seven-point statement which represented, in effect, a unilateralist declaration. From this point on, the TGWU and Frank Cousins were the spearhead of the attack on the leadership's nuclear policy. It would be mistaken to suggest, however, that Cousins imposed his view upon the TWGU. There is no doubt, of course, that Cousins, as a forceful leader and a committed unilateralist,

> fought hard to swing his Union's policy towards unilateralism . . . But the decision of the 1959 Conference, marking a distinct break with Party policy, was part of a genuine upsurge of unilateralist sentiment, an upsurge which paralleled a similar development in the General and Municipal Workers' Union. The difference between the two Unions was undoubtedly a matter of leadership. The General and Municipal Workers' Union successfully resisted the tide; Cousins encouraged it.[25]

At the TUC Conference of 1959 the TGWU motion was defeated, but a motion protesting against the installation of missile bases was narrowly carried. Because of the General Election there was no Labour Party Conference in the autumn of 1959 (although a special post-electoral conference was held in December) – but at the end of July it had been reported that over one-third of the resolutions submitted for the conference advocated unilateral nuclear disarmament (and of the 141 resolutions on disarmament, 117 called for unilateral nuclear disarmament and only one supported the TUC/Labour proposals).[26] The confrontation which was to take place in 1960 had thus already taken shape in 1959.

Why did the tide of trade union opinion begin to swing behind the unilateralist policy during 1959? Relatively few trade union members were Labour Left supporters: the rank and file pressure towards unilateralism resulted rather from other factors. First, the rise in public awareness and concern over the dangers inherent in nuclear weapons had its effect in trade union circles, as elsewhere. Second, the coincidental rise of more radically-minded trade union leaders, in particular Frank Cousins, gave a considerable impetus to the Movement.[27]

This predominantly emotive commitment to unilateralism, which was not linked organisationally to CND, was deeply felt, but was more easily swayed by other, political, considerations during 1961 and 1962. Indeed, the relative ease with which Gaitskell's campaign to reverse the 1960 decision of Conference was accomplished, testified, among other things, to the politically superficial commitment of trade unionists on the nuclear disarmament issue. One of the major weaknesses of the Movement as a whole was its lack of political understanding and commitment on the nuclear issue. Nowhere was this political weakness more crucial than in the trade unions' attitudes and responses from 1959 to 1961.

However, in 1959, it was evident that Labour Movement opinion was moving strongly towards the unilateralist view, from whatever motivations. Throughout 1960 the trade union commitment to unilateralism increased rapidly: of the 'big six' trade unions the TGWU, AEU, USDAW and NUR all came out in support of unilateralist policies, leaving only the GMWU and NUM backing the NEC/TUC policy.

Thus, by the time of the Conference, the bulk of trade union votes was mandated in favour of both the TGWU and AEU resolutions. The total voting of the 'big six' for the Scarborough debate was mandated as follows:

For the AEU resolution: 2,298,000
against: 1,292,000
For the TGWU resolution: 2,026,000
against: 1,546,000

If the mandated votes of several of the smaller trade unions are added to this, it was virtually certain before the Conference took place at Scarborough that the NEC/TUC policy would be defeated.

Labour defence policy 1958–60

Before discussing the 1960 Conference and its aftermath, however, attention must be turned to the twists and turns of the Labour Party's defence policy. The key figure was Hugh Gaitskell, who was just as committed, emotionally and politically, to the maintenance of the British independent nuclear deterrent as was the Conservative Government. All the shifts and compromises of the Labour leadership have to be seen against this commitment: Gaitskell regarded any compromise on the independent deterrent principle as, at best, a regrettable political necessity.

The Labour Party policy document 'Disarmament and Nuclear War', was issued on 6 March 1958, following the leadership's decisive victory at the 1957 Conference, and adhered strongly to the principle of deterrence, to the maintenance of the British deterrent, and to the importance of maintaining the NATO alliance.

In response to the mounting pressure through late 1958 and early 1959 (particularly on the trade union front), the Labour Party published a new declaration on 24 June 1959: 'Disarmament and Nuclear War: The Next Step'. This was a complex and comprehensive document which laid out a rather grandiose list of objectives 'as laudable as they were impracticable'.[28]

The central proposal was for the formation of a non-nuclear club, with Britain agreeing to abandon her nuclear weapons unilaterally, *provided* that all other nations except the USA and USSR agreed to a document banning nuclear weapons. The intention, and the immediate impression, of this proposal was that Britain would take the lead in a great and dramatic moral movement to rid the world of nuclear weapons. In reality the picture was rather different: Britain would only develop the non-nuclear club if all other nations agreed not to develop nuclear weapons – and there was no chance whatsoever that other nations, France and China most obviously, would agree to such a proposal.

The proposal was in reality a straightforward tactical attempt by the leadership to head off the growing challenge of unilateralism. Having established the 'camouflage' of the 'non-nuclear club', the document rejected unilateralism on the grounds that there was no evidence that such action by Britain would have any effect on either the USA or the USSR, but that it *would* lead to the break-up of NATO, the possibility of US isolationism, and thus be a threat to world peace.

The combination of the leadership's approach, and the imminence of the General Election, saved the day for the NEC/TUC policy at the TUC (where the AEU, NUM and NUR supported the leadership). But the reasoning behind the policy statement was transparent, and seen to be so: in the aftermath of the election defeat, Gaitskell could not stem the tide of revolt.

The existing trend towards unilateralism in the Labour Movement was considerably reinforced by the final collapse of the last remnants of Britain's nuclear credibility when, in April 1960, the Government was compelled to announce the abandonment of the Blue Streak project, and thus, *de facto,* the independent deterrent. Before this announcement the Co-operative Party, USDAW and AEU had all passed unilateralist resolutions, and by June the NUR, TGWU, and NUM had passed similar resolutions. Gaitskell was forced to abandon his rigid stance, and the Labour Party adopted a new policy. The new document, 'Foreign Policy and Defence', was published on 1 July 1960. Prior to this, in March 1960, only a month before the announcement of the abandonment of Blue Streak, Gaitskell had argued that the real case for Britain's maintenance of the independent deterrent was to prevent Britain's total dependence on the USA. (This was hardly compatible with the non-nuclear club policy of a few months before, which had supposedly formed the central thrust of Labour's policy.) The new policy thus had to cope with a chaotic defence situation: the Blue Streak decision had rendered Gaitskell's central adherence to the British independent deterrent redundant. Moreover, the non-nuclear club proposals had proved to be manifestly unworkable by 1960 and had to be discarded. In the event the new policy provided little fresh hope of compromise: it argued clearly for Britain remaining in NATO, although it stated that Britain should press for revisions of NATO policy. It acknowledged that the 'Blue Streak fiasco' had shown that Britain could not maintain herself as an independent nuclear power. (And this finally and explicitly differentiated the Labour Party policy from that of the Conservatives, who were attempting to negotiate for Skybolt to replace Blue Streak, and thus preserve the independent deterrent.) The document reiterated Labour Party opposition to nuclear tests and to Thor missile bases, but introduced no new formulations which might have won over the unilateralists.

The upshot of the new situation was 'a sort of half triumph for CND but the decision stemmed far more from impracticability than from a political or ethical decision'.[29] The independent deterrent had been abandoned by circumstance rather than by design: thus a part of the CND case had been gained by default.

The nature of the argument changed radically after the Blue Streak announcement: no longer could a 'simple' demand to 'Ban the Bomb' be countered by an equally 'simple' reiteration of Britain's need to be 'independent', to maintain the nuclear wherewithal for her own defence. After 1960 the argument on both sides became more complex and, necessarily, more political. As far as the Labour leadership was concerned the new situation enabled Gaitskell to interpret the NEC's policy as belligerently anti-unilateralist and to concentrate the attack even more than he had in 1959 on the extent to which support for the *moral* cause of unilateral nuclear disarmament would entail the *political* consequence of withdrawal from NATO.

By the 1960 Conference it was clear that the nuclear issue had become 'inevitably one of confidence in the party leadership'.[30]

The Labour Party Conference of 1960

Given the pre-determined outcome of the debate, because of the mandated trade union votes, the bulk of the speeches were of a somewhat ritualistic and anticlimactic tenor.

The debate centred, on the unilateralists' side, largely on questions of Britain's potential influence through a moral lead, the horrific effects of nuclear war, and the dangers of remaining firmly committed to the American Alliance in NATO and the bases in Britain that this involved.

Those supporting the Executive's policy concentrated on the need to back NATO to preserve world stability and the 'Western way of life', and on the disastrous consequences that the adoption of unilateralism would have on the unity, and on the electoral chances, of the Labour Party.

By far the most significant contribution to the debate was the concluding speech by Gaitskell. It was by any measure an outstandingly important speech: according to one, admittedly partisan, commentator, it was 'one of the boldest and most forthright in the whole history of British party leadership'.[31] Having outlined the considerable areas of agreement over defence policy (including support for the UN, reform of NATO policy on nuclear weapons, and on opposition to German rearmament with nuclear weapons, opposition to the independent British deterrent, and to the Thor missile bases, and support for the Test Ban negotiations), Gaitskell moved on to the nub of the disagreement: unilateral nuclear disarmament. On the issue of the independent deterrent Gaitskell reaffirmed two points: first, that he had supported the independent nuclear deterrent because it 'gave us . . . a certain degree of independence – additional independence – from the USA';[32] and second, that the possession of nuclear weapons by Britain was 'not, in my opinion, a matter of principle but a matter of the balance of arguments, economic, military and technical, on which a cool re-examination and reappraisal was certainly necessary from time to time'. Gaitskell then moved to the heart of his argument: that the policy of unilateralism logically and morally entailed withdrawal from the NATO alliance, because it was a *nuclear* alliance. CND, he pointed out, had adopted this commitment to withdrawal from NATO into its programme of aims earlier in 1960 – yet neither Cousins nor Foot had recommended this line of action in the debate.

Gaitskell then went on to defend the theory of deterrence, and make the case against neutralism and for NATO (arguing as he had before that British withdrawal would lead either to the break-up of NATO and American isolationism, or to the dominance within NATO of Germany).

In the closing stages of his speech Gaitskell moved on to consider the view that 'the issue here is not really defence at all but the leadership of the Party . . . (but) . . . The place to decide the leadership of this party is not here but in the PLP.' Finally, Gaitskell made the crucial point that even if the NEC policy were defeated, the PLP itself would have to decide its future policy. Conference could not be allowed to dictate policy to the Parliamentary Labour Party (PLP), whose primary loyalty must be to the election pledges on which MPs had been returned to parliament, and to the electorate which had voted them into parliament. Dismissing his opponents as 'pacificists, unilateralists and fellow travellers', Gaitskell declared that 'we will fight and fight and fight again to save the Party we love. We will fight and fight and fight again to bring back sanity and honesty and dignity, so that our Party with its great past may retain its glory and its greatness.'

The AEU and TGWU resolutions were duly carried, and the NEC/ TUC Defence Policy statement duly lost. However, it is important to note that CLP delegate opinion at the 1960 Conference gave substantial support to the leadership's policy. Approximately two-thirds of CLP delegates in fact backed the party leadership and rejected unilateralism.[33] It is significant, too, that despite Gaitskell's triumphant reversal of the unilateralist decision of the 1961 Conference, CLP delegate support for unilateralism *increased,* albeit marginally, in 1961.

This debate, and particularly Gaitskell's speech, marked a turning point – some would say *the* turning point – for CND. And it certainly had a profound effect on CND's relationship with the Labour Movement. In a sense, the victory had come too early for CND:[34] neither CND nor the Labour Left was used to *winning* in the Labour Party, and now that the whole machine was ranged against them, how were they to defend and secure their victory? In particular, how were the trade unions to be held to the unilateralist line?

Whilst most in the Labour Left and the CND leadership (though by no means the whole Peace Movement) generally supported the demand for withdrawal from NATO,[35] neither the majority of the Labour Movement, nor the majority of the electorate, was willing to accept such a policy. Gaitskell astutely emphasised this aspect of CND policy, to drive a wedge between what he saw as the 'soft' moral centre of CND support, and the 'harder' Left elements. Take away the simple emotive appeal of 'Ban the Bomb' and replace it with the more political, more complex and more left-wing notion of 'neutralism' – and, Gaitskell and his allies argued, the mass support for CND would fade away, not least in the trade union movement, which, as far as the Labour Movement was concerned, was where the power lay.

Gaitskell's stance, and his emotive and effective conference speech, also raised the issues of confidence in his leadership and of the ultimate sovereignty of the PLP. Such an appeal was a strong influence on the trade unions, always characterised by collective loyalty to the duly constituted leadership. Moreover, the Left had nobody of sufficient political weight to challenge Gaitskell for the leadership, as he well realised.

The aftermath of the 1960 Conference and the campaign to reverse the decision

How did CND and the Labour Left react? 'Nobody had a clue as to what to do with the victory in the Labour Party – absolutely not a clue as to how to make that real!'[36] CND was in fact not able to give its full support to the Labour Left in its fight through from October 1960 to the Labour Conference the following autumn. It was not only that CND was not strategically prepared for the victory: more importantly, CND was not an organisation capable of mounting the hard internal battle at trade union and constituency party level. To confront and take over the Party machine was a major task that would have required the total commitment of the CND organisation to working through the Labour Movement, and strong links between the Peace and Labour Movements at all levels. This was not the case: there was always, in CND, ambiguity about the Labour Party. Many in the Peace Movement were extremely suspicious of the Labour Party for political reasons, and directly hostile to it for ideological reasons. As Stuart Hall has said, 'there was no way that the whole weight of the Movement could have been swung to that kind of detailed penetration.'[37] The links between the two organisations were also weak. CND was essentially a *middle-class* movement,[38] and had relatively little working-class and trade union backing.

Gaitskell's campaign to reverse the 1960 decision thus took place in propitious circumstances. Gaitskell's campaigning organisation, the Campaign for Democratic Socialism (CDS), although not formally inaugurated until October 1960, had begun to take shape in the winter of 1959. Based on a group of MPs friendly with Gaitskell, some academics and party workers in Oxford, and a group of parliamentary candidates in the London area, the CDS had three principal objectives: to influence the trade unions to reverse their support for unilateralism; to increase the volume of media pressure in support of Gaitskell and against the policy of unilateralism and the implied political extremism of those supporting the unilateralist position; and to encourage the 'silent majority' in constituency parties and trade unions to involve themselves in the issue and defeat the Left. In the first two of these objectives they were certainly successful; and in the third, partially so.

It is hard to quantify the influence and importance of a group such as the CDS, which by its very nature worked informally. Yet it seems reasonable to suppose that its role *was* of some significance. By identifying the unilateralist campaign as essentially a politically *leftist* campaign, the CDS helped Gaitskell to outflank the unilateralists.

Gaitskell was thus able to win over, with the active co-operation of their leaderships, three of the 'big six' trade unions (the NUR, AEU and USDAW). The GMWU and NUM already supported Gaitskell's policy, of course.[39] Doubtful though some union leaders were of both Gaitskell's leadership, and of his intransigent views on defence policy, they were persuaded to support him above all else by the dangers of 'civil war' within the Labour Movement over the defence issue.

More important than any of these considerations, however, was the changed context of the debate, as already noted. Through force of circumstance the independent deterrent had been abandoned *de facto* with the cancellation of Blue Streak. 'Once the question of Britain's own deterrent was out of the way the issue could be focused clearly on the question of neutralism and NATO bases.'[40] The unilateralists in the Party were placed in a very awkward position: whilst most, though not all, supported such a stance they realised that the espousal of such a policy would ensure their defeat. The problem was exacerbated by the Crossman–Padley compromise proposals which, though not unilateralist, moved closer to CND's position. Some in the Labour Movement, including Cousins, were prepared to accept such a compromise, although the Peace Movement as a whole was far more doubtful. In the event such agonising was irrelevant: Gaitskell refused to compromise at all. And the official policy was adopted by both the NEC and the TUC General Council.

Gaitskell had won the tactical battle, and the unilateralists were left in disarray. In the end, Gaitskell succeeded in virtually isolating the TGWU at the 1961 Conference, and the margin of his victory was substantial.[41]

CND and the Labour Movement 1961–64

The CND leadership had based its whole strategy on winning over the Labour Party to a unilateralist policy. Having apparently succeeded in capturing the Party in 1960, and then having lost the vote so decisively in 1961 (after being continuously outmanoeuvred through 1961), what alternative strategy could now be adopted? As Peggy Duff wryly observed: 'they decided to go on doing the same thing'.[42] And, as the 'Labour tactic' appeared less and less viable, and the leadership floundered, so the Movement began to splinter into its various constituent parts, and, subsequently, to disintegrate.

The immediate effect of the Blackpool Conference was to confirm Gaitskell's position as Party leader, and he was never again challenged seriously. The resentment and anger felt by the Left at the Blackpool decision, and the arbitrary way in which it had been taken, manifested itself in demonstrations against Gaitskell, and in condemnations of his support for the American Government's decision to resume nuclear tests in response to a similar announcement by the USSR. Gaitskell was acting in flat contradiction of a unanimous Conference decision opposing nuclear tests by any country.[43]

But, despite its vigour, the campaign against Gaitskell had a hollow ring: the political Left may have been just as solid for CND (or perhaps even more so – certainly the Campaign as a whole was attracting more and more support through 1962: the Aldermaston March of 1962 was the biggest yet); but the battle in the Labour Party had been lost, and everyone, 'Tribunites' as well as 'Gaitskellites', realised this. The debate on this issue in the Labour Movement was over, and did not arise again until 1973.[44]

Support in the trade unions subsided as quickly as it had arisen, and for the same combination of factors that has been discussed earlier. Those in and around the CND leadership who were most closely associated with the perspective of 'victory through the Labour Party' joined forces with the 'Tribune Left' through 1961, 1962 and into 1963 to put pressure on the Labour Party at Conference time and, where possible, at parliamentary and local levels. But, in this period, the 'Labour Party perspective' lost its central place. It was natural for CND to become more independent of the Labour Party following the reversal in 1961. However, it would be wrong to attribute this entirely to the 1961 decision: there were forces at work on both the libertarian and

Socialist wings of the Movement which were intent, in their very different ways, on breaking the Peace Movement/Labour Movement link.[45]

Indeed, just as many people in CND had joined the Labour Party in the 1957 to 1961 period on the issue of unilateralism itself, so many Labour unilateralists began gradually to leave the Party or become inactive CLP members in the years following the 1961 reversal of policy. In part cause and in part effect of this distancing of CND from the Labour Party, the Movement as a whole moved in political directions radically at odds with the traditions and practices of the parliamentary democratic Labour Party.

Following Gaitskell's death in January 1963 the Labour Left showed a decreasing interest in CND. To quite a large extent the issue of unilateralism and support for CND had been bound up with the personal and ideological animosity which the Left had felt, and shown, for Gaitskell. With Gaitskell gone and Harold Wilson, a leader at first more attractive to the Left, in command, there was a decreasing incentive for Labour Left involvement in CND. However, this was by no means the only reason for the fairly rapid withdrawal of Labour Left leaders from active support for CND.[46] The first and most important reason was the style of Wilson's leadership. Whatever may have been the subsequent disillusionments for the Left in the 1964–70 Labour governments and beyond, there can be no doubt that in 1963 Wilson seemed to represent a new and more radical Socialist perspective.

Although Wilson's foreign and defence policy was in all essentials the same as Gaitskell's, the conciliatory, and at the same time radical, way in which he expressed the commitments, created a quite different ethos. Moreover, most of those on the Left who had suspicions or reservations about his ability and/or will, to deliver the 'socialist goods', reasoned that they would be able to exert pressure once the Government had been elected. And anyway, it was argued, Wilson was a leader as far to the Left as could be hoped for, given the balance of forces in the PLP (the alternatives had, after all, been James Callaghan or George Brown). This was thus another example of the dilemma for the minority left wing in the Labour Party: how far should the Left compromise its socialism in order to achieve some influence in a future social democratic administration?

There were other factors which also contributed to the slackening of the ideological and organisational ties between CND and the Labour

Party. The increasing division in the Movement – over INDEC and the Committee of 100, and the subsequent extra-parliamentary orientation of much of the Movement – led to a distancing between CND and the Labour Left. Moreover, by 1963, many of the initial leaders of CND had themselves resigned, and the Labourist and elite nature of the leadership had decreased considerably. Trade union involvement in CND had also been steadily decreasing since 1961, not least because of the increasingly militant politics of a substantial section of the Committee of 100. Finally, on the domestic scene, the moral appeal of defence issues had declined, as noted earlier, since the cancellation of Blue Streak in 1960 had made all the issues concerned so much more complex and technical.

Internationally, both the Cuban crisis and the Partial Test Ban Treaty of 1963 had, in their different ways, a profoundly negative effect on the Movement, and tended to downgrade the issue's importance in the eyes of the Labour Left (and other former activists and supporters).

These developments of course affected the Movement as a whole – not just the Labour Left; but the combination of these factors with the replacement of Gaitskell by Wilson, plus the approach of an election and the need to 'close ranks', all contributed to the tactical withdrawal of the Labour Left from the leadership of CND.

With Wilson installed as leader, and an election in the offing, the whole context was changed. Wilson was concerned above all to avoid a split. He echoed the opinions he attributed to Bevan: 'Nye saw . . . that these were decent, fine, morally committed people'; and like Bevan, he was not prepared to initiate or to condone purges against CND supporters. 'I was not looking for splits, for I would say they're all good chaps, essential to the Party, and it was my job to keep links around them all, which I did.'[47]

It is clear from Wilson's own comments (and from his actions in power) that he had a real concern with the problems of world peace and disarmament. It is, however, equally clear that he had little interest, and certainly no belief, in CND's policies for Britain. Wilson was firmly committed to the Atlantic Alliance and to NATO, and he would countenance no policy which might threaten that relationship (*vide* his consistent support of American policy in Vietnam). More than this, Wilson had an antipathy to the whole approach to politics which CND represented. Unlike many who had had some experience on the Left of the Party, Wilson had never relished extra-parliamentary politics and had no empathy with 'radical movements' *per se*.

Once in office Wilson became more distanced from CND's perspective. Moving in the world of international *realpolitik* he could see no political or strategic justification for Britain unilaterally disarming. There were, from the Labour leadership's point of view, overwhelmingly strong political and economic reasons for Britain's rejecting any weakening of the economic, political and military ties with the USA. This certainly formed the cornerstone of the Labour Government's Foreign and Defence Policy between 1964 and 1970. The degree of influence which Britain was thereby able to exert on US foreign (or economic or political or military) policy was, arguably, negligible: and the implication of this sort of statement – that Labour was concerned to push US policy into more liberally-inclined channels – would also appear to be questionable, given the historical record of the 1964–70 governments. Be this as it may, it is clear that, from this perspective, there could be no question of Wilson giving any consideration to CND's case for unilateral nuclear disarmament and its political consequences.

By the time Wilson became leader CND was, anyway, a spent force as far as the Labour Party was concerned. He regarded the CND lobby in the Party as a manageable and relatively unimportant pressure group, although he did not underestimate the strength of feeling in the Party about the need for peace and disarmament, nor did he fail to appreciate the latent anti-Americanism of many of his colleagues. But, shrewd tactician that he was, he calculated that he would be able to accommodate and contain any potential rebels on defence and foreign policy issues. And so it proved – even over the Vietnam War.

The resurgence of CND: the Peace Movement and the Labour Party 1979–85

From the mid-1960s until the late 1970s, the Peace Movement in Britain faded from national prominence and became a small and relatively minor pressure group, increasingly concerned with the complexities of strategic and disarmament issues, and dominated by Communist Party (and some Christian) activists.

During this period of relative quiescence CND's relationship with the Left generally was dominated by the Vietnam issue. From the mid-1960s the Anti-Vietnam War Movement and the subsequent rise of the extra-parliamentary, Marxist and sectarian Left, enveloped CND as it did other radical groupings (see Chapter 8). In the heady days of militant protest, when revolution seemed to be in the air, both CND and the whole edifice of established Labour Movement politics seemed somewhat dull, unadventurous and *passé*.

The Labour Party showed little interest in nuclear disarmament issues in either the 1970 or 1974 General Elections. The 1970 Manifesto made no mention of defence and foreign policy until the last of eight sections. Reference was made to the need for Britain to 'maintain her defences and her firm commitment to NATO', and for NATO to 'work positively for a relaxation of tension and reduction of forces'. There was also a call for a 'comprehensive ban on the testing of nuclear weapons', and an agreement to outlaw biological weapons and to prevent 'the depths of the sea from being used for warlike purposes'.

In 1972 and 1973 Labour Party Conference resolutions were passed which moved the Party towards the policies advocated by CND. In 1972 Conference carried a resolution calling for 'the removal of all nuclear bases' from Britain; and, in 1973, despite NEC opposition, a resolution opposing any 'British defence policy which is based on the use or threatened use of nuclear weapons either by this country or its allies', and reaffirming opposition to nuclear bases, was carried by 3,166,000 to 2,462,000 votes.

Such debates did not, however, constitute major areas of dissension and division in the Party. The nuclear question was simply not an issue between Left and Right in the way that it had been in 1960/61. The 1974 manifestos reflected this low-key attitude, and, whilst advocating the removal of American Polaris bases from Britain, and a reduction in defence expenditure, unequivocally reiterated a multilateralist and centrist attitude to the problems of defence and disarmament.

All in all, it is not surprising to learn that Zoë Fairbairns, as editor of *Sanity* in 1973–74, felt that this was 'a fairly lean time for CND. When strangers asked me who I worked for, I always felt I had to spell it out: "CND, that's the Campaign for Nuclear Disarmament, yes, it is still going." '[48]

In 1979 everything changed. CND national membership grew from 4,287 in 1979 to 9,000 in 1980, 20,000 in 1981, and, by 1985, to 110,000. And of course, these national membership figures do not reflect accurately the total level of support for CND. At least five to ten times that number are involved in the Peace Movement as a whole, in all its forms. (Moreover, there were other significant areas of growth in the Peace Movement – the World Disarmament Campaign, for example – which did not support CND.) Massive demonstrations were held in London through the early 1980s. Opposition to Cruise Missiles and the proposed Trident missile system mounted rapidly from 1980 onwards; and defence issues again became of central importance.

In part cause and in part effect of this resurgence in the Peace Movement and the priority given generally to the nuclear issue, the Labour Movement moved decisively to a pro-CND policy position, and defence and disarmament became priority issues. Both the 'Peace, Jobs and Freedom' policy statement of the Labour Party in May 1980, and the 1980 autumn Conference, committed the Party unequivocally to such policies; and, most important of all, the 1983 Election Manifesto gave prominence to defence and disarmament issues, and committed the party unequivocally to opposition to Cruise and Trident, and to a policy of unilateral nuclear disarmament.[49]

The reasons for this whole upsurge of feeling on the nuclear issue, within both the Labour Party and the population as a whole, are no doubt diverse, and are discussed in Chapter 12.

In this context it is the marked swing to the Left in the Labour Movement generally which is of particular concern. CND's longstanding objective of winning over the Labour Party was accomplished – but led in fact to a whole series of other problems.[50] With the defection of a substantial section of Labour's erstwhile Right Wing to the SDP, and the increasing dominance of Thatcherism, Labour's standing in the country following the 1979 election fell sharply. Moreover, many analysts argued that, for ideological, demographic and sociological reasons, the Labour Party was in long-term, and virtually inevitable, decline. Paradoxically, therefore, the question arose as to whether a mass movement with the huge and wide-ranging popular appeal of CND should, tactically, accept an alliance and identification with the Labour Party. Given the weakness of the Labour Party, and its increasingly leftward policy orientations, should CND *distance* itself from such an alliance?

Related to this, and equally important, was the media treatment of CND and the Labour Party's defence policy position during the 1983 election. Not only was CND's policy merged in the media with the overall position of the Labour Left, and therefore ridiculed and attacked consistently; its policy was also wholly misrepresented. The central campaigning issues of opposition to Cruise and Trident were almost wholly ignored (as were the mass rallies and meetings called by CND), and attention concentrated rather on what was projected as CND's 'one-sided disarmament' policies, and the implied links to pro-Soviet attitudes.[51] Midway through the campaign, the interventions of Denis Healey and James Callaghan, explicitly dissociating themselves from official Labour policy, finally destroyed any surviving credibility in Labour's position over defence. Such was the effect of the débâcle of Labour's defeat on CND that Michael Heseltine, and the media, declared the Peace Movement to be dead and buried. Whilst this was of course wildly inaccurate, as the subsequent growth and intensification of Peace Movement activity demonstrated, there is no doubt that Labour's crushing defeat, and the débâcle over defence, had a temporarily severe effect on CND too.

By the mid-1980s, the new Labour leadership, though committed to CND policies, was displaying some ambivalence over defence and nuclear issues in the light of the deep divisions that still persisted within the Party. And the question of the advisability for CND of retaining its longstanding link with the Labour Party remained a major tactical question. It was, however, *more* than a tactical question: it related to fundamental ideological and political analysis concerning the nature of the demands being made by the Peace Movement, their linkage, if any, to socialist politics, and the debate on the Left over 'agency' – over whether structural socialist change can be achieved by a social reform party of the Labour Party mould.[52]

The Labour Left and the 'Little Englander' outlook

Before turning, finally, to some of these questions, brief note should be taken of the *nature* of the Labour Left's longstanding concern with disarmament and related issues. The belief in Britain's potential for taking the 'moral lead' through unilateral initiatives – which was so strong a motivating force in CND as a whole in the 1958 to 1965 period[53] – stemmed in part from the long tradition of quasi-pacifist, and Socialist, internationalism which had formed a persistent minority dimension of the Labour Left from the early years of the Independent Labour Party onwards. This tradition embodied also a moral nationalism, stemming from nineteenth-century radicalism, emphasising the importance of national sovereignty, parliamentary democracy, and the rights of free individuals, and free nations, to determine their own futures. It thus saw the role of Britain and other liberal democracies as the basis of an international movement for the spread of suffrage and civil liberties. And it was thus firmly anti-colonialist and pro-national independence. It is from within this tradition, for example, that both Aneurin Bevan and Michael Foot have drawn their definitions of socialism, and its order of priorities.

In some respects, though, this Labour Left perspective has been contradictory, advocating both an internationalist, and often pacifist, policy, and yet failing to move beyond the national ideological framework, with its stress upon the actions and interests of the nation state rather than the international working-class, socialist movement.

It is outside our scope here to analyse in any depth either the historical or theoretical aspects of this ideological stance. Two observations may be made, however, which have direct relevance for the relationship between the Peace Movement and the various sections of socialist opinion. The first is that the inconsistencies and ambiguities of the Labour Left/ILP attitude and policy towards the central issue of socialism and nationalism, have been characteristic of the overall failure of socialism since 1914, in all its forms, to transcend nationalism and national consciousness. And the only 'international' to forge some disciplined, international, socialist movement – the Third International – suffered quite other, and far more drastically unsocialist, problems. The second observation is that the Labour Left/ILP internationalist perspective was founded ultimately upon the moral socialism which formed the basis of the ILP's overall socialist framework, and took insufficient account of a structural analysis which could explain the connections between the capitalist system, class struggle and the phenomenon of war between modern nation states. Because it was in this sense 'under theorised' the Labour Left has always tended to see all problems discretely. Thus, in the context of nuclear weapons, there was no attempt to make the structural links between the struggle for nuclear disarmament, the class struggle, and the international structure of capitalist dominance. The upshot of this incomplete ideological framework was thus an inability to break from the dominant culture and the processes and institutions that inhered within it: the nation state, the orthodox institutional structure, etc. Hence, too, it could be argued that the Labour Left adopted the Great Power morality, and translated it into its own quasi-pacifist moral framework. The result was thus to espouse both the morality of internationalism and the nationalism of the 'Britain must lead' position.

Be this as it may, there is no doubt that this 'moral imperialism' has been a major force throughout CND, especially in the 1958 to 1965 period. The need for Britain to reassert her importance on the world's stage – following her rapid demotion from Great Power status after 1945 – was seen as important on the Left as well as on the Right, and was a powerful motivating force, psychologically as well as politically and tactically.

CND and the Labour Movement: some conclusions

Three distinct groupings have seen the relationship between CND, unilateralism and the Labour Movement as important: the dominant group within the CND leadership and a substantial section of CND's supporters;[54] the Labour Left; and the Labour Right, both in the earlier period when Gaitskell was dominant, and in the 1980s.

For the Labour Left, the Movement was in the grand tradition of morally inspired Labour peace movements, embodying the socialist commitment to 'peace and brotherhood'. Reference has already been made to the Labour Left's tendency to adopt 'Little Englander' attitudes, and the concept of unilateralism satisfied its ideological, and perhaps psychological, need to believe that 'Britain still has the power to change its destiny at will'.[55]

There was, too, a suspicion bordering on rejection of the NATO alliance and the so-called American/British special relationship, and an antipathy towards both American imperialism and American capitalism.

On the Labour Left the combination of these quasi-Socialist objections with the 'Little Englander' mentality has resulted in a strong and continuing opposition to American bases in Britain. Thus the Labour Party Conference in 1961, and for several years thereafter, carried resolutions rejecting Polaris, after the CND case for unilateral nuclear disarmament had been voted down.

More generally, the Labour Left has always argued strongly, too, that the social and economic policies that it saw as being essential to the creation of a democratic socialist society were being dismissed or disregarded by the leadership, at least in part because of the assumption that so large a proportion of government expenditure should be devoted to 'defence', and especially to nuclear weapons.

On the other side, as it were, the CND/Labour Movement relationship has been just as important to the Right. Again, both the substantive issues connected with unilateralism and NATO, and the questions concerning the ideological direction of the Party and the leadership, have been intertwined.

The issue should be seen in the wider context of the Labour Right's commitment to an overall revisionist perspective. Gaitskell saw the struggle against the Left as the price that had to be paid if the Labour Party were to be 'modernised' – which he saw as crucial if it was to appeal to the new, supposedly increasingly classless, electorate. This problem became particularly acute after Labour lost their third successive General Election in 1959. And Gaitskell saw as central to this process the defeat of the Left and the final rejection of the old 'pacifist/neutralist' image of the Labour Party. A further aspect of this modernisation process was to bring the Labour Party firmly into the parliamentarist fold and to remove the damaging image of trade union control through Conference.

In the 1980s such divisions have persisted, but with the crucial difference that the Left has become more dominant, and the Right, or a section of it, seceded and became the core of the SDP. Moreover, as the ideological lines became drawn more firmly, and as the central issue in the 1980s became the American Cruise missiles, so the nature of the division became even more integrated into the overall debate concerning the nature of socialism, the means of advance, and the mechanism whereby the Labour Party could be both regenerated and radicalised.[56]

These, then, were the basic dimensions of the CND/Labour Movement relationship. There have undoubtedly been major problems for the Peace Movement in the strategy of allying itself with a Labour Left that has always been weak – whether within the context of the Labour Party balance of power (as in 1958 to 1965), or in the more general forms of the balance of political forces in the wider society (as in the 1980s).

Cogent cases have been put, of course, by those in the Peace Movement who believe in working outside the conventional parliamentary framework altogether, as the 'anarchists' on the one hand, and the 'apolitical moralists' on the other, argued. There was, too, a case to be made for converting the Movement into a mass extra-parliamentary force, with Labour Movement links, but not tied to the parliamentarist strategy.[57]

For both those on the Labour Left who supported CND, however, and those in CND who believed in a Labourist strategy, there was an overwhelmingly strong case in principle and in practice to be made for working in and through the Labour Party. These perspectives were not wholly dominant in the Peace Movement and have not succeeded, at least as yet, in terms of either the specific policy objectives of the Movement, or wider radical societal and ideological change.

All that can be asserted here is that, despite its dramatic successes in 1959–60, and its prominence as an issue through the early 1960s, the CND/Labour Left axis failed to hold the Labour Party to a 'CND line', and that this failure was a major factor in the decline of the Movement from 1963/64 onwards. With the resurgence of the Movement in the 1980s, and the adoption by Labour of firmly CND policies, the position may seem far better, in many ways, for the Peace Movement. But there remain the two intrinsic problems: how to secure electoral victory for a Left-inclined Labour Party; and, much more fundamentally, whether a socialist restructuring, of which the implementation of the Peace Movement's objectives would be a major part, is possible through the mechanism of social reformism. Whether such progress can be achieved will be among the most important political questions facing both the Peace Movement and the Left in Britain in the remaining years of this century.

References

1 Ian Mikardo, in conversation with Richard Taylor, April 1978.
2 CND's inaugural meeting was held at the Central Hall, Westminster on 17 Feburary 1958, but moves were afoot from late 1957 onwards to launch a new organisation.
3 Jacquetta Hawkes, in conversation with Richard Taylor, January 1978.
4 Canon L. John Collins, *Faith Under Fire*, Leslie Frewin, London, 1966, p. 326.
5 The Left had been campaigning on the issue of nuclear weapons and defence expenditure from the time of the first Atom Bomb and before; and *Tribune* had been conducting a campaign for unilateral nuclear disarmament from 1957 onwards.
6 In this chapter, 'Labour Movement' signifies the Labour Party and affiliated organisations, and the trade unions, and does not refer to those socialist groups and organisations outside the orthodox framework, the Communist Party and the various Marxist groupings. These are discussed, in their relationship to the Peace Movement, in Chapter 8.
7 For full accounts of this period and its political implications see Ralph Miliband, *Parliamentary Socialism*, 2nd edn, Merlin Press, London, 1973; David Coates, *The*

Labour Party and the Struggle for Socialism, Cambridge University Press, 1975, Ch. 4; and Michael Foot, *Aneurin Bevan* (2 vols.), Vol. 1, McGibbon and Kee, London, 1962, and Vol. 2, Davis-Poynter, London, 1973.

8 Bevan, cited in Foot, *Aneurin Bevan,* Vol. 2, p. 552.

9 Cited in *ibid.*

10 Mikardo, in conversation.

11 *Ibid.*

12 This, and the extracts below quoted from Bevan's speech, are from LPACR, 1957, pp. 165 ff.

13 Coates, *The Labour Party,* p. 193.

14 Foot, *Aneurin Bevan,* p. 584.

15 Peggy Duff, *Left, Left, Left,* Allison and Busby, London, 1971, p. 71.

16 *Ibid.,* p. 74.

17 Michael Foot wrote a reply to Bevan in *Tribune,* 11 October 1957.

18 Olive Gibbs was 'upset by Nye Bevan, horribly upset. And I haven't a good word to say for him now: all this veneration quite honestly makes me *sick*! How any man who had held the views he had could make a statement of that sort . . . Everything was finished for me.' Olive Gibbs, in conversation with Richard Taylor, January 1978.

19 Frank Allaun, in conversation with Richard Taylor, January 1978.

20 The *New Statesman* relegated the 'Bevan debate' to the third item on page 2, and its attitude was at most lukewarm (*New Statesman,* 12 October 1957).

21 Correspondence in *New Statesman,* 9 November 1957, 16 November 1957, 23 November 1957.

22 Emrys Hughes remarked in the same debate that Bevan's speech 'was so statesmanlike that it reminded one of Mr. Asquith'. LPACR, 1958, p. 199.

23 Duff, *Left, Left, Left,* p. 186.

24 Lewis Minkin, *The Labour Party Conference,* Manchester University Press, 1978, p. 100, has noted that the debate was weighted heavily in the GMWU leadership's favour.

25 Lewis Minkin,' 'The Labour Party Conference and Intra-Party Democracy', unpublished PhD thesis, University of York, 1975, p. 322.

26 *Tribune,* 31 July 1959.

27 Cousins, however, was not involved with CND *per se* (though he did sometimes appear on Aldermaston marches). His support for unilateralism stemmed essentially from moral rather than political motivations. As A. J. P. Taylor has recalled, 'Cousins never worked with us in any way: he simply took his own line and expected us to follow him.' A. J. P. Taylor, in conversation with Richard Taylor, April 1978.

28 A. J. R. Groom, *British Thinking About Nuclear Weapons,* Francis Pinter, London, 1974, p. 314.
These objectives included the withdrawal of foreign forces from Europe and the subsequent reunification of Germany, the withdrawal of Germany from NATO, and of Poland, Czechoslavakia and Hungary from the Warsaw Pact. On nuclear weapons the document urged a complete and permanent ban on nuclear tests and a general and wholesale de-escalation to take place multilaterally. No suggestion was made as to how these major but, in the immediate context, impracticable policy proposals might be effected. It does not seem unduly cynical to dismiss these proposals as 'window-dressing': at all events this was the reaction of CND and the Labour Left.

29 Duff, *Left, Left, Left*, pp. 187–8.
30 *New Statesman*, editorial, 'An issue of Confidence', 1 October 1960.
31 R. T. McKenzie, *British Political Parties*, Mercury Books, London, 1963, p. 615.
32 LPACR, 1960.
33 Minkin, *The Labour Party Conference*, p. 89, states that 'in 1960 and 1961 (there were) substantial CLP majorities (67% in 1960 and 63% in 1961) in favour of the Party leadership and against unilateralism'. However, caution should be exercised here. Minkin's source was a survey of CLP opinion conducted by Keith Hindell and Philip Williams, the latter Gaitskell's biographer and an ardent Labour right-winger.
34 Jacquetta Hawkes, for example, recalled that 'we were absolutely astonished . . . we didn't realise what was happening in the Labour Party . . .'. Hawkes, in conversation.
35 Some in the CND leadership did not support withdrawal from NATO. Jacquetta Hawkes and Arthur Goss were particularly vehement on this point in conversation with the author.
36 Stuart Hall, in conversation with Richard Taylor, April 1978.
37 *Ibid*.
38 See Frank Parkin, *Middle Class Radicalism: the Social Bases of the Campaign for Nuclear Disarmament*, Manchester University Press, 1968; and Part II (the survey) of Richard Taylor and Colin Pritchard, *The Protest Makers: the British Nuclear Disarmament Movement of 1958 to 1965, Twenty Years On*, Pergamon Press, Oxford, 1980.
39 'Unquestionably, the greatest asset which Gaitskell possessed in the long run struggle to assert himself over Conference was the political commitment of senior Trade Union leaders.' Minkin, PhD thesis, p. 117.
40 Minkin, *The Labour Party Conference*, p. 59 (although it should be noted that Polaris, too, became a focus of attention).
41 The offical 'Policy for Peace' was carried by 4,526,000 to 1,756,000; the TGWU policy was defeated by 4,309,000 to 1,891,000.
   For details of the ways in which the major trade unions were 'converted' to Gaitskell's policies in 1961, see Minkin (both book and PhD thesis); and Richard Taylor, 'The British Nuclear Disarmament Movement of 1958 to 1965 and its legacy to the Left', unpublished PhD thesis, Department of Politics, University of Leeds, 1983, Ch. 4, pp. 333–9.
42 Duff, *Left, Left, Left*, p. 193.
43 LPACR, 1961. ('Policy for Peace' declaration; and George Brown's speech on behalf of the NEC resolution in 1961.)
44 Thus the only motion debated on nuclear weapons at the Labour Party Conference of 1962 was that moved by Counsins calling for a reiteration of the 1961 condemnation of all nuclear weapons tests by the Party. After a short debate this was passed unanimously. LPACR, 1962, pp. 225–32.
45 Most notably the Committee of 100; but also INDEC (the Independent Nuclear Disarmament Election Committee). For detailed discussion of both these areas of the campaign's activities, see Taylor, PhD thesis, Chs. 3 and 8.
46 Michael Foot, Judith Hart and Anthony Greenwood did not stand for re-election to the CND Executive in 1963.
47 Harold Wilson, in conversation with Colin Pritchard, June 1978, cited in Taylor and Pritchard, *The Protest Makers*.

48 Zoë Fairbairns, 'Study War No More', in John Minnion and Philip Bolsover (eds.), *The CND Story*, Allison and Busby, London, 1983, p. 68.

49 It was of some significance that the Party was led, in 1983, by Michael Foot, one of the founders of CND and a passionate advocate of unilateral nuclear disarmament.

50 It should be noted also that, although the leadership of the Liberal Party remained resolutely opposed to CND's policies, the Liberal Party Conference adopted unilateralist anti-Cruise and anti-Trident resolutions at its conferences in the 1980s. (And many leading Liberals were prominent in CND activities: Paddy Ashdown and Michael Meadowcroft, for example.)

51 For detailed discussion of the whole issue, see Richard Taylor, 'CND and the 1983 Election', in Ivor Crewe and Martin Harrop (eds.), *Political Communication: the General Election Campaign of 1983*, Cambridge University Press, 1986, pp. 207–16.

52 For further discussion, see Ch. 11. See also Richard Taylor, 'The British Peace Movement and Socialist Change', in Ralph Miliband and John Saville (eds.), *Socialist Register 1983*, Merlin Press, London, 1983; and Raymond Williams, The Politics of Nuclear Disarmament, *New Left Review*, No. 24, 1981, reprinted in Thompson *et al.*, *Exterminism and Cold War*, Verso and New Left Books, London, 1982.

53 See, for example, J. B. Priestley's original *New Statesman* article which was one of the key precipitants of CND. ('Britain and the nuclear bombs', *New Statesman*, 2 November 1957.)

54 This was confirmed in many of the conversations the author had with leading CND figures, e.g. Peggy Duff, Canon Collins, Ian Mikardo, Frank Allaun and Olive Gibbs, amongst others. (This was denied by others in the Campaign with at least equal vehemence: e.g. Pat Arrowsmith, Hugh Brock and George Clark.)

   Support for the Labour Party was also one of the major characteristics of rank and file disarmament Movement supporters, although there were significant numbers of activists who opposed the 'Labourist view'. For a detailed discussion see Taylor and Pritchard, *The Protest Makers*, Part II.

55 Alastair Buchan, 'The odds against Gaitskell', *Reporter*, 22 December 1960, XXIII, pp. 30–3.

56 For further discussion of these issues in the context of the Labour Party's defence and foreign policy stance in 1986/7, see Richard Taylor, 'The British Peace Movement and radical change: problems of agency', *Peace Magazine*, January 1987, Toronto, Canada.

57 See Ch. 8.

7

Non-violent direct action in the 1950s and 1960s

MICHAEL RANDLE

FOR HUGH BROCK
pioneer of non-violent direct action
in Britain, who died in April 1985

Non-violent direct action (NVDA) for anti-militarist ends has experienced a revival with the rise of the new Peace Movement in the 1980s – most dramatically with the women's sustained protest at Greenham Common, but also with other direct action demonstrations against nuclear weapons. It is an appropriate moment, therefore, to review the direct action of the earlier phase of the anti-nuclear campaign in the late 1950s and early 1960s.

The events themselves have been described elsewhere: I shall recapitulate them only briefly here, concentrating instead on certain key issues, principally the question of whether NVDA is morally justified in a parliamentary democracy, and whether it was an effective political strategy.

The development of non-violent direct action in the 1950s and 1960s

There were four principal phases in the development of post-war anti-militarist direct action in Britain. The first, lasting from around 1951 to 1957, was the precursor to effective public action; the second saw the development of NVDA on a scale that had significant public impact, starting with the first Aldermaston March of Easter 1958 and concluding with the Direct Action Committee's protests at Holy Loch in mid-1961. The third phase, overlapping to some extent with the second, saw the mass non-violent action and civil disobedience of the Committee of 100 during 1961. Finally, in the period 1962–68, there was a return to smaller scale actions at bases, and also non-violent direct action on social and political issues not directly related to the nuclear issue.

Phase I: The embryonic movement

During this phase small-scale demonstrations were undertaken which provided models for the later campaigns, ideas were developed and a network established, small in numbers but international in scope. However, the impact on the public, or on political thinking generally, was marginal.

The key figure in this early period was Hugh Brock, who had been a conscientious objector during the war and who became, in the late 1940s, Assistant Editor of the pacifist weekly *Peace News*. What differentiated him and the small group of activists working with him from mainstream British pacifism was the conviction that the methods of non-violent action at the group and collective level, as exemplified by Gandhi's campaigns in India, could and should be applied in Britain in the struggle against war. Hugh became Secretary of a small group, Operation Gandhi, which organised a sit-down in January 1952 outside the War Office in London. A dozen or so people were arrested and fined. It was the dream and conviction of Hugh and those of us working with him that one day mass non-violent demonstrations might be staged in Britain.

Operation Gandhi – which soon changed its name to the Non-Violent Resistance Group – went on to organise further demonstrations over the next two or three years, including two at the Atomic Energy Research Establishment at Aldermaston. My own involvement in the movement began soon after the War Office sit-down in 1952.

The connection with *Peace News* during these early years was critical, providing the advocates of non-violent action with an organisational base and a forum for ideas. It helped also to give the emerging movement a distinctly internationalist character. *Peace News* during this period strongly supported the anti-colonial struggle and Hugh and others established contacts with several future African leaders such as Julius Nyerere and Kenneth Kaunda. During the Mau Mau rebellion in Kenya the paper exposed the horrors of the Hola detention camps, to the profound embarrassment of the British Government. When the Civil Rights campaign organised by Luther King in the US began, *Peace News* recognised its importance and helped to make it known in this country. Bayard Rustin, one of King's close associates, established strong links with the group around *Peace News*, and he and other visitors, notably from the US and India, spoke to the Non-Violent Resistance Group about their activities and ideas. Among the visitors was another American black radical, Bill Sutherland, who subsequently went to work as an assistant to the Finance Minister, Mr Gbedemah, in the Nkrumah Government in Ghana, and played a crucial role in the Sahara Protest Expedition against French nuclear tests during the Direct Action Committee period.

Phase II: The development of public protest

The second phase in the development of non-violent direct action began with the formation of the Emergency Committee for Direct Action (later changing its name to the Direct Action Committee against Nuclear War – DAC) in November 1957. It came into existence following the (ultimately unsuccessful) efforts of a Quaker, Harold Steele, and others, to sail into the British nuclear testing area at Christmas Island in the Pacific. *Peace News* had provided the organisational base for this project, and on Harold Steele's return a meeting of supporters was held at which the new organisation was formed and plans made to hold a three-day march from London to Aldermaston. The interest in this march, and its eventual size, exceeded by far the expectations of all of us involved in organising it. It was to prove, in effect, the first major public action in a campaign which has had its ups and downs, but is unlikely to go away until nuclear weapons themselves have been abolished.

The success of the march was due to a convergence of factors, most of them outside the control of the organisers. Firstly, the mood in the country had changed in the aftermath of the Suez and Hungary crises in the previous year. The Suez adventure, and the massive Trafalgar Square demonstration against it, had broken the comfortable post-war consensus on foreign and defence policy. Hungary had emphasised the imperialist and reactionary role of the Soviet Union in Eastern Europe, and led to important resignations from the Communist Party in Britain, most notably those of Edward Thompson and John Saville who, having been prevented from expressing dissent within the Party through their journal *The Reasoner*, resigned and founded an important new theoretical magazine, *The New Reasoner*. Secondly, the journal *Universities and Left Review* (ULR) had recently been launched, together with the associated New Left Clubs, and the New Left gave enthusiastic support to the march. Finally, in February 1958, the CND was launched at a huge meeting at Central Hall, London and, despite the reservations of some of the CND Executive, the forthcoming march received publicity and support.

To acknowledge the importance of these factors is not to take anything away from the main organisers of the march – Hugh Brock, the committee's chairman, and Pat Arrowsmith, its secretary and sole paid worker. The response to the call for the march made enormous demands on the small group of people who initiated it, but it was nevertheless organised with an efficiency that surprised and impressed the rather sceptical press of the day.

I recall particularly the day when a Twickenham artist, Gerald Holtom, arranged to see Hugh Brock, Pat Arrowsmith and myself in the small *Peace News* offices in Blackstock Road, and showed us the enigmatic symbol he had designed and which he urged us to adopt. He also brought sketches of how he envisaged the march, with long banners stretching across the road with his symbol at either end of it, and such was his enthusiasm and persuasiveness that we immediately agreed to his proposal. This was how the now famous nuclear disarmament symbol came to be adopted.[1]

The DAC also sought allies outside its ranks. Thus the Labour MP, Frank Allaun, a friend of Hugh's, and Walter Wolfgang, another figure on the Labour Left, were brought on to the march sub-committee. After the march, too, the Committee was reconstituted and enlarged, notably with the addition of two people active in the New Left, Bill Crampton, an LSE student, and Alan Lovell, a founder member of ULR and a member of its Editorial Board.

The DAC remained in existence for a little under four years, until the middle of 1961. Its best known and most characteristic actions, aside from Aldermaston, were the non-violent sit-downs and occupations, commencing with the demonstrations at the Thor intermediate-range rocket base near Swaffham in Norfolk in December 1961. In the first of these actions the participants used their banner to make a bridge across the barbed-wire entanglements surrounding the base, and obstructed the work going on inside. No arrests were made, but the demonstrators were doused with water hoses by those working on the site and endured other forms of harassment. Two weeks later eighty participants in a second demonstration were arrested and about fifty of them remanded in custody over Christmas. They were led on that occasion by the Revd

Michael Scott, the only well-known member of the Committee, who had been expelled from South Africa for his opposition to apartheid and his campaign at the UN on behalf of the Herero tribe at Namibia.

The response to those first major sit-down demonstrations was enormous. They made front-page headlines in virtually every newspaper, and the prisoners remanded over Christmas (of which I was one) were inundated with thousands of cards and food parcels. Like the Aldermaston March, the demonstrations had struck a chord to which thousands responded. As Gene Sharp was to argue in one of the spate of articles in *Peace News* that followed the demonstrations, they were a kind of propaganda by the deed, juxtaposing the social and military reality of the base not simply with an argument but with a visible and dramatic alternative.[2]

Inevitably, perhaps, some of the later actions of the same kind, such as the demonstrations at the base at Harrington in 1959, did not get quite the same attention. However, the dramatic Holy Loch demonstrations in the summer of 1961, when demonstrators in boats attempted to board the supply ship for the Polaris submarine fleet, did make headline news. It had been preceded by a six-week march from London to Glasgow which received support from various bodies including trade unions, trades councils and constituency labour parties along the route.

It is important to stress that the demonstrations which made the headlines were invariably preceded by intensive 'field work' carried out by full-time DAC workers and local sympathisers, and usually focused on the Trade Union and Labour Movement.[3]

The most tangible success in the work among rank and file trade unionists came at the end of a two-week campaign in Stevenage, where the Blue Streak missile intended as the delivery vehicle for Britain's H-Bomb was being built and where most of the other work available in the town was connected with military production. There, Pat Arrowsmith and I, and a team of volunteer workers, received a sympathetic hearing from many local trade unionists: we were particularly well received within the building trade union, AUBTW, whose members we addressed both at branch and shop-floor meetings. At the end of the two-week period AUBTW members staged a token one-hour stoppage to lead a protest demonstration into the city centre. Following this significant, if small-scale, success, the DAC carried out an industrial action campaign in the summer of 1960 focused on industrial armaments locations at Woodford in the Manchester area, at Chertsey and Weybridge in Surrey, in Bristol, and in Slough. It has to be acknowledged that for the most part these campaigns had only marginal effect and could not be counted as 'successes'.

The DAC was also involved in several international actions. One of the most important of these was the Sahara Protest Expedition in which twenty people from Britain, France, the US and various African countries set out from Ghana in an attempt to reach the French atomic testing site at Reggan in the Algerian Sahara.[4] Although the French authorities prevented the team from getting far beyond the Ghanaian border, the protest received enormous support within Ghana, where mass rallies involving tens of thousands of people were organised. Bayard Rustin, Bill Sutherland, and the veteran American pacifist, A. J. Muste, were among those who participated and helped organise the action. Another key figure was the Revd Michael Scott, who had enormous prestige in Africa, and was carried shoulder-high from the airport in Accra by a huge crowd when he came to join the project. The two other British participants were the artist Francis Hoyland and myself.

When the expedition itself came to an end, President Nkrumah of Ghana, at the suggestion of Michael Scott, called a Pan-African conference in Accra in which independent governments and liberation movements from all over Africa participated, and affirmed their opposition not only to colonialism but to nuclear imperialism. I stayed on in Ghana helping with the organisation of the conference which made, I think, a significant contribution to consolidating African opinion against the spread of nuclear weapons to that continent.

Another major action was the San Francisco–Moscow march of 1960–61 organised jointly by the Committee for Non-Violent Action in the US and the Direct Action Committee in Britain. In January 1962 a new body to co-ordinate transnational non-violent action, the World Peace Bridgade, was established at a meeting in Beirut, largely at the initiative of British, American, and Indian activists, with organisational support from the London based non-violent international, War Resisters International.[5]

Phase III: mass civil disobedience
The third phase, 1961 to early 1962, was the period of the Committee of 100 and non-violent action involving thousands of people. It

coincided with a renaissance in British cultural and artistic life, and it is no coincidence that the majority of those involved in this cultural renaissance, especially the playwrights, but also poets, critics, producers, and singers, were either members of the Committee of 100 or actively involved in its campaigns. In fact the Committee's activities should be seen in the context of this wider cultural and artistic movement which itself represented a rebellion and a demand for radical change. To view either in isolation is to misjudge their overall impact.

There were three major demonstrations in London in the course of 1961 involving NVDA. The first, in February, was a sit-down outside the Ministry of Defence in Whitehall, led by Russell, in which around 5,000 people participated. Despite prior warnings to the Committee from the police, no arrests were made and the demonstration dispersed after three hours. The second, in April, actually attracted fewer people (probably about half the number that had taken part in the first action) but was rescued, in terms of its impact, by the action of the police in arresting nearly 1,000 people as they sat down in Whitehall. In August a dignified and well-ordered demonstration at the Cenotaph did not involve any obstruction or arrests, and yet in its own way was quite as effective as any of the earlier demonstrations. It shows also that the Committee was not interested solely in mass confrontation with the authorities, but was also thinking of ways in which it might communicate its message effectively to people. A further major 'Assembly' in Parliament Square was planned for 17 September.

Before it could take place, however, the authorities made what was probably their biggest ever mistake in handling civil disobedience demonstrations in this country. They arrested about fifty members of the Committee, including Russell and other well-known figures, most of whom were sent to prison for a month. Russell's imprisonment at the age of eighty-nine made headlines not only in this country but round the world and messages of support came from far and wide, including a telegram from Albert Schweitzer. The authorities also invoked the Public Order Act to ban the initial rally in Trafalgar Square, thereby probably recruiting thousands more to the demonstration. In the event, a crowd estimated variously between 12,000 and 17,000 took part in the action. The previous day a direct action demonstration at the Holy Loch Polaris base in Scotland, organised by the recently formed Scottish Committee of 100, attracted some 500 supporters, despite appalling weather conditions. A measure of the impact the demonstrations were having can perhaps by gauged from the fact that on 17 September ITV set aside most of the afternoon for live coverage of the events in Trafalgar Square – something unique in terms of media coverage for any demonstration either before or since.

Two developments at this point were to prove critical for the future of the Committee's activities. First was the process of decentralisation within the organisation, which had taken place more or less spontaneously in the autumn of 1961, though it accorded with the political emphasis within the Committee of 100 and DAC on decentralisation. Not only had national committees been established in Scotland and Wales, but a number of regional committees had also sprung up. These were, naturally, keen to organise actions in their own areas, though preferably in conjunction with a national demonstration and other regional actions.

Second, there was a debate about whether demonstrations should continue to be held in city centres or move to the bases. The DAC had always concentrated on the latter and there was an obvious logic to non-violent obstruction in and around bases which did not apply to causing traffic jams in city centres. The success of the DAC Holy Loch demonstration in the summer, and of the Scottish Committee of 100 demonstration there on 16–17 September, helped to persuade some of those who were dubious about switching to bases that it was worth trying. It was also tempting to consider what might be achieved if the thousands who had sat down in Central London on 17 September – or even larger numbers – were to occupy or blockade a military base.

The problem was that, following the heady success of 17 September, the Committee overestimated its strength. It called for 50,000 people to take part in a day of action, and under pressure of the regional committees decided to hold simultaneous demonstrations at seven locations – Wethersfield, Ruislip, Bristol, Brize Norton, York, Cardiff and Manchester. Most of the public attention, however, was focused on the plan to occupy the USAF base at Wethersfield, which was unfenced, and to sit down on the runways, to prevent aircraft presumed to be carrying nuclear weapons from taking off.

Again the authorities took preventive action, but this time with greater discrimination. All the staff employed at the Committee office were arrested and charged under the Official Secrets Act, and the Attorney-General warned that anyone taking part in the demonstrations at the bases could face similar charges. Those charged under the act were Helen Allegranza, Terry Chandler, Ian Dixon, Trevor Hatton, Pat Pottle and myself.

My own arrest was somewhat dramatic. In the middle of a Press Conference in a room above a pub in Fleet Street, I had just commented that the threat by the Attorney-General in the House the previous day that demonstrators at Wethersfield could face prosecution under the Oficial Secrets Act was either bluff or the prelude to a serious breach of civil liberties, when I was called to the telephone to be told that Helen, Terry, Ian and Trevor had been arrested and charged under the Official Secrets Act and that warrants were out for Pat Pottle and myself. When I came back into the room and gave the news there was a stampede for the door as journalists rushed to telephone the news to their papers; I do not think I have ever seen a room empty so fast. I then went with a number of journalists and photographers to a pub, and about half an hour later received a tap on the shoulder from Detective-Inspector Stratton (the Inspector assigned to keep tabs on the Committee) and I was led off amid a volley of flashes from the cameras of press photographers. I don't doubt that it was some of the journalists who tipped the police off about my whereabouts so that they could be present when the arrest was made. But this suited our purposes too, and the arrests and charges made front-page headlines in the following day's newspapers.

Meanwhile the authorities had taken further steps to hamper the demonstration. A barbed-wire entanglement was hastily thrown round the Wethersfield base and at the last minute the bus company which had been hired to take demonstrators to Wethersfield announced that it was no longer prepared to fulfil the contract. This was a strategem we should have foreseen, but in the event it made, in my judgement, little difference to the numbers attending the demonstration. But the numbers were disappointing. The most optimistic estimates put the total number of demonstrators at the seven locations at 7,000, of whom a total of 840 were arrested. Wetherfield, which had been seen as the centre of the action, actually attracted the smallest number (600), of whom seventy were arrested. The combination of moving out of central London, of dispersing the demonstrations, and of calling for massive numbers meant that the expectations that had been built up were not met.

I am not convinced that going to the bases was in itself a mistake, but given the added difficulty of organising demonstrations in the countryside we should have planned a more modest start, perhaps following the pattern of the 17 September demonstration by having a demonstration in central London (or in a number of city centres) plus an action at a military base on a smaller scale. As it was, the lesson that was deduced from the December demonstrations was that demonstrations should move back to city centres. But when this was tried, it, too, was relatively unsuccessful, perhaps because it seemed unimaginative, perhaps partly because the authorities were taking more repressive action, but perhaps too because the 17 September demonstrations marked a climax which could not be repeated for some time in terms of mass action.

If the outcome of the December demonstrations marked a psychological success for the authorities, it was the Committee that had the moral and political edge in the Official Secrets Act trial which began at the Old Bailey in February 1962 with the Attorney-General, Reginald Manningham Buller, conducting the prosecution. Witnesses for the defence included a Nobel prize-winner in physics, Linus Pauling, the inventor of radar, Sir Robert Watson Watt (both of them flown over specially from the US), Archbishop Roberts, the former Roman Catholic Archbishop of Bombay, and of course Bertrand Russell. The gist of the defence was that though we had indeed planned a demonstration to occupy and immobilise the airbase at Wethersfield, the purpose was not, as the Act specified, 'for a purpose contrary to the safety and interest of the state' but to save the state (in the sense of the community) from grave peril and from involvement in the crime of genocide. That defence was ruled out of order by the judge in the opening two days, but it did not prevent it being introduced in one guise or another throughout the trial, especially by Pat Pottle, who defended himself. The most dramatic and important moment of the trial, in fact, came, when, under cross-examination from Pat, the prosecution witness Air Commodore Magill, Director of Operations at the Air Ministry, stated that he would if necessary be prepared to press the nuclear button, despite Pat's reminder to him that this would involve killing millions of innocent people.

The defendants were sentenced to eighteen months' imprisonment, except for Helen, who was sentenced to twelve months'. Courageously, she interrupted the judge in mid-flow and asked to be given the same sentence as everyone else.

Prison proved a particularly gruelling experience for Helen. The rest of us were to see her on two subsequent occasions, at the Appeal Court and House of Lords Appeal hearings. (Both appeals failed, though Lord Devlin, in his judgement in the Lords, put in an important marker for the general right of citizens to challenge the Government on whether or not the interests of the state were being put in jeopardy in any given instance.) On both occasions she put a brave face on things, yet after the Lords hearing she was clearly feeling lonely and isolated as she was led off on her own back to Holloway. A month before my own release I received a telegram from her urging me to stick it out for the final period. A week later we were stunned to learn that she was dead, having taken a drug overdose. I have no doubt that it was the strain of her ordeal that led to this and it is a reminder that the campaign could take a heavy toll in personal terms and impose strains that could become unbearable.

Attempts to hold further mass demonstrations in London during 1962 had, at best, limited success. Then in October came the Cuba crisis, when for a time nuclear war seemed imminent. Despite the fact that Khrushchev chose to use Russell to announce his climb-down on the stationing of missiles, and despite hastily organised demonstrations in London, the effect of Cuba on the Committee, and indeed on the Peace Movement as a whole, was demoralising. There was a feeling that, regardless of all the protests, the fate of the world remained in the hands of a small number of people whom it was exceedingly difficult to influence. But I also think that it is not possible to sustain a campaign at the level of intensity that was achieved in 1961, and that campaigns seeking radical goals have to pace their efforts so that morale is maintained during the periods between peak activity.

Phase IV: the spread of NVDA as a method of protest

After the 17 September demonstration the Committee never again mounted a really *mass* demonstration on the nuclear issue, though it was centrally involved in a large demonstration against the visit of the King and Queen of Greece to Britain in 1963. In September and October 1961 it had mounted a series of lightning demonstrations outside the Soviet Embassy following the Soviet resumption of nuclear tests in the atmosphere, and in July 1962 it carried out a dramatic protest action in Red Square in Moscow in the course of an international peace conference. And the anonymous 'Spies for Peace' group also undoubtedly included individuals from the Committee of 100.[6]

In general, from around mid-1963 to its demise in 1968, the Committee tended to concentrate on actions at military bases which often resembled in style and scale the earlier campaigns of the DAC. But it also adopted a wider range of radical goals and became involved in a number of political and social struggles not directly related to nuclear weapons.[7]

In general, the late 1960s and the 1970s saw the flourishing of grass-roots community, ethnic, and political organisations, and, most importantly, of the Women's Movement, and a much more widespread use of NVDA. Sometimes former Committee of 100 or DAC people were directly involved: more often, groups and organisations adopted NVDA because it was an effective means of protest. Thus, while the Committee of 100 and the DAC never came near to achieving their ambitious major goals, they did help establish, or revive in a new guise, a tradition that has proved of profound and lasting importance to British political and cultural life, and to the prospects of further change and reform.

The moral and political rationale for NVDA

One central objection that the direct actionists had to face, not only from their political opponents but from many within the Peace Movement, was that direct action was unjustified in a democratic (or even approximately democratic) society.[8] The nub of our answer was that while rule by the majority was an important principle in a democratic society, respect for fundamental human rights was even more central. No government, for instance, however much public support it enjoyed, had the right to persecute ethnic or national minorities within the society, and if it did so those who resisted it could fairly claim to be upholding the democratic tradition.

In the case of nuclear weapons, it was the human rights of people outside the national territory that were being threatened, but the principle still applied. The use of nuclear weapons would have involved genocide on an even greater scale than the Nazi concentration camps. Governments certainly hoped that they would not be used, but as Air Commodore Magill had dramatically testified, if the circumstances demanded it they would be used. In a sense our protests were directed against a crime in contemplation rather than in the act of commission, and this certainly is an important difference in context to the situation in the American deep South, for instance, where Blacks were daily facing discrimination and persecution. Yet if nuclear weapons were to be opposed, this had to be done before war broke out, and, as far as possible, before we were on the brink of war.

But in democratic political theory governments do have a right, indeed an obligation, to provide a reasonable system of defence for their territories. And in terms of strategic rationale, if not of morality, the British Government and its supporters also had a case when they argued that reliance on nuclear weapons at some level was necessary as long as potential adversaries possessed them. Was it right then, and did it make campaigning sense, for a minority to attempt to change government policy by coercive or semi-coercive tactics? Would not this give the green light to extremist groups of Right and Left to pursue their objectives by the same methods, though perhaps with a less scrupulous observation of non-violent discipline? Can a democracy function if groups of citizens claim the right not simply to refuse co-operation with policies they regard as fundamentally wrong, but actively to obstruct them – albeit by non-violent tactics?

These are issues which have to be confronted if the practitioners of direct action are not to lose public support and to find themselves increasingly isolated. Given the constraints of space I will restrict my observations to the issues which seem to me to be central to the debate.

First, direct actionists do have to recognise in some sense the right of duly elected governments to legislate and enforce legislation: this obviously includes the right to decide on a defence policy for the country. (I leave aside here the question of whether the present system of representative democracy within a framework of capitalist economics is genuinely democratic; the issues of principle apply to almost any kind of society one can imagine, no matter how decentralised or democratically run.) Those, therefore, who claim a moral right to refuse to give a particular policy their co-operation on grounds of principle, and even physically to obstruct it by non-violent means, must also be prepared to accept the legal consequences of their actions. Yet society too, if it is sensitive to the issues at stake, will recognise the potential contribution to social and political progress of what we might term *conscientious resisters,* even if it cannot make explicit exceptions for them in its legislation. It will impose penalties, but it will not *persecute* the resisters or seek to suppress them altogether.

Second, though obstruction is involved in many kinds of non-violent action, it is not obstruction *per se* that is important, but the symbolism of the action, its power to communicate and its potential to create moral and political dilemmas for a government. If simple obstruction of, say, a military base was the prime objective, this could be achieved more effectively than by having people sitting down at the entrances – for instance, as I have occasionally heard proposed, by dumping lorry-loads of wet concrete at the entrances, or driving up to them in old vehicles and letting down the tyres. Work at the base might indeed be held up for longer periods by such tactics, but in terms of gaining public support they would almost certainly be counter-productive. (Indeed, I confess that some of the tactics that have been adopted in recent actions seem to me to be highly questionable from this point of view.)

Mass NVDA can of course present a government with extremely difficult physical problems. Removing tens of thousands of demonstrators becomes a major police operation. The courts may not be able to cope with the numbers or the prisons, to hold them. Yet even in this extreme situation, which the Committee of 100 would like to have brought about but never succeeded in doing, it is the moral and political struggle that is decisive. Physically, the government can always cope by introducing special measures – setting up special courts, erecting detention camps and so on. The point is that *provided the demonstrators have managed to retain a large measure of public sympathy* these draconian measures will have a political cost for the Government. It may be seen as repressive and the whole range of its policies subjected to more intensive scrutiny; it may even lose support in parliament and be forced to go to the country where the whole issue would be put to the test of an election. However, if the demonstrators come to be widely regarded as people with no regard for democratic process, the majority of the public is likely to rally to the side of the Government and to support it in whatever measures it decides to take to restore order. In short, the notion that an elected government could be coerced *physically* into changing the whole basis of its defence and foreign policy by the sheer weight of numbers of demonstrators, is an illusion.

In the DAC period especially, those involved stressed the power of non-violent action to communicate and to mobilise. The drama of the action, its particular appropriateness to the immediate aims and broader objectives, was seen, as noted above, as a kind of propaganda by the deed for the views we espoused. The very willingness of the demonstrators to endure hardship, fines and imprisonment was integral to the process. This did not mean that traditional forms of campaigning were unnecessary, only that by themselves they were unlikely to be sufficient.

NVDA was also seen by some as demonstrating an alternative form of resistance which might eventually replace military preparations in the defence of a community and its values, and this was frequently linked to a broader project to build a new non-violent community within the old and bring about a radical transformation of society from below.

The direct actionists and political strategy

If the direct actionists could provide moral justification for their methods, did they have a political strategy – and how successful were they in implementing it? What was their legacy to the movement of the present time, and to British politics in general?

In considering these questions something needs to be said of the strategy and achievements of the disarmament movement as a whole. First, however, a caveat about the pitfalls of trying to categorise and label too precisely the various tendencies within the overall movement, or any particular wing of it. This was a period of intense political activism and debate in which not only did individual views change and develop, but the consensus within a given wing of the movement was also liable to shift. The political perspective of the core activists in the DAC, for instance, shifted perceptibly between the period of its inception in 1957 and its dissolution in mid-1961 – by which time they were mainly involved in the Committee of 100. Similarly, the New Left movement of, say, 1957 to 1961 was very different in character – and much closer to the disarmament movement as such – than that of the *New Left Review* circle from around 1962–63 onwards, which was by then committed to a highly theoretical and specifically Marxist political analysis. Moreover, the division that opened up within the New Left between those of a particular Marxist tendency and critics of this tendency, notably Edward Thompson, was far greater than that between the direct actionists and the New Left of the earlier period.[9]

Organisationally there were orginally three main groupings that can be regarded as constituting the broad disarmament movement: the Campaign for Nuclear Disarmament – CND; the New Left; and the DAC – which was eventually replaced in 1961, after a short overlap period, by the Committee of 100. The New Left movement revolved around two publications, the *Universities and Left Review* and the *New Reasoner*; these amalgamated in 1960 to form the *New Left Review*. While the New Left movement was not organised specifically around the issue of nuclear weapons, it gave strong support to both the DAC and CND, and made nuclear disarmament a central demand in its own policies, and it is therefore reasonable to treat it as part of the broad movement. All three wings shared a rejection on moral grounds of nuclear weapons, though probably the specifically moral issue was most strongly emphasised by the direct actionists.

The leadership of CND adopted by and large a 'Labour-path' strategy: the Labour Party was to be won over to the cause of unilateralism by the efforts of its left wing and by the pressure of a public campaign, to secure victory at the polls and then implement British nuclear disarmament.[10] For a brief period it looked as though this strategy might succeed, when the Labour Party Conference in 1960 passed a unilateralist resolution. But, after Hugh Gaitskell's pledge at that conference to 'fight, fight, and fight again', the policy was reversed in the following year.

The strategy of the New Left on the disarmament issue is harder to pin down, partly because there were various influences at work within it. (See Chapter 8 for a more detailed discussion of the New Left.) There was strong sympathy, for instance, within New Left circles for direct action; and later it was an alliance of individuals within the New Left, CND and DAC that led to the formation of the Independent Nuclear Disarmament Election Committee – INDEC – the campaign to field independent nuclear disarmament candidates at elections. Nevertheless the majority tendency, in terms of political strategy, within the New Left was again strongly oriented towards the electoral victory of a reformed Labour Party which was seen as having the possibility of bringing about not only nuclear disarmament but a more open, democratic and participatory form of socialism.

For the most part the DAC rejected the Labour-path strategy – though certainly among active supporters many would have been Labour voters or even members of the party. First, we argued that the political divisions within the Labour Party, the strength of the centre and right, and the role of trade-union bloc votes at the party conferences, made it unlikely that the Labour Party as it was then constituted could be the vehicle for nuclear disarmament. Second, we argued that nuclear disarmament would represent such a radical change in the direction of British politics that it could not be achieved by winning over a party machine, but required a fundamental shift in British political culture at the base; and for this a popular campaign involving new methods of protest and resistance was required.

This is not to say that the DAC at any stage of its history was an apolitical campaign; it was in fact strongly influenced by ideas inherited from the Independent Labour Party, Guild Socialism, anarchism, and the libertarian left in general. There was thus both an overlap, and a natural rapport, with a significant wing of the New Left, and, as noted earlier, the enthusiastic support of New Left activists was one of the critical factors in the success of the first Aldermaston March.

There were two central figures in the DAC who articulated most clearly and forcibly the critique of the Labour-path strategy. Allen Skinner analysed the weakness of the political left within the Labour Party, arguing, among other things, that ultimately the Labour leadership could count on the support of the parliamentary Left in the Commons and on the votes of left-wing Labour supporters in the country, and that while this situation obtained, there was little hope of change. It was Allen Skinner who was largely instrumental in persuading the DAC to launch the 'Voters' Veto' campaign referred to earlier.[11]

The second influential critic of the Labour-path strategy was Alan Lovell. He pressed the point that, without a strong political force at the base, even a government that had included nuclear disarmament in its election programme would be liable to succumb to pressures from the Establishment and to retreat from its anti-nuclear commitment.

On the question of how ultimately nuclear disarmament would be achieved, there were within the DAC several viewpoints. A few looked to a reformed and radicalised Labour Party, though I think this approach was more widely favoured among DAC supporters than among the actual Committee members. Allen Skinner looked towards a split in Labour producing a new radical party. Neither of these perspectives implied a radical change in the parliamentary system as such. Others, however, nourished hopes that the practice of non-violent direct action and agitation at the grass roots, not only on the Bomb but on a range of social and political issues, would throw up new structures of democratic political organisation. But we were for the most part open-minded (and hence also vague) as to the precise nature of the structural and political changes that would be necessary, and we were not against seeking what support and help we could get from within the ranks of existing parties and institutions. Perhaps the major political tendency could be described as 'sceptical libertarian' rather than, for instance, straightforward anarchist or Marxist. Discussion within the DAC was marked by an absense of political dogmatism, and this, plus the consensus in favour of some kind of non-violent, libertarian approach, made for a viable working relationship, despite differences of emphasis. There was in fact a broad agreement on the campaigning strategy required for the foreseeable future – a grass-roots campaign which would challenge the consciences of those working on nuclear-related projects, would mobilise opinion against nuclear weapons, and would be capable of putting pressure on governments of whatever complexion to change or modify their policies.

It is important to stress that last aim for it indicates the principal way in which we expected to have a direct political impact in the short and medium term. Essentially, we aimed to put pressure on governments and political parties from the outside, mobilising opinion for or against particular government actions, while at the same time laying the foundations through direct action for more fundamental change.

With the formation of the Committee of 100, the range of political perspectives within the direct action wing broadened. On the one hand there were those like Bertrand Russell who saw direct action simply as a way of drawing media and public attention to the nuclear issue, and were not looking towards any radical change in the existing political structures and institutions. On the other, there were those like the 'Solidarity' group[12] which had a well-articulated quasi-syndicalist position – a position associated for over eighty years with direct action. 'Solidarity' saw the Committee campaigns as contributing to a programme of radical change that would affect almost every aspect of social and political life. Anarchist ideas were also more prominent and were given persuasive expression in the pages of a new monthly journal, *Anarchy,* edited by Colin Ward. But again there was an overlap of views between the varying perspectives and room for differences provided agreement could be maintained on campaigning priorities.

Probably the main threat to that consensus came, following the formation of the Committee of 100, from the debate about whether actions should continue to focus on military bases or at symbolic sites in city centres, especially London. The latter approach was strongly favoured by, among others, Ralph Schoenman, the dynamic young

American who played a central role in the setting-up of the Committee of 100. His preference for city-centre demonstrations is sometimes seen as a direct reflection of his belief that ultimate success for the Movement would be brought about by a quasi-insurrection at the centre of government power.[13] But I think this is a simplification: the arguments about where demonstrations should be held focused more on the short term and on tactical questions – on where, on the one hand, we could expect to attract large-scale participation, and, on the other, where demonstrations involving obstruction would have the kind of clear symbolism and logic that would be understood by those not already committed to the cause.

It is true that on the whole it was the DAC members who most strongly favoured action at bases and expressed most unease about actions whose main effect would be to block civilian traffic in city centres. But, after all, the first major action of the Committee of 100 was a sit-down on the pavements around the Ministry of Defence in Whitehall, an action which echoed that of the Operation Gandhi demonstration outside the War Office back in early 1952. Moreover, Schoenman himself was impressed by the very successful DAC demonstration at the Holy Loch base at Whitsun 1961, following the London to Glasgow march, and was not opposed to demonstrations at bases if these could be on a large scale and had a significant public impact. And as we have seen, one of the first major actions by the Scottish Committee of 100, in fact, was a non-violent blockade involving 500 people at the Holy Loch base on 16 September 1961.

Of course political perspectives do colour the view one takes about the appropriate place for demonstrations. When, for instance, the CND took over the Aldermaston march from the DAC at Easter 1959 they reversed its direction, so that it went from Aldermaston to London, and this was clearly intended as a statement of where political responsibility for nuclear policy lay and where pressure needed to be brought to bear if things were to change. No doubt Ralph Schoenman and other Committee of 100 activists who favoured demonstrations in London did think that this was the appropriate place politically for them to happen and they no doubt saw them as models of the kind of agitation that could eventually inaugurate a new political era. However, I do not think anyone, Schoenman included, expected the demonstration on the scale we could hope to mount during 1961 would bring about the collapse of the central Government: they had a symbolic and mobilising value of much the same kind as the demonstrations at bases, and their great advantage over the latter was not that they prefigured the form of ultimate revolt that would overthrow the existing system, but that they more readily attracted large numbers of participants.

Did the 'radical' direct actionists have a strategy at all? Perhaps in one sense we did not – at least if by a strategy is meant a programme of action leading step by step to the establishment in the short term of a unilateralist government. But we analysed, in my judgement quite correctly, the weakness and superficiality of the Labour-path strategy at that period, and argued in effect that the preconditions for the election of the committed unilateralist Government did not exist. Our efforts were focused, as already noted, on putting pressure on the government of the day, whatever its political complexion, and we hoped that in that very process, through the campaigning methods used, we would help to change the conditions and the attitudes in society at large.

The approach was also strongly internationalist. If the project was to succeed there had to be similar movements at the base in other countries, not only to get rid of nuclear weapons but to ensure that structures of domination and repression were replaced by genuinely democratic ones which would allow people a real say in the running of their lives at every level.

Richard Taylor's critique of the direct action approach

I want to consider briefly certain criticisms of the direct action approach in the 1950s and 1960s made by Richard Taylor in his writings.[14] The reason for focusing on his critique in particular is partly that he has written extensively on the period, and the perspective he puts forward could, if unchallenged, come to exercise a considerable, and in my view unwarranted, influence, and partly because he raises serious issues which deserve consideration. Finally, some of his criticims are representative of those made by other critics of the direct action approach.

His judgements of the direct action approach are harshly dismissive. Thus we are informed of 'the marginality and incoherence' of the direct action position, and of direct action representing 'the politics of immaturity: the desire and belief that dramatic and immediate antiauthority political action would secure the objectives'.[15]

Much of Taylor's own material suggests that a more generous appraisal of the achievements of the direct actionists, and of the earlier

Movement as a whole, is called for, but his final verdicts on the politics and strategy of NVDA are generally dismissive.

There are three specific criticisms made by Taylor that I want to consider here. First, that a major weakness of the direct actionist wing and of the nuclear disarmament campaign as a whole, was its essentially middle-class style and ethos, and its failure to establish solid links with the organised working-class movement or with the radical tradition of protest and dissent in British politics. Second, that the direct actionists ignored the problem of agency, i.e. the problem of specifying, or creating a political party or organisation to carry through its programme. Third, that the Movement as a whole pursued a mistaken strategy by remaining an essentially single issue, moral, campaign.

The 'class issue' is a major one and only a few central aspects can be considered here. It is true that although the direct action wing was far from being exclusively middle-class, it never gained mass working-class support or the active allegiance of trade unions and constituency Labour parties. Taylor himself, however, suggests an explanation for this, namely the predominance throughout every sector of society of an essentially conservative culture and ideology. Although his expositions tend to be over-schematic, leading him to overstate this cultural and ideological 'hegemony' of the Right, he is surely correct in concluding that it was the very radicalism of the Peace Movement's demands and its style of action that excluded the possibility of mass working-class support.[16]

But if it was virtually out of the question for the Movement to mobilise mass working-class support, it is pointless taking the Movement to task for not succeeding in doing so. Taylor, however, never lets his left hand know what his ultra-left hand is doing, and subsequently suggests that there was a possibility of the New Left bringing together the direct actionists and the working-class movement to create a radical extra-parliamentary mass movement based on the industrial trade unions and constituency Labour parties. In fact Taylor's own analysis indicates that in the time span under consideration this was never a serious possibility.

Taylor argues that the direct actionist approach, with its strong emphasis on the moral issue and on individual responsibility, is essentially alien to the radical working-class tradition which emphasises *collective* action and is strongly focused on economic issues. His own ideological position leads him to underestimate the importance of the broad radical and working-class tradition of principled opposition to what is regarded as unjust and therefore intolerable.[17]

One of the most significant social/political developments during and since the 1960s has been the emergence of influential radical movements not rooted in the class issue *per se*. The Women's Movement, and the campaigns by ethnic minorities and others against discrimination and harassment, are obvious examples. As a result there is now a greater awareness of the fact that social injustice does not operate only along the dimension of class, and that therefore many movements of resistance and reconstruction cut across class lines. It would be perverse, too, not to recognise the major contribution of sections of the middle class to these movements.

This does not, of course, imply that there should not be attempts to create links between different, though related, struggles to end injustice and oppression of various kinds – on the contrary, this is clearly a vital task. But because there are clashes of style, ideas and sometimes too of particular interests, a broad alliance of separate organisations is called for, rather than simply a single organisation or political party that attempts to reconcile all differences in the formulation of a common policy.

If, then, it was virtually impossible at the time for the Movement to gain mass working-class support, the establishment (or the re-establishment under a significantly different guise) of a tradition of NVDA that would be available to groups struggling against oppression or immoral policies, was about as important a contribution as the Movement could have made to the radicalisation of British politics. It is clear, too, from the spate of sit-ins, occupations and similar protests against factory closures, homelessness and other developments affecting the lives of working people, that the influence of the direct actionists did extend to the working-class movement and, together with other influences, contributed to a shift in the political and cultural ethos in Britain during the 1960s.

The second question – that of the agency for achieving reform or radical change – is again a crucial one. But if 'agency' implies a political party, then there was only one serious candidate for this role at the time, namely the Labour Party. Neither the Communist Party, nor the splinter Trotskyist or other leftist parties, offered a real possibility.[18] Taylor acknowledges this last point but he is even more insistent in his rejection of what he terms the Labourist strategy; indeed he argues that following Aneurin Bevan's rejection of unilateralism at the Brighton Labour Party conference in 1957, the Labourist approach favoured by the CND Executive was doomed even before CND had been formed. Moreover, he suggests that the central weakness of the New Left was its commitment in the last analysis to a Labourist approach and 'parliamentarism'.[19]

In principle, of course, there was a further option – that of creating a new political party. It can scarcely be doubted, however, that unless this was the outcome of a split in an existing major party – which in practice would have had to be the Labour Party – no new party could hope to attract more than a tiny minority vote. (The experience of the INDEC campaign at Parliamentary by-elections was that even committed nuclear disarmament supporters within the Labour Party were not prepared to switch their traditional allegiance, and the INDEC candidates never attracted significant electoral support.)

But if, as Taylor insists, the question of agency is central, and the direct actionists' failure to specify one was a crucial weakness of their politics, what in his view could have provided such an agency? The nearest we get to an answer is the following passage in *The Protest Makers*:

> Despite the fatalistic assumptions of the Labour Left view, the Labour Party is not a static, immovable monolith: there, *are*, potentially, other avenues to both power and socialism. And one of the most attractive and potentially realisable of these, in the UK, is a new alliance, on an NL basis of some description. There is nothing inherently foolish or ridiculous in the notion of an NL regrouping leading to a reformation of the organised working-class movement around a socialistically oriented party, or grouping.[20]

Here the very movement of the prose indicates Taylor's uncertainty whether to opt for the reformation of the Labour Party (since it is not 'a static, immovable monolith') or for 'other avenues'. And it is difficult to know what is meant by the 'notion of an NL regrouping' which could lead to 'a socialistically oriented party, or grouping'. Given Taylor's insistence on the crucial importance of political agency, this confusion, and his failure to specify concretely at any point what agency he thinks was required, is fatal to the cohesion of his critique. I draw attention to it to underline the genuine difficulty that any radical movement of that time faced, and that, to a considerable extent, is still to be faced today.

If there was little or no chance of either changing or splitting the

Labour Party in the time period we are considering; if neither the Communist Party nor the minority Trotskyist and other leftist parties offered any hope, and if creating a new party from scratch could only at best be an exercise in protest, then there was no way forward at the electoral level at that time, and therefore no chance of bringing about the election of a unilateralist government before the political situation in the country as a whole had changed.[21] This meant essentially that the main campaigning work had to be done outside the political parties – though of course it could be complemented by campaigning work from inside them.

During 1961 when the momentum of protest was building up, we entertained the hope that things might change very rapidly. In retrospect it is clear that that hope was misplaced – and indeed, after 1962, I would say that the Committee resigned itself to the necessity of a longer-term campaign in which direct action would take its place alongside other forms of action. But in arguing that the campaign must be taken to the people as a whole and that dynamic new methods of protest and resistance were necessary, I think we on the direct action wing were right. In the short to medium term there was no 'agency' for change in the sense of a political party or organisation that would implement change in the total defence strategy of the country.

Finally, there is the criticism that the Movement as a whole, and the direct action wing in particular, focused too much on the moral issue and failed to realise the crucial political dimension of the problem. I think this criticism is misplaced. A perusal of the literature produced in the period by the Movement and associated publications like *Peace News*, indicates that certainly the majority of leaders and activists were fully aware of the political dimensions, though of course there were differences about how the campaign would eventually resolve itself at the political level.

What neither the CND nor the two direct action organisations were willing to do was to link their organisation to any particular political party. In this special sense they were apolitical, but quite rightly so, since it is clearly essential to have a campaign broad enough to include anyone from Conservatives to Marxists or anarchists who are convinced for moral and/or political reasons that nuclear weapons should be rejected. What one can expect is the growth of parallel political organisations, working either within or outside the existing mainstream parties, for whom nuclear disarmament is the central element in a broader programme. One can also expect a political consensus, or centre of gravity, to be defined within the disarmament movement as such – and it is also reasonable to expect that the centre of gravity will be well to the left. But this is a very different thing from the Movement defining itself as a specifically Socialist (or Marxist or anarchist) organisation and requiring members to assent to a whole set of political beliefs when joining it. What was needed, and what broadly speaking evolved, was not so much a 'single issue' campaign as a 'broad church movement', – i.e. a movement which had certain definable political characteristics but was not so ideologically narrow as to exclude opponents of nuclear weapons coming from different political traditions.

It is true that the Committee of 100 in its latter period came close to defining itself as a political, rather than simply an anti-Bomb, campaign and took up issues other than those connected with nuclear weapons. But it defined its politics in very broad, if decidedly radical, terms, and the Bomb still remained the central issue. Thus it was far removed in character and organisation from a political party. In any case CND remained as the broad church anti-nuclear campaign to attract people of all political persuasions who rejected the Bomb.

The perspective which came to predominate within the Committee of 100 and other NVDA movements, especially after the heady excitement of 1961 had subsided, was that a variety of grass-roots movements and groups, using direct action and other forms of protest and resistance, could bring about political change from below. These groups and organisations would be expected to work together in a loose alliance rather than attempting to form a unified political organisation or party. Thus in the mid- and late sixties there was a considerable emphasis on community politics, and on the efforts of oppressed sections of society to take matters into their own hands in the struggle to change their situation. At the same time national and international protest was necessary to put constraints on governments and, at least indirectly, affect their policies. (Vietnam is the clearest example of the latter.)

Taylor contends that movements that focus primarily on the moral issue are too concerned with their own internal purity and consistency to operate effectively at the political level – being unwilling in particular to join in alliances to campaign for limited objectives in line with their broader goal. This is sometimes true, but is far from being universally so. Certainly the DAC was quite positive towards the idea of co-operation with other groups, and in the Sahara Protest Action against

French nuclear tests, for instance, it co-operated with a variety of organisations and bodies, including, informally, the Ghanaian Government of Kwame Nkrumah. In both the US and Europe, pacifist organisations whose primary emphasis is clearly a moral one have played an important role, in mobilising action against the war in Vietnam, and against Cruise and Pershing deployments.

Many questions relating to the strategy and tactics of direct action politics remain to be explored. Furthermore, it is clear that in the 1950s and 1960s mistakes were made – inevitably so indeed. (The 'Voters' Veto' campaign, for example, was, I think, a tactical error.)

Probably many of us on the direct action wing, particularly during the Committee of 100 period, took insufficient account of what was, or might have been, politically possible at the time in terms of parties and governments, and were perhaps too dismissive of the possibilities of working from within the Labour Party, or other political parties. We were right in thinking there was no possibility of a unilateralist Labour (or any other) government being elected in the short or medium term, and we were right in surmising that there would not be a unilateralist Labour Party without a political split of the kind that was eventually to occur with the formation of the SDP. But in the end it was not a 'Voters' Veto' that brought about that split, or a Labour Party committed at least to British nuclear disarmament, but the combined pressure of the Peace Movement able to mount mass public demonstrations, and committed unilateralists working within the Party.

To elaborate the point at a more general level, if one has very radical goals which would involve the restructuring of the whole political system, one cannot expect this to happen overnight, especially if one is committed to a non-violent approach. Given that fact, it is necessary to plan with short-term possibilities as well as the long-term goal in view. Movements at the base can, over time, extend the options at the government and party level by introducing and popularising new concepts and new modes of organisation. But they do also have to be aware of the political possibilities at any given moment and of the potential allies they can recruit for particular demands within mainstream politics. In brief, radical campaigns must by their nature 'demand the impossible', but they must do so with an understanding of what *is* possible and sometimes focus their immediate efforts on short-term goals. I am not saying the DAC and the Committee of 100 never did this – indeed they could not have obtained the degree of support they did if they had not at times focused on issues – such as the construction of Thor rocket bases or the establishment of the US submarine base at Holy Loch – that touched a political nerve in the country. But perhaps in the latter stages not enough attention was paid to this aspect of campaign strategy.

Assessing the achievement of NVDA in the 1950s and 1960s

How then should one assess the achievements of the earlier Movement and the contribution of its direct action wing? In many ways, because of my strong personal involvement, I am not the right person to make that assessment, and my comments must be read with that in mind. Clearly, the central goal of the Movement – that of getting Britain to renounce nuclear weapons and to secure their removal altogether from its territory – was not achieved. There is, however, as I have noted, good reason to believe that, whatever strategy or approach had been used, this was not a realisable goal at that time.

Educationally the effect of the campaign was enormous, and not in Britain alone. (This is a point which Taylor acknowledges.) For the first time in the post-war period there was a major public debate on the moral and political issues surrounding nuclear weapons. This, and the fact that the Movement at its height was in a position to bring tens of thousands of people on to the streets willing to engage in non-violent action, altered, if only to a certain degree, the background against which governments made their decisions. The usually well-informed British columnist, Chapman Pincher, suggested, in an article in 1961, that the Kennedy Administration seriously considered cancelling its decision to base its Polaris-carrying submarine fleet at Holy Loch for fear of the popular protest this would arouse in Britain. However, according to Pincher, Macmillan insisted that the plans should go ahead because he was concerned that any change would be regarded as a victory by the Peace Movement. If this is true, it suggests that governments took a great deal of notice of what the Peace Movement was doing and how it would respond to particular decisions. Moreover, the decision to prosecute leading activists in the Committee of 100 under the Official Secrets Act was clearly taken at the highest level.

The most tangible effect within Britain of the activities of the DAC and Committee of 100 was to establish a tradition of NVDA within the political culture. It is difficult now to realise just how controversial such action was in the late 1950s: if it is far less so today that is because its use has become so much more widespread, and because the intellectual case for the discriminate use of non-violent direct action in a democratic society has largely been won. Today, for instance, CND itself can organise demonstrations involving non-violent obstruction without causing a split in the movement, or even any particularly sharp controversy. This itself is a measure of the impact of the direct actionists of the earlier period.

Did the Movement as a whole have any influence on the military, foreign and disarmament policies of British, or any other, governments? Possibly the pressure of the campaign helped to push the British and US governments to negotiate the Partial Test Ban Treaty of 1963 – if only as a way of taking the wind out of the Movement's sails; but one cannot be sure even of this. But certainly there were no major changes of direction in Western policy. Nevertheless the existence of the Movement is part of the background against which particular decisions are taken by governments. Is it possible, then, that this actually tipped the balance between peace and war, or between a decision to use or not to use nuclear weapons on particular occasions? This might well have been the case on at least two specific occasions: the Cuban missile crisis of 1962, and the influence of the anti-war movement in tempering Nixon's actions in Vietnam in 1969.

The secrecy surrounding government decisions means that it is rarely possible to show conclusively that particular government decisions, or changes in decisions, are attributable to the pressure of peace movements. But it is certainly possible to judge when the scale and nature of popular protest is beginning to have an impact on government leaders – if only by the energy they put into refuting the criticisms of their policies and the ploys they use to deflect or undermine the peace movements. (As, for example, in the Ministry of Defence propaganda campaign against the Peace Movement in the 1980s.)

On that basis I think that there is little doubt that the spate of mass anti-war protest that began on a significant scale in Britain in the late 1950s, and spread to a number of West European countries and to the US and Canada, did have a political impact – just as the rejuvenated and still more extensive movement of the 1980s is doing. The first priority of a Peace Movement is not disarmament but the prevention of war. And I have no doubt that if we are to avoid the nuclear holocaust, as well as to achieve the longer-term goals, an international Movement of conscientious resistance and NVDA will play a crucial role.

References

1 These original sketches were kept by Hugh Brock, and were donated by his widow Eileen on his death in 1985 to the School of Peace Studies at Bradford University.

2 See Gene Sharp, 'A time for action', *Peace News*, 30 January 1959.

3 Thus, before the North Pickenham demonstrations, five field workers lobbied in the area with some success, enlisting the support of a number of trade unions and constituency labour parties. Several trade union secretaries and Labour Party agents assisted the DAC in organising the campaign. In subsequent campaigns Will Warren spent months living on his own in a caravan in Norfolk doing work of this kind and travelling round in an old jeep that the Committee had bought. Pat Arrowsmith and I similarly worked from a caravan parked in a field near Wollaston in Northamptonshire. Later during the campaign against Polaris in Scotland, Douglas Brewood (Senior), a trade union activist who had taken part in the hunger marches in the thirties, campaigned in the Glasgow area and made many valuable contacts for us in the Labour and Trade Union Movements in that city.

4 See April Carter, 'The Sahara Protest Team', in A. P. Hare and H. H. Blumberg (eds.), *Liberation Without Violence*, Collins, London, 1977.

5 The Brigade went on to organise several actions, including a Delhi–Peking Friendship March in 1963; it also campaigned in South-East Africa and made detailed preparations for an international march from Dar Es Salaam to the border with Zambia in opposition to the British Government's plans to create a Central African Federation. This had the active support of both Julius Nyerere and Kenneth Kaunda, and was called off only at the last minute when the British Government announced the scrapping of the Federation plans.

6 This was the group that obtained and released a secret official document revealing the existence of underground 'Regional Seats of Government' across the country, from which authorities with sweeping powers would rule the country in the aftermath of a nuclear war.

7 Its involvement in demonstrations against the state visit of the King and Queen of Greece to Britain has been mentioned. Another action that was small in scale but had a dramatic impact was the demonstration at a church in Brighton in 1967 where, as a protest against British complicity in the war in Vietnam, demonstrators interrupted the Prime Minister Harold Wilson when he was reading the Lesson.

   The Committee, or active members of it, also took up issues related to domestic politics. The squatters' movement by homeless people in the mid-1960s was initiated largely by Committee activists, notably Jim Radford and Ron Bailey. George Clark developed a programme for community action in Notting Hill, while Ernest Rodker became closely involved in community politics in South London.

8 For a fuller discussion of the issue, see April Carter, *Direct Action and Liberal Democracy*, Routledge and Kegan Paul, London, 1973.

9 See Perry Anderson, 'The origins of the present crisis', *New Left Review,* reprinted in Anderson and Nairn (eds.), *Towards Socialism,* Fontana and New Left Books, 1965; and E. P. Thompson's attack on their position in his essay 'The Peculiarities of the English', *Socialist Register 1965,* Merlin Press, 1965.

10 The term 'Labourist' is sometimes used to denote this approach (for instance by Richard Taylor in his writings). But it has a distinctly pejorative tone. I use the term

'Labour-path' because it is more neutral in connotation.

11 Allen Skinner, although a founder member of the DAC and an influential voice within it, never supported the use of non-violent obstruction (such as sit-downs and blockades) in a Parliamentary democracy like Britain. On the other hand, he strongly supported taking the Campaign directly to the people and appealing on grounds of conscience to those working on projects to do with nuclear weapons to give up their work.

12 A left socialist grouping considerably influenced by the writings of Paul Cardan of the *Socialisme ou Barbarie* group in France. 'Solidarity' had a strongly class-based analysis but were highly critical of aspects of Marx's analysis and often scathing in their attacks on present-day Marxism in its various forms, taking a broadly libertarian view of Marxist politics.

13 Richard Taylor, for instance, interprets Schoeman's preference for demonstrations at city centres in this way.

14 One of the co-editors of this book, Richard Taylor, has undertaken research into the Peace Movement of the 1950s and 1960s. My comments are made on the basis of three pieces:

   i) (Jointly with Colin Pritchard), *The Protest Makers: the British Nuclear Disarmament Movement of 1958 to 1965, Twenty Years on*, Pergamon Press, 1980.

   ii) 'The British Nuclear Disarmament Movement of 1958 to 1965 and its legacy to the Left', unpublished PhD thesis (2 vols.), University of Leeds, 1983 (available also for consultation at the Commonweal Collection, J. B. Priestley Library, University of Bradford).

   iii) 'The British Peace Movement and Socialist Change', in R. Miliband and J. Saville (eds.), *Socialist Register 1983*, Merlin Press, London, 1983.

   Taylor is highly critical of direct action strategy and politics and, although this is not the place for a detailed critique of his approach, I wish to take issue with his critique, defend the direct action approach, and draw attention to what I see as weaknesses and inconsistencies in his argument which, in my judgement, largely invalidate his analysis.

   (Note – although the first of these works is co-authored I shall refer, for simplicity's sake, to Taylor as author when citing from it.)

15 The first of these quotations is taken from Taylor's PhD thesis, p. 931, and *Socialist Register*, p. 132, and the second from *The Protest Makers*, p. 127.

16 See, for example, *The Protest Makers*, pp. 116, 129.

17 The successful year-long strike in Dublin in 1984–85 by women shop assistants in a leading supermarket who refused to handle South African goods, is a dramatic illustration of the fact that economic self-interest is not always involved in radical working-class action. See Claire Reed, 'Counter offensive', the *Guardian*, 23 July 1985, which traces the development of the campaign during the first eleven months.

18 Taylor notes that the political initiative in the late fifties and early sixties lay with the direct actionists and the New Left, not with the Communist Party or the splinter Marxist parties. (This despite the fact that from his point of view these parties had a more correct political analysis than the direct actionists.)

19 See PhD thesis, p. 939 and *Socialist Register* article, p. 138.

20 *The Protest Makers*, pp. 123–4.

21 Ironically, Taylor and Pritchard in *The Protest Makers* concur with Stuart Hall's

judgement that the Bomb 'was the one thing that we (the movement) couldn't do anything about'. This does not deter them from taking the movement to task for not achieving nuclear disarmament and attributing this to weaknesses in the Movement's strategy – though, as I have argued, without proposing an even remotely viable alternative strategy.

8

The Marxist Left and the Peace Movement in Britain since 1945

RICHARD TAYLOR

'Only the destruction of the capitalist system and its replacement by a socialist one will put an end to wars and human sufferings.' (Bolshevik leaflet, November 1916, cited in *Socialist Worker Diary* 1985)

Introduction

Marxists have had a significant impact on the Peace Movement since the onset of the anti-nuclear protests. In both the first and the second waves of the anti-nuclear movement the Communist Party (CP) has been prominent within the leadership and activist sections of CND. Moreover, the CP gained a dominant influence within CND during its 'fallow years' (from the late 1960s to the late 1970s). Whilst the Trotskyist Movement was very small in the late 1950s and early 1960s it was of some importance within the early stages of the Movement, and, from the late 1970s, the various Trotskyist and quasi-Trotskyist groups, especially the Socialist Workers' Party (SWP), have been a sizeable grouping within the Peace Movement.

Perhaps most significant of all within this context has been the 'New Left' which emerged originally in the aftermath of the 1956 events, and has subsequently developed, in a variety of organisational forms, the politics of socialist humanism.

The Marxists' role in the Movement has been important not only for their activism and support, but also because in various forms they have presented a structural analysis of the H-Bomb issue and the political questions surrounding it which opposed fundamentally many of the assumptions on which the mainstream of the Movement has been based. For all Marxists, whatever their differences in orientation, the issue of the Bomb has been inseparably linked to the structure of existing society, and for them the unilateralist movement has been intimately involved with the struggle to create a socialist system. This chapter thus analyses the perspectives of the various Marxist groupings on the Peace Movement since 1945 and discusses their significance in the context of the overall development of the Movement's politics.

The Communist Party and the Peace Movement

In the late 1950s, when CND was inaugurated, the CP was at first somewhat sceptical of both the policy and the political orientation of the new campaign. The CP had been engaged, through the British Peace Committee (the British branch of the World Peace Council), since the early 1950s, in a concentrated international drive for disarmament. The Stockholm Appeal, the Campaign against German Rearmament, and the constant pressure, in the context of the Cold War, for international disarmament negotiations, had been high priorities for the CP in the years immediately prior to CND's creation.

The crucial question for the CP in the late 1950s was the 'fight for an international agreement . . . which would get rid of the Russian and American bomb'.[1] In order to attain this end the CP saw its role primarily as one of mounting a propaganda campaign for summit talks between Russia and the USA. Combined with this was the strong desire for Britain to renounce the Western Alliance and, more specifically, to refuse the USA the right to bases in Britain.

It is in this context of continued and mounting CP pressure around what were seen as the two major issues – summit talks and the ending of the US 'presence' in Britain – that the CP's attitude to CND must be seen. Contrary to popular opinion both inside and outside CND, the *Daily Worker* had given considerable coverage to Peace Movement activities prior to the formation of CND. It continued to give far greater prominence to CND activities than any other national newspaper.

There were, however, qualifications to CP support for the Movement. The concentration of CND upon British unilateral action was seen as, at best, a diversion from the central issues. There was thus no overt hostility to CND but a 'certain amount of emphasis on criticising the unilateral aspects of its policy'.[2]

This was the central area of disagreement – but it was exacerbated by what the CP saw as the reactionary element within CND: those unilateralists who advocated renunciation by Britain of the Bomb, but adhered to the theory of the deterrent and, above all, wanted Britain to remain a loyal member of NATO and 'concentrate . . . on the establishment of highly mobile conventional forces'.[3] Such advocates took the view, it was argued, that America could defend the West alone, and that Britain's best contribution to the Western alliance would be through conventional armaments. This, noted the CP, 'fits in with the outlook of a certain section of the British imperialists, who are mainly concerned with repressing the liberation struggle of the colonial peoples, for which purpose atomic weapons are not useful'.[4] Others in CND were, in the CP's view, motivated by a 'moral defeatism', and seemed to advocate empty gestures rather than concentrating on the complex business of securing international agreement.

The differences with CND were, however, according to the CP, 'a question of tactics, of estimating what was the best campaigning demand, or series of demands . . .'.[5] One of the major reasons for the CP's reluctance to accept CND's unilateralist policy on tactical grounds was its belief that 'maximalist' demands would serve to divide the wider Peace Movement. An editorial in the *Daily Worker* of 28 February 1958, put the point bluntly: 'to raise instead the question of unilateralism, against which the (Labour) Conference decided by a seven-to-one vote and which the later Gallup Poll shows is supported by only a fifth of the British people is likely to divert attention from the main job', i.e. for Britain to stop the tests, for international agreement to ban the Bomb, for progressive disarmament, and for a European security pact.

This question of 'unity' over a minimum set of demands is indicative of the whole CP philosophy in relation to the Peace Movement (and to later 'single-issue' campaigns). The CP viewed CND very much as a specific single-issue campaign, both before and after the CP's 'change of heart' on unilateralism. In this the Party agreed far more with Canon Collins and the leadership than it did with other more radical disarmament movement political activists, who saw the campaign, in one sense or another, as part of a wider social and political struggle. The CP was willing, indeed eager, to depoliticise the Peace Movement in the sense of presenting a set of specific policy objectives which could be agreed to by as wide a range as possible of the general public. 'We've always . . . been prepared to cooperate, on the question of peace, with *anybody,* including Tories – who want peace. Whereas that is regarded as "betraying the revolution" and so on by some of these ultra-Left sects.'[6]

A further and even more fundamental cause of tension between the CP and the disarmament movement was inherent in this same question of 'unity'. Basic to the whole approach of the 'British Road to Socialism' – in all its many revised versions since its first appearance as the CP's official programme in 1951 – has been the idea of building a socialist unity between the Left of the Labour Party and industrial movement, and the CP – in both industrial and political terms. The whole strategy, including the much debated 'Parliamentary Road', has hinged on the CP's ability to forge this alliance and to make itself appear both acceptable and viable to Labour.

CND, in 1958, showed little sign of attracting majority Labour Movement and trade union support. It was quite clearly a middle-class radical movement, and its support lacked any significant working-class or Labour Movement component. For the CP, therefore, to divert campaigning for peace into support for CND, in terms both of policy and organisation, would have been tactically incorrect. 'In the last resort it is the relation of class forces which will decide whether there is peace or war. The degree to which the working class and its allies are active in the fight for peace is the crucial question.'[7] This was at the heart of the CP's belief. If CND did not accept the rudiments of class analysis it is not surprising that the CP, in CND's early years, regarded the campaign with some suspicion.

The CP, however, has good grounds for maintaining that it never *opposed* CND – indeed both the *Daily Worker* and the various Executive statements from 1958 testify to the publicity and qualified support given by the CP to CND activities. The publicity given to the 1958 Aldermaston March by the *Daily Worker* was, for example, fuller and more enthusiastic than the coverage of any other national newspaper.

This general relationship – supportive but somewhat critical and distanced – continued through 1958 and early 1959. CP policy began to change in the early summer of 1959. At the BPC's 'March for Life' rally in Trafalgar Square on 28 May 1959, whilst the text of the resolution still emphasised the cessation of nuclear testing and the need for a Summit meeting, there was also a commitment to asking Britain *to take the initiative for agreement to end the manufacture of nuclear weapons,* to destroy stocks, and to renounce their use, *being prepared if necessary*

itself to set the example' (my emphasis).[8] The CP's change of policy
evolved over the summer and was spelled out in fuller form in a BPC
policy statement reported in the *Daily Worker* of 7 July 1959. This
statement reaffirmed the BPC's 'resolute opposition to the declared
policy of the British government to use nuclear weapons as the basis of
British defence'. It welcomed the demand for an end to the manufacture
of the Bomb in Britain, but pointed out that, for this to be effective, it
must be coupled with the withdrawal of US rockets and H-Bomb bases
from Britain. The BPC thus condemned the Labour leadership's
proposals for a non-nuclear club, and called for opposition to
continued British membership of NATO. Thus, whilst the *emphasis* of
CP policy remained as before, the CP (via the BPC) was beginning to
move further towards a unilateralist position by early July 1959.

Immediately following this statement, the Transport and General
Workers' Union carried a resolution at its conference which, although
somewhat complicated in its expression and implications, was beyond
doubt unilateralist and clearly opposed to the Labour Party leadership's proposals.

The CP reacted swiftly to this and, in a special report on 12 July
1959, the Party came out firmly in favour of backing the TGWU line. In
an article in the *Daily Worker,* John Gollan put the issue starkly: '. . .
the Movement is confronted with two sharply conflicting policies. To
vote for the TGWU resolution is to vote against the Bomb and the Cold
War. To vote for the TUC/Labour Party Executive statement is to vote
for the Bomb and the Cold War.'[9]

This change on the part of the CP was quite consistent with the
overall strategy. As George Matthews has put it: 'around the middle of
1959 we came to the conclusion that whether or not we had been right
earlier on about the issue of unilateralism . . . the situation had
developed as far as public opinion, and opinion in the Labour
Movement, was concerned where the issue was combining the two:
that is, calling for Britain to renounce the Bomb as a step to
international agreement. We saw that as the big issue for the
Conferences of the Labour Movement in 1959 and 1960. . . .'[10]

The CP's two most basic objections to full support for CND had thus
been neutralised by events. With the TGWU (and other trade unions
during 1959) moving towards a unilateralist stance, there could no
longer be any doubt about the increasing involvement of the organised
working class in the general unilateralist movement. Even more

important was the related point of 'unity': far from the TGWU package resolution being regarded as 'maximalist', the CP, rightly, took it as a unifying call around which, during 1959 and 1960, all the forces within the Labour Movement opposed to the Bomb could be gathered. Thus, from a position in 1958 where the CP could argue that CND was unrepresentative of the working class and potentially divisive, things had sufficiently changed by late 1959 for the CP to see a potential unifying theme in the combining of their own consistently held demand for summit talks leading to international agreement, with CND's unilateralism.

In the aftermath of Labour's defeat in the 1959 election, the heightening of tension between Left and Right in the Party, and the increasing focus on the issue of nuclear disarmament, the CP came out four-square behind CND in May 1960, encouraging its members to participate fully and actively in the campaign.

Secretary Gollan's statement to the Executive Committee of the CP (reported in the *Daily Worker* on 16 May 1960) outlined in some detail both the contents of the 'new policy' and the reasons for its adoption.

> Britain's national security and national independence alike demand a new independent British peace policy, a policy which renounces nuclear weapons and nuclear strategy, a policy based on peaceful coexistence . . . we want Britain to take its own independent action on nuclear weapons now and at the same time to ally itself with the Soviet Union in the international negotiations for agreement to end all tests, outlaw all nuclear weapons with international inspection and control and for agreement on comprehensive disarmament including so-called conventional weapons. Both steps are needed . . . our Party, which has consistently campaigned against the manufacture of the H-Bomb and the whole nuclear strategy and for real summit negotiations, now calls for a supreme effort to win the whole Labour Movement for the new policy. This is the key to victory.

Whilst it is true that the CP moved, in this declaration of policy, towards CND's unilateralist line, it is equally true that CND policy had itself changed during 1960 and come much closer to that of the CP on some issues (*vide* CND's adoption of withdrawal from NATO in its policy aims at its 1960 Conference).

The two organisations had thus moved somewhat closer together by 1960, although of course this was also the period of developing Direct Action politics in the Committee of 100 – an ideology and a political

practice with which the CP had little sympathy.[11] The primary motivation for the change of CP policy, though, lay in the shift of opinion
within the organised Labour Movement: just as the TGWU decision in
1959 to back a unilateralist policy had been the decisive factor in the
CP's more favourable attitude to CND policy, so the decisive factor in
1960 was the rapidly snowballing campaign for this policy in the wider
trade union movement. Moreover, the huge success of the 1960 Aldermaston March probably provided the final proof to the CP leadership
that the CP could no longer afford to remain 'distanced' in any way
from such a rapidly growing movement.

The CP thus achieved its initial political objective in 1960 when a
united Left faced the right-wing leadership at the Labour Conference –
and won the day. The CP of course had to acknowledge that, in the
event, the Left was not strong enough to maintain the 1960 victory.
This was a political tragedy for the CP as for the Labour Left generally.
In this context, however, the salient point is that the CP's strategy was
neither confirmed nor denied by events in the Labour Party post-Scar-
borough.

From this time onwards the CP has been consistently involved with
CND and its campaigning. With the decline of CND as a mass
movement in the mid-1960s, the CP's relationship with the Peace
Movement became considerably closer. In part, this was due to the
dominance of the Vietnam War issue. Through the late 1960s the
international movement of protest against American involvement in
Vietnam gathered momentum, and demonstrations in Britain, as elsewhere, had an explicitly socialist dimension. CND became merely one
of a plethora of supporting organisations within the mass movement of
opposition to American policy, which was dominated by two organisations – the British Campaign for Peace in Vietnam (in which the CP
was well-represented) and the Vietnam Solidarity Campaign (ultimately the larger and the more influential of the two, and the breeding
ground for the 'Second New Left' of student radical neo-Marxism and
the ultra-Left Trotskyist groupings – in particular the International
Socialists, later to become the Socialist Workers' Party). Apart from
their disparate political bases of support, the two organisations differed
in their orientations and aims, with the BCPV oriented towards
attaining a negotiated solution, and the VSC taking a militant pro-
National Liberation Front (NLF) line.

The Peace Movement *per se* was dramatically reduced in strength:

nuclear weapons seemed, to most people on the Left, of less immediate importance than the horrific confrontation between the forces of American imperialism, as it was seen, and the apparently indigenous movement of popular opposition, the National Liberation Front (NLF), backed by Communist North Vietnam and its allies.

In these circumstances it is not surprising that the CP assumed a greater dominance within the Peace Movement (though it is important to note, too, that they did *not* so dominate the anti-Vietnam War movement: after 1967 the initiative here lay increasingly with the VSC). As CND declined, and became by the 1970s a small and specialist pressure group, so the CP influence increased. Nigel Young has noted how, from the mid-1960s, the CP came to exercise 'virtual control over the CND national office, its newspaper and its major committees. . . . Dedicated, manoeuvring and repetitious, the Party "bored from within" in every sense . . .'.[12]

Whatever the justification for such critical analyses of the CP's role in CND, there is no doubt that, from the later 1960s onwards, CND, whilst maintaining its central commitment to British unilateral nuclear disarmament, gave more emphasis than previously to withdrawal from NATO, the dismantling of US bases and the economic problems of transition to a peace-oriented economy. Moreover, all this has been couched within the context of a programme for world-wide nuclear disarmament, with British unilateralism being seen as the first stage in this process. Whilst this was always the CND policy, it has been given far more emphasis since the 1970s (not least, of course, because of the decline in importance of Britain as a world power, and hence the decreasing significance of any British unilateral act *per se*). In part cause and in part effect has been the return to a more *generalised* Peace Movement campaign since the 1970s, with strong similarities to the pre-CND Movement in terms of general orientations. Moreover, with the rebirth since 1979 of the mass Peace Movement and the strong focus of protest on the Cruise and Trident issues, considerable prominence has been given to opposition to the domination of the USA and the NATO alliance.

For various reasons, therefore, the Peace Movement and the CP have moved closer together in the period since the later 1960s. The CP has been fully supportive of CND policies. A statement of the Executive Committee of the CP in 1976, for example, declared that the CP 'would draw special attention to the need to end the arms race, take serious measures towards complete disarmament, work for the dismantling of all foreign military bases, end the production of nuclear weapons, destroy existing stocks and call on the British government to withdraw from NATO and work for the dissolution of NATO and the Warsaw treaty organization'.[13]

The 'British Road to Socialism' makes the policy arguments for a unilateral nuclear initiative in terms very similar to those of CND itself. Of more significance than these policy considerations, however, has been the CP strategy of the 'broad alliance', arguing that the transition to socialism in Britain will be accomplished, not by exclusive reliance upon the traditional male, manual working class and its trade union movement, but by a variegated collaborative movement encompassing the broad range of progressive political forces. 'The basic force for change in our society is the class struggle between workers and capitalists. However, capitalism not only exploits people at work, it impinges on every aspect of their lives. . . . Hence the broad democratic alliance needs to be not only an expression of class forces, but of other important forces in society which emerge out of areas of oppression not always directly connected with the relations of production.'[14] Within this amalgam the Peace Movement has a major role to play. A prominent CND activist (Chairman of CND from 1971–7) and long-standing member of the CP, John Cox, has argued that the Peace Movement must remain broadly based, and not become identified with any particular political stance. Moreover, the Movement should concentrate upon immediate, urgent, and popular issues – in particular, in the mid-1980s, Cruise and Trident. This provides the basis for a genuinely *popular* movement. Thus, perhaps surprisingly for the CP, Cox argues that 'we do not advocate that opposition to NATO should be a major campaigning priority at the moment, or that CND should challenge NATO as an imperialist alliance . . . the nature of NATO and what it represents is a *conclusion* to be drawn from campaigning around nuclear weapons – not a starting point'.[15]

The CP in the 1980s is also very eclectic and tolerant about methods of protest. In Cox's view all the major methods of protest have a legitimate role to play. The orthodox political movement, the more anarchic politics of the Greens and the Women's Movement, industrial action, and non-violent direct action, whilst none is 'a panacea for success . . . all have proven value and should be encouraged'.[16] (This is in contrast to CP attitudes to the Committee of 100 in the earlier period.)

Through the 1970s, therefore, the CP not only became increasingly influential in CND, but there was also a coming together over policy and general political alignments. In the 1970s CND was a small, pressure group organisation with a national membership of between 2,000 and 2,600 up to 1977. (This rose to 4,287 in 1979, and subsequently of course has grown dramatically, reaching 110,000 in 1985.) In this lean period of the 1970s CND was dominated by a mixture of 'veteran' CND campaigners, CP members and supporters, and Christian activists (mainly Quakers). Whilst there was some overlap between these groupings, there were clear and obvious philosophical and ideological differences. Nevertheless, the campaign operated in relative harmony, symbolised perhaps by the effective working relationship of Bruce Kent, a Roman Catholic priest, and Duncan Rees, a CP member, who together led CND in the late 1970s.

There were, however, major underlying tensions between CP and CND perspectives, even though they remained largely latent in the 1970s. Essentially, these resided in two interrelated areas: the CP's attitude to the USSR, and the cultural dissonance between the CP and the Peace Movement. Whilst it is true that the CP in the 1970s and 1980s has been markedly less 'pro-Soviet' than had been the case previously (hence, in part, the bitter divisions in the Party throughout both the 1970s and the 1980s), it remains the case that, for the bulk of the CP, it is quite erroneous to apportion equal blame for the arms race and the Cold War on the two superpowers. 'It is . . . quite wrong to pose the situation in the world as between two super powers, the USA and the USSR, both being regarded as acting on the same level. This totally ignores the fact that the USA is an imperialist power, and the USSR a socialist country.'[17] This is in striking contrast to the prevailing policies and mood of the Peace Movement as a whole. Whilst there is in the Peace Movement of the 1980s a general acknowledgement that the USA with its military might and generally hawkish policies has been the pace-setter in the arms race, there is an explicit condemnation of *all* nuclear weapons and *all* nuclear bases. There is the further realisation, in the 1980s, that the drastic reduction of the Super Powers' involvement in other areas of the world is an essential corollary of nuclear disarmament. In this context, the politics of 'positive neutralism' have assumed a far greater dominance in the 1980s Peace Movement than was the case in the 1950s and 1960s. Partly for this reason, therefore, the CP has found itself somewhat at odds with the prevailing priorities and perspectives within the Peace Movement of the 1980s.

This directly political tension is only a part of the explanation, however. Equally important have been the broader cultural and ideological influences within the Peace Movement since its second mass movement phase. In this context the influence of the Women's Movement and the Greens have been especially important. And a further crucial dimension in the 1980s has been the presence and influence of a number of Socialists whose formative political years were spent in either the 'first New Left' of the 1958–63 period or in the 'second New Left' of the post-1967/8 years. This is not the place to enter into the political analysis of these and other perspectives. But the nature of this combination, its deep-rooted antipathy, for a variety of reasons, to the CP, and its importance in determining a new political style and profile for the Peace Movement in the 1980s, should not be underestimated. The result has been that, in the 1980s, the CP has worked relatively harmoniously within the Peace Movement, in the broad coalition of perspectives which has been led so skilfully and sensitively by both elected and paid officials (in particular, Bruce Kent and Joan Ruddock), but has no longer been dominant. CND has steered a resolutely independent line and, despite the attempts to persuade the public otherwise by the Government, has successfully repudiated any charge of being either pro-Soviet or crypto-Communist.

The CP's role in the Peace Movement of the post-1958 period has thus been one of consistent involvement, after an initial period of doubt in 1958/9. This initial reluctance was logical, given the CP's ideological assumptions; though whether these were or are *correct* assumptions is obviously a much larger question. With the decline of CND in the mid-sixties the CP, largely because of its diligence and the growing together of CND and CP policies, became more influential. With the resurgence of the mass movement, however, this influence has waned, despite a much more eclectic and tolerant attitude on the part of the CP leadership. This change in CP attitude is itself a part of the growth of the influence of the 'Eurocommunist' wing of the Party. The inability of the CP, even with this changed approach, to attain greater influence in the Peace Movement of the 1980s, testifies to its persistent failure in the wider context of British politics to widen its appeal and its cultural and political base. In the public mind it remains associated with the authoritarian politics of the USSR and the undemocratic structures and practices of Communist regimes throughout the world. On the Left, such views are not held in quite such crude forms. But there is a residual belief that the CP in general is pro-Soviet and anti-American, rather than fully supportive of peace politics. Added to this there is – again despite the evidence of Eurocommunist activities to the contrary – a persistent image of cultural conservatism, and a continuing reality of political failure, which renders the CP an unattractive political vehicle for most Peace Movement activists. Declining membership – in 1985 down to below 16,000 – and internal divisions have brought the CP close to disaster, at just the time when the Peace Movement has enjoyed its greatest levels of support and public attention. The CP, despite its most earnest endeavours, thus remains a relatively minor force within the Peace Movement and seems likely to decline in influence still further in future years.

The Trotskyists[18]

Trotskyism was a very minor force in British left-wing politics until the later 1950s. And even then, following the shattering of the international Communist monolith in the wake of Stalin's death, Khrushchev's 1956 'revelations', and the Soviet suppression of the Hungarian 1956 uprising, Trotskyism in all its varieties had only a relative handful of adherents. It was not until the post-1968 explosion of radical protest that, in Britain as elsewhere, Trotskyism became a relatively significant political force.

Nevertheless, despite their minuscule size, the Trotskyist groupings were of some significance in the Peace Movement of the late 1950s and early 1960s. The Socialist Labour League (SLL), subsequently to become the Workers' Revolutionary Party (WRP) in 1973, grew out of the *Newsletter* group, formed after the exodus from the CP following the Hungarian uprising in 1956. It was composed partly of long-standing Trotskyists from the 1940s and 1950s, and partly of ex-CP members – notably Peter Fryer of the *Daily Worker* – disillusioned with the CP. Throughout 1957 the *Newsletter* focused its campaign against the Labour Party leadership on the nuclear issue; and it was Vivienne Mendelson, a Trotskyist CLP delegate, who moved the unilateral nuclear disarmament motion at the 1957 Labour Party Conference.[19]

In 1959 the SLL came formally into existence. Its views on the nuclear issue were clear. There was support for unilateral nuclear disarmament and all that went with it, but an insistence on working-class action to achieve this, and an equally vigorous rejection of both non-political and CP orientations.[20] The SLL believed that the USSR, despite its 'degeneration', had to be defended from the imperialist powers.

The SLL thus defended the Soviet Union's right to maintain nuclear weapons and its possession of the 'workers' Bomb'. In common with all Trotskyists, the SLL believed that, if socialism were to be attained in Western industrialised societies, revolutionary movements of the working class must be built, led by the Leninist/Trotskyist vanguard party. Trotskyists had no faith whatever in the potential for reformist change, and they opposed the CP both for its reformism and for its adherence to the USSR. All efforts had therefore to be directed to building the alternative, revolutionary Socialist, political party, concentrating upon rank and file, trade unionist, working-class activists, rather than the Trade Union bureaucracies and the elite groups which, the Trotskyists maintained, were the CP's 'bureaucratised' points of contact with the working class. Trotskyists were divided, then as in later years, over whether to adopt 'entryism' (i.e. working as Trotskyists within the Labour Party to achieve either a split in the Party or, less likely, a Trotskyist takeover), or to work for the creation of a separate and autonomous working-class revolutionary party. But in both cases Trotskyists believed that only through class struggle, political education, and thus heightened working-class political consciousness, could the necessary revolutionary cadres be created. One key context in which such political experience could be gained was that of extra-parliamentary, mass movement action. From such initial political contact, it was hoped, working-class and other militants could be drawn into the ultimately more crucial arena of revolutionary socialist politics within the Trotskyist revolutionary party.

Within this context the *Newsletter*/SLL group saw the unilateralist campaign of CND as a major opportunity for mobilising political forces *outside* the conventional political arena on an issue which could command substantial support. From the outset the SLL emphasised that only the organised working-class movement, engaging in Direct Action industrially and politically, could bring success to CND's campaign. Thus, whilst supportive of CND's initiative, the *Newsletter* pointed out that 'one element is missing from the "moral lead" of the CND. That element is working-class internationalism . . . we are confident that once the example has been set the gravity of the H-Bomb menace and the power of the workers' solidarity will ensure that it is followed.'[21]

The SLL conducted a consistent campaign around the slogan 'Black the H-Bomb! Black the Bases!' Only through industrial action could the movement against the Bomb really begin to bite. The SLL grew steadily more critical of the CND leadership and its refusal to link the CND issue with a wider militant strategy centring on the working class and socialism.[22] Unofficial strikes at the point of production supported by socialist militants were viewed as the primary focus of activity for opposition to the Bomb.

In the early days the *Newsletter* group had favoured the direct industrial action strategy for two reasons: tactically, the movement against the Bomb had been seen as a potential catalyst for the creation of a revolutionary socialist movement; but there was also a strong *ideological* conviction that the Bomb was 'the ultimate custodian of the capitalists' political and economic power'.[23] The Bomb was seen as the final, obscene product of a fundamentally irrational and immoral social system. As with the CP, it is too simplistic to view the Marxist activists of the *Newsletter*/SLL as being interested in CND and the issue of nuclear weapons *solely* as a means of recruiting new members. There was, at least in the early days, a genuine concern with the issue, coupled with a strongly felt and strongly expressed conviction that only through the adoption of a socialist/Trotskyist perspective and strategy could the objectives of the Movement be attained.[24]

From early 1959 the SLL in fact began to move away from close involvement in the disarmament movement, for political reasons related not to the Peace Movement but rather to internal Trotskyist ideology and strategy.[25] Under Gerry Healy's control, the SLL rapidly assumed a rigid, vanguardist structure and sectarian ideology. A part of the process of turning the SLL into a more disciplined and 'hard-line' political force was the toughening up of the attitude to the Peace Movement. Thus, for example, on the occasion of the Soviet resumption of nuclear tests in 1961 when the Committee of 100 held a demonstration outside the Soviet Embassy, the SLL took a very critical line. By 1963 this had 'hardened' still further and Jack Gale could write: 'to call today for the "utmost unity" in the Peace Movement, as the "Daily Worker" does, is totally wrong. Without a decisive break with all forms of pacifism, the movement against nuclear weapons will fizzle out.'[26]

From this time onwards the SLL, and later the WRP, became increasingly rigid and sectarian, distancing itself from *all* other Marxist parties, and devoting much of its energies to polemics against other groupings. In common with its attitude to other issue movements, the WRP has shown no support for the Peace Movement in the 1970s and 1980s.

The SLL/WRP has thus been an isolated force and, since 1963, has taken no active role in the Peace Movement.

How important was the SLL to the Movement? One of its main areas of significance lay, as Parkin has noted,[27] in its involvement in the Young Socialist Movement. Over and above this, there are perhaps four reasons for regarding the SLL 'line' in the disarmament Movement as worthy of analysis. The first is that, despite all its manifest shortcomings, the early SLL did represent one of the first attempts, albeit limited, to break with the prevailing Cold War orthodoxies of the post-war period. The second is that the Peace Movement provided the major focus of attention for the *Newsletter* group in its early days: it was around the specific issue of nuclear weapons policy and the relationship of the Trotskyist movement to the Peace Movement that the general ideological framework of the SLL began to crystallise. For an understanding of the evolution of the SLL/WRP, then, an understanding of the SLL/WRP/Peace Movement relationship is essential. As far as impact on the disarmament Movement itself was concerned there were two further important areas: the SLL made a serious attempt in the early days to link Marxism with the Direct Action militancy of the campaign's radical wing. With hindsight the attempt can perhaps be seen as doomed to failure from the outset: the ideological gulf was too wide. But the clarification of perspectives that resulted from the interchange of polemics was important both for an understanding of the Movement at the time, and for the attempt at subsequent analysis. Finally, the concerted attempts by the SLL (and the DAC) to stimulate *working-class* Direct Action provided a unique dimension to the campaign. In the virtual absence of CP advocacy of working-class industrial action, it was the SLL activists who took the lead in trying to instil nuclear campaign militancy amongst the rank and file workers. Their almost total failure in this aim did not render the attempt unimportant, but, rather, underlined the wider problems inherent in involving the working class in the Peace Movement.

In many ways there were similarities between the SLL and IS in their attitude to the disarmament movement. Both organisations based their unilateralist campaigns on attracting the working class; both were highly critical of the CND leadership for its non-political stance; and both were deeply hostile to the CP.[28]

IS thus paralleled the SLL's critical attitude to the Labour Party, but IS, in relation to CND, always placed emphasis on developing a *political* movement against the Bomb, whilst the SLL, as has been argued, concentrated upon the *industrial* struggle and the central role of the industrial working class.[29]

IS's contribution to the analytical aspects of the Peace Movement, in its early years, lay in the formulation of the 'Permanent Arms Economy' theory, which claimed to provide a *structural,* economic, and Marxist explanation for the arms race and the Cold War. It posited a *necessary,* rather than a purely politically contingent, link between the struggle for socialist restructuring and the Movement to abolish nuclear weapons.[30] Moreover, this integrated, dual Movement was essential in the Communist East as well as the capitalist West. The theory thus complemented and added further weight to the fundamental IS ideological contention concerning the 'state capitalist' nature of the USSR,[31] and the need for Socialists to divorce themselves entirely from identification with the USSR's position in the Cold War struggle.

Subsequent analysis, and indeed political events and processes, have resulted in a considerable modification to the theory in its pure form; most Marxists would perhaps agree with Stuart Hall's judgement that, although subsequently shown to be fundamentally incorrect, the theory may well have 'played a pivotal part in thinking about those essentially *war*-oriented economies becoming essentially *peace*-oriented ones . . . it's not that it's not important, but [it was] made the single, central explicator for everything, which I think was not true'.[32]

Although IS had little power or influence within the practical politics of the Peace Movement, it did have some marginal involvement with the Committee of 100.[33] And its advocacy of a socialist version of 'positive neutralism', linking together its total rejection of the USSR with its advocacy of a new and more militant form of worker-controlled socialism, had affinities with the 'plague on both your houses' orientation which was an important element in the mainstream Movement.

Overall, though, its influence in the years of the Movement's prominence in the late 1950s and early 1960s was minimal. As IS began, slowly, to grow in the later 1960s, and as CND declined and other issues (especially Vietnam) grew into prominence for Marxists, so the connections between the organisations, and IS's concern to influence CND policy, declined. IS shared the disillusionment of most of the Marxist groups (except the CP) as CND refused to opt for a class-oriented line through 1962 and 1963. Thus, as IS gradually formulated itself into a somewhat more orthodox Far Left, quasi-Leninist group, concentrating on questions of traditionally central concern to Marxist activists, so the radical wing of the disarmament Movement moved over towards a more explicitly anarchist/syndicalist conception of action. By 1964 CND and IS had gone their separate ways – CND down a slow divisive path towards fragmentation and decline (though never extinction), and IS beginning its fairly dramatic growth to become the most significant of the Far Left groupings by the 1970s.

Not until the revival of the Peace Movement in the late 1970s did the SWP show any renewed concern with the nuclear issue (though it had been prominent in the anti-nuclear *power* movement in the mid-1970s). In its initial phase of growth, IS had been an informal propaganda group, placing 'a good deal of emphasis on political ideas and discussion'.[34] But with its rapid growth, and with a leadership committed firmly to the orthodox Marxist–Leninist view of the centrality of the working class, attention was turned away from both ideological and foreign policy issues, and directed towards building strength and credibility in the working class ('the turn to the class'). Thus, throughout its period of growth and consolidation, IS/SWP had little or no contact with the Peace Movement.

Since the resurgence of the Peace Movement in 1979 the SWP, somewhat weaker than in the earlier 1970s, has been vociferous in its involvement. Although still a relatively small organisation, its membership has remained highly activist and large enough to exert some influence within the Movement at all levels. In keeping with the SWP's overall orientation, the emphasis has been heavily upon the practical links between the economic effects of capitalism upon the working class, and the gross waste of military expenditure: hence the SWP slogan, 'Jobs not Bombs'.

The SWP, unlike some other Trotskyist groups (principally 'Militant'), has maintained its strong criticism of the Labour Party on the nuclear issue as on general ideological and political perspectives. Drawing attention to Labour's record of continuous involvement in nuclear weapons development when in government, the SWP rejects the claim made by many that Labour is, in the 1980s, fully committed to Peace Movement policies. The Labour Party is still fully committed to the NATO alliance; it backed the Falklands escapade; and it argues for greater expenditure on conventional defence. Above all, the SWP has argued, the Labour Party leadership still contains powerful figures who are wholly opposed to the policies of the Peace Movement. 'Healey, Hattersley and the rest of them clearly do not take Labour's commitment to unilateral nuclear disarmament seriously. Why should anyone else?'[36] For the SWP the root causes of the Peace Movement's failure in the 1960s were twofold: the failure to involve 'millions of ordinary working people in the campaign',[37] and the Movement's reliance on the Labour Party.

And, for the SWP, a similar fate awaits the Movement of the 1980s unless these same dangers are avoided. 'Unless within that Campaign there is a growing nucleus of people who understand the need to make the connections with the other issues, who see nuclear weapons as a *class* issue, then at the end of the day the Movement will tragically fail as much this time as it did last. . . . The alternatives are Socialism or nuclear annihilation. . . .'[38]

And yet the very insistence of the SWP on an orthodox Marxist approach has debarred the Party from any decisive influence within the Peace Movement. The level of popular support for Marxist politics remains infinitesimal in Britain: whilst the support for the Peace Movement is very substantial indeed. The reluctance of the SWP to acknowledge the viability of *other* ideological approaches, and its central commitment to building its own strength (often seen as cynically opportunist by others), have ensured that its influence within the Peace Movement has remained marginal in the 1980s.

The New Left

In reality, the Peace Movement of the 1980s has a number of new and important influences when compared with the Movement of the late 1950s and early 1960s. In addition to the strong pacifist presence, and the markedly changed Labour Party influence discussed in Chapter 6, three perspectives stand out as of particular importance, though they shade into one another at various levels: the Greens, the Women's Movement, and the independent Marxist Left. The first and second of these lie outside the scope of this chapter.[39] The third category, which includes some of the most notable figures in the 1980s Peace Movement, stems from a mix of the 'first and second New Lefts': that is, those around the New Left movement of the 1957 to 1962 period; and those who were politically active in the late 1960s and early 1970s, usually in one of the Trotskyist groups (IS, IMG, *et al.*), but who have resigned since such groups became increasingly rigid and 'orthodox' within the Marxist context.

The New Left which emerged in 1957 was grouped initially around two journals: the *New Reasoner,* and the *Universities and Left Review.* The former of these, which began life as *The Reasoner,* an internal CP 'dissident' journal edited by Edward Thompson and John Saville, was the focus for a group of CP members who left the Party after 1956 partly because of frustration with the CP's undemocratic and hierarchical structure, but mainly because of the failure of the Party to condemn the suppression by the USSR of the Hungarian uprising in 1956.

The CP legacy was centrally important in the evolution of the *New Reasoner.* Up until its merger with the *Universities and Left Review,* to form *New Left Review* in 1960, the *New Reasoner* 'maintained a dissident Communist identity of sorts . . . with the merger the *New Reasoner* gave up certain formal attributes of ex-Communism'. This Communist tradition 'brought into the fusion far more than it shed: an explicit commitment to class-struggle, an iteration of the role of human agency as against impersonal historic process . . .'.[40]

A crucial aspect of this CP legacy was the adherence of the *New Reasoner* group to a Labourist strategy. The strategy of the CP, so reviled by other sections of the Marxist Left, was implicitly accepted by the *New Reasoner* and every effort was made to forge a link with the theoretically inclined sector of the Labour Left.

From the beginning the *New Reasoner* was in favour of British withdrawal from NATO, unilateral nuclear disarmament, and the adoption of a neutralist foreign policy. The theme of international agreement to break the deadlock of the Cold War was seen as absolutely central. The *New Reasoner* linked up the international theme – the need to end the Cold War and develop a neutralist bloc – with the international role of British Labour – the opportunity for Britain to take the lead through unilateral nuclear disarmament, a withdrawal from NATO, and the espousal of a neutralist foreign policy.

One of the major contributions of the NL to the Peace Movement was to bring home the connection between unilateralism and withdrawal from NATO. In 1960 CND officially adopted the withdrawal from NATO into its statement of aims and the influence of the NL in this process of persuasion was central. (However, most Peace Movement supporters were motivated to give support to such a policy after 1960 because of the perceived illogicality of a unilaterally disarmed Britain remaining within a nuclear alliance, NATO, rather than because of ideological commitment to positive neutralism.)

A further dimension of the *New Reasoner*'s advocacy of neutralism was its conviction that through a unilateralist initiative 'Britain could again lead the world'. This was different in spirit from the populist moralism of J. B. Priestley and much of the CND leadership. E. P. Thompson in particular was a passionate advocate of the radical working-class tradition which, he argued, had done so much to define and to put into practice a genuinely democratic socialism.

It was the guiding principle of moral revolt, in which the struggle for democratic and social rights has always been intertwined, that brought together Thompson's and the *New Reasoner*'s, belief that the essentially *moral* campaign of the disarmament movement could be fused with the radical tradition of the British Labour Movement, to produce a major innovative force on the radical Left. And this led logically to the demand for a policy of positive neutralism. If unilateralism entailed withdrawal from NATO, and if the USSR and its alliances were rejected too, as they were by all except the CP and the SLL, then the logical next step was to define a role for a neutralist Britain. As Thompson outlined,[41] the implications of such a policy were not confined to major changes in international relations and foreign policy. It was quite possible too that, on a domino theory scenario, the adoption of a unilateralist/neutralist policy might lead to the socialist revolution.

The other part of the NL partnership offered somewhat different, though broadly complementary, ideological perspectives. The *Universities and Left Review* group was in many ways the natural nucleus for disaffected students and other young radicals, and its concentration was more upon cultural and literary processes, particularly as they affected social consciousness amongst the working class. If the *New Reasoner* provided the Labour Movement and Marxist experience, and, substantially, the bedrock of *political* theory for the NL, the *ULR* fulfilled the equally vital role of providing a bridgehead to non-Marxist, but Left-oriented, students and radicals, and to the rapidly growing radical pacifist movement. And it was from those within the ambit of this group, at the beginning of the NL movement in 1957/58, that there developed an involvement in community organisation and activity in Notting Hill and elsewhere.

The merger between the two groups, to form *New Left Review*, took place in late 1959, and, under the editorship of Stuart Hall, the first edition of *NLR* appeared in January 1960. In relation to the Peace Movement the *NLR* pursued its policy of positive neutralism with some enthusiasm. But there is no doubt that the concern with 'conventional' politics as exemplified by the *NLR*'s neutralist policy, contrasted with the *ULR*'s earlier and less structured approach. There was an even wider ideological gap, of course, between this approach and that of IS, and, far more importantly, the whole decentralised, quasi-anarchistic perspective of the Committee of 100. The *NLR* politics was not conventional in the sense of supporting conventional political policies and objectives (NATO and so on), but rather in the more fundamental sense of the conceptual framework of political thought within which policies were formulated: in this context, thinking in nation state, diplomatic and international relations terms, and in the orthodox organisational forms of parliamentarism and party politics (and this was evidenced by the policy documents produced by the NLR in the early 1960s). The legacy of the CP perspective on foreign policy, and politics generally, was writ large in the NL: again, the political arguments, whilst not acceptable to all on the Labour Left, were couched in the same political context. For very different reasons, both the Far Left and the Committee of 100 rejected the suppositions of the arguments, as well as the specific policies themselves.

Was there any alternative strategy that the NL could have adopted which would have brought it success in terms of creating a wider socialist, extra-parliamentary political formation, based upon the nuclear disarmament movement? When asked why the NL activists had failed to convince the disarmament movement of the need for the wider socialist struggle along the lines it advocated, Peggy Duff replied: 'they did *try* you know – they did try'.[42] They were not, however, able to unite around a particular strategy for action and work for it. There was a striking gap between the coherence, originality and appeal of their ideological perspective, and the ambivalence, confusion, lack of clarity, and genuine differences, over their political strategy. The crucial link between these two facets of the NL was, of course, its inability to reach any clear decision about its attitude, at a number of levels, to Labourism. The NL acknowledged the centrality of the Labour Movement to CND's effectiveness – and it was aware of the need to build inside as well as outside that Movement – but it had no detailed plans for achieving such links, and showed no serious, practical intention of working to convert the industrial and political sections. There were of course enormous political and cultural barriers to building such links; and in purely organisational and numerical terms the NL was never a major force *vis-à-vis* the Labour Movement. Nevertheless the almost total lack of a serious *attempt* to realise what was, after all, the cornerstone of the framework and hence of the strategy, would seem to testify to the view that NL activists saw themselves as in some ways above the rough and tumble of political in-fighting. Psychologically they thought of themselves as something of an elite – not altogether unlike the Fabians' self-perception *vis-à-vis* the Trade Union Right of the Labour Movement. In terms of CND, too, there was a failure to come to grips with the perspectives of the 'ordinary supporters' – a failure to take seriously the task of converting to a socialist perspective a mass organisation based on a moral, single issue motivation.

Yet the NL perspectives had a number of distinct advantages over other socialist positions within the Peace Movement.[43] It gave to the cause of the Peace Movement a genuine centrality which was lacking in the approach of both the Labour Party and the Marxist groupings. The NL's humanistic socialism found its central focus and ideological articulation in the cause of nuclear disarmament. There was, too, a commitment to *extra-parliamentary* politics within the NL, not in the sense of Trotskyist vanguardism, but rather linking in to the radical traditions of the British Labour Movement. Because of these, and other related political attributes, the NL was, potentially, in a unique position to act as the bridgehead and the catalyst within the Peace Movement. But, of course, it failed because of its own internal weaknesses, *and* because of the unpropitious political environment of the times.

Since the early 1970s, however, circumstances have changed considerably, and the politics espoused by the NL and its successors have developed within a far more receptive climate. No longer is the governing class so confident in its assertion of the need for a British independent nuclear deterrent, given Britain's declining status as a world power, and given the huge and escalating costs of nuclear development. Indeed, many prominent military figures – Lord Mountbatten and Lord Carver amongst them – have questioned seriously the wisdom of the nuclear deterrence theory itself. Potentially more significant, however, is the effect of the economic crisis on the stability of the socio-economic basis of British society. The material base of the 1950s and 1960s has been severely eroded. If this process continues and deepens, continued political stability is by no means certain. What forms political polarisation may take is an open question: but the previous consensus is unlikely to remain viable.

A second major development which bears upon the argument has been the rapid growth of the 'middle class' within British society in the period since the 1950s. Whilst major sectors of the class are of course opposed to radical political ideas and remain quite separate from the Labour Movement, it is also true that there has been a considerable expansion in the number of radical, tertiary educated, professional and intellectual employees, whose public sector occupations and general background of 'critical thinking' have resulted in an ideological stance opposed to the market individualism of competitive capitalism.[44]

There have been three major groupings involved in this radical middle-class growth: trade union activists in the white-collar unions (white-collar membership has grown from 1·9m in 1948, to 2·68m in 1964, and 4·26m in 1974); new artisans (the 'alternative society' radicals); and welfare bureaucrats (those working in schools, hospitals, welfare agencies, etc).

What was once a 'marginal constituency' for the Left has thus become a major sub-section of the class structure of contemporary Britain. In this sense, too, therefore, the context for a New Left politics is considerably more favourable in the 1970s and 1980s than was the case in the 1958 to 1965 period. The strength of this radical middle-class Left has manifested itself in numerous ways: most notably through the growth of ecological/environmentalist politics, the Women's Movement, and the Peace Movement itself.

Finally, as was discussed in Chapter 6, the Labour Left has itself undergone profound change since the 1960s – in part cause and in part effect of the developments already discussed. The change represents a qualitative move away from the exclusively parliamentarist preoccupations of orthodox Labourism and has emphasised far more the concept of the wider, partially extra-parliamentary, Labour

Movement, giving more centrality to issue-based campaigns and the need for a broad socialist alliance. All this has not signified, of course, the collapse of orthodox, parliamentarist Labourism. But it has meant a real advance within the Labour Left, for the politics espoused by the New Left and its successors.

There has thus been a resurgence of an extra-parliamentary, alternative Left culture in the 1970s and 1980s, which has been combined with a *structural* strengthening of the basis of the radical middle-class Left. Britain still has, of course, a profoundly conservative political culture, and a very securely based capitalist socio-economic system. Yet challenges to this structure and its ideology can be made. The original nuclear disarmament movement of 1958 to 1965 was a major attempt to challenge an important aspect of this structure. Subsequent developments have made far more favourable the prospects for a New Left politics, centred on 'Third Way' concepts of humanistic socialism.

Conclusion

Although numerically Marxists have been a relatively minor part of the Peace Movement 'coalition', they have played, in their highly disparate ways, a significant role in its political development and direction. Socialism of any description, let alone Marxism, remains a minor sub-culture within a predominantly Conservative and consensual society. The Peace Movement in the 1980s is a mass movement – hence its strength and importance – and the large majority of its supporters are *non*-Socialists, though most have a generally radical perspective.[45] Yet this societal political stability is increasingly under threat, and the Peace Movement is a more politicised and more sophisticated movement than was the case in the 1958–65 period. The impact and importance of humanistic socialist politics, and the emphases upon the need for 'Third Way' socialism, positive neutralism and the inter-connections between peace, justice and freedom, within an internationalist context, have been notable features of the revitalised Movement of the 1980s. And these developments have been the direct result of the ideological contributions to the Peace Movement – since the 1950s – of the socialist movements analysed in this chapter. If the socio-economic and political crisis of Western capitalism persists and deepens, the role of this 'socialist legacy' may assume a far greater dominance in both the Peace Movement and the wider political context.

References

1 George Matthews, formerly Assistant Secretary of the CP, and also former Editor of the *Daily Worker*, now the *Morning Star*, in conversation with Richard Taylor, January 1978.

2 *Ibid.*

3 George Matthews, 'Unilateralism and the fight for peace', *World News*, 14 March 1958.

4 *Ibid.*

5 Matthews, in conversation.

6 Matthews, in conversation.

7 Matthews, *World News*.

8 *Daily Worker*, 28 May 1959.

9 *Daily Worker*, 18 July 1959 (article by John Gollan).

10 Matthews, in conversation.

11 As George Matthews recalled, 'we were never terribly keen on the Committee of 100' (Matthews, in conversation).

12 Nigel Young, *An Infantile Disorder? The Crisis and Decline of the New Left*, Routledge and Kegan Paul, London, 1977, p. 155.

13 Statement of the Executive Committee, CP, August 1976.

14 See 'The British Road to Socialism' (the Communist Party's policy statement, first issued in 1951, and subsequently revised), March 1978, p. 29.

15 John Cox, *War and Peace: the Nuclear Edition*, CP publications, London, 1984, p. 11.

16 *Ibid.*, p. 12.

17 Tony Chater, 'The Case for Peace and Disarmament', CP pamphlet, 1980, pp. 27–8.

18 The term 'Trotskyist' is used here to refer to the whole range of far Left socialist groupings, excluding those of anarachistic or Maoist persuasion, which have at least a connection with Trotskyism *per se*. Thus, attention here is upon the International Socialists (Socialist Workers' Party) amongst others, even though this group has been, and remains, ideologically unorthodox in Trotskyist terms.

   For discussion of Trotskyism in Britain, see Peter Shipley, *Revolutionaries in Modern Britain*, Bodley Head, Oxford, 1977; and John Callaghan, *British Trotskyism: Theory and Practice*, Blackwell, Oxford, 1984.

19 For discussion of this, see Ch. 6.

20 The SLL believed that the USSR had become, since the coming to power of Stalin, a 'degenerated workers' state': the SLL believed, therefore, that the USSR was capable of reform, and was at least potentially a socialist state.

21 *Newsletter*, Vol. 2, No. 45, 22 March 1958.

22 See, for example, Peter Fryer's speech to Aldermaston marchers in 1959 where he exhorted the Campaign to adopt a more militant and class-conscious approach. *Newsletter*, 4 April 1959.

23 *Newsletter*, 28 March 1959.

24 Whilst there were superficial similarities between the SLL's demands for industrial action and the industrial campaign of the Direct Action Committee (see Ch. 7), there were fundamental divisions between the two perspectives. Most notably, the DAC rejected wholly the class analysis of the Trotskyists and their strategy of revolutionary violence. See, for example, the article by Pat Arrowsmith, *Newsletter*, 24 June 1961.

25 Principally, Healy's determination to create a new political force for Trotskyism in the SLL following the proscription by the Labour Party of both the *Newsletter* and the SLL in early 1959. For details of this development and its relationship to the wider splits in international Trotskyism and the Fourth International, see Shipley, *Revolutionaries in Modern Britain*.

26 *Newsletter*, 20 April 1963.

27 Frank Parkin, *Middle Class Radicalism: the social bases of the British Campaign for Nuclear Disarmament*, Manchester University Press, 1968.

28 For an account of the origins and development of the International Socialists, see Martin Shaw, 'The Making of a Party? The International Socialists 1965–1976', in Ralph Miliband and John Saville (eds.), *Socialist Register 1978*, Merlin Press, London, 1978.

29 For the political emphasis in IS, see Dave Peers, 'The impasse of CND', *IS Journal*, No. 12, 1963.

30 For a brief statement of the elements of the theory, see Michael Kidron, 'Capitalism, the latest stage', in Nigel Harris and John Palmer (eds.), *World Crisis*, Hutchinson, London, 1971. For the full explication of the theory, see Michael Kidron, *Western Capitalism since the war*, Pelican, London, 1970. (The original idea derived from the work of the American Trotskyist Movement.) For a critique of the theory, see David Yaffé, 'The Marxian theory of crisis, capital and the state', *Economy and Society*, 2, No. 2, May 1973.

  For a discussion of the whole debate, see Richard Taylor, 'The British Nuclear Disarmament Movement of 1958 to 1965 and its legacy to the Left', unpublished PhD thesis, University of Leeds, 1983, Appendix to Ch. V, pp. 448–53.

31 The categorisation of the USSR as 'state capitalist' – a more critical view than that of the more orthodox Trotskyist 'degenerated workers' state' concept of the SLL/WRP – had been the initial ideological focus for the formation of the Socialist Review Group, which became the IS in 1962.

32 Stuart Hall, in conversation with Richard Taylor, March 1978.

33 See Notes of the Quarter, *International Socialism*, No. 5, Summer 1961.

34 Shaw, 'The Making of a Party?', p. 121.

35 See, for example, the Conference resolutions at the 1984 Labour Party Conference, and the explicit commitment to NATO given by Denzil Davies, MP, Shadow Spokesman on Defence (interview with END Journal, reported in the *Guardian*, 21 June 1985).

36 Extract from 'Socialism and War', Socialist Worker 1985 Diary.

37 Peter Binns, 'Missile Madness', SWP pamphlet, 2nd edn, December 1981.

38 *Ibid.*, p. 36.

39 On the Women's Movement and the Peace Movement, see Ch. 10 of this book; on the Greens, see *Embrace the Earth: a Green View of CND*, CND Publications, 1983; Richard Taylor, 'Green Politics and the Peace Movement', in David Coates *et al.* (eds.), *A Socialist Anatomy of Britain*, Polity Press, Cambridge, 1985, pp. 160–70; and Ch. 12 of this book.

40 Peter Sedgwick 'The Two New Lefts', in David Widgery (ed.), *The Left in Britain 1956–1968*, Penguin, London, 1976, p. 135.

41 See E. P. Thompson, Revolution, in Thompson (ed.), *Out of Apathy*, Stevens and Sons, London, 1960.

42 Peggy Duff, in conversation with Richard Taylor, January 1978.
43 See Richard Taylor, 'The British Peace Movement and Socialist Change', in Ralph
   Miliband and John Saville (eds.), *Socialist Register 1983*, Merlin Press, London, 1985,
   for detailed explication of this argument.
44 See David Coates, *The Context of British Politics*, Hutchinson, London, 1984, for a
   discussion of this.
45 For the 1958–65 Movement, see Part II of Richard Taylor and Colin Pritchard, *The
   Protest Makers: the British Nuclear Disarmament Movement of 1958–1965, Twenty
   Years On*, Pergamon, Oxford, 1980; for the Movement of the 1980s, see John
   Mattausch, 'The Sociology of CND' (paper given at the 1985 British Sociological
   Association Conference, Hull, April 1985) to be published in Martin Shaw (ed.), *The
   Sociology of War and Peace*, Macmillan, 1987.

9

The churches and the
nuclear arms race, 1945–85

DAVID ORMROD

From the standpoint of the 1980s, the attitude of the churches in Britain towards the relentless build-up of nuclear arms appears to have been divided and marked by periods of strange indifference. In 1959, Karl Barth suggested that the most vital issue confronting Christianity was the inability of the church to take a definite stand against nuclear weapons. 'How', he asked, 'do you explain the fact that the large Christian bodies cannot pronounce a definite yes or no on the matter of atomic war?'[1] Four years earlier the prominent Christian Socialist, Canon Stanley Evans, described this same failure as a 'paralysis which is gripping contemporary Christian "morality" ' and an abdication of the Church's position of moral leadership.[2]

Barth's question is perhaps easier to answer in 1987 than it was in 1959, and it may well be that history supplies more clues than theology. To an historian surveying the church debates and events of these years, two closely-related points are immediately obvious. In the first place, the churches (in common with society at large) were slow to grasp the full implications of the military use of nuclear energy, in terms of new military strategies, the multiple risks of radioactive fall-out, and the pace of leap-frogging 'modernisation'. Secondly, and as a direct consequence, the reports which they produced invariably referred to a body of Christian ethics which was fashioned in a different and relatively static historical reality, whilst the arms race entered new and unexpected stages. To appreciate the full force of this problem, it is necessary to remind ourselves briefly of the history of the arms race, before examining the content of the official church debates, the prophetic voices which questioned them, and the radical reassessments which began from diverse quarters in the early 1980s.

1 Stages in the history of the arms race

During the first three centuries of the Christian era, Christians normally abstained from military service. It was after the conversion of Constantine (312–316 A.D.) that the compromise with pacifism occurred. If Christians were to share in decision-making in society, it was argued, they must also be prepared to share the moral ambiguities of power. By the early fifth century, St Augustine outlined the notion of the just war at a time of pagan accusations that Christian principles of non-violence were weakening the Empire in the face of barbarian aggression. The aim of a just war was deliverance from evil and a better state of peace. By the time of the Reformation, the refinements of Aquinas and Vitoria had produced a doctrine which stressed the following six principles as requirements for a just war: (1) it must be waged by a legitimate authority; (2) it must be in a just cause proportionate to the evils which arise from its waging; (3) it must be undertaken with the right intention, which ultimately is a just and lasting peace; (4) it should be a last resort, when all peaceful remedies are exhausted; (5) there should be a reasonable expectation of success; and (6), the conduct of the war should be morally legitimate so that non-combatants should be immune from slaughter, and the war must not result in disproportionate evils to the parties involved and to the international community.[3]

The just war doctrine was concerned primarily with the circumstances in which resort to war was made, with the justice of the cause, rather than with the destructive potential of the weapons used. Fashioned in a largely pre-industrial world to contain the ambitions of emerging nation states, its utility in the present century of total war has not surprisingly come into question. It assumed, of course, hand-to-hand combat using conventional weapons and it permitted, in Charles Raven's words, the image of 'the Christian warrior as an ideal type of manhood . . . military efficiency [was] accepted as the proof of a civilization's worth and the arbitrament of arms as the ultimate test of righteousness'.[4] In other words, the arbitration of arms was linked directly with the individual's capacity for self-sacrifice – and so in a one-sided way could be seen as being connected with a central theme of the crucifixion drama. What the just war doctrine did not assume was the war technology of a 'mature' industrial society, barbarian in its destructiveness, but 'advanced' in the sense that it might develop its own momentum and create its own destabilising effects in the international arena.

As early as 1924 the COPEC Conference, meeting in Birmingham, received a report on Christianity and War which suggested that 'the mode of conducting war since 1914, and much of the sentiment shown since the peace, derive far more obviously from the Old Testament, even from the standards of our pagan forefathers, than from the Gospel of Christ'.[5] But, as one of the authors of that statement admitted many years later, the time was not quite ripe for a far-reaching reassessment of the Christian attitude to war, since 'No man who has offered his life for a cause and is still bearing the psychic and physical evidence paid, can, while the wounds are still fresh, discuss whether his offering was a mistake.'[6] Not until the late 1920s, after the tenth anniversary of the Armistice had unleashed a torrent of anti-war literature, did a powerful wave of pacifism sweep through the churches, as through society at large. In October 1929, the 'Christ and Peace' Campaign was launched which held twenty-five meetings and conferences over seventeen months; its main achievement was the Lambeth Conference declaration of 1930 that 'war as a method of settling international disputes is incompatible with the teaching and example of our Lord Jesus Christ'. Also in 1929, the Church of Scotland Peace Society was reconstituted, and recruitment to the somewhat quietest Fellowship of Reconciliation (founded in 1914) increased. The formation of pacifist movements by Congregationalists and Methodists soon followed. The Anglican Pacifist Fellowship emerged only in 1937, in the wake of the 'New Pacifist Movement' of the mid-1930s dominated by Canon Dick Sheppard's Peace Pledge Union.[7]

Yet official church opinion preferred to live with the existing doctrine of the just war throughout the inter-war period and beyond, neither fully accepting nor decisively rejecting it. Assemblies of several denominations during the 1930s revealed deep divisions on the duty of Christians to undertake military service.[8] In 1940, a resolution was moved in the Convocation of Canterbury asking for a ruling as to the applicability of the just war doctrine in the war against Germany. A solemn decision was taken that the resolution should lie on the table until after the war![9] Had that debate been continued in 1945, a digest of the full ethical and practical implications of the obliteration bombing of

German cities, opposed during the war by the lone voice of Dr George
Bell, Bishop of Chichester, might well have prevented the church from
following public opinion and policy down the nuclear slide.[10]

In concentrating attention on the morality of warfare rather than on
the changing material means by which war is conducted, mainstream
Christian thinking on war and peace has shown itself ill-prepared to
face the crisis of the twentieth century, in which the arms race has
passed through two historic phases, and has recently entered a third.
With the decision to use atomic weapons against Japan in 1945, coming
in the wake of mass aerial bombardment of civilian as well as military
targets in Europe, the epoch of conventional war-fighting was oversha-
dowed by a new phase, subsequently known as 'nuclear deterrence'.
According to its proponents, if stocks of nuclear weapons are kept at
sufficient levels to enable the victim of nuclear attack to retaliate and
inflict heavy damage on the attacker, such a state of preparedness will
itself provide security against nuclear attack. Deterrence based on the
threat of 'Mutual Assured Destruction', backed by a developed nuclear
capability, clearly depends upon a society's scientific and technological
ingenuity rather than the impulse towards noble acts of self-sacrifice on
the part of its individual members. Between the collective suicide pact of
Mutual Assured Destruction and 'the Christian warrior as an ideal type
of manhood', there lies no continuity of commitment. In this respect,
and because of the total lack of non-combatant immunity and disproportionate damage threatened, nuclear deterrence plainly lies outside the framework of earlier Christian thinking in the just war tradition. It was not until the early 1980s, however, that the churches
squarely faced these new difficulties and contradictions. Public concern
about the siting of American tactical nuclear missiles in Britain and
Europe generated new thinking from several quarters. Some attempted
to construct a 'nuclear pacifism', whilst others suggested the outlines of
a 'theology of deterrence'.

But by the early 1980s, the inner dynamics of the arms race had
overtaken the capacity of many in the churches to comprehend it. In the
late 1950s and early 1960s, the strategy of massive retaliation was
replaced by that of 'graduated response' – a more flexible nuclear war
fighting capability proportionate to the scale of the expected attack.
The search for 'appropriate' weapons has subsequently continued, and
the increasing mobility, accuracy and speed of nuclear missiles has led
to greater reliance upon automated decision-making, and the race to

deploy usable 'first strike' weapons against military targets. Nuclear strategy has thus moved beyond deterrence to that of nuclear war-fighting capability. American planners have now evolved the doctrine of 'counterforce' which envisages the continuation of nuclear war-fighting well beyond the initial exchanges. But because there is neces-sarily a gap between the evolution of a military strategy and the development of appropriate weapons, there is some disagreement as to the point at which the nuclear arms race shifted decisively 'beyond deterrence'. A 1981 publication of the International Institute of Stra-tegic Studies summarises the change as follows:

> For the greater part of the nuclear age, Western strategic thought focused on deterrence and other means of avoiding strategic nuclear war. The principal concerns of the strategic studies community were the conditions of viable mutual deterrence and crisis stability, the prevention of accidental nuclear war, and the promotion of nuclear non-proliferation to limit the danger of catalytic war. . . . During the last decade, however, there has been a radical shift in this thinking. Today, the principal concerns of the strategic studies community relate to the period following the initiation of a strategic nuclear exchange – i.e. to questions of nuclear war-fighting, such as targeting plans and policies, the dynamics of escalation during the strategic nuclear exchange, and the termination of an such exchange. Controlled escalation has become the central operational concept in current US strategic doctrine.[11]

This third stage in the twentieth-century arms race has yet to find a name. The strategists would doubtless prefer 'controlled escalation', or 'counterforce' to Edward Thompson's 'exterminism'. What is certain, however, is that many within the churches have failed to recognise this third phase in the arms race, which involves a decisive lowering of the nuclear threshold, first crossed in 1945. Indeed, it seems that in the official church debates and statements on peace and disarmament, there is an almost inescapable tendency for theology and Christian ethics to depend upon and fall behind existing historical reality. This may be indicated somewhat schematically:

Period	Conduct of war	Official Christian doctrine
Early Christian centuries	Conventional weapons	Original pacifism
Fourth century–1945	Conventional weapons	Just war doctrine
1945–?1980	Nuclear deterrence + conventional weapons	Just war doctrine
?1980s–	Counterforce +	Redundancy of just war accepted by some
	Nuclear deterrence +	(Theology of deterrence as unofficial stance)
	Conventional weapons	Just war doctrine

2 Official church debates, 1946–73

During the three decades following the atomic bombing of Hiroshima, the British Council of Churches developed a stance towards nuclear weapons which permitted, and in effect encouraged their acceptance by Christians. The periodic working party report, produced by the BCC's International Department, became the established vehicle for communicating the 'official' Christian, non-Catholic, approach to the nuclear arms race. The first three reports of 1946, 1959 and 1963 were concerned exclusively with nuclear armaments, and their titles reflect the general shift in public understanding of nuclear capability in terms of weapons ('the bomb') to that of deterrence. The fourth report of 1973 was concerned with nuclear and conventional weapons, though the distinction was sometimes blurred in the report.[12]

The reports were ostensibly intended to guide discussion within the churches, as 'the necessary basis of responsible statements by church groups, whether local or national'. But in practice, their authors addressed themselves to public opinion in general: secular language and utilitarian ethics took precedence over a theologically-based approach. Indeed, an important and expressed secondary objective was the parliamentary lobby. *The British Nuclear Deterrent* of 1963 was produced rapidly in the run-up to a general election and spent some time considering the question 'whether Christians should intrude on the discussion'. The three political parties purchased copies for distribution in both Houses of Parliament, and the deterrent proved to be a major election issue. *The Search for Security* of 1973 was a more thoroughly prepared report, the result of thirty-two meetings, spread over a period of three years, but was published early in 1973, less than a year before the February 1974 general election, and concluded with a number of questions addressed to the incoming government in the area of arms control. The reports were undoubtedly seen as representing the mainstream Christian voice in the nuclear debate, and their influence was felt at the political level – in spite of the authors' more modest pretensions.

All four reports were produced by male-dominated bodies composed of roughly equal numbers of lay Christians and clergy, ranging from twelve to twenty members. The 1946 Commission contained no military, strategic or technical experts, but two women members participated. (Women were entirely absent from the Commissions of 1958 and 1973, with the exception of the Secretary of the latter!) Specialist expertise bulked larger in the later reports, particularly through the participation of Rear Admiral Sir Anthony Buzzard, the only individual to serve on three successive commissions. A former Chief of Naval Intelligence and director of Vickers—Armstrong, Buzzard seems to have exercised a powerful influence. The Chairman of the 1973 Commission commented, 'Much that is in this report comes from his specialised, knowledge, his constructive criticism, and his assiduous industry.'[13] Another prominent member of the 1963 and 1973 Commissions was Sir Michael Wright, head of the British delegation to the Nuclear Test Ban and Disarmament Conferences in Geneva from 1948–62. The need for a progressively technical approach was a direct consequence of the BCC's policy of conditional acceptance of deterrence – conditional upon international control and reduction of nuclear weapons and therefore upon increasingly complex disarmament and non-proliferation negotiations. From 1963, following the conclusion of the Partial Test Ban Treaty and the first stirrings of *détente,* the BCC concentrated its attention more intensely on the trend of national policy – as the report of 1973 admitted.[14]

The basis for official Christian acquiescence to nuclear deterrence was laid in the 1946 Commission's report edited by Dr J. H. Oldham. Although the fifteen-strong working party was exploring uncharted territory, discussion was confined to three weekend meetings, and members provided written comments on drafts and memoranda in circulation. The complete report was submitted within three months of the first meeting. It was philosophical and speculative in tone, and in the aftermath of Hiroshima addressed the question, 'What has happened?' The participation of Dr George Bell, Bishop of Chichester, was insufficient to ensure that the question was squarely faced. The word *hibakusha* was as yet unknown, and perhaps the Commission was too deeply shocked to contemplate what R. J. Lifton termed 'the indelible imprint of death immersion'.[15] At any rate, they viewed the event with Western eyes. Western civilisation was seen to be in danger of losing its sense of social purpose, and feelings of insecurity, anxiety and futility, it was suggested, might generate recklessness and possibly even a decline in the birth rate. 'The mere discovery of the atomic bomb itself, even if it is never used, might well create such strains in our society as to destroy it.'[16] Questions about the consequences for Japanese society did not arise, since the Commission believed 'The argument that on balance the use of the atomic bomb saved hundreds of thousands of lives, both in the forces of the United Nations and in Japan itself, undoubtedly has weight.'[17] Evidence available at the time that a negotiated surrender could have been achieved was either overlooked or ignored.[18] Unlike the Federal Council of Churches of Christ in the USA, the BCC refused to condemn the allied decision to use the Atomic Bomb on the grounds that they were not in full possession of the facts.[19]

The Commission's ignorance of the immediate and long term genetic effects of radiation and fallout is glaringly apparent in its comparison of the effects of the obliteration bombing of German cities with the devastation of Hiroshima, noting that the latter was not greater than that of the thousand-bomber raids. It was felt that the Atom Bomb did not introduce a new ethical problem, in spite of the fact that it seemed to rule out the possibility of precision bombing. Nuclear weapons were regarded simply as an extremely efficient explosive, 'another kind of big bomb'. The deterioration of public sensitiveness to the indiscriminate massacre of non-combatants was condemned and it was recognised that the emergence of total warfare had caused the restraints required by the just war doctrine to disappear.[20] But in a colossal failure of logic and responsibility, the commission did nothing to fill the theological vacuum or to oppose the new instruments of total warfare which it so deplored. It escaped from the dilemma by suggesting firstly, that Christian opposition to the use of atomic weapons was merely optional:

'Some members of the Commission take the view that in no circum-stances whatever should a Christian approve the use of the atomic bomb or similar weapon of wholesale massacre.' By strong implication however, others did approve not merely the possession of nuclear bombs, but their actual use. For against such Christian disapproval, the report continued, must be set the no less insistent Christian responsi-bility to defend fundamental rights and liberties.

> The main stream of Christian tradition has recognised the legitimacy of war for a just cause. If there is a responsibility of the secular power which Christians must acknowledge, to defend the right, if necessary by force of arms, this responsibility is not, it may be argued, and cannot be, diminished or altered by technical advances [sic] and the introduction of new weapons, even though the resulting problems may be far more acute.[21]

Within the space of five paragraphs, the apparently moribund just war doctrine had been rehabilitated.

In the second place, the Commission felt that it was difficult 'even if it were desirable' for the general public to comment on military decisions in wartime. Nor was it right 'for Christians to weaken the hands of their government by announcing in advance that, if hostilities take place, they will have no part in them'.[22] Security considerations dictated that Christians should keep their objections to themselves. In the third place, the report suggested, at a time when it was barely understood, that 'the atomic bomb ought in the future to be used for one purpose, and one purpose alone, to deter by the threat, and if necessary by the execution, of reprisals [against] a nation which attempted to use it for aggressive purposes'.[23] The principle of deterrence was itself thought of as a restrained approach at this early stage.

In 1946, few people could envisage the huge increase in potential destructive nuclear capability of the following decade, and it was expected that the US monopoly of nuclear weapons would continue for some time.[24] Nevertheless, the Oldham Report was especially notable for its willing acquiescence in the West's possession and development of nuclear weapons, underpinned by an awe-inspired belief that the atomic scientist had opened up a new frontier for humanity. The dangers were seen as counterbalanced by a 'new power to promote human well-being' in medical, chemical and industrial research and alternative power sources. The Hiroshima event itself was described as a turning point in history, 'with illimitable potentialities for good or evil'.[25] By exaggerating or making unfounded claims about the possible social uses of atomic energy, Christians enabled themselves to comply more easily with its military use – a tendency which persisted for at least two decades. In 1955 for example, the Christian pacifist physicist C. A. Coulson, who had in 1945 refused to work on a nuclear-related research project, felt able to support such work on the grounds that production of nuclear weapons was by then established and irreversible. Whilst admitting that, 'in relation to large-scale government science . . . the appeals of novelty and priority and loyalty combine to make responsible decision difficult', Coulson appears to have been swayed by his belief that the world's energy needs could be met only by the development of atomic power, and that its discovery had 'come only just in time'.[26]

In retrospect, the conclusions of the Oldham Report found much of their justification in the deliberate ambiguities and resonance of the word 'Power' given in its title, and obsessively repeated in the text. The promise of a new energy source, economic recovery, the Allied victory and the prospect of a new era of Anglo-American hegemony formed the basis of its appeal: 'power mysticism' in its extreme manifestations 'revolts us', but 'all of us are in greater or less degree infected with the virus'.[27] The Commission was most seriously infected at the point where Britain's Great Power status and imperial responsibilities were seen as being under threat. In a dangerous analogy, Britain's renunciation of the use of the Atomic Bomb was seen to involve immediate renunciation of her Great Power status, 'equivalent to an attempt, in the naval age, to wage naval war without the use of capital ships'.[28]

The Oldham Report was followed in 1948 by that of a Church of England Commission on the moral and theological aspects of nuclear war, which confirmed the basic assumption of 1946 that 'today the possession of atomic weapons is generally necessary for national self-preservation, [and] a government which is responsible for the safety of the community committed to its charge, is entitled to manufacture them and hold them in readiness'.[29] The Cold War was now well under way, and the following year saw the establishment of NATO and the USSR in possession of the atomic bomb. In 1952, Britain carried out a series of test explosions off the coast of Western Australia and joined the 'nuclear club'. But it was not until 1954, when it became clear that a decision had been taken to make a British H-Bomb, that the interest of the churches revived.

Early in the year, the horrifying effects of radiation resulting from the American Pacific H-Bomb tests were widely reported in the Press. The BCC registered dismay at its April meeting and in August, the World Council of Churches called for a pledge from nations to refrain from the threat or the use of hydrogen, atomic and all other weapons of mass destruction.[30] This represented a challenge to the BCC's existing policy which it was, however, unwilling to meet. Behind the rhetoric of the next formal statement of the BCC's International Department (April 1955) lay the suggestion that any further resolution would 'add little' and that opposition to the H-Bomb was a matter for the individual Christian conscience 'before God'.[31] This was gratuitous advice, for Christians had already begun to campaign against the H-Bomb tests. Dr Donald Soper led his Methodist congregation and choir in a protest march through London and chaired the first meeting of the National Hydrogen Bomb Campaign. Many others supported the National Council for the Abolition of Nuclear Weapon Tests, initiated by Gertrude Fishwick of the Anglican Pacifist Fellowship. Sponsors included the Bishop of Chichester, the Revd George Macleod and Dr Soper.[32] But by April 1957, the BCC took the step of opposing the forthcoming series of British H-Bomb tests, by a narrow vote, against the advice of its Chairman, the Archbishop of Canterbury. This represented the limit of official Church opposition in the years leading up to the formation of CND in 1958. A. J. R. Groom describes it as merely 'an exception to an embarrassed silence'.[33]

More typical were the pro-nuclear sentiments of the Anglican hierarchy expressed at the May 1954 meeting of the Convocation of Canterbury. The Bishop of Southwell claimed that the H-Bomb raised no new question, and the Bishop of Derby compared it to a hand-grenade. A more extremist line was taken by the Bishop of Winchester who suggested, 'It might be better to perish than submit to the parody of civilisation which seems to be the alternative presented from the other side of the Iron Curtain.'[34] As opinions polarised in the late 1950s, the 'better dead than red' argument became increasingly fashionable and vehement, and the Archbishop of Canterbury was forced to intervene and publicly condemn such speeches by the Bishops of Peterborough and Willesden as 'appalling'. By 1958, only twelve per cent of Anglican bishops and suffragans took a unilateralist position.[35]

The BCC's 1959 Report, *Christians and Atomic War*, was thus produced against the background of mounting public anxiety about nuclear testing, the emergence of an organised anti-nuclear movement and polarisation of opinion both inside and outside the churches. The Report opened by conceding that the Christian case for refusal to participate in war had acquired much greater recognition 'in the light of nuclear armament', but suggested that the use of political and military power was necessary to protect 'our standard of living' and democratic freedoms which depended upon 'the present position of Britain in the world'.[36] The difficulty was conceived as a dilemma rather than a problem capable of definite solution, although its unfortunate effects might be mitigated, particularly if defence and disarmament could be understood as being interlinked. The fact that they were handled by different government departments was regarded as a practical obstacle. The Commission noted 'with the gravest attention' that Western strategy dictated the first use of nuclear weapons, and felt that policies should be found to get the West out of this position as quickly as possible.[37] Reliance upon conventional in place of nuclear weapons, realisation that 'the race for supremacy in total war is vain', increased provision of information about defence matters, the application of measures of political and military restraint, and the reduction of claims to national sovereignty were recommended as practical policy steps.[38] The report also commented on personal commitment, recognising that conscientious objection should be respected, but without indicating the forms that this could take in the nuclear age. Even more anachronistic was the suggestion that it was 'the duty and privilege' of Christians to participate in civil defence work.[39]

The theological content of the 1959 Report was somewhat thin. Like its successor of 1963, it rested upon an 'immanentist' view of God's activity within as well as beyond the present order. In one sense, this was interpreted in a deeply pessimistic way: 'A thousand acts of disobedience create a tangle which demands the patience of a thousand acts of faithfulness to begin to unravel.'[40] Decisive and responsive action seemed to be ruled out. Yet the authors were prepared for the transformation of disobedience into virtue, believing that 'the Atomic bomb is exerting a discipline over men's minds', that awareness of new dangers would discourage humankind from violating the moral order.[41] Insofar as these two conclusions represent a discontinuity of thought the latter was derived directly from the earlier report, that of 1946, and therefore from its short-lived optimism about the manifold benefits of atomic power. Discussion of the relevance of the just war doctrine, briefly dealt with in 1946, was virtually omitted from the 1959 Report.[42] The authors agreed that methods of unrestrained warfare during the two world wars had called into question the role of force in international affairs, and 'Nuclear weapons have brought us to the end of that road.' But the implications of this momentous change for Christian ethics in relation to nuclear deterrence were not spelt out.

In spite of its weaknesses, *Christians and Atomic War* provoked widespread interest amongst the churches and the general public. Several commentators in the national Press expressed horror that Christians could envisage 'living with the Bomb', so the BCC commissioned a shorter and more readable text from Canon T. R. Milford. Published in October 1961 as *The Valley of Decision*, the Milford pamphlet sought to provide a more convincing justification of the Report's recommendations.[43]

The period which separated these two publications from the BCC's next report of 1963 was one of heightened interest in the nuclear issue. The temporary suspension of nuclear testing by the USSR, USA and UK was agreed in 1959, but international tension mounted with the building of the Berlin Wall in August 1961 and the Cuban missile crisis of 1962 when Khrushchev tried to use the USSR's newly-acquired nuclear capability to political advantage. The Partial Test Ban Treaty of August 1963 was a response to the gravity of the situation. In welcoming the Test Ban, the BCC passed a resolution which reflected this increased concern and affected a more radical stance than anything shown hitherto, in three respects. In the first place, it looked forward to joint control of nuclear weapons, believing that Britain 'should express her willingness to forego the claim to independent nuclear action'; secondly, it described the West's policy of first use of nuclear weapons as intolerable; and thirdly, it condemned them as 'an offence to God and a denial of His purpose for man'.[44] Nevertheless it came nowhere near to demanding unilateral renunciation. The resolution in fact derived from arguments presented in the BCC's latest working party report, *The British Nuclear Deterrent* of October 1963, which in its underlying principles and approach followed its predecessors. As already noted, the report was produced in the period leading up to a general election.

The 1963 working party was dominated by strategic expertise to a greater degree than its predecessors, and its apparent concessions towards shared control and disapproval of first strike weapons represented little more than a justification of Britain's approaching dependence on the American-built Polaris missile system. (The chief characteristic of Polaris, as a submarine-launched missile, was and is its second strike capability). The report suggested that the Test Ban Treaty had been facilitated by 'negotiation from strength' and that the possession of thermonuclear armaments and a voice in their use 'confers political influence'. Furthermore, it claimed, nuclear deterrence had succeeded in preventing major wars.[45] Insofar as the Report adopted the rhetoric of the World Council of Churches statement, in which nuclear weapons were described as 'an affront to the Creator and a denial of the very purposes of the Creation', abolition was viewed as a far-distant objective – 'the Ultimate Goal'. In common with society at large, however, the churches seem to have felt a genuine optimism that 1963 test ban would mark the opening of a new era in East–West relations, and that 'internal developments within Russian society [may have] started a slow reversal of Russian policy, in which a series of agreements, sought fruitlessly for a decade, [may] now become possible'[46] Indeed, a number of Christian groups and organisations played an important role in facilitating improved East–West understanding when the Christian–Marxist dialogue developed after the Second Vatican Council, well before the full emergence of *détente* in the 1970s. The BCC, for example, participated in the activities of the Prague-based Christian Peace Conference before the crisis of 1968.

The Chairman of the Division of International Affairs of the BCC, Sydney Bailey, has suggested that from the mid-1960s, the ground of the Council's discussions began to shift.

> It was the manifest failure of the policy of retaining nuclear weapons in order to promote their abolition that led the BCC to question the notion from the mid 1960s. While British governments continued to pay occasional lip service to the goal of ultimate abolition, it was increasingly clear that complete abolition was becoming less rather than more likely with every month that passed and that nuclear weapons had been proliferating both horizontally and vertically.[47]

This increasing uneasiness led the Council to propose radical disarmament measures which stopped short of demanding total renunciation (unlike the Papal Encyclical of 1963, *Pacem in Terris,* which called for the banning of nuclear weapons). In 1967, for example, a resolution was passed suggesting that Britain should be prepared to 'forgo the possession of national nuclear weapons' provided this would secure a satisfactory non-proliferation agreement.[48] However, by the time the BCC had produced its 1973 report, *The Search for Security*, a stock of non-proliferation agreements, including SALT 1, had accumulated without resort to unilateral action. *Détente* seemed well-established and, believing that 'there are visible signs of nuclear sanity in the wary attitude of the two greatest nuclear powers towards each other', the authors felt confident enough to tackle the question of the just war doctrine in some detail.[49]

The Search for Security devoted a complete chapter to 'Restrictions on and in War' embodied in the two main streams of the law of armed conflict, the so-called Law of the Hague and the Law of Geneva. But the authors failed to distinguish clearly between conventional and nuclear weapons and grossly underestimated the consequences of nuclear war, which they described merely as making 'the thought of war less romantic and more repulsive'.[50] Of course the phenomenon of 'nuclear winter' was not understood at this time, yet the working party's view that the extension of international law was sufficient to preserve prudential restraints on war in the nuclear age appears crazily optimistic. The possibility of working within NATO to secure 'a policy of deterrence designed to spare non-combatants' was seen as entirely realistic.[51] But the Report's most serious weakness was that which plagued the whole series of BCC reports on the nuclear issue, which was an insistence on dismissing the anti-nuclear case by equating it with the pacifist objection to war in general. By failing to acknowledge that the nuclear threat involved a qualitatively different threat to the created order from that presented by conventional warfare, and therefore negated the conditions required for a just war, the BCC was unable to do anything other than underwrite the continuation of the arms race. Typically, the 1973 Report asserted: 'the pacifism of the Christian pacifist does not originate in revulsion from the vision of fifty million deaths in a nuclear holocaust. He is against war; war waged with any sort of weapons. He accepts the refusal to participate in war as a personal vocation.'[52] The practical impossibility of withdrawing personal consent from nuclear deterrence was never considered.

3 Prophetic voices, 1945–70

The BCC reports described above increasingly made a clear separation between 'unilateralism' and 'gradualism' and tended to simplify and limit the objections of anti-nuclear Christians in their midst. The 1963 Report admitted a lack of consensus within the working party on the moral issues involved, and agreed that this reflected deep divisions of opinion among Christians in general on the nuclear issue. But instead of examining the technical, political, ideological and theological grounds for these differences, those responsible for drafting the reports uniformly equated unilateral nuclear disarmament with traditional pacifism which, they asserted, was not capable of being translated into a political option. The spectrum of non-nuclear defence alternatives was ignored, and the position of those Christians who participated in these discussions but were unable to assent to nuclear deterrence was marginalised. In 1959, they were described as 'contracting out of some of their obligations to society'.[53] In 1963, their contribution was valued as 'a protest against the iniquity of our present situation' but dismissed as politically impracticable 'and even possibly disastrous', since it was assumed without question that a non-nuclear Britain would necessarily disengage from NATO.[54] The report of 1973 argued that unilateral disarmament had only small support in Parliament and the country as a whole and, whilst the same could no doubt have been said of Christianity, the authors felt 'we do not deem it necessary to examine in depth subtly varying differences in both pacifist and non-pacifist judgements'.[55]

Not surprisingly, some members and former members of the BCC Commissions publicly voiced their unease about the drift of these official debates. Dr John Vincent, for example, author of *Christ in a Nuclear World* (1962) criticised the BCC's dual standard which divided Christians into the few, prepared to follow all Christ's commands, and the many, involved with the ambiguities of their worldly situation. On the contrary, Vincent argued, 'Christians are called to live the life of the few without abdicating the duties of the many'.[56] The BCC responded by co-opting him on to its next working party! Professor Donald Mackinnon, the Cambridge theologian who participated in the 1946 discussions, voiced his own misgivings many years later, at the same time as Vincent. In a 1962 lecture, he suggested that 'because the very high-minded persons who move in these exalted circles [of the BCC] are at all costs anxious to avoid an open breach between Christ and Caesar, the perils, even the likelihood, of escalation have been much under-emphasised'.[57] Far from keeping the peace, Mackinnon claimed that the deterrent had introduced 'radical instability' into international relations.

Mackinnon's criticisms pointed to the fundamental flaw of the entire series of BCC discussions which was that they depended upon the trend of government policy and military strategy, and were based on assumptions which were invalidated by each stage of the upward spiralling arms race. The 1973 report, for example, made no reference to the introduction of multiple independently targetable re-entry vehicles (MIRV-ed missiles) which totally altered the existing basis of arms limitation efforts, and therefore of the BCC's conditions for the acceptance of deterrence. As another critic, Christopher Driver, put it in 1964, non-unilateralist Christian thinkers 'who are normally prepared to underwrite particular solutions of current problems, expose themselves to more serious dismay when these solutions are outpaced by technological or political change, or simply shown to be wrong'.[58]

To an extent, it seems that official Christian acceptance of nuclear deterrence, with its uncertain and contingent quality, provided a foil against which individual Christians and groups could develop a prophetic response. Their chief difficulty, however, was to avoid falling back on a kind of inflexible absolutism which was blind to the dangers of nuclear as distinct from conventional weapons, which 'rendered obsolete the accumulated wisdom of centuries'.[59] Many Christians drawn into the early anti-nuclear movement had been and still were associated with pacifist organisations established during the inter-war years, such as the Anglican Pacifist Fellowship and the Fellowship of Reconciliation. Whilst some doubtless adjusted their thinking after 1945, others were slow to do so. In 1958, both the Peace Pledge Union and the Fellowship of Reconciliation officially withheld support from CND on the grounds that if it were successful it might encourage outbreaks of conventional warfare.[60] (This apparently outweighed the reverse proposition that nuclear deterrence has actually shifted the locus of global conflict and encouraged conventional wars in the periphery.) In his autobiography, Canon John Collins explained the ineffectiveness of the peace organisations in terms of three persistent problems: the general feeling that pacifists had enfeebled resistance to Hitler; disagreements between the peace organisations themselves; and the fact that until 1958, 'most peace organisations were still so preoccupied with their pacifist activities that they failed to realise that

Hiroshima demanded a new approach'.[61] The dangers of nuclear escalation substantially invalidated the old debate between absolute pacifists and non-pacifists (or 'pacificists'), but the division exercised a debilitating influence for some time.[62]

From 1945 to 1958, differences in the thinking of these two groups were reflected in their relative willingness to act and organise opposition to the nuclear arms race. The absolutists, such as Dr Donald Soper and the Revd George Macleod, were prepared to take early action, in campaigning against nuclear tests, promoting abolitionist resolutions at the annual Methodist Conference, and in their public pronouncements.[63] As leading Christian pacifists however, Soper and Macleod, together with Canon Charles Raven, had been banned from broadcasting by the BBC from 1941 to 1945, and Soper had been associated with the discredited wartime People's Convention for Peace.[64] This undoubtedly reduced their credibility for the majority of Christians, who saw the war against Hitler as a just war. In the late 1940s and early 1950s, Soper believed that the Methodist Church should take an unqualified pacifist position on the nuclear issue – 'a forty-million strong pacifist protest'. At the 1950 Methodist Conference, he suggested that there was a difference between 'the use of a hydrogen bomb and the bayonet, but that the distinction lay not in ethics but in logistics and the strategy of war'. He went on to make the much-publicised remark that if he had to choose between a Third World War and the Russian occupation of Britain, he would choose the latter as preferable to complete annihilation.[65] Christian non-pacifists, pacificists or 'nuclear pacifists' were in a better position to gain public support for an anti-nuclear campaign, but were sluggish in organising. Canon John Collins, ex-RAF Chaplain and first Chairman of CND, withdrew his support from the Hydrogen Bomb National Campaign and its great Albert Hall rally of April 1954 feeling that it was premature. In 1957, he refused to allow Christian Action to sponsor a National Campaign for unilateral nuclear disarmament, though this was on grounds of Christian Action's overall purpose as much as timing.[66] When CND was formed in 1958, it was the product of decidedly secular initiatives. J. B. Priestley's 1957 article in the *New Statesman* was the catalyst which generated a flood of readers' correspondence, canalised into a forceful movement by Kingsley Martin and Bertrand Russell.[67] Collins was invited to act as chairman out of 'a latent respect for the Churches, and a wistful hope that they might yet, against all precedent, start living up to their profession'.[68]

Collins himself was not an absolute pacifist and took up a position of self-confessed ambivalence. 'I say that I am not an absolute pacifist', he commented in his autobiography, 'but where nuclear, biological, or any other indiscriminate or mass destructive weapons are concerned, I have never doubted, certainly not since 1945, that their manufacture, let alone the threat to use them or their actual use, is not only wholly contrary to the Christian Gospel but ought to be actively opposed by every Christian.'[69] By occupying this 'kind of no-man's land', Collins felt enabled to bring together Christian pacifists and non-pacifists with a common interest in disarmament and peace. From 1951 to 1959, Christian Action served, *inter alia,* as a vehicle for this purpose when a working relationship between that body and the Friends' Peace Committee was established, culminating in a great meeting at the Royal Albert Hall, 'Modern War: a Challenge to Christians', in May 1959.[70] Speakers and participants included Mervyn Stockwood, Victor Gollancz, Trevor Huddleston, Richard Acland and Pamela Frankau, with Collins in the chair. According to Peggy Duff, CND's first Secretary, Christian Action had up to this point been 'always a little frightened of the CND' and never unilateralist.[71] The *Socialist Christian* described the meeting as over-organised and lacking in unity of conviction.[72] Shortly after the Albert Hall meeting therefore, Christian CND was set up by Francis Jude of the Friends' Peace Committee 'to put a reasoned case for nuclear disarmament within Church circles'.[73] Christian CND produced materials which were widely used by CND groups and sympathisers in the churches.[74] Its first pamphlet of 1960 gave seven reasons why Christians should support nuclear disarmament: (1) nuclear weapons are not weapons of defence; (2) they would involve indiscriminate mass extermination; (3) there would be fall-out on neutrals; (4) there would be genetic effects on future generations; (5) deterrence depends on a willingness to inflict mass extermination; (6) nuclear war is suicidal and, therefore, indefensible; (7) 'tactical' nuclear weapons were greatly destructive in themselves and would inevitably lead to escalation.[75] By confronting the requirements of the Just War doctrine with the reality of nuclear war, this statement provided a means of breaking down the moral isolation of traditional Christian pacifism.

Further pamphlets followed by Pamela Frankau, Herbert Butterfield and Canon Stanley Evans, which questioned the BCC's conditional acceptance of nuclear deterrence as lacking a firm ethical and theological basis.[76] Stanley Evans's *Nuclear Deterrent and Christian Conscience* provided a powerful criticism of Canon Milford's BCC-sponsored pamphlet, *The Valley of Decision*. Evans argued the anti-nuclear case on non-pacifist grounds, and showed that nuclear weapons differed from earlier weapons not merely in their destructiveness but in two important respects. First, use of a *single* nuclear weapon necessarily involved the crime of genocide; and secondly, the necessary consequence of fallout was that *creativity itself was destroyed*. 'But creativity is an expression of the nature of God and if this is not the ultimate blasphemy then words have no meaning.'[77] Evans went on to condemn nuclear diplomacy as 'a system of world relations based on violence with annihilation as its final possibility', and as such incapable of Christian support. Whilst the conditions for a just war as outlined in *The Valley of Decision* could not possibly be fulfilled in the case of nuclear war, the antithesis of limited warfare, 'what has not yet been adequately realised is that the nuclear armament race makes free diplomatic discussion impossible'.[78]

After an early spate of pamphleteering, Christian CND continued to debate the Christian grounds for the anti-nuclear case in its quarterly magazine *Rushlight* from 1964 to 1967. The official BCC policy again provided the main target as set out in the 1963 report *The British Nuclear Deterrent*; and there was concern that the Christian demand for immediate abandonment of the British deterrent might be in danger of being written off, or writing itself off as pacifist. One contributor went so far as to suggest that Christian opposition should not be based on moral or theological grounds at all, but on practical considerations alone: 'Christ did not teach Christian morality, still less Christian theology – he told his followers to keep the laws of Moses ... the question should be "What are the consequences of not pretending to rely on the nuclear deterrent?" and "How do we deal with these consequences?" '[79] But the organising committee of Christian CND continued to maintain that the basis of its opposition to the BCC view lay in the latter's military and strategic form of reasoning. The very title of its 1963 report, claimed Stanley Evans, 'has done all it can to align the Churches with official propaganda'.[80]

During the first three years of its life, Christian CND concentrated on small group activity such as vigils and pilgrimages to cathedral towns rather than nuclear bases, regional conferences, and the formation of a

Christian Group section in the annual Aldermaston march.[81] After the 1963 march for example, 600 people attended prayers in Westminster Abbey. But this campaigning work tended to be haphazard, and often occurred outside local CND group activity, 'the whole tending to create amongst individuals a feeling of frustration and sometimes a "segregationalist" attitude towards CND in its local and national activity', according to a Christian Group report to CND's national council in September 1963. 'It is time', the report continued, 'now that some Church leaders are coming into the light, that the movement took on a more dynamic and cohesive form.'[82] In fact the mid-1960s were to see a period of fairly vigorous activity for Christian CND at a time when national CND was experiencing crisis and decline following divisions over non-violent civil disobedience. In a circular of September 1967, it was reported that 'in recent years Christian CND has grown from a handful of Christian nuclear disarmers into a movement of some hundreds ... it is no longer the predominantly Anglican organisation it once was and the adhesion of Roman Catholics and Free Churchmen has already altered its character.'[83] The publication of Rushlight, from February 1964, subtitled 'A Journal of the Christian Peace Movement', evidenced this growth, as did the mushrooming of local groups. The majority were established as Christian CND branches but some, such as the Sevenoaks 'Nuclear Prayer Group', were set up as an amalgam of older peace groups like the Anglican Pacifist Fellowship and the Methodist Peace Fellowship.[84] The Encyclical of John XXIII of April 1963, Pacem in Terris, undoubtedly strengthened the movement with its declaration that 'Justice, right reason and the realisation of man's dignity cry out insistently for a cessation to the arms race. Nuclear weapons must be banned.'

At the same time, the tone of Christian protest became more insistent, although it stopped short of non-violent civil disobedience. Pilgrimages were more strategically planned and became more frequent. The Revd Sidney Hinkes, Christian CND Chairman from 1963 to 1966 encouraged the movement with the text from Luke xiii, 'I must walk today, and tomorrow, and the day following: for it cannot be that a prophet perish out of Jerusalem.'[85] The 1964 Whitsuntide pilgrimage of London Christian CND from Southwark to Canterbury carried 'The Complaint of Canterbury' before them, which accused the Church of failing because of its own unbelief.[86] Two years later, Christian groups were setting up their banners at Napthill HQ Bomber Command, and in

February 1967 several hundred Christians demonstrated at the launching of the second Polaris nuclear submarine at Birkenhead, led by Dr John Vincent.[87] But protest was kept within limited bounds so as to maintain the credibility of anti-nuclear Christians within the churches. Christian members of London CND branches frequently visited church services to put their case in small groups, and a report of February 1964 stressed that 'The non-aggressive bearing of the visitors restored – and continues to restore – the bad CND image created by the press and by the obstructionists in Whitehall on Easter Monday.'[88] John Vincent emphasised that healing was greater than peace and more useful than protesting: 'whereas protest widens the gap between person and person, the way is open to peacemakers to become one with the person against whom the protest is made. This is better medicine than bleating peace protests.'[89] Christian CND was clearly anxious to avoid the divisions which had developed within national CND, and when the latter faced the possibility of closure under financial pressure in 1966, the Christian Group declared it would continue the campaign 'under whatever title seems right'. Doubters were assured of the group's respectability by the clouds of distinguished advisers and sponsors – bishops, academics and writers – whose names graced its letter-headings.[90]

4 New perspectives, 1979–85

From 1967 onwards, the Anti-Vietnam War Movement drained the energies of many anti-nuclear campaigners and Christian CND entered a period of decline. The arms control treaties of the late 1960s and early 1970s and the emergence of *détente* reduced earlier feelings of insecurity, in spite of the fact that the SALT agreements had no practical effect in preventing the upward twist of the arms race.[91] The Helsinki Agreement of 1975, which recognised the permanence of existing European frontiers, seemed to promise a measure of political stabilisation which was at least more conspicuous than the development of MIRV arms technology. In 1979, however, the renewal of the Cold War and the NATO decision to deploy Pershing II and Cruise missiles in Europe gave birth to a massive revival in the British and European peace movements. But the new cold war differs from its predecessor in that lesser economic and political tensions have been magnified by the nuclear arms race itself; the assumptions of deterrence and the sheer accumulation of nuclear weaponry have themselves generated sufficient mistrust and instability to provide a certain political momentum.[92] The churches have been quick to perceive this and, recognising that earlier compromises with deterrence were based on unrealistic expectations about disarmament, have been more ready to promote trust-building and Christian peacemaking initiatives. The Church of England and the BCC are still reluctant to demonstrate outright opposition to nuclear deterrence, but polarisation of opinion within the churches, and between the BCC and the Christian anti-nuclear movement has been much reduced.[93] In 1979, the Council for Christian Approaches to Defence and Disarmament (CADD), an advisory body closely related to the BCC, acknowledged 'the sinfulness of even a conditional intention' to use nuclear weapons. In November 1983, the BCC urged that Britain 'should progressively phase out British nuclear weapons, and in particular should not replace Polaris with Trident missiles'.[94] Christian opposition to nuclear deterrence can no longer be considered as a marginal protest or a pacifist option.

Nevertheless, ambiguities still remain about approaches to nuclear disarmament, alternative forms of non-nuclear defence, and what are considered to be appropriate forms of demonstrating Christian opposition to nuclear deterrence. The churches have generally stopped short of providing resources for peace movements within their own denominations or of associating themselves with secular peace movements – although twenty-three per cent of national CND members were practising Christians in 1982 (11,500 individuals). Not until 1983 did the BCC decide to establish and finance a 'Peace Desk'.[95] To date, none of the mainstream churches, apart from the Society of Friends, has reached a formal unilateralist position: the nearest approach is that of the General Assembly of the Church of Scotland which in 1983 called upon the government to 'negotiate . . . with energy to achieve an immediate freeze on further research, development and deployment of [nuclear] weapons'.[96]

From 1979 to 1982, the Anglican Church considered the nuclear issue and provided a major force for debate in its Board of Social Responsibility working party report, *The Church and the Bomb*. The report recommended British renunciation of the independent nuclear deterrent, immediate cancellation of Trident and the phasing out of Polaris missiles and submarines.[97] The decisive but realistic approach of the report contrasted with the hesitant and convoluted arguments of

ealier BCC documents, and it excited widespread interest ranging well
beyond church circles. Far from occupying an absolutist position, *The
Church and the Bomb* advocated a course of practical unilateralism. In
language which refused to polarise 'unilateral' and 'multilateral'
options, it recommended British renunciation as a 'unilateral stage
within a multilateral process' – that is, a phased series of unilateral
reductions designed to secure reciprocation according to principles
suggested by the North American strategist Charles Osgood. By
remaining within NATO, it was suggested that Britain would work for
a genuine reduction in the West's nuclear capability as a whole, and
would not assume the status of a 'free rider'.[98] But in February 1983,
under conditions of intense publicity, the Church of England's General
Synod rejected such a course of action. Instead, it approved a motion
calling for 'no first use' of nuclear weapons which differed little from the
position adopted by the BCC twenty years earlier. Although the synod
vote appeared as a short-run defeat for the nuclear disarmament
movement, the entire *Church and the Bomb* debate generated several
positive developments. In the first place, the report itself survives as a
more permanent and far-reaching contribution to the effort to halt the
arms race than the largely-forgotten synod debate. Secondly, the report
clarified the issues and increased the commitment of large numbers of
Christians to nuclear disarmament. Insofar as these people 'cannot
reconcile the possession of nuclear weapons with Christian disci-
pleship [they] find themselves looking for support and leadership outside the official churches'. This must either strengthen the anti-nuclear
movement or tend towards a closer integration of the Christian and
secular peace movements.[99] Thirdly, the debate served to draw out the
arguments of the Christian pro-deterrence lobby, and to crystallise
certain ideas which were only loosely formulated, but commonly
expressed, in the earlier BCC discussions and official reports.

   In the interval between publication of *The Church and the Bomb* and
the synod vote, intensive lobbying took place. A number of polemical
exchanges occurred in *The Times* led by Paul Johnson and Graham
Leonard, Bishop of London, in which the former portrayed the Soviet
Union as a 'kingdom of darkness' with a 'structural propensity to evil';
at the same time a conference of 'Christian Conservatives' was hastily
arranged in London.[100] From this unpromising milieu a new theological label emerged for an older political option – the theology of
deterrence. Other proponents include Richard Harries, now Bishop of

Oxford, Fr Gerard Hughes of Heythrop College and Keith Ward, Professor of Moral Philosophy at King's College, London, who together provided a more reasoned case in a collection of essays entitled *The Cross and the Bomb* (1983). Significantly, the 'theologians of deterrence' see themselves as responding to a 'trend towards unilateralism in the churches'.[101] Their deeply pessimistic Niebuhrian view of humankind's irredeemably fallen state suggests that insofar as the prime consequence of the possession of nuclear weapons is the prevention of the outbreak of nuclear war, nuclear deterrence must be ethically sound. And some suggest that deterrence represents not merely the lesser of two evils, but is actually a force for good. According to Harries, the divine 'mercy of deterrence' is turned against war itself, as the 1946 and 1959 BCC Reports had suggested in the phrase 'the atomic bomb is exerting a discipline over men's minds'.[102] A debilitating and anti-historical fatalism unites the theologians of deterrence in their assurance that 'what cannot be disinvented must be endured'.[103] Nevertheless, their reasoning possesses one striking merit – it gives formal recognition to the fact that acceptance of the ethical basis of the just war doctrine is incompatible with the conditional acceptance of deterrence. Successive BCC commissions refused to face this difficulty in their anxiety to avoid both a radical revision of Christian ethics and a radical questioning of government policy. The 'theology of deterrence', however, decisively rejects the just war doctrine as inapplicable in the nuclear age: the criteria of discrimination and proportion cannot be seriously upheld, and 'the axis of war theology, therefore, now revolves around the notion of peace by deterrence'.[104] The authors of *The Church and the Bomb* likewise perceived a threatening crisis in Christian ethics but emphasised that 'the cause of right cannot be upheld by fighting a nuclear war. . . . This is the moral challenge, new in human history, which nuclear weapons pose.'[105] Their response, in advocating practical unilateralism, represented a decisive break from all previous official church statements.

This new realism and level of concern in official church circles has been matched by a unity of conviction, enhanced confidence and improved organisation amongst Christian peace groups and movements since the early 1980s. Interest in Christian CND revived in the mid-1970s, but steady growth dates from May 1979 when a service of thanksgiving in Westminster Abbey to mark the thirtieth anniversary of NATO brought together Christian CND activists and protesters from the older Christian peace organisations: the Anglican Pacifist Fellowship, Pax Christi, the Fellowship of Reconciliation and Quaker Peace and Service.[106] In 1981, over 900 people attended Christian CND's conference 'Profess and Survive' at Coventry Cathedral, and by 1985, the Movement's quarterly magazine *Ploughshare* reached a circulation of 5,000.[107] Several new groups and movements began to emerge between these years: Clergy Against Nuclear Arms (CANA), Catholic Peace Action, the Gloucestershire Churches Freeze Campaign and the Dunamis project at St James, Piccadilly, amongst many others. This dense growth of Christian peace networks and the publications which it generated indicates that Christians are no longer content to wait for radical statements by Church Synods but are undertaking their own peacemaking initiatives at a variety of levels. Christian CND has perceived this in terms of developing 'Dialogue and Resistance': dialogue particularly inside the churches, but also within the political arena, and resistance through developing alternative forms of personal and social behaviour, and through symbolic and direct forms of protest.[108]

In common with the secular peace movement, the Christian peace movement in the 1980s has developed a broad consensus on the desirability of non-violent direct action and disciplined forms of civil disobedience, in contrast to the 1960s. Since the first 'Peace Pentecost' of May 1983 when Christians scaled the barbed wire perimeter at USAF Upper Heyford and arranged a liturgy beside the runway of a nuclear bomber base, 'holy disobedience' at places of war-preparation has become a regular occurrence. Barbara Eggleston, national organiser of Christian CND, suggests that

> This is in the ancient Christian tradition of praying in evil places as well as good – many of the cathedrals of Europe are on the site of pagan temples, or on places of execution . . . Christian peace activists worship at (and inside) nuclear bases and establishments as a way of breaking out of the reservation of private worship . . . This activity has always been noticed, and sometimes been criticised. It is criticised because Christians have for so long been relied on to be silent on these issues, to know their place and to keep to it.[109]

Besides drawing on their own pacifist tradition, Christians practising non-violent direct action in the 1980s have moved closer to other sections of the Peace Movement, particularly the peace camps, women and Greens. Furthermore, the former isolationism of Christian pacifism has been partially broken down by affinity group and peace camp organisation which has generated small non-violent communities. The personal vocation of the pacifist is being slowly translated into the social option of non-violence.

It is too early to make further generalisations about these new perspectives within the churches and the Christian peace movement, or to predict the likely course of future developments. But it seems clear that few Christians, except the most hierarchically-minded, expect the churches to behave as 'an authoritative, autonomous institution, capable of deciding what the "law" of Christ is and enforcing it.'[110] In the case of the nuclear arms race, past mistakes and a failure of vision have created such an accumulation of misunderstanding that synodical statements and official resolutions nowadays appear increasingly suspect. Secrecy about decisions relating to nuclear weapons is now much more difficult to maintain, and information about weapons systems and strategy has become plentiful and accessible. Christians are therefore beginning to realise that militarism takes a variety of forms, and that morality in defence matters cannot be divorced from practical questions about weapons and military strategy. With the lowering of the nuclear threshold, at least one church has accepted a campaigning role. In May 1985, the Church of Scotland General Assembly agreed to commend the nuclear freeze campaign, and a petition urging the government to intitiate a nuclear freeze was placed in all churches during a 'Freeze Endorsement Week'. Over 150,000 signatures were collected.[111] Within the Church of England, the Bishop of Dudley has recently suggested that new directions should encompass 'opening up discussion on such subjects as a European defence strategy independent of the American deterrent, a European nuclear-free zone, a reassessment of our relations with and attitude to the Warsaw Pact countries, and an immediate freeze on the British deterrent'.[112] The moment has passed when the churches could afford the time to observe, in the manner of the 1946 Oldham Report or *The Search for Security* of 1973, that the arms race and the discoveries of science represent a far less serious threat than the contradictions of human nature itself.[113]

References

(Place of publication London unless otherwise stated.)

1 In *Christianity Today*, 1959, quoted in J. Garrison, *The Darkness of God: Theology*

after Hiroshima, 1982, p. 1.

2 S. G. Evans, *Return to Reality*, 1954, pp. 280, 283.

3 R. Ruston OP, *Nuclear Deterrence – Right or Wrong?*, 1981, pp. 13–15.

4 C. E. Raven, *War and the Christian*, 1938, p. 44.

5 *Christianity and War*, Vol. VIII, COPEC Commission Report (Conference on Christian Politics, Economics and Citizenship), 1924, p. 23.

6 Raven, *War and the Christian*, p. 19.

7 M. Ceadel, *Pacifism in Britain 1914–1945: The Defining of a Faith*, Oxford, 1980, pp. 63–70, 210; Raven, *War and the Christian*, pp. 19–21.

8 Raven, *War and the Christian*, p. 93.

9 Evans, *Return to Reality*, p. 280.

10 See G. K. A. Bell's published wartime speeches, *The Church and Humanity (1939–1946)*, 1946, especially pp. 129–41. Bell vigorously opposed the H-Bomb on the grounds that it 'negated the conditions for a just war and would cause genetic effects of unprecedented and unpredictable magnitude', in 'Nuclear War and Peace', Peace Aims Pamphlet No. 60, 1955, quoted in A. J. R. Groom, *British Thinking About Nuclear Weapons*, 1974, p. 199.

11 D. Ball, *Can Nuclear War be Controlled?*, Adelphi Papers (169), International Institute of Strategic Studies, p. 1.

12 British Council of Churches: *The Era of Atomic Power*, May 1946; *Christians and Atomic War, A Discussion of the Moral Aspects of Defence and Disarmament in the Nuclear Age*, 1959; *The British Nuclear Deterrent*, 1963; *The Search for Security, A Christian Appraisal*, 1973.

13 *The Search for Security*, p. xii. Buzzard, a professional strategist and the author of several papers on nuclear deterrence, played a key role in arguing the case for graduated deterrence as a response to successive Defence White Papers which favoured massive retaliation. Graduated deterrence, Buzzard claimed, was preferable on grounds of morality, the fact that it facilitated disarmament, and economy (Groom, *British Thinking About Nuclear Weapons*, pp. 75–82).

14 *The Search for Security*, p. 20.

15 R. J. Lifton, *Death in Life, Survivors of Hiroshima*, New York, 1967, quoted in Garrison, *The Darkness of God*, p. 69.

16 *The Era of Atomic Power*, p. 17.

17 *Ibid.*, p. 50. The qualification was added that this argument could 'justify any kind of barbarity'.

18 G. Prins (ed.), *Defended to Death, a Study of the Nuclear Arms Race from the Cambridge University Disarmament Seminar*, Penguin, 1983, p. 70.

19 *The Era of Atomic Power*, p. 49.

20 *Ibid.*, pp. 50–1.

21 *Ibid.*, p. 53.

22 *Ibid.*, p. 56.

23 *Ibid.*, p. 54.

24 A. J. P. Taylor, *English History, 1914–1945*, Oxford, 1965, p. 601.

25 *The Era of Atomic Power*, pp. 7, 12.

26 C. A. Coulson, 'Responsibility', the Second Tawney Memorial Lecture, Christian Socialist Movement, 1966, p. 16; C. A. Coulson, 'Some Problems of the Atomic Age', The Second Scott Lidgett Memorial Lecture, Free Church Federal Council, 1957,

p. 9.

27 *The Era of Atomic Power*, p. 26.

28 *Ibid.*, p. 41.

29 Press and Publications Board of the Church Assembly, *The Church and the Atom*, 1948, summary of conclusions quoted by Evans, *Return to Reality*, pp. 281–2.

30 British Council of Churches, *The Churches and the Hydrogen Bomb*, n.d. (1955?), pp. 4–6.

31 *Ibid.*, p. 6.

32 H. Greer, *Mud Pie, The CND Story*, 1964, p. 19; C. Driver, *The Disarmers, A Study in Protest*, 1964, p. 26. I am grateful to Dr Sheila Jones for information about the National Council for Abolition of Nuclear Weapon Tests.

33 Groom, *British Thinking About Nuclear Weapons*, p. 327.

34 Driver, *The Disarmers*, p. 198.

35 *Ibid.*, pp. 199–200.

36 *Christians and Atomic War*, p. 3.

37 *Ibid.*, p. 27.

38 *Ibid.*, pp. 32–4.

39 *Ibid.*, p. 35.

40 *Ibid.*, p. 22.

41 *Ibid.*, p. 5.

42 *Ibid.*, p. 27.

43 British Council of Churches, *The Valley of Decision: The Christian Dilemma in the Nuclear Age*, by T. R. Milford, 1961. Summarised in *The Search for Security*, pp. 12–15.

44 *The British Nuclear Deterrent*, pp. 5–6.

45 *Ibid.*, pp. 19, 22, 23.

46 *Ibid.*, p. 25.

47 S. D. Bailey, *Christian Perspectives on Nuclear Weapons*, Division of International Affairs, British Council of Churches, 1981, p. 38.

48 *The Search for Security*, Appendix 6, p. 129.

49 *Ibid.*, p. 43.

50 *Ibid.*, p. 77.

51 *Ibid.*, p. 94.

52 *Ibid.*, p. 77.

53 *Christians and Atomic War*, p. 2.

54 *The British Nuclear Deterrent*, p. 28.

55 *The Search for Security*, pp. 77–8.

56 Quoted by Driver, *The Disarmers*, p. 213.

57 D. M. Mackinnon *et al.*, *God, Sex and War*, 1963, p. 18.

58 Driver, *The Disarmers*, p. 214.

59 *Ibid.*, p. 195.

60 L. J. Collins, *Faith Under Fire*, 1966, p. 268.

61 *Ibid.*, p. 267.

62 M. Ceadel, following A. J. P. Taylor's usage, distinguishes between pacifism (the belief that all war is always wrong and should never be resorted to, whatever the consequences of abstaining from fighting) and pacificism (the assumption that war, though sometimes necessary, is always an irrational and inhumane way to solve

disputes, and that its prevention should always be an overriding political priority), *Pacifism in Britain*, p. 3.

63 D. Thompson, *Donald Soper: A Biography*, 1971, pp. 100–1; Driver, *The Disarmers*, p. 200.

64 Thompson, *Donald Soper*, pp. 73–4.

65 *Ibid.*, p. 133.

66 Collins, *Faith Under Fire*, pp. 294, 296.

67 *Ibid.*, p. 302.

68 Driver, *The Disarmers*, p. 194.

69 Collins, *Faith Under Fire*, p. 277.

70 Christian Action had been formed in Oxford in December 1946, and was initiated by and embodied the aims of some of those who had organised the movement for 'ethical socialism' during the war years. Sir Richard Acland, Victor Gollancz, Barbara Ward, the Bishop of Chichester and Canon Collins launched Christian Action at a large meeting in Oxford Town Hall. *Ibid.*, p. 111; D. J. Ormrod, 'The Christian Left and the Beginnings of Christian Marxist Dialogue', in J. Obelkevich, L. Roper and R. Samuel, *Disciplines of Faith, Studies in Religion, Politics and Patriarchy*, 1987, pp. 435–50.

71 Peggy Duff, *Left, Left, Left: A Personal Account of Six Protest Campaigns*, 1971, pp. 156–7.

72 *Socialist Christian*, Vol. XXIII, No. 1, New Series, September 1959, report by Stewart Purkis, p. 3.

73 Collins, *Faith Under Fire*, p. 299.

74 Duff, *Left, Left, Left*, p. 157.

75 Christian Group of the Campaign for Nuclear Disarmament, *Questions and Answers for Christians on Nuclear Disarmament*, quoted by Groom, *British Thinking About Nuclear Weapons*, p. 463.

76 Pamela Frankau, *Letter to a Parish Priest*; Herbert Butterfield, *Human Nature and the Domination of Fear*; Stanley Evans, *The Nuclear Deterrent and Christian Conscience*. Dates not indicated, but all 1960–63.

77 Evans, *The Nuclear Deterrent*, pp. 2–3.

78 *Ibid.*, p. 5.

79 Ralph Clark, 'Render unto Caesar', *The Rushlight*, No. 2, Summer 1964.

80 Stanley Evans, 'An answer by Christian CND to the British Council of Churches' new pamphlet, "The British Nuclear Deterrent" ', *The Rushlight*, No. 2, summer 1964.

81 British Library of Political and Economic Science, Archives of the Campaign for Nuclear Disarmament. CND 1/7, Report of the Sub-Committee to consider the Structure of the Campaign, 20 May 1962; Annual Report, 14 October 1963. The status of Christian CND was that of the 'Christian Group', a specialist section within national CND, comparable with the Women's Group and the Scientists' Group.

82 BLPES, CND 1/7, Report of the Christian Group to National Council, 8 September 1963.

83 BLPES, CND 1/7, Christian Group circular (Simon Blake), September 1967.

84 Established in 1962. *The Rushlight*, No. 2, Summer 1964.

85 Sidney Hinkes, 'A marcher looks at the Gospels', *The Rushlight*, No. 6, Summer 1965.

86 *The Rushlight*, No. 2, Summer 1964. Fifty-five people carried 'The Complaint of Canterbury' from Southwark to Canterbury Cathedral, which ran:

ONE   That the vision of the Risen Christ has become blurred, because the Church has compromised with war, and because of this has left the Prince of Peace hanging on his cross.
TWO   That the Church fails to demand nuclear disarmament.
THREE   That the Church has no plan to cast out fear from the Nations.
FOUR   That the Church fails to release the power of the love of God.
FIVE   That the Church knows how to promote lasting peace; how to abolish famine; how to abolish poverty; how to cure diseases; how to change the lives of men and women, but it fails because of its own unbelief.

87 *The Rushlight*, No. 9, Spring 1966; Stanley Dyke, 'From the peace front', *The Christian Socialist*, No. 39, July–August, 1967, pp. 14–15.
88 Jack Bowles, 'CND church visiting', *The Rushlight*, No. 1, Winter 1964.
89 Charles Stimson, 'Obedience', quoting John Vincent speaking at Spode House, October 1964. *The Rushlight*, No. 4, Winter 1965.
90 CND Christian Group Newsletter, No. 2, October 1966. I must thank Barbara Eggleston, national organiser of Christian CND, for making this and other documents available to me at CND's national office.
91 G. Prins, *Defended to Death*, Ch. 4 *passim*, pp. 83–132.
92 H. Davis, 'The New Cold War', in H. Davis (ed.), *Ethics and Defence. Power and Responsibility in the Nuclear Age*, Oxford, 1986, pp. 173–87.
93 W. B. Johnston, 'The Churches' Role in the Nuclear Debate', in Davis, *Ethics and Defence*, pp. 241–56.
94 Bailey, *Christian Perspectives on Nuclear Weapons*, p. 52.
95 B. Eggleston (ed.), *Christian Initiatives in Peacemaking*, NACCCAN, Birmingham, 1983, pp. 3–4.
96 Johnston, 'The Churches' Role', p. 248.
97 Report of a Working Party under the Chairmanship of the Bishop of Salisbury, *The Church and the Bomb, Nuclear Weapons and Christian Conscience*, 1982, p. 160.
98 *Ibid.*, pp. 133, 139.
99 T. Dumper, 'Nuclear Weapons and the Quest for True Peace', in B. Kent *et al.*, *In God We Trust: Christian Reflections on the Nuclear Arms Race*, 1986, p. 12.
100 Sparked off by Johnson's article, 'Christians awake', in *The Times*, 29 January 1983.
101 Editor's introduction to F. Bridger (ed.), *The Cross and the Bomb, Christian Ethics and the Nuclear Debate*, London and Oxford, 1983, pp. 1–2.
102 Expressed in Harries's contribution to J. Gladwin (ed.), *Dropping the Bomb*, London, 1985, criticised by B. Eggleston, 'In God We Trust – A Question of Idolatry', in B. Kent *et al.*, *In God We Trust*, p. 51.
103 See, for example, M. Quinlan, 'The Meaning of Deterrence', in Bridger (ed.), *The Cross and the Bomb*, p. 148; and the criticisms made by B. Eggleston, 'In God We Trust', pp. 49–53.
104 Johnson, 'Christians awake'.
105 *The Church and the Bomb*, p. 162.
106 Information provided by Barbara Eggleston.
107 D. Pybus, 'Christian CND', in B. Eggleston, *Christian Initiatives in Peacemaking*, pp. 14–17.
108 Eggleston, 'In God We Trust', pp. 54–5.
109 *Ibid.*, p. 56.

110 Driver, *The Disarmers*, p. 214.
111 W. B. Johnston, 'The Churches' Role in the Nuclear Debate', in Davis, *Ethics and Defence*, p. 251.
112 Dumper, 'Nuclear Weapons and the Quest for True Peace', in B. Kent, *In God We Trust*, p. 12.
113 *The Era of Atomic Power*, pp. 66–7; *The Search for Security*, p. 43; *The British Nuclear Deterrent*, p. 41.

10

Women and peace: from the Suffragists to the Greenham women

JOSEPHINE EGLIN

Twice in the twentieth century women's actions for peace have made dramatic impact. In 1915 British Suffragists formed part of an International Congress of Women who met at the Hague, in an inspiring attempt to halt World War I.[1] In the 1980s members of the women's peace camp at Greenham Common have maintained a courageous opposition to the siting and use of Cruise missiles. Knowledge of the actions of women at Greenham Common has spread world-wide, as did that of the Suffragists at the Hague. These were not, however, isolated incidents and since 1915 there has always been a women's peace movement in Britain, although sometimes during the intervening years it has been relatively quiescent, and at all times its history has been inadequately recorded.

This chapter seeks to provide a necessarily brief account of British women in the Peace Movement, locating the specifically female tradition within the wider Movement. This will be combined with an investigation of the extent to which these women's activities throughout the century were informed by their perceptions of themselves as women, as mothers and as feminists. The ideas that women have a 'civilising mission' stemming from their motherhood role, and that there are particular female ways of looking at and dealing with conflict situations, will be examined. Both the institutional links between the female suffrage movement and the anti-war movement, and later between the Women's Liberation Movement (WLM) and the Peace Movement, and the theoretical relationships between feminism and pacifism,[2] will be investigated. An attempt will be made to assess the effectiveness of the women's actions, and the question of the future of their movement will be raised.

1 The first wave: The Women's Peace Movement 1915 to the 1930s

The period 1870–1914 has been described as the Golden Age of peace movements.[3] Most peace movements of this period were, however, due to the initiatives of men and had male leaders and executives. Women were more conspicuous in movements for social reform, socialist politics, and female suffrage. They were leaders of the Temperance Movement and of the campaign to combat the state regulation of prostitution. The Women's Trade Union League was founded in 1874, the Women's Co-operative Guild in 1883, and the Women's Labour League in 1906. Above all, women were working for female suffrage. In 1897 the National Union of Women's Suffrage Societies (NUWSS), the constitutional wing of the suffrage movement, was formed by the federation of existing suffrage societies having close links with the Liberal Party. By the twentieth century the NUWSS's more radical members had extended their programme to include demands for equal wages, job opportunities, and trade union representation for women. Some were also concerned to debate the role of women in the home, divorce, birth control, and child allowance. They had developed close connections with the Independent Labour Party (ILP), the Women's Co-operative Guild and the trade unions. These radical suffragists[4] comprised the executive of the NUWSS with the exception of the President, Millicent Fawcett, and the Treasurer, Margery Corbett Ashby. They were also very powerful amongst the rank and file in the north of England and in Scotland.[5] In 1903 the second largest female suffrage group, the militant Women's Social and Political Union (WSPU, or the Suffragettes) came together under Emmeline and Christabel Pankhurst. This group began its life with a socialist affiliation, but moved decisively towards the right after 1906. From 1909 onwards it adopted the tactic of violence against property.

The majority of these women's organisations, including the women's section of the ILP, the Women's Co-operative Guild and the female suffrage societies, expressed a strong commitment to peace during the opening years of the twentieth century, but they did not become actively involved in the Peace Movement prior to 1914. With the growing threat of the First World War, however, women began to translate their words into actions. In July 1914 leaders of the International Woman Suffrage Alliance (IWSA) delivered a manifesto to the Foreign Office and Foreign Embassies in London appealing for conciliation and arbitration to settle international differences. On 4 August 1914, the day that war was declared, a peace rally was organised by combined women's socialist, trade union, and suffrage organisations in Kingsway Hall, London.

Following the declaration of war, many of the existing peace groups fell into disarray. Socialist internationalists failed to organise the world-wide strike to prevent war and the majority supported their national governments.

The incipient women's peace movement was divided: some women greatly increased their activities for peace whilst others performed a *volte-face* and, sometimes reluctantly, sometimes eagerly, lent their support to the war effort. The NUWSS was split, with the radical Suffragists and Socialists committing themselves to peace, whilst Fawcett and other Liberals supported the war effort. Emmeline Pankhurst announced that her organisation would suspend all its activities for the duration. She and Christabel organised the 'Women's Right to Serve' march and made speeches on the need to combat the 'German Peril'.[6] Their supporters gave white feathers to young men not in uniform and demanded the internment of those of 'enemy race'. There were, however, a number of smaller militant groups and individuals who had broken away or been expelled from the WSPU in earlier years because they favoured more democratic forms of organisation, contact with the ILP, and less violent tactics. They included Charlotte Despard's Women's Freedom League, Sylvia Pankhurst's East End Federation of Suffragettes, and the unique Pethick-Lawrences, all of whom had held and continued to hold pacifist views.

It was, then, from the ranks of the suffrage movement and from the Labour party that a women's peace movement emerged as a distinct entity in Britain during the years of the First World War.

In November 1914 Emmeline Pethick-Lawrence toured America, which was still neutral, urging women's suffrage groups to unite in a world-wide 'women's war against war'. Pethick-Lawrence frequently spoke on the same platform as Rosika Schwimmer, leader of the Hungarian women's suffrage movement. Since the two were technically enemies, their joint appeal for peace was particularly poignant. They were instrumental in the establishment of the Women's Peace

Party in America which drew its membership largely from women's suffrage societies and from women social workers.

While Pethick-Lawrence was in America, Crystal Macmillan, Catherine Marshall and Kathleen Courtney were in Amsterdam. These three women had all been members of the executive of the NUWSS, but had resigned when Fawcett committed the organisation to supporting the war effort. They met with fellow Suffragists to arrange a Congress of Women to be held *in lieu* of the 1915 IWSA conference which had been cancelled because of the war. The Congress was held in April 1915. A total of 1,336 women Suffragists, social workers and Social Democrats from the Netherlands, America, Scandinavia, Germany, Hungary, Austria and Italy met at the Hague to express solidarity against the war and to discuss ways of ending it quickly and preventing future wars.

The women drew up a plan for an immediate halt to the fighting and the institution of a process of continuous mediation, with a neutral country like America as arbiter, to resolve the dispute. They sent two delegates to carry their resolutions to each of the belligerent and neutral countries. The envoys were politely received by statesmen in all countries, but their suggestions were ignored.[7]

Unwilling to abandon their plan, Schwimmer, Macmillan, Ethel Snowden – another member of the NUWSS executive who had resigned – and Aletta Jacobs – a member of the IWSA executive who was also the first woman doctor in the Netherlands – journeyed to America. There Snowden and Schwimmer organised a campaign involving 10,000 women's organisations, each of which sent a telegram to President Wilson asking him to support continuous mediation. On the day the telegrams were delivered Schwimmer and Snowden visited Wilson with the same request. Again they were rebuffed.

The women's activities received tremendous publicity, although much of it was of a critical nature. Many national papers reported rows and poor attendances at the Hague – accounts belied by the women's own reports – and vilified and condemned the women as traitors and pro-Germans.[8]

Before disbanding, the women at the Hague had established the International Committee of Women for Permanent Peace (ICWPP), later to be renamed the Women's International League for Peace and Freedom (WILPF). They agreed to return home and work in their own countries for peace, and to meet again after the war. At a conference in

Westminster in 1915, the British branch of the WILPF was established, incorporating thirty-four branches with between 2,000 and 3,000 members. Members produced pamphlets and organised public meetings all over Britain seeking to educate women for a future peace, to promote a future League of Nations and to organise relief work.[9] For this their telephones were tapped, their letters opened, public halls in London banned their meetings, and they suffered attacks by their pro-war opponents.

Obviously, only middle-class women could afford to travel to the Hague and America. In the north of England and in Scotland, however, another women's peace organisation emerged amongst the working-class women of the Labour Movement[10] and the radical northern suffrage societies. In June 1916 Agnes Dollan and Helen Crawford, both Socialists from Glasgow and members of the Women's Labour League, founded the radical, grass-roots Women's Peace Crusade (WPC). The WPC co-operated with local branches of the WIL and membership of the two organisations overlapped considerably. WIL members often spoke at WPC meetings: Charlotte Despard, in particular, worked extensively for the Crusade. The WPC organised anti-war demonstrations, especially in Yorkshire, Lancashire, and Scotland. Their activities too met with public hostility and their first leaflet, 'Casualties', was seized from the printers by the police.[11]

Sylvia Pankhurst, in addition to supporting WIL, organised her own East London Federation of Suffragettes into a pressure group for peace similar to the WPC. In April 1916 the Federation marched from the East End to Trafalgar Square to protest against the Second Military Service Act which was to extend conscription to married men. The women were attacked by soldiers who tore their banners, stormed their platform, and threw objects at them. In December 1916, following the announcement that Germany was prepared to negotiate peace because she feared American intervention in the war, Sylvia Pankhurst organised daily peace meetings in the East End. To advertise these meetings she distributed leaflets, chalked pavements and summoned her audience with a bell. Again, women attending these meetings were continually harassed: they were pelted with vegetable peelings and their platforms were pushed over.[12]

In 1919 WILPF members met again at Zurich in parallel with the statesmen meeting at Versailles. One hundred and fifty women assembled, twenty-six of them British women who had received passports from their government only after promising 'to indulge in no socialist propaganda'.[13] The WILPF was the first public body to criticise the Treaty of Versailles for its cruel reparations and the continued food blockade.

In the 1920s and early 1930s women's movements for peace increased in size and numbers as women determined that there should never be another war like that of 1914–18. The British section of WILPF had 4,000 members in fifty branches in 1919, and was growing. During the immediate post-war years the chief concerns of its members were to end the famine, to raise the food blockades, and to make the League of Nations a more representative body. In 1926 WILPF members organised a Women's Peace Pilgrimage modelled on the NUWSS pilgrimage of 1913: 10,000 women from all over the country converged on Hyde Park.[14] Similar local demonstrations were held in other parts of the country by women unable to travel to London.[15]

Both the WIL and the WPC had always drawn support from members of the Women's Co-operative Guild. This organisation, though always sympathetic towards peace and internationalism, had previously concentrated most of its own energies in attempts to alleviate the social hardships of the workers. As an organisation it began to work actively for peace in the 1920s. Its members sought an end to the arms trade, and disarmament by mutual consent. Guild members addressed themselves particularly to the possibilities of education for peace: they pressed local authorities to introduce 'peace days' in schools, with peace plays and addresses.[16]

Similarly, members of the women's section of the British Labour Party resolved in the inter-war era that internationalism should be promoted in every way in the hope of averting another war: they gave active support to the League of Nations, the study of Esperanto, and to all movements for international solidarity. Right up until the late 1930s, when rearmament began, they supported the German socialist women against Fascism.

In the summer of 1934, in response to the growing threat of Fascism, Women Against War and Fascism (WAWF) was established as the British section of the Women's World Committee Against War and Fascism. British sponsors included women from the Labour Party, the Co-operative Guild, the trade unions, and the Communist Party,[17] but they tried to make the charter appeal to as broad a range of women as possible irrespective of race, religion, or political party.[18] Their stated

aims included peace, freedom, the disbandment of all Fascist organisations, support for the League, rights of women and the conversion of
armaments production to production for social use.[19] They held
regular international congresses in Paris during the mid-1930s.

In addition to developing their own peace groups women had also
played an increasingly important role in those mixed peace initiatives
which had emerged between 1914 and 1918, in response to the particular problems of the war years.[20] Frequently the same women were
active in both women's and mixed groups. The No Conscription Fellowship was founded in 1914 by Fenner Brockway at the prompting of
his wife,[21] to mobilise men of military age against conscription. In
1916, when many of the original members had been imprisoned as
conscientious objectors, Marshall, aided by other Suffragists, took over
the secretaryship of the organisation. She was succeeded by Lilla Brockway. Lucy Gardner was a founder, and later took over the leadership, of
the Fellowship of Reconciliation (FOR), a Christian pacifist organisation founded in December 1914. Members included Maude Royden,
the pioneering woman preacher. Alice and Hetty Wheeldon, who were
members of the Derby Socialist Party, and had been members of the
WSPU, joined an underground network designed to help conscientious
objectors to escape.[22] Socialist and suffragist women played a leading
role in the Union of Democratic Control (UDC) during its most active
period from 1914 to 1925.

In the ensuing inter-war years women were active in the new mixed
groups which emerged alongside their own now flourishing peace
traditions. The NCF wound itself up in 1919 when all COs had been
released, but its predominantly ILP Socialist members established the
No More War Movement (NMWM) as its successor in 1920. This in
turn merged with the Peace Pledge Union (PPU) in 1936. The early
sponsors of the PPU, founded in 1934, with a philosophy mid-way
between that of FOR and the NMWM,[23] included the ex-Suffragette
Sybil Morrison, the ILP Socialist Ethel Mannin, Maude Royden and
Vera Brittain. Ellen Wilkinson, Storm Jameson, and Rose Macaulay
were also members. Royden was a prime mover in the instigation of the
short-lived Peace Army in February 1932.[24] Women were also active in
War Resisters' International (WRI) and in the League of Nations:
Marshall and Brittain were amongst the League's leading speakers.
Often these diverse groups would come together for joint actions.

2 Why a women's peace movement?

Although women had by no means eschewed mixed organisations for peace during the First World War, the 1920s and the 1930s, they had been conscious of certain practical advantages inherent in a movement specifically for women. They realised that the network of women's organisations which had grown up in the previous decades could greatly facilitate their attempts to obtain peace. In particular, the global network of the IWSA provided them with a world-wide platform from which to conduct their conciliation attempts.

Women's reasons for organising in exclusively female groups were not, however, confined to the practical. Women put forward at least four different ideological reasons why they felt that as women they had something special to contribute to the Peace Movement. These reasons were: their commitment to peace as physical mothers; their commitment by virtue of their conditioning in nurturing and caring roles; their position outside the major power hierarchies which enabled them to look critically at the latter; and their understanding of the interdependence of peace and the emancipation of women. Despite the apparently incompatible nature of some of these beliefs, they were not in practice regarded as mutually exclusive: many women expressed more than one, or even all four, views.

In the late nineteenth century a belief in their own moral transcendence rooted in their child-bearing and nurturing roles had informed women's activities for social reform. By the early twentieth century this widely accepted rhetoric had incorporated the view that women had a special commitment to ridding the world of war. Members of the female suffrage societies had reasoned, either from expediency or from a genuine belief, or possibly both, that women, thinking and acting as mothers, would use their vote to end war.

Ironically, when the war broke out many of these erstwhile female pacifists had displayed a dramatic change of heart. Inspired then by a combination of patriotism and expediency, they had replaced the argument that female enfranchisement would promote peace with the hope that their contribution to the war effort would prove an overwhelming case for female suffrage.[25] Notwithstanding this defection, those women who remained active for peace during the First World War continued to articulate their conviction of the moral superiority of women *qua* mothers, and of their consequent hatred of war. Pethick-Lawrence claimed that war was especially abhorrent to women because 'Women the world over have but one passion and one vocation – the creation and preservation of human life'.[26] Helena Swanwick, the leading theorist of the British WIL, argued in speeches and pamphlets that women were more revolted by war than were men because 'In war women do not see the good work of their guns, but babies who die of starvation and young lives destroyed, each one having cost the travail and care of a mother.'[27] When one woman at the Hague Congress questioned women's innate peacefulness she was aggressively hissed![28]

In the inter-war era this stance endured. Sylvia Pankhurst was almost a lone voice in arguing that the First World War itself had shown these beliefs to be unfounded: 'Gone was the mirage of a society regenerated by enfranchised womanhood as by a magic word . . . The profound divergences of war and peace had been shown to know no sex.'[29] For the majority of WIL members, however, the mirage had not gone, and they, along with members of the women's section of the British Labour Party, the Women's Co-operative Guild and WAWF, still reasoned that they were opposed to war by virtue of the instincts of motherhood.[30]

Nonetheless it is possible that women did not always intend claims to their unique commitment to peace on the basis of inherent sex differences to be taken literally. They may simply have been repeating the rhetoric of an earlier generation, making use of a powerful and emotive rallying call, or explaining the prime motivation – their concern for their children – which had drawn them as individuals into the peace movement. Certainly, Swanwick and others were not always consistent in their arguments, and on occasion gainsaid themselves. (In the same pamphlet in which she wrote of women leading the struggle for peace on account of their biological mothering functions, Swanwick also admitted that not all women were peace-loving.)[31]

Many women attempted to make positive use of their particular education and learned skills in food production, child-care, and health care to promote their wartime relief work. Sylvia Pankhurst organised a subsidised restaurant and nursery in the East End, whilst Eva Gore-Booth worked with German children, women and old people living in the north of England. At the same time women exploited their tradition of concern and sharing to combat the dominant warlike male stereotype. Marshall understood a close relationship between the use of women's learned nuturing skills and the special contribution which they could make towards ending war. She always ended her talks on relief work by urging women to strive for an atmosphere in which real peace could be made at the end of the war, and friendship established between the British and German people.[32]

Similarly, after the war, women in WIL and the Women's Co-operative Guild consciously availed themselves of their nurturing traditions in working for famine relief and peace education. In the 1930s members of WAWF repeatedly condemned the waste of money on armaments whilst families lacked adequate housing, health care and education.[33]

The idea of making deliberate use of the prescriptive female role was closely related to the argument that women, being excluded from the political and military status quo, would perforce view the latter more critically than men. Women pacifists reasoned that being in a structurally different position from men, with their experiences predominantly confined to the private sphere, women would experience contradictions between their own values and the dominant political and military ones. In particular, they reasoned that as non-combatants women had a special duty to assume the role of peace makers: 'It is much more difficult for men to meet in conference; they are in the silent armies. Women as non-combatants have this right, and as guardians of the race they have this duty'.[34]

Moreover, they argued that paradoxically, women's very exclusion from national arenas had enabled them to bypass those arenas and the struggles going on within them, and to commit themselves instead to a global union. Through organisations like the World Young Women's Christian Association, the World Women's Christian Temperance Union, the International Council of Women, the Women's Section of the Socialist International and the International Women's Suffrage Association, they had created systems of communication and action with their fellow women in other countries via non-governmental channels. Pethick-Lawrence expressed their consciousness of this: 'In our own and many countries the idea of the solidarity of women had taken a deep hold upon many of us: so deep that it could not be shaken off even by the fact that the men of many nations were at war.'[35]

It is significant that when world governments refused the women's appeal for a neutral mediation conference in 1915, the women set up a non-governmental conference of experts instead. The WILPF itself exemplified a new non-governmental global approach to international relations.

This argument that women, by virtue of their peripheral position in society, interpreted the world in a different way from men and had different values, was voiced with a new eloquence and urgency in the 1930s by Virginia Woolf. She accepted that women were opposed to war both by training and by the instincts of motherhood. Her main argument, however, was that men generally favoured war because they had a vested interest in fighting to maintain their positions and power. Women, on the other hand, being excluded from power, had no interested motives in war. They were therefore free from patriotism and unreal loyalties to their nation and were able to understand war as the barbarous institution it was. Woolf railed against men who claimed to be fighting to protect herself and her country. She argued that it was not 'her country' for she did not own its wealth, land or property, and would indeed become a foreigner were she to marry one. Moreover, she affirmed the sense of global solidarity which had been so remarkable amongst women active for peace during and since the First World War:

> If you insist upon fighting to protect me, or 'our' country, let it be understood soberly and rationally between us, that you are fighting to gratify a sex-instinct which I cannot share, to procure benefits which I have not shared and probably will not share; but not to gratify my instincts or to protect either myself or my country. For . . . in fact as a woman I have no country. As a woman I want no country. As a woman my country is the whole world.[36]

Woolf cautioned that as women entered public life they would have to take care to retain their humanity and their different sense of values. She concluded that although women were at one with men who formed societies to end war, still they should proceed independently and by different methods: 'Since we are different our help must be different . . . we can best help you to prevent war not by repeating your words and following your methods but by finding new words and creating new methods.'[37]

Woolf's cogent argument gained increasing popularity in the 1930s amongst members of the International Women's Co-operative Guild,[38] the Women's Labour League and the Women's World Committee Against War and Fascism. The latter emphasised that whilst the governments of many countries seemed bent on world suicide, the people, especially the women, were anxious for peace.[39] The presence of women from China, North Africa, Czechoslovakia, Switzerland, Holland, Britain, Belgium, Scandinavia, Spain, France and the Soviet

Union at their Paris Congress in July 1937, bore witness to their belief in the global solidarity of women.[40] The sense of sisterhood which existed between British and German members of the Committee was not destroyed even by the outbreak of the Second World War.[41]

Women also justified their 'different help' on the basis of the inter-dependence which they understood to exist between peace and the freedom of women. WILPF's very name expressed this belief, and its first constitution declared its objectives to be 'peace, internationalism, and the freedom of women'. Not only had the women's peace movement grown out of the infrastructure of the women's suffrage movement, but there were in addition important theoretical links between the two movements. The two planks of the Hague Congress to which all women had had to agree were that all disputes should be solved by pacific means and that parliamentary franchise should be extended to women. In her pamphlets Swanwick explained the Suffragists' belief that their freedom was bound up with the defeat of militarism. She drew analogies between militarism and anti-suffragism, arguing that militarism was the enthronement of physical force as an arbiter of nations, and women, being weaker than men, were in the same position as weak nations oppressed by belligerent ones. As long as the sanctions of brute force continued to dominate the world, men would continue to dominate women. Peace and the enfranchisement of women would go together because they both represented the control of physical by moral force. Therefore 'Each suffrage society ought to be a pacifist society, and realise that pacifist propaganda is an integral part of suffrage propaganda. If there are some suffragists who do not yet see this, they are matched by some pacifists who do not see that their creed removes the only obstacle to the enfranchisement of women.'[42]

When Suffragists talked of freedom they naturally emphasised the freedom of women, but they were conscious that this was only one of many freedoms. Marshall, for example, always envisaged her work for peace, women's suffrage and socialism as part of the same struggle for liberty. She always hoped that the example of the conscientious objectors with whom she worked would act as a catalyst for an international socialist revolution. Like many socialist–pacifists she identified with the Russian Revolution of March 1917. The Revolution had begun with the opposition of workers and peasants to war and its concomitant militarism, hunger and death.[43] For some months Marshall hoped that the same revolt against war and militarism would sweep across Britain.[44] Members of the WPC shared this hope: in July 1917, 14,000 people gathered on Glasgow Green to acclaim the peace policy of the new Russian regime, and similar meetings were held elsewhere. The Revolution itself, however, became militarised as the Civil War led to the creation of the Red Army and the instigation of war Communism. At first seen as a temporary necessity, this quickly subverted socialism–pacifism in Russia, and a total distinction was made between imperialist and revolutionary war.[45]

Despite this disappointment, the tradition which recognised socialism, women's emancipation and peace as interdependent, survived the inter-war years in Britain, finding expression amongst members of WILPF and WAWF. The latter emphasised the links between Fascism and war, and the threat which Fascism posed to women's rights.[46]

It may be, however, that the failure of socialist–pacifism in Russia influenced those women pacifists who during the inter-war years began to place a more exclusive emphasis on feminist–pacifism, hinting that there was something fundamental in the relationship between the particular freedom of women (as opposed to that of any other oppressed group) and peace. Woolf widened the analogy which Swanwick had drawn between militarism and the oppression of women,[47] and she described militarism as an expression of patriarchy,[48] but she did not develop this. Only Dora Russell in Britain in the 1920s attempted to pursue this argument. In 1922, following a trip to Russia, and acutely conscious of the dangers of the lack of understanding between East and West, Russell wrote that a dominant 'male ideology' was responsible for promoting the inhuman political structures of patriarchal society which underpinned war and militarism. Discussion of partriarchy evoked little response, however, at this time and Russell did not take up the theme again until the 1980s.[49]

3 The Second World War and after: the decline of the independent women's peace tradition

The advance of Fascism challenged all branches of the Peace Movement as members sought a means to reconcile their opposition to war with their abhorrence of totalitarianism.

Between 1934 and 1935 hopes of avoiding military entanglement by internationalism and collective security remained high, especially amongst members of the League of Nations.[50] Later, when doubts spread about the efficacy of the League, hopes were transferred to economic sanctions and non-violent resistance.[51] During the early 1930s many peace groups had studied theories of non-violent resistance which had been developed by Gandhi in India and popularised in the West through the works of Gregg[52] and de Ligt.[53] Between 1936 and 1937, therefore, some members of the PPU, WRI, WILPF, and WAWF advocated the imposition of moral, diplomatic and economic sanctions against aggressor nations. WAWF repeatedly appealed for the boycott of Japanese goods – especially silk stockings.[54] The possibility of a wider application of the boycott was never seriously considered, however, and many members of peace societies acknowledged that they did not know enough nor have enough power in the world to persuade people that non-violent methods could work.[55]

By 1939, with the rise of Fascism, the experience of the Spanish Civil War and the growing menace of Hitler, general support for pacifism had declined in Britain. However, there is some indication that a continuing commitment to pacifism may have been more widespread amongst women than amongst men during the late 1930s[56] and the early years of the war. Brittain, Morrison and Kathleen Lonsdale were conspicuous amongst those who remained morally committed to absolute pacifism even after 1939. A special Women's Peace Campaign was instigated by Morrison and Mary Gamble to stop the war and organise a negotiated peace. This campaign reached a peak in March 1940.[57] Between 1938 and 1948, Morrison spoke for the PPU every Monday at Tower Hill . . . except when she was in prison. Lonsdale was also imprisoned because of her refusal to undertake compulsory fire-watching.[58]

Mannin abandoned her anti-militarism in her enthusiasm for the Republican cause in Spain, but later reverted to strict pacifism.[59] Similarly, WAWF members reasoned that in the circumstances the only way to preserve liberty in Spain was, through the use of force, to destroy Fascism. From 1937 onwards they organised aid for the Republicans fighting Fascism in Spain and condemned the government policy of non-intervention there which allowed large numbers of innocent people to be slaughtered, and which increased the threat of European war.[60] They condemned the Munich Settlement as paving the way for future threats and conquests by Fascist states.[61] When Britain finally entered the war in 1939, however, they argued that entry came too late, and for base motives. Their suspicions were that the Government was not fighting for democracy, as it might have done in Spain, but for the profits of armaments manufacturers. Therefore they opposed conscription and criticised the conduct of the war.[62] They condemned both the British and theGerman governments for making a war in which the poor of both countries suffered. On 31 January 1940 they organised a Stop the War meeting at Kingsway Hall.[63] They were met with the accusation that WAWF was a Communist Front Organisation,[64] and after February 1940 their periodical, *Women Today,* was suspended.

In contrast to the situation in 1918, the decline in membership of the Peace Movement continued and even accelerated in the immediate post-Second World War years. The focus and some of the urgency of wartime pacifists was lost.[65] Keynesian techniques of economic management had apparently secured full employment and economic growth at home; and Socialists were disillusioned by the conduct of Soviet Russia[66] and the Cold War. The Peace Movement, socialism and feminism were all in decline.[67] The position of women was compounded by the fact that after 1945 the Government was anxious to find jobs for men returning from the front and manufacturers were eager to turn women into consumers of their new products. Social pressure and advertising propaganda located women firmly in the domestic context. Of all the radical traditions, feminism was consequently the last to recover, and during the ensuing two decades women ceased to be so conspicuous in public life, and the women's movement and the independent women's peace tradition virtually disappeared.

The most prominent peace group of the early post-war years was the British Peace Committee, which in 1950 organised the Stockholm Peace Appeal, demanding the unconditional prohibition of nuclear weapons. Many were, however, blind to the merits of this appeal because it was backed by the Communist-led World Peace Council.[68]

When peace groups did manage to maintain their traditions during these bleak years they represented one of the few areas of public life where women were actively involved. In 1948 Morrison was appointed organiser of a new PPU recruitment campaign.[69] Between 1948 and 1952 she held outdoor meetings at Lincoln's Inn every Thursday, as well as organising rallies in Trafalgar Square and in provincial towns. Myrtle Solomon became the London area organiser of the PPU, whilst Lonsdale concentrated on drawing attention to the inadequacy of civil defence. Brittain and Mannin also worked extensively for the PPU and for the World Disarmament Campaign.

It was not until 1956–58, however, that a widespread new idealism, combined with political interest and will crystallised around the Campaign for Nuclear Disarmament (CND) and the Direct Action Committee (DAC). A new peace tradition emerged whose members, reacting against the specific horrors of nuclear war, were often nuclear pacifists rather than absolute pacifists.[70] Women were again prominent in these new peace groups.

Gertrude Fishwick was the effective founder of CND. Fishwick, a member of the Labour Party and an ex-Suffragette, heard about the radiation risks from H-Bomb tests at a meeting of her local Women's Co-operative Guild. She established a local Committee for the Abolition of Nuclear Weapons Tests. Other committees followed and merged in 1957 to form the National Council for the Abolition of Nuclear Weapons Tests (NCANWT). Members included Pat Arrowsmith, April Carter and Peggy Duff, who organised 2,000 women with black sashes and flags to march from Hyde Park to Trafalgar Square in protest against these tests. In 1958, when it was decided to form a mass movement against nuclear weapons, rather than just nuclear weapons tests, NCANWT transferred its staff and funds to the new body – CND.

In the early years CND was dominated by Bertrand Russell, Canon Collins and Peggy Duff, who has been described as 'the mainspring of C.N.D. in so far as any one person could be'.[71] Duff was the organising Secretary of CND throughout the years 1958–67. Other women holding major offices in the Movement were Olive Gibbs who was Chairman (sic) from 1964 to 1967, Sheila Oakes who held this position from 1967 to 1968 and April Carter from 1970 to 1971.

The DAC (which is discussed in some detail in Chapter 7) organised a number of obstructions at nuclear bases, and the first march to Aldermaston at Easter 1958. Duff managed to persuade other CND members to support this march, and from 1959 onwards CND took over its organisation. Prominent amongst DAC organisers were Arrowsmith, who organised the first Aldermaston march, and April Carter, who was Secretary of the DAC between 1958–61 and the major theorist of the movement.[72] (Both she and Arrowsmith were active in the Committee of 100 from 1960 to 1962/63. The Committee is, again, discussed in some detail in Chapter 7.)

Despite the revival of radical peace traditions and of New Left socialism, and despite the leading role assumed by women in mixed peace groups, feminism was still dormant and there were few specifically female initiatives for peace during the years following the Second World War.

The WIL continued to exist but its membership was much diminished for not only had the Second World War caused many resignations but many of the original WIL members were now very old and some had died. Nonetheless WIL members, joined by Women for World Disarmament, a branch of the World Disarmament Campaign, continued their activities of research, the distribution of information and lobbying for disarmament.

In 1958 Dora Russell organised a Women's Peace Caravan to tour East and West Europe for twelve months. In the same year Jacquetta Hawkes organised the Women's Committee of CND and they held their first all-women rally in June 1959. The Women's Committee and the Women's Co-operative Guild were together responsible for exposing the inadequacy and inaccuracies of civil defence lectures being propounded by Women's Voluntary Service (WVS) speakers. Olive Gibbs had attended one of these lectures – which urged women to whitewash their windows and stack up sandbags during the four-minute warning which would precede a nuclear attack – in response to an invitation brought home from school by her son. Gibbs and Antoinette Pirie – an expert on fall-out – compiled a memorandum, which was circulated by the Women's Co-operative Guild, comparing what the WVS said with reality. They then consulted with the Atomic Scientists Committee of the British Association, which offered an accurate series of lectures for WVS speakers. The Women's Committee of CND organised a deputation to present this offer to Lady Reading (Chairman of the WVS) but she refused to see them.[73]

In 1961, in response to the Berlin Crisis, the Women's Committee organised a demonstration of 800 Women Against the Bomb outside the Russian and American Embassies. At the same time Judith Cook founded Voice of Women, and in the ensuing years several other women's groups emerged.

The actions of these groups were, however, on a smaller scale than those of women pacifists between 1915 and the late 1930s, and female peace groups did not emerge in large numbers again until the late 1970s.

4 A mothers' movement

It comes as no particular surprise, in the absence of a strong feminist tradition, to discover that when women did organise *qua* women for peace during the years following the Second World War, their motivation was either practical or else expressed almost exclusively in terms of women's particular concern for their children. The popular pre-war beliefs that women, because they stood outside the political arena, were more clear-sighted than men, and that peace and the freedom of women were interdependent, were no longer voiced.

In 1945, WILPF members rejected a suggestion that their organisation should be dissolved because peace and freedom were not the specific concerns of women. Their rejection, however, was based on the grounds that WILPF had long international experience and influence combined with a comprehensive programme, and that nothing should be done to weaken the Peace Movement, and on the grounds that women's co-operation was required in building a world in which 'children may grow up safely and happily'.[74] There was no mention of the relationship between peace and the freedom of women which had been such a vital consideration for the Suffragists who founded WILPF.

Similarly, in the 1950s Dora Russell stressed her belief in the life-preserving and nurturing functions of women, but found no opportunity to discuss the connections between feminism and peace.

The Women's Committee of CND always stressed that theirs was an emotional and moral response to nuclear weapons.[75] Warning women of the genetic dangers of radiation, Winifred de Kok said, 'you should not listen to the arguments at all but follow your feelings. Every woman knows that a deformed baby is a tragedy which she would not wish on any other woman.'[76] The protest organised by this group outside the Russian and American Embassies in 1961 was exclusively a mothers' protest.

Judith Cook, herself a young mother, founded Voice of Women in response to 1,000 letters, mainly from other women with children,[77] again expressing their concern specifically as mothers. Cook herself defined the typical VOW member, not in terms of her own achievements, but in terms of her husband and children: '(she) would be about thirty, with perhaps two children at school and a baby, married to a teacher . . .'.[78]

Similarly, the prominent female activists in large, mixed peace groups did not express any understanding of a relationship between peace and feminism. Duff, Arrowsmith and Carter did not act specifically as women or as feminists. Duff was herself openly sceptical of feminism.[79] Carter, when she talked of the interdependence of peace and freedom, emphasised, like Duff, freedom from capitalism, colonialism and racism, but did not mention the oppression of women.[80] Even Arrowsmith, who was a feminist, found little opportunity, during these years, to discuss the relationship between war and the oppression of women (except in her novel – *Jericho* (London, 1965)).

The absence of a feminist tradition, the residue of the wider conservatism of 1948–56/7, meant that there was an unsympathetic climate towards the expression of any feminist sentiment, including a feminist position on peace. Thus women organising independently still defined themselves exclusively in terms of their motherhood. It was not until after the revival of the feminist movement in the late 1960s that a new period of female activism heralded the re-emergence of a significant female peace tradition as opposed to a small and sporadic mothers' movement.

5 The second wave: the women's peace movement in the 1980s

Throughout the 1960s women remained prominent in mixed peace groups like the PPU and CND, but there was no significant, independent female peace tradition. During this decade, however, a new Women's Movement was gestating.

In 1963, in America, Betty Friedan expressed the discontent of middle-class women deprived of equal economic and political rights with men.[81] Her supporters formed the National Organisation of Women to lobby for an Equal Rights Amendment. The Women's Liberation Movement (WLM), the more radical branch of the Women's Movement, also emerged first in America. Activist women were disillusioned by their treatment in the peace, civil rights and anti-Vietnam War movements. They had discovered a discrepancy between the egalitarian rhetoric of the New Left, and the sex-role divisions within it. When they reacted against this they were variously ignored, insulted and physically attacked.[82] WLM groups sprang up as women attempted to analyse and overcome this treatment.

By 1969 similar groups had emerged in Britain, stimulated partly by the American example, and partly by British women's own experience in male-dominated movements. As in America, women had found that even within the supposedly radical left-wing groups, which took on a new lease of life after 1968, their demands for an equal role were ignored. This applied in academe, in political parties and on the shop floor.[83]

Two main groups were distinguished within WLM in the early 1970s: the radical feminists who interpreted women's oppression as the primary form of oppression, and the socialist feminists who were convinced of the primary importance of Marx's analysis of class conflict.[84]

The years 1968–75 were comparable with the 1900s in that both were times when women concentrated upon their own emancipation, although they differed in the breadth of women's demands. In the later period demands for contraception, abortion, nurseries and a different personal life-style – in addition to equal pay and equal work – were voiced by the majority of WLM adherents rather than by just a small minority of radical Suffragists.

As in the 1900s, although nominally committed to peace, women *qua* women and feminists were not actively involved in the Peace Movement between 1968 and 1975. Indeed, many feminists expressed some reluctance to act on what they interpreted as the 'male issues' of war and militarism until after they had achieved their own emancipation.

In the late 1970s the series of events which led to the resurrection of the mass, anti-nuclear Peace Movement heralded also the revival of the women's peace tradition, just as the threat of the First World War had spurred women to action in 1914.

By no means all the women's peace groups which sprang up were initiated by members of the Women's Movement, but it seems unlikely that they would have proliferated to the same extent without the political consciousness generated amongst women as a result of a decade of experience in WLM, and without the atmosphere of renewed female activity generated by that movement.

In the early 1980s branches of Women for Peace, an organisation first formed in the Netherlands as *Vrouwen Voor Vrede,* sprang up throughout Britain. Members were committed to disarmament, especially of nuclear weapons.[85] Branches of WIL which had been on the point of closing down suddenly found themselves with new members.[86]

In 1980 Marie Bowland made a dramatic round-the-world journey to talk with other women about peace.[87] Two pensioners, Marian Mansurgh and Lucy Behenna, pooled their life savings to send two groups of four Mothers for Peace to the USA and the USSR respectively to press for peace. Since then annual exchanges of Mothers for Peace have taken place.[88] Manchester Women's Movement for Peace and Oxford Mothers for Nuclear Disarmament began to organise local women's activities in 1981. Nationally, Babies Against the Bomb and Families Against the Bomb were founded in 1982.

The International Feminism and Non-violence Study Group (IFNV) first came together in France in 1976, and its members held a conference at Laurieston, Scotland, in August 1980. Women Oppose Nuclear Threat (WONT) grew directly out of WLM: the first WONT group was founded by Erika Dwek of Leeds WLM in 1980, and WONT groups have since proliferated in other towns.[89] Members often use street theatre to communicate their message.

International Women's peace marches were organised by Scandinavian Women for Peace from Copenhagen to Paris and from Copenhagen to Minsk in 1981 and 1982 respectively.

The most dramatic and influential of all women's activities for peace in the 1980s was the establishment and maintenance of the Greenham Common Women's Peace Camp. During August–September 1981 the eco-feminist group Women for Life on Earth (WFLOE) organised a march from Cardiff to the US airbase at Greenham Common, in Newbury, Berkshire. They were protesting against the proposed siting of Cruise missiles there. Their march was largely ignored by the media, and, unwilling to accept this, some of the marchers spontaneously decided to establish a camp at Greenham. The march to Greenham and the original camp were women's initiatives, but the camp did not become 'women only' until February 1982. On 21 March 1982, against a background of threats of eviction by Newbury District Council, women organised a festival at Greenham which both men and women attended. The following day a twenty-four-hour women-only blockade took place. In May the Council attempted to evict the women and their camp was razed to the ground by bulldozers. The women moved to Ministry of Transport Land 100 yards from the main gate of the airbase. Women were arrested and imprisoned for 'breach of the peace'! In September 1982 a second attempt at eviction, this time by the Ministry of Transport, left the women without caravans or tents, so they continued to live in the open. They organised direct actions both at

Greenham and elsewhere, including a 'Die-In' outside the Stock Exchange in June 1982. On 12 December 1982, at least 30,000 women converged on the Greenham base to encircle the nine-mile fence, and the following day there was another blockade. On New Year's Day 1983 women climbed the perimeter fence and danced on missile silos. Throughout that year, living in the open, women continued to scale the fences, blockade military personnel, and to keep Greenham in the public eye. After the arrival of the missiles in December 1983 they maintained their presence and, notwithstanding many arrests, they have been alert to blockade and track convoys every time the missiles are taken out on exercises.[90]

Like the women at the Hague in 1915, the women at Greenham managed to turn an initial indifference by the media into headline news. Again, as in 1915, media reports were mixed, and whilst some newspapers praised the courage and objectives of the women, others condemned them as traitors and pro-Russians, or evaded the issue entirely by writing only about their clothes and conditions at the camp.[91] Similarly, whilst benefiting from many support groups, women at Greenham were also, like women pacifists in the First World War, subject to verbal and physical attacks by vigilante groups.[92]

As women's peace groups and *ad hoc* activities again became a major phenomenon within the Peace Movement, the Women's Peace Alliance was established in November 1981. The Alliance recognised the value of diversity within the Women's Peace Movement and sought to co-ordinate the various groups, to liaise between them, and to provide an information network, support, advice and publicity functions.

In addition to its success in attracting both publicity and persecution, the Women's Peace Movement of the 1980s was again comparable with that of the First World War, the 1920s and the 1930s in that its members were frequently middle-class. Inevitably, middle-class women were the ones with the leisure and the economic security which enabled them to work for peace. As earlier in the century, however, this tendency was by no means universal, and from the beginning women in the 1980s worked to break down this barrier.[93]

Members of the new Women's Peace Movement, like those of earlier in the century, frequently had a leading role in mixed, as well as women only, peace groups. The political situation of the late 1970s had not only revitalised women's peace groups, but existing mixed groups whose membership had been ebbing in the late 1960s and early 1970s also took on a new lease of life.[94] In 1980 national membership of CND doubled,[95] and women like Meg Beresford, and Joan Ruddock, who was Chairperson from 1981 to 1985, continued to play a prominent role. In 1980 European Nuclear Disarmament (END) was formed to provide an international response to an international threat.[96] Its founding committee included Mary Kaldor of the Armament and Disarmament Information Unit at Sussex University. Joint actions were sometimes organised between mixed and women only groups, for example the human chain formed from Burghfield through Aldermaston to Greenham at Easter 1983.

6 The ideological revival

The similarities between the first and second wave of the Women's Peace Movement also included women's reasons for organising independently.

In the 1980s, as earlier, this independent organisation was often only a matter of convenience or strategy rather than one of principle. Groups such as Oxford Mothers for Nuclear Disarmament, Families Against the Bomb, and Babies Against the Bomb came together as women's groups partly because only in that way were they able to meet at times of day suitable for the mothers of young children and to provide facilities for those children.[97] Others came together as women because they sought a chance to develop their own skills, strength, and confidence, and to draw into the Peace Movement women who had not previously been involved in politics. Both these objectives, they believed, were best achieved in a supportive, non-competitive atmosphere without men.[98] The Greenham Women considered it politic to resist the involvement of men in direct actions like the blockades, on the basis that there was a reduced possibility of violent attacks by the police and of violent responses by the demonstrators themselves if men were not involved.[99]

Often, however, ideological rationale replaced what had earlier been a tactical decision as women began to experience the benefits of organising alone.[100] Women then put forward the same ideological reasons for organising autonomously as they had done early in the century. Again, not all their proponents regarded these reasons as being mutually exclusive. They are discussed separately here only as a matter of convenience.

Perhaps surprisingly, against the background of an active Women's

Movement, the view that women as biological mothers have a special concern for peace retained its popularity in the 1980s.[101] When pressed, many women have qualified this view, though clearly their concern for their children's future, combined with the hardships which they and their children suffered as a result of government spending on warfare rather then welfare, was frequently their prime motivation for becoming involved in the Peace Movement.

The view that, although they are not inherently peace-orientated, women have something positive to offer the Peace Movement by virtue of the nurturing skills which they have learned in the home, was widely adopted by socialist feminists in the 1980s.[102] They reasoned that by virtue of their conditioning women were less aggressive and more caring than men. At Greenham, women deliberately promoted those emotional caring qualities traditionally labelled 'feminine' and 'inferior',[103] developing an atmosphere of co-operation, mutual support and creativity. The most remarkable expression of these qualities came at the Greenham demonstration in December 1982 referred to earlier. The women surrounded the base and decorated the perimeter fence with photographs, children's toys, paintings and craft-work. In late afternoon candles were lit and women spontaneously began to walk around the base or to gather in groups to sing.

As earlier in the century, the belief that gender role socialisation conditioned women away from militarism and war was closely linked with the idea that being largely excluded from positions of power in the state, in industry, in science and in the military, women could view these hierarchies more critically than men. The women who marched to Greenham stressed that this exclusion gave them a special role to play in opposing nuclear weapons.[104] Moreover, women suggested that as a result of this very exclusion they had been especially successful in developing organisational forms and methods which were particularly suited to the promotion of peace.

In 1914 this had been manifested mainly through women's commitment to a global unity bypassing national loyalties and differences. This element was still present in the 1980s: WILPF maintained its global network; the IFNV conference at Laurieston in 1980 was attended by women from fourteen countries; and Women for Peace developed branches in Britain, Switzerland, Denmark, Norway, Sweden, Germany, Italy and Finland. The women's peace marches from Copenhagen to Paris and Minsk spoke of a commitment to trans-nationalism.

The activities of Mothers for Peace and Marie Bowland represented deliberate atempts to break down national barriers. Greenham women have travelled and lectured all over the world: in 1983 alone women from the camp visited Belfast, Comiso in Sicily, America and Hungary. In return, women of all nationalities have been attracted to Greenham, and the Greenham example has stimulated the establishment of new camps world-wide. It should not, of course, be assumed that globalism has ever been peculiar to women: both international Socialists in the earlier period and END members in the later, have shared this commitment. Women do, however, have a good case for arguing that they have been particularly successful in building up non-governmental contacts all over the world.

In addition, women in the 1980s developed local grass-roots actions not only as a practical means of involving more women in individual villages and towns, but also in conscious opposition to their exclusion from power at the national level. Such activities, for example the peace picnics of Oxford Mothers for Nuclear Disarmament and the street theatre of Nottingham WONT, mirrored the local actions of the WPC and the Women's Co-operative Guild in the 1920s.

Women's International Day of Disarmament, celebrated annually since 1982 on 24 May, is a tribute to both the transnationalism and the localism of the Women's Peace Movement. Activities like one-day strikes, the wearing of armbands, rallies, vigils, prayers and phone-ins are organised by *ad hoc* groups of women and individuals in towns, villages and communities world-wide.[105] The web has become a symbol of the networking which draws together and strengthens the activities of local groups throughout the world:

> A web with a few threads is weak and can be broken, but the more threads it is composed of, the greater its strength. It makes a very good analogy for the way in which women have rejuvenated the peace movement. By connections made through many diverse channels, a widespread network has grown up of women committed to working for peace.[106]

Thirdly, in the 1980s many women in the Peace Movement adopted the democratic methods of organisation developed by WLM. Believing that means relate to ends, the latter had always favoured small, democratic, decentralised egalitarian groups with no permanent officers and with an emphasis on participation and adaptability. The acceptance of leaders, hierarchies, and bureaucracies would have implied a movement concerned to seize power and to become part of the very dominance structure which they were seeking to eliminate. Their priority was to develop the self-confidence and autonomy of the women involved, not their unquestioning obedience to received wisdom.[107] Like members of WLM, women in the peace movement did not argue that these forms of organisation were unique to themselves,[108] but that no one had ever promoted them so successfully before. This success, they reasoned, stemmed from their virtual exclusion from, and consequent lack of commitment to, traditional power hierarchies. Many members of WONT had been involved in mixed groups like CND where they had become frustrated with 'male methods' of organising. In WONT by contrast, they met as equals in small groups without rigid structures or officers and they reached decisions by consensus.[109] Similarly, the women of Greenham felt that their very lack of structure was their greatest strength. They believed it was conducive to trust, co-operation, and achievement. They reasoned that bureaucratic institutions on the other hand promoted role-playing and wastage of energies and talents: 'We don't have a steering committee or hierarchy or all that kind of thing. My C.N.D. group did and spent most of its time organising jumble sales and never doing anything.'[110] Whilst this picture is by no means representative of all branches of CND, and whilst not all women experienced frustration with CND hierarchy, this reaction against bureaucracy in mixed peace groups was sufficiently widespread to merit quotation.

The events of 12 and 13 December 1982 at Greenham illustrated the success of decentralised organisation. Leaflets about the proposed gathering were sent to Greenham supporters who photocopied them and sent them on. As a result the base was surrounded in a mass demonstration, followed the next day by blockades organised by autonomous groups of women at the different gates. Many sympathisers who had previously been critical of the Greenham Women's methods of decentralised organisation now changed their minds.[111] Even those women's peace groups which were not specifically feminist adopted the methods of organisation popularised amongst women by WLM, and avoided leaders and committees in favour of shared jobs and ideas.[112] Indeed, members of mixed groups suggested that they too could learn from the values of WLM.[113]

In the 1980s, as in 1915, the Women's Peace Movement had roots in the women's own movement: WONT, like WILPF, had grown directly out of the Women's Movement, and just as the infrastructure and skills of the Women's Suffrage Movement had been at the command of women at the Hague, so the political experience and forms of organisation of WLM had benefited women's peace groups in the 1980s. Moreover, as earlier in the century, the links between the two movements were not only institutional but also theoretical: belief in the interdependence of peace and the freedom of women was widespread amongst female peace activists in the 1980s.

During the 1970s the concept of patriarchy had been incorporated into feminist theory in an attempt to describe and analyse the principles underlying and maintaining women's subordination as a sex. Increasingly, between 1968 and 1975, radical feminists in particular had emphasised the way in which violence, and more especially the threat and fear of violence (for example the threat and fear of rape), were used to keep women in a subordinate position. From this emerged their interpretation of patriarchy as itself a system of violence against women, incorporating both the physical violence of rape and wife-beating, and the psychological or structural violence of social and familial oppression. The interpretation of female subjugation in these terms had led many feminists to the adoption of a pacifist position by the 1980s: war and militarism had ceased to be 'male issues'.

Women at the IFNV Conference in 1980 reasoned, like Swanwick in 1915, 'we see our stand against violence, exploitation and injustice, as the basis of our feminist–pacifism and our anti-militarist-feminism'.[114] They produced a considerable volume of literature investigating the relationship between feminism and non-violence.[115] They argued that the oppression of women, both overtly via increases in the incidence of rape, and covertly via their representation in pornographic films, was more likely to occur in a warlike atmosphere. Similarly, WONT members regarded their demonstrations outside recruiting centres and those outside cinemas showing pornography as part of the same struggle against violence and oppression.

Feminist–pacifists did not ignore the fact that militarism, for example as manifested in the nuclear arms race, oppressed and exploited all minorities. And, like Marshall during the First World War, they recognised the interdependence of peace, feminism and socialism: 'Peace isn't just about removing a few pieces of war furniture, or bringing about an international ceasefire; it is about the condition of our lives. Peace is the absence of greed and domination by a few over the rest of us.'[116]

Nonetheless, radical feminist–pacifists did place particular emphasis on the relationship between war and the oppression of women, and increasingly they reasoned that there was something fundamental about patriarchal oppression. They reasoned that men's control over women by the threat and fear of violence, and the consequent promotion of the aggressive male stereotype over the female one, cut across all society and was the paradigm of all dominance and submission. The women's peace movement thus represented a widening of the feminist struggle:

> The nuclear industry is the epitome of the patriarchal state. The decision to go ahead with the nuclear programme was made by men in traditional male ways of thinking and working. Women were not considered or consulted. It seems to me that this is an extreme example of the way women are expected to 'support their men and family', to maintain the nuclear family, to be silent victims on the receiving end of decisions which some man has decided are right for us.[117]

A just and peaceful world could only be achieved after the violent patriarchal ideology had first been eradicated and changes had been made in human relations so that the dominance of one sex over the other was eliminated.[118]

This view achieved growing popularity as many women who had entered the Peace Movement motivated by their concern for their children's future, found that as feminist–pacifist theory evolved their own views developed along with it. Many of the women who contacted Angela Phillips when she was organising the original march to Greenham stressed that they were not feminists. Indeed Phillips expressed her own doubt at the time as to whether the nuclear issue was a feminist one,[119] and she sought to avoid alienating anyone by organising a specifically feminist event. Nonetheless by the time the final handout for the march was produced it read:

> We see the development of all weapons of mass destruction as a product of a hierarchical and militarist society which is based on competition and aggression. Compassion and consideration for the needs of others are labelled as 'feminine' qualities and are therefore seen as irrelevant to the real world. Men are encouraged to be 'detached' and objective and this further promotes a war mentality. . . . We see the nuclear issue as a feminist issue.[120]

From February 1982 onwards this belief was increasingly acclaimed at Greenham.

Radical feminists opposed the patriarchal system rather than men as individuals. They stressed that in organising in separate groups they were not writing off men as peacemakers. They sought to combine the tenderness and compassion traditionally associated with women, with the assertion and competence traditionally associated with men. At the same time they wanted to avoid both the violence and the passivity respectively associated with the two gender roles. Few women in the Peace Movement in Britain adopted the revolutionary feminist position, which went further in attributing violence to men as individuals and whose exponents sought the elimination or suppression of men *per se*.

The expression of militarism as a function of patriarchy invoked a language which was virtually unheard in Britain prior to the flowering of the WLM in the 1970s.[121] This popular new mode of expression did not, however, represent a totally new argument in support of specifically female activities for peace. Rather it was a restatement of old arguments in new language. The biological reductionism of the revolutionary feminists in viewing men as inherently violent exactly mirrored the belief in women's inherent peacefulness expressed throughout the century by those who emphasised women's moral superiority based on their biological motherhood. The radical feminists' denial that men were inherently violent left their theory of war as an expression of patriarchy as merely a re-statement of the old arguments, that by virtue of their training and position in society men and women view war and peace in different lights.[122]

British women active for peace in the 1980s differed from those of the First World War, the 1920s and the 1930s in their vocabulary, with their much wider use of terms such as patriarchy; in their wider interpretation of the freedom of women to include a critique of the nuclear family,[123] in their knowledge of the theory and practice of nonviolence; and in their non-hierarchical methods of organisation learned from their experience in WLM. Their essential reasons for organising as women for peace did not, however, change.

7 Inconclusive evidence and controversial statements

Only by making very selective use of the empirical evidence can it be argued that the caring, peace-loving virtues are, for any reason, more apparent in women. It is true that, although there have been exceptions, women have not led military states nor initiated wars to the extent that men have done. On the other hand, women have sanctioned wars as readily as men and women's 'nurturance' has often consisted in raising patriotic sons to fight and die for their country rather than to counteract militarism. Many women opposed the pacifist position of their sons in the First World War, and the campaign of handing out white feathers was initiated by Emmeline Pankhurst. Women's enfranchisement, as Sylvia Pankhurst acknowledged, brought none of the promised changes for peace.

Similar ambiguities exist in the assumption that women may be more critical of the status quo on account of their virtual exclusion from centres of power. Women are not the only outsiders: exclusion from high office is a function of class, colour, and race, as well as one of sex. The jingoism of Emmeline and Christabel Pankhurst and their followers has to be offset against the activities of women at the Hague in 1915, and the activities of Olga Maitland and Women for Defence[124] against those of the Greenham women.

If women monopolise the compassionate virtues they may fail to unlock these in men, legitimise the male stereotype as natural and unavoidable, lose potential allies, and drive a wedge between the male and female exponents of peace. In the wake of the new women's peace movement both men and women have protested that to explain all wars in terms of male aggression is intellectually untenable and morally defective, and that men are more likely to contribute to a future peace if they are not suffering from self-contempt and collective guilt.[125]

Moreover, when women pacifists emphasise their motherhood and domestic role as opposed to men's public and political role, and their emotional rather than rational stimulus, they run the risk that their movement may be trivialised. The caring, nurturing qualities which they have brought to the Peace Movement are vitally important, but these qualities alone may prove insufficiently powerful to influence mainstream politics. The socially determined male role may be one of aggression, intolerance and inflexibility, but it is also one of intellect, assertion and strength. These qualities too are needed for an effective movement. The problem is exacerbated by the methods of decentralist organisation which the women have made their own. Difficulties in decision-making may result in political impotence and the evasion of responsibility. Preoccupation with method may preclude the achievement of real change.[126]

Similarly, the women's emphasis on transnationalism and localism, bypassing national centres of power, may further reinforce the dangers of political irrelevance. For, unless very great numbers of people are prepared to act, such an approach may leave the real centres of power untouched.

A more general, but equally serious, potential problem is that, in reducing war to an expression of patriarchy, women may confound the feminist and the pacifist movements to the detriment of one or the other. This could result in their ignoring the possibility of reciprocal relationships between peace and freedom, and in failure to combat the war system itself. Alternatively, a specifically women's peace movement could actually divert energy away from WLM and postpone women's liberation. Some radical and revolutionary feminists argue that the first women's movement in Britain was swallowed up in the women's peace movement of the First World War, the 1920s and the 1930s, and fear that this may happen again.[127]

This chapter has dealt briefly with the history of women in the Peace Movement in twentieth-century Britain, and has attempted to describe the reasons why women often chose to act in women-only groups for peace. It has been seen that the same motivations have recurred. No attempt has been made to quantify accurately the strength of sentiment in each category at different times,[128] but a certain pattern has emerged.

The conviction of women's moral superiority expressed as a belief in women's special commitment, as mothers, to peace has survived throughout the century. Only when there was a background of powerful feminism, however, did independent women's peace groups emerge on a large scale as in 1915 and the ensuing years, and again in the 1980s. Such groups were often feminist and their members were conscious of the interdependence of peace and their own emancipation.

It is not questioned that women's reasons for joining the Peace Movement included concern for their children and a consciousness of the interdependence of peace and freedom. The evidence for their having a special commitment to peace, or a special role to play in the Peace Movement, has, however, been shown to be inconclusive. More importantly, it has been suggested that certain incongruities are inherent in such arguments which may in fact weaken both the Peace Movement and the feminist movement.

This is not to deny the remarkable achievements of women-only peace groups. They have raised awareness of individual responsibility for world peace, and of the need to rehabilitate the emotional, caring qualities. They have drawn many previously apolitical women into the Peace Movement, and sometimes thence into other political movements. In addition, those groups which flourished alongside a powerful feminism also developed a vital analysis of the theoretical relationship between peace and freedom, including the freedom of women. Moreover, it is not questioned that there may always be certain practical reasons for women's autonomous organisation and action.

Doubts are raised, however, as to the wisdom of women, or indeed any other exclusive group, claiming a special prerogative for peace, and deliberately excluding men from their actions, even though they may participate in joint movements too. If such claims can be traced ultimately to a belief in biological reductionism, then women should logically be seeking to eliminate men entirely,[129] which surely few would contemplate. If, on the other hand, they are based on socially and culturally enforced gender roles, then it is suggested that perhaps the undesirable features of the male role, and those of the female one, may be overcome more effectively by contact rather than by avoidance. At the same time the equally vital emotional and intellectual qualities of the respective stereotypes may be promoted in both sexes.

Any risk of women being dominated by men in mixed peace groups is surely minimal provided WLM groups continue to provide a sympathetic and supportive forum in which women can develop confidence, political skills, and an analysis of their own oppression. Analogies may then be drawn between the feminist and Peace Movements, and their interdependence recognised without their being confused, or either one subordinated to the other.

Finally, women at Greenham reason that approaches to peace via international bargaining have always failed because of the recalcitrance of those in traditional positions of power. Their own most impressive achievements have been their use of non-violent direct action and decentralist forms of organisation. They have promoted a non-governmental approach to international relations using alternative methods, bypassing national centres of power in favour of local and global contact by autonomous groups. Both the successes, and the difficulties and potential pitfalls, faced by such groups have been discussed above. It is suggested that future success in promoting peace by these methods is dependent upon the development of a dialectical relationship between intellect and emotion on the part of protagonists, and, perhaps more than anything else, upon the numbers of people prepared to act. So far, women pacifists have failed in their ultimate objectives. They have acknowledged that their methods are not exclusively female, and to exploit their potential fully surely they must welcome the support of sympathetic men? For surely only a united grass-roots movement can produce an historical change from a war-orientated world to a peace-orientated one?

References

1 G. Bussey and M. Tims, *Pioneers for Peace*, first published 1965, reissued London, 1980, provides the most comprehensive history available of the Women's International League for Peace and Freedom, the women's peace group which has had continuous existence since 1915.

2 The etymology of the term 'pacifism' has been elaborated by M. Ceadel, *Pacifism in Britain 1914–45*, Oxford, 1980, pp. 3–5; and see Chapter 5 of this volume. Some authorities have distinguished between pacifism and pacificism (see A. J. P. Taylor, *The Trouble Makers*, London, 1957, p. 51 and Ceadel, *Pacifism in Britain*, p. 3), using the latter to describe a commitment to the prevention of war which, however, accepts that the controlled use of armed force may be necessary to achieve this. Pacificism thus accounts for different degrees and even kinds of pacifism other than absolute pacifism. In this chapter it is assumed that it will be obvious from the context when people who describe themselves as pacifists are in fact pacificists.

3 C. Chickering, *Imperial Germany and a World Without War*, Princeton, 1975, p. 8.

4 The term 'radical suffragists' was coined by J. Liddington and J. Norris, *One Hand Tied Behind Us*, London, 1978, p. 15, to describe these particular suffragists.

5 See Liddington and Norris, *One Hand Tied Behind Us*, especially pp. 15–17, 143; E. S. Pankhurst, *The Suffragette Movement*, first published 1931, reprinted London, 1977, p. 593; D. Nield Chew, *Ada Nield Chew*, London, 1982, *passim*. In a foreward to Chew's work A. Davin points out that although Ada Nield Chew contributed to the *Common Cause*, the organ of the NUWSS, since her views were generally more radical than theirs her articles were usually preceded by a disclaimer. They found a more sympathetic reception in *Freewoman*, the radical suffragist journal edited by Dora Marsden.

6 For example, E. Pankhurst, 'Why women must be mobilised', *The Sketch*, 23 March 1915, p. 10; C. Pankhurst, *The War: A Speech Delivered at the London Opera House*, London, 1914, 16 pp.

7 For details of the Hague Congress, see *Towards a Permanent Peace, A Record of the Women's Congress at the Hague*, London, 1915, 24 pp.; M. M. Randall, *Highlights in W.I.L.P.F. History: From the Hague to Luxembourg, 1915–1946*, Philadelphia, 1946, n.p.; J. Addams, E. Balch and A. Hamilton, *Women at the Hague*, first published 1915, reprinted London and New York, 1972; J. Addams, *Peace and Bread in Time of War*, first published 1922, reprinted London and New York, 1971; Bussey and Tims, *Pioneers for Peace*, pp. 17–24.

8 For an annotated summary of press reports see E. Sharp, 'The Congress and the press', *Towards a Permanent Peace*, pp. 22–3.

9 For details of the activities of British WIL during the war years see H. Ward, *A Venture in Goodwill*, London, 1929, especially pp. 19–21; Bussey and Tims, *Pioneers for Peace*, pp. 25–34; Randall, *Highlights in W.I.L.P.F. History*.

10 The Labour Movement encompasses not only members of the ILP, but also those involved in union activity, the Women's Co-operative Guild and on the Board of Guardians.

11 For details of the WPC's activities see J. Liddington, 'The Women's Peace Crusade', in D. Thompson (ed.), *Over Our Dead Bodies*, London, 1983, pp. 180–98.

12 For details see Pankhurst, *The Suffragette Movement*, pp. 592–9.

13 The extent to which they complied with this injunction may be judged from Florence Kelly's remarks in a letter which she wrote home to America from the Congress: 'The English leaders amazed everyone by emphasising at every opportunity that they were all socialists. This included Mrs Pethick-Lawrence, Crystal Macmillan, Mrs Snowden (of course) and all the lesser lights.' Letter in Schwimmer/Lloyd collection, New York, quoted in A. Wiltsher, *Brave Women Against the Great War*, forthcoming.

14 For details of WILPF activities during the 1920s and 1930s see WILPF, British section, annual reports; Ward, *A Venture in Goodwill*; Randall, *Highlights of W.I.L.P.F. History*; Bussey and Tims, *Pioneers for Peace*, pp. 34–167.

15 See, for example, J. Liddington, *The Life and Times of a Respectable Rebel: Selina Cooper 1864–1946*, London 1984, pp. 406–7.

16 For details of their activities see *Caring and Sharing*, the journal of the Women's Co-operative Guild; J. Melichar, 'White Poppies', *The Pacifist*, XX, n.p.

17 See *Woman Today*, October 1937, p. 6.

18 See H. Vernon, 'Your movement abroad', *Woman Today*, September 1937, p. 7.

19 See, for example, E. Tuckfield, 'I appeal to the women', *Woman Today*, October 1937, p. 4; E. Rathbone, letter, *Woman Today*, December 1937, p. 4; K. Gibbons, 'Women who march for peace', *Woman Today*, December 1937, p. 7.

20 J. A. Berkman, *Pacifism in England 1914–1939*, unpublished PhD thesis, Yale University, 1967, esp. p. 55.

21 Ceadel, *Pacifism in Britain*, p. 33.

22 The colourful story of the Wheeldons was unearthed, mainly from the Derby local press, by Sheila Rowbotham. Rowbotham presented a paper on the Wheeldons at Bradford Women's Local History Conference, May 1983. She suggested that there may have been other similar networks to the Derbyshire one, but that by virtue of their local, and even more their underground nature, it is difficult to discover details of them.

23 Ceadel, *Pacifism in Britain*, p. 274.

24 *Ibid.*, pp. 93–6.

25 See M. G. Fawcett, *What I remember*, London, 1924, pp. 226–9.

26 E. Pethick-Lawrence, 'Motherhood and war', *Harpers Weekly*, LIX, 1914, p. 542. See also E. Pethick-Lawrence, *My Part in a Changing World*, London, 1938, p. 308.

27 H. Swanwick, *War In Its Effects Upon Women*, first published 1916, reprinted New York and London, 1971, p. 4. See also p. 32, and H. Swanwick, *Women and War*, first published 1915, reprinted New York and London, 1971, especially pp. 2,

13–14.

28 C. Macmillan, *The History of the Congress*, London, 1915, pp. 128–9.

29 Pankhurst, *The Suffragette Movement*, p. 608.

30 See, for example, M. L. Davies (ed.), *Life As We Have Known It*, first published 1930, reprinted London, 1977, p. 65; H. Vernon, 'Your movement abroad', *Woman Today*, September 1937, p. 7; G. Duchene, 'Appeal', *Woman Today*, October 1937, p. 4.

31 Swanwick, *War In Its Effects*.

32 See J. Vellacott-Newberry, 'Anti-war suffragists', *History*, LXII, 1977, p. 417.

33 See, for example, editorial, *Woman Today*, April 1937, p. 2; anon. 'Food, good health and employment: a better defence than armaments', *Woman Today*, May 1937, pp. 8–9.

34 *Manifesto of the Hague Congress*, The Hague, 1915.

35 Pethick-Lawrence, *My Part in a Changing World*, pp. 307–8.

36 V. Woolf, *The Three Guineas*, first published London, 1938, reprinted London, 1982, p. 135.

37 *Ibid.*, p. 164.

38 See Davies, *Life As We Have Known It*, p. 107.

39 See, for example, H. Vernon, 'The future: peace or war', *Woman Today*, October 1936, p. 3; editorial, 'Innocent people bear the burden of wars that are not theirs', *Woman Today*, March 1937, p. 2.

40 See H. Vernon, 'Your movement abroad', *Woman Today*, September 1937, p. 7; D. Tuckfield, 'I met my friends abroad', *Woman Today*, January 1939, p. 20.

41 See anon., 'How German Women are fighting Hitler', *Woman Today*, October 1939, p. 12.

42 Swanwick, *Woman and War*, p. 11. See also Swanwick, *War In Its Effects*, p. 2.

43 Shaw, *Socialism and Militarism*, p. 10.

44 Vellacott-Newberry, 'Anti-war suffragists', pp. 422–3.

45 Shaw, *Socialism and Militarism*, esp. pp. 8–16. See also N. Young, 'Why peace movements fail', *Social Alternatives*, Vol. IV, No. 1, 1984, pp. 9–16. (After 1918 the military consolidation of the Russian State ended in a dominant military tradition of socialism there.)

46 See, for example, anon., 'Women must choose', *Woman Today*, October 1937, p. 7; H. Vernon, 'Women demand the right to happy motherhood, work and education', *Woman Today*, December 1937, p. 10.

47 Woolf, *The Three Guineas*, esp. p. 162.

48 V. Woolf, *A Room of One's Own*, first published London, 1929, reprinted 1984, pp. 34–6, 38.

49 The ideas which Dora Russell had begun to develop in 1922 were eventually published in 1983: D. Russell, *The Religion of the Machine Age*, London, 1983. See also M. Johnstone, 'The religion of the machine age: an interview with Dora Russell', *Undercurrents*, 59, 1983, pp. 24–7. Dora Russell also discussed these ideas at a meeting of the Women's Peace Alliance, Newbury, November 1982.

50 Ceadel, *Pacifism in Britain*, p. 147.

51 *Ibid.*, p. 101.

52 R. Gregg, *The Power of Nonviolence*, London, 1935.

53 B. de Ligt, *The Conquest of Violence*, London, 1937.

54 Editorial, *Woman Today*, October 1937, p. 2. WAWF members continued to advocate economic boycotts long after others had abandoned the idea; see, 'Yes it would look nice – but stop and think', *Woman Today*, November 1938, p. 2; 'Sex appeal without silk', *Woman Today*, March 1939, p. 22.

55 See, for example, S. Morrison, *I Renounce War*, London, 1962, p. 60.

56 A *Peace News* reader of 13 August 1938 warned against pacifist demonstrations being 'too predominantly female', cited in Ceadel, *Pacifism in Britain*, p. 233.

57 Ceadel, *Pacifism in Britain*, p. 296.

58 Morrison, *I Renounce War*.

59 Ceadel, *Pacifism in Britain*, p. 229.

60 *Woman Today*, December 1937, p. 4.

61 Editorial, *Woman Today*, November 1938, p. 2.

62 See, for example, 'My son a soldier', *Woman Today*, November 1939, p. 10; editorial, *Woman Today*, January 1940, p. 2.

63 For a summary of the speeches made at this meeting see *Woman Today*, February 1940, p. 20.

64 Liddington, *The Life and Times of a Respectable Rebel*, p. 416.

65 Morrison, *I Renounce War*, p. 65,

66 C. Driver, *The Disarmers*, London, 1964, p. 16.

67 R. Taylor and C. Pritchard, *The Protest Makers, The British Nuclear Disarmament Movement of 1958–1965, Twenty Years On*, Oxford, 1980, p. 2.

68 J. Minnion and P. Bolsover (eds.), *The CND Story*, London, 1983, p. 9.

69 Morrison, *I Renounce War*, p. 75.

70 Taylor and Pritchard, *The Protest Makers*.

71 Minnion and Bolsover, *The CND Story*, p. 30.

72 See for example, A. Carter, *Direct Action*, London, 1962; *Authority and Democracy*, London, 1979; *The Political Theory of Anarchism*, London, 1971.

73 Driver, *The Disarmers*, p. 187.

74 Bussey and Tims, *Pioneers for Peace*, p. 24.

75 Driver, *The Disarmers*, p. 186; Taylor and Pritchard, *The Protest Makers*, pp. 114, 171–3.

76 Quoted in C. Driver, *The Disarmers*, London, 1964, p. 54.

77 Cook had published her own fears in the *Guardian* after seeing an American colonel on television at the time of the Berlin crisis, saying that nuclear weapons could be in use within a week. The letters she received were in response to her article.

78 Quoted in C. Driver, *The Disarmers*, p. 127.

79 E. Cappizi, 'Goodbye to Peggy Duff', *Spare Rib*, 107, 1981, p. 17.

80 See, for example, A. Carter, *Direct Action*, p. 2.

81 B. Friedan, *The Feminine Mystique*, New York, 1963.

82 For details see S. Evans, *Personal Politics*, New York, 1983; J. Hole and J. Levine, *The Rebirth of Feminism*, New York, 1971.

83 A. Coote and B. Campbell, *Sweet Freedom*, Oxford, 1982, pp. 15–18; S. Rowbotham *et al.*, *Beyond the Fragments*, London, 1979, pp. 34–6.

84 For an elaboration of this distinction see Coote and Campbell, *Sweet Freedom*, pp. 27–33.

85 *Women for Peace: Who Are We?* A statement in translation of *Vrouwen Voor Vrede*, Netherlands, 1981.

86 At the beginning the 1980s Worthing WILPF, for example, had only six active members and was on the point of closing down. After 1982, however, membership revived dramatically – probably due to the influence of the Greenham demonstration of December 1982 – to exceed thirty active members in 1984, with many other women who never actually joined the organisation nonetheless attending its meetings.

87 See M. Bowland, *Chain of Hope Newsletter*, 1981, n.p.

88 See J. McMinn and others, *Report: Mothers for Peace*, 1981, n.p.

89 See WONT newsletter (irregular), Nottingham WONT, 'Working as a group', in L. Jones (ed.), *Keeping the Peace*, London, 1983, pp. 22–8; C. Bradshaw, 'W.O.N.T. is growing stronger', *Spare Rib*, 1981, p. 13.

90 For details of the peace camp see L. Jones, 'On common ground', in Jones, *Keeping the Peace*, pp. 79–98; A. Cook and G. Kirk, *Greenham Women Everywhere*, London, 1983; reports in the *Guardian, Peace News* and *Sanity* since September 1981.

91 See, for example, A. Leslie, 'The fantasy of Greenham Common', *Daily Mail*, 13 January 1983, pp. 16–17; see also Cook and Kirk, *Greenham Women Everywhere*, pp. 91–108, for a comprehensive survey of media reaction.

92 See, for example, P. Brown, 'Greenham women are kept on the move', the *Guardian*, 7 April 1984, p. 2.

93 B. Harford and S. Hopkins (eds.), *Greenham Common: Women at the Wire*, London, 1984, p. 2, claim that there has been considerable success in involving working-class women in the Peace Movement, especially at Greenham.

94 Young, 'Why peace movements fail', Fig. 3, p. 12.

95 Minnion and Bolsover, *The CND Story*, p. 34.

96 E. P. Thompson, 'Resurgence in Europe and the role of E.N.D.', in Minnion and Bolsover, *The CND Story*, p. 81.

97 See T. Swade, 'Babies Against the Bomb', in Jones, *Keeping the Peace*, pp. 64–5; J. Lavelle, 'Children need smiles not missiles', in Jones, *Keeping the Peace*, p. 7; A. Tutton, 'Families Against the Bomb', in Jones, *Keeping the Peace*, p. 120.

98 See, for example, letter from A. Phillips, July 1981; L. Caldicott, 'Keep out: reserved for the exclusive sisters', the *Guardian*, 4 January 1983; Lavelle, 'Children need smiles', p. 69; K. Howse, quoted in Cook and Kirk, *Greenham Women Everywhere*, p. 80.

99 See, for example, letter to the *Guardian*, 15 December 1982, p. 2; Harford and Hopkins, *Women at the Wire*, p. 31.

100 Harford and Hopkins, *Women at the Wire*, p. 4.

101 See, for example, A. Whyte, 'Mothers for peace mission', *Sanity*, 4, 1981, p. 9; McMinn, *Report: Mothers for Peace*; Lavelle, 'Children need smiles', p. 70; Tutton, 'Families Against the Bomb', p. 120; J. Jacobs, 'Interview with Doreen Henshaw of Manchester Women's Movement for Peace', *CND Broadsheet*, 1981, n.p.; Swade, 'Babies Against the Bomb', pp. 65–7; Bowland, *Chain of Hope Newsletter*, n.p.

102 See, for example, P. Strange, *It'll Make a Man of You*, Nottingham, 1983, p. 28.

103 See, for example, L. Jones, 'Afterword', in Jones, *Keeping the Peace*, pp. 153–4; S. Riddell, 'Hell no: we won't glow', *Spare Rib*, 119, 1982, pp. 22–3.

104 Handout of WFLOE to advertise the march to Greenham, August 1981. See also R.

Wallsgrove, 'The reasons why Greenham should be a women's world', the *Guardian*, 15 December 1982, p. 12.

105 See. M. Miller and L. Jones, 'Notes on organising a decentralised international action', in Jones, *Keeping the Peace*, pp. 108–12.

106 Cook and Kirk, *Greenham Women Everywhere*, p. 126.

107 On the use of these methods by WLM members see H. Wainwright, 'Introduction' in Rowbotham *et al., Beyond the Fragments*, p. 13; L. Segal, 'A local experiment', in Rowbotham *et al., Beyond the Fragments*, pp. 164, 167; S. Rowbotham, 'The women's movement and organising for socialism', in Rowbotham, *Beyond the Fragments*, especially pp. 30, 40, 50, 75, 133. On their use by women in the Peace Movement see Harford and Hopkins, *Women at the Wire*, p. 3; Cook and Kirk, *Greenham Women Everywhere*, pp. 83–5.

108 These forms of organisation had precedents in, for example, the classical Left literature of the First and Second Internationals, the Utopian Socialists, Rosa Luxemburg, Pannakok and the Dutch Socialists.

109 See R. Wallsgrove, 'Why W.O.N.T.? A feminist view of the disarmament movement', *Sanity*, 4, 1981, p. 5; L. Whitman and R. Wallsgrove, 'Why we W.O.N.T.', *Spare Rib*, 113, 1981, p. 3; Nottingham WONT, 'Working as a group', pp. 22–8.

110 Shushu, quoted in L. Jones, 'On common ground', in Jones, *Keeping the Peace*, p. 83. For an interesting example of the dangers of hierarchies in promoting role-playing see J. Vellacott-Newbury, 'Women, peace and power', in P. McAllister (ed.), *Reweaving the web of Life*, Philadelphia, 1982, pp. 36–7.

111 See, for example, R. Gott, 'A man at Greenham', the *Guardian*, 15 December 1982, p. 10; P. Brown, 'Leaderless peace movement keeps law at arm's length', the *Guardian*, 31 March 1983, p. 10.

112 See Lavelle, 'Children need smiles', p. 70.

113 M. Beresford, 'Women and nuclear disarmament', *CND Broadsheet*, 1981, n.p.

114 Conference statement of IFNV, Laurieston, Scotland, August 1980.

115 See, for example, 'Feminism and nonviolence', *Shrew*, 1978, 36 pp.; *International Feminism and Nonviolence Newsletter* (bimonthly); D. Shelley, 'Women against militarism', *Peace News*, 1980, pp. 8–9; Feminism and Nonviolence Study Group, *Piecing It Together*, London, 1983.

116 Harford and Hopkins, *Women at the Wire*, p. 3.

117 Letter from Marion Levitt, organiser of the women's and children's action at Torness, May 1981. See also Wallsgrove, 'Why we W.O.N.T.'; Bradshaw, 'W.O.N.T. is growing stronger'.

118 See, for example, L. Whitman, 'Stay home and die', *Spare Rib*, 99, 1980, 50–1.

119 Letter from Angela Phillips, 1 July 1981.

120 Handout of WFLOE to advertise their march, August 1981.

121 Although some German suffragists had made these connections in the 1920s. See A. Hackett, *The Politics of Feminism in Wilhelmine, Germany*, unpublished PhD thesis, Columbia, 1976, esp. pp. 768, 845; R. S. Evans, *The Feminist Movement in Germany*, London and Beverley Hills, 1976, esp. pp. 214–19.

122 Compare Rowbotham, 'The trouble with patriarchy', where she argues that the concept of any fixed structure of patriarchy leads inevitably to the biological reductionism of revolutionary feminists. Contrast, however, S. Alexander and B. Taylor,

'In defence of patriarchy', *New Statesman*, XCVIII, 1980, p. 161.

123 It should be remembered, however, that even in the 1900s and 1920s radical suffragists had criticised the nuclear family.

124 Maitland founded Women for Defence, a women's organisation in support of the stockpiling of nuclear weapons for 'defence purposes' in 1982, in reaction against the growing Women's Peace Movement.

125 M. Randle, letter in the *Guardian*, 11 December 1983, p. 10. See also N. Walter, 'The women only debate', *Peace News*, 2188, 1983, pp. 14–15; S. Spiller, 'Women and peace', *Sanity*, 5, 1983, pp. 14–15; A. Tunnicliffe, 'Let's get on with it together', *Sanity*, 2, 1983, pp. 10–11; N. Vittachi, 'The trouble starts at Greenham Common', the *Guardian*, 16 July 1985, p. 6. But contrast J. Cade, letter in *Peace News*, 2189, 1983, pp. 20–1.

126 See Rowbotham, 'The women's movement and organising for socialism', pp. 41, 71, 76; J. Freeman, 'The Tyranny of structurelessness', *The Second Wave*, II, 1975, J. Freeman, 'Political organisations in the feminist movement', *Acta Sociologica*, XVIII, 1975, pp. 222–44.

127 See *Breaching the Peace: A collection of Radical Feminist Papers*, London, 1983.

128 Such a quantification would probably be impossible, since the membership figures are not available for all women's peace groups and political organisations discussed, and it is difficult to estimate just how much support each group had. There are certainly no 'membership figures' for Greenham women. Some women activists may not have belonged to any organised group. Moreover, a whole range of motivation is commonly expressed even within one group. Finally, for the early part of the century the evidence of motivation depends largely upon whether women left written records or not, and upon the accuracy and reliability of those records. Allowance must always be made for the possibilities of rhetoric, for discrepancy of views between leaders and rank and file, and between those who had time to write and those who did not.

129 Compare Rowbotham, 'The trouble with patriarchy', pp. 970–1.

11

Critics and criticisms
of the British Peace Movement

PETER VAN DEN DUNGEN

Not all that long ago advocates of peace and the societies which they formed were criticised and ridiculed for their attachment to this idea. Whereas some critics accepted the desirability of peace but doubted the possibility of its immediate (or even distant) realisation, others rejected altogether the notion that peace would be an incontrovertible benefit to mankind. Helmut von Moltke's oft-quoted view, 'eternal peace is a dream, and not even a beautiful dream and war is a link in God's order of the world. . . . Without war the world would bog down in a quagmire of materialism', is symptomatic of an entire school of thought, as old as history, which proclaims that in the life of society and in the unfolding of history, conflict, including war, is necessary and desirable.[1] In this respect Social Darwinian notions only reinforced, in the second half of the nineteenth century, a long-established and widely-held belief. As a leading historian of war has written: 'before 1914 war was almost universally considered an acceptable, perhaps an inevitable and for many people a desirable way of settling international differences'.[2]

It is interesting to observe that when in the 1920s P. A. Sorokin undertook, as one of the first sociologists to do so, to study the phenomenon of war in an objective manner, unencumbered by traditional metaphysical and opinionated beliefs, he focused almost exclusively on the 'functions' (i.e. consequences) of war, and virtually ignored its 'factors' (i.e. causes).[3] He found that neither the claims of those who suggested that war was wholly beneficial nor those of their opponents who argued that it was always detrimental to the individual and the society which engaged in the practice were true. Those peace researchers who followed in his footsteps barely a generation later are, by contrast, overwhelmingly concerned with uncovering the correlates and causes of war in the hope of preventing and ultimately eliminating it. To the extent that the consequences of war are discussed (a major preoccupation, now as before, of the Peace Movement), an almost complete consensus prevails: war between the major powers will be suicidal and everything should be done to prevent it from occurring. Whatever benefits may have accrued from warfare in the past, in the nuclear age the balance sheet has only one side to it. Within a few generations, therefore, one kind of critic of the peace idea has become extinct; peace has become, at least in much of the world, a consensual value. The mass conversion to peace also embraces the traditional arch-opponent of the pacifist, the military man. It is very unlikely that in the nineteenth century or before the military profession would ever have contemplated inscribing its instruments with mottoes such as can be found today ('Peace is our profession', 'Peacekeeper'). Although cynics regard this merely as an illustration of the modern corruption of language and of the depravity of the military mind, it cannot be doubted that at least Western military establishments now regard their primary function to be not the prosecution but the prevention of war.[4]

It is not surprising therefore that contemporary critics of the Peace Movement resent the exclusiveness which this term suggests, especially in view of their claim that the policies advocated by the Peace Movement are likely to result in war. Hence they prefer to speak of the 'Peace' Movement, the so-called Peace Movement, the protest movement or the anti-nuclear movement. In the words of one prominent critic:

> It is reasonable to assume that the avoidance of war and the preservation of peace are aspirations shared by most reasonable and intelligent human beings. . . . A debate about nuclear weapons is, or should be, a debate about the most effective way of achieving peace with freedom and security. It is likely to be entirely abortive if, in its early stages, one side is allowed blandly to describe itself as the 'peace movement', implying the simple-minded corollary that those who disagree with it must be in favour of war.[5]

Many critics also share the conviction of Franz Joseph Strauss 'that the existence of NATO and the effect it has had is the greatest peace movement in the history of mankind'.[6] The proprietorial tug of war today concerning the word peace has a parallel in the debates of the

1930s concerning the definition of a pacifist. Fifty years before Chalfont wrote, Frank Hardie, the president of the Oxford Union (and the initiator of the 'King and Country' motion debated in February 1933), noted: 'In the sense of preferring peace to war, we are all pacifists now.'[7] A few years later Wickham Steed, the Editor of The Times, could similarly say: 'I hate war and want to put an end to it. To this extent, you may call me a pacifist' – thereby incurring the ire of Lord Ponsonby, the chairman of the War Resisters International.[8]

One of the first historians of the organised movement for international peace, writing in the inter-war years, could rightly claim 'that many of its aspirations had been at last realised'.[9] The codification of international law, arbitration treaties between governments, the establishment of a League of Nations, disarmament and the outlawry of war – these were the issues which the nineteenth-century Peace Movement propagated and which gradually also became the concerns of states and the emerging international community. Henceforth, 'the burden of the Movement was lighter. It was crusading, for the first time, in a Peace setting, and with Peace the leading topic of the day.' Thus, at least since the end of the First World War, the disagreement between the Peace Movement and its critics is no longer about the desirability of peace, but whether and in what way it can be achieved.

Since each of the parties in the debate is an amalgam of groups and individuals[10] whose views often sharply differ among themselves, it is inevitable that in a general discussion no justice can be done to the subtleties of the position and argument of both the intelligent peace dissenter and his critic. Indeed, there is no doubt that the complexity of the debate is an important reason for the frequent claim of deliberate falsification or involuntary misrepresentation which each party has levelled at the other. On a subject which is intellectually complex and emotionally-laden, it is not surprising that the tendency to create a straw-man adversary or the temptation to approach the issue in Manichaean terms, is even stronger than usual. Polarisation is no respecter of differentiation; in this atmosphere the Peace Movement and its critics are needlessly driven further apart. In fact, it is the belief of some critics that even at the best of times little real dialogue can take place between the two sides 'since they can agree neither on the nature of man, nor on the role of the state, neither on Soviet intentions and capabilities nor on the function of weapons in the international system'.[11] What follows is an overview of some of the objections most frequently encountered among those who criticise the Peace Movement in varying degrees. The arguments themselves can be of a general (and time-honoured) nature or can be specific, changing with the circumstances of time and place. We shall largely confine ourselves to the current Peace Movement and its opponents. Among the latter we include only those who can generally be assumed to belong to the conservative side of the political spectrum. Those on the Left who deplore the liberal, reformist character of much of the contemporary Peace Movement[12] are disregarded here because lack of space warrants a concentration on critics from without rather than from within. Moreover, it is this kind of critic who most readily comes to mind, and is the most common.

At a fundamental level, the identification of peace with disarmament (irrespective of the mode of disarmament), a deeply-held and virtually axiomatic belief as well as an explicit strategy, is questioned. The point critics make here is that disarmament is a Utopian idea because 'general and complete disarmament' (GCD) is impossible. It is true that at least some members of the Peace Movement would characterise this objective in similar terms; on the other hand, it appears at times in the rhetoric of political leaders and in disarmament plans submitted by countries to international fora. On these latter occasions it has often been implied, however, that disarmament would not really be absolute but implemented only to the extent that it would be compatible with the maintenance of domestic law and order. It is evident that this problem is not the same in all countries, some being more conflict-ridden than others and having to rely on greater coercive force to maintain domestic peace. Some countries, by virtue of their size and population, may maintain forces which would dwarf those of their smaller neighbours. In both cases the potential threat which such superior power presents to rivals and neighbours in an unreconstructed international system will make GCD difficult to achieve. Another problem with this notion resides in the fact that, even if all manufactured instruments of war were eliminated, the process of disarmament could never be complete (because we arm ourselves when we raise a fist) or irreversible. It is also observed that the advantages accruing to a party which infringes a disarmament agreement are directly related to the scope of the latter: the more wide-ranging and thorough the measure, the greater will be the resultant shift in the balance of power between those who implement the agreement and those who do not. For this reason, and contrary to what is often asserted, GCD makes the issues of trust, inspection and verification even more vital than is the case with partial measures of disarmament.

The automatic juxtaposition of peace and disarmament by the Peace Movement makes it oblivious of any problems which disarmament may bring in its wake. That such problems can be considerable and that we must investigate them, as Michael Howard has argued, will strike many as perverse at a time when the only problem which seems to matter is that of an intolerable arms burden and a dangerous arms race. Likewise, his conclusion – 'that it may not be possible to have both disarmament, and that degree of peaceful order which, with all its many imperfections, so much of the world enjoys today'[13] – is bound to be rejected by most members of the Peace Movement as both wholly incredible and unwelcome. Reviewing Philip Noel-Baker's *The Arms Race* (1958), Hedley Bull finds, like Howard, that there are 'serious objections to the notions both of the possibility and the desirability of disarmament'. The arms race is a cause as well as a consequence of international tension, he writes, 'but the fact that the arms race contributes to political tension does not diminish the difficulty that it cannot be brought to an end without the ending of this tension'.[14] According to Bull, the most notable acts of disarmament are those which occur spontaneously (and often unilaterally) in response to a lowering of political pressures, without the need for any formal treaty. The latter involves the giving of a promise to disarm, and this implies a suggestion of distrust – and so does, of course, the insistence on verification.[15]

Bull, like so many other critics of nuclear disarmament, draws attention to the paradoxical situation created by the existence of nuclear weapons. Under present conditions, he writes, 'the objective of a reduction in the frightfulness of war, and the objective of reducing the incidence of war, appear to conflict with one another: to make war less frightful may be to make it more probable'. This view is echoed by Michael Howard: 'I find it hard to believe that the abolition of nuclear weapons, even if it were possible, would be an unmixed blessing. Nothing that makes it easier for statesmen to regard war as a feasible instrument of state policy, one from which they stand to gain rather than lose, is likely to contribute to a lasting peace.'[16] It is interesting to observe that in the Peace Movement of the pre-nuclear era there were those who, despairing of the moral improvement of mankind, put their hope for peace in a monster weapon.[17] They rarely faced up to the fact that such a device would be able to exercise its peace-preserving function only for as long as it was kept in existence, and that such a situation was morally, psychologically and intellectually bound to be an uncomfortable one. It was generally assumed that the invention of such a weapon would simply inaugurate, at long last, general and complete disarmament. By some magical process the horror weapon, as soon as it was invented, would be disinvented, and with it, all other weapons.

Many in the Peace Movement will regard as bizarre Bull's conclusion that in the present world, states are unlikely to agree to measures of general and complete disarmament and that they 'are behaving rationally in refusing to do so'.[18] To the question 'Does disarmament mean peace?', an equally distinguished student of war and peace, Hans Morgenthau, answers that a direct relation between the possession of arms and the issue of war and peace exists but it is not the one assumed by advocates of disarmament: 'Men do not fight because they have arms. They have arms because they deem it necessary to fight.'[19] Referring to the disarmament of Germany under the terms of the Treaty of Versailles, he illustrates the thesis that disarmament affects the technology and strategy, but not the incidence, of war. Like other commentators Morgenthau agrees that disarmament has a vital part to play in a general settlement of international conflict, but that it cannot be the first step: 'Competition for armaments reflects, and is an instrument of, competition for power. . . . Therefore, a mutually satisfactory settlement of the power contest is a precondition for disarmament.' Disarmament, in other words, is not inevitably and invariably to be welcomed since it may disturb a precarious balance of power and thus destroy an equally fragile peace based on it.

Critics of the Peace Movement frequently point out that the war-weariness and pacifist disposition of the Western liberal democracies – of which the Peace Movement is the most obvious manifestation – are too often assumed also to exist outside this relatively small, stable and homogeneous enclave. This is not only argued today (cf. below) but also with respect to the past. This thesis, as well as the one referred to above concerning the relationship between armament and war, is often illustrated by the events of the inter-war period. The experience of the First World War, which in many ways provided a demonstration of the suicidal nature of modern warfare, greatly stimulated the pacifist sentiment of the peoples affected and resulted in large-scale demobilisation and disarmament. The Western democracies, especially France and Great Britain, were slow in recognising the emerging dangers of Nazism and Fascism and in building up their defences. It is now widely accepted that the failure to stem the rise of the dictators in the 1930s ultimately made war inevitable. If they had been confronted with a determined opposition, adequately armed not only for its own protection but also for upholding the basic principles of international law (and the integrity of the League of Nations), no appeasement would have been necessary[20] and very likely, no war would have ensued. Idealist illusions and a parochial attitude had to be paid for dearly: a mere two decades after the conclusion of 'the war to end all war' another great war engulfed Europe and the rest of the world. The belief in the efficacy of unilateral measures of restraint and of benign statesmanship, through appeasement, and the unwillingness to engage in an arms build up (in order to avoid war rather than engage in one), proved to be counterproductive.

While these conclusions are legitimate it is not correct to blame – as critics of the contemporary Peace Movement are wont to do – 'the' Peace Movement of the period for what happened. Firstly, as Arthur Salter, a prominent participant in the political events of the inter-war years, later observed: ' "Munich" . . . was . . . not the weakness of a moment or a man. It was the climax of a long period of blindness and inadequate preparation . . . It was indeed much more than that. It was a phase of weakness in the life of the democracies of the world.'[21] Secondly, the 'largest and most influential society in the British peace movement'[22] of this period was the League of Nations Union (LNU). At its peak in 1931 it collected over 400,000 subscriptions, whereas the number of pledges for its nearest rival, Dick Sheppard's Peace Pledge Union (PPU), formed in 1935–36, amounted to only one-fifth of this number.[23] The popularity of the LNU derived from the goodwill which its parent body, the League of Nations, experienced in the aftermath of the Great War when it was seen by many as the best hope for a world without war, or at least a world in which the use of arms would be constrained by, and in the service of, the Covenant. Because the LNU did not espouse unilateral disarmament but advocated both general disarmament and the strengthening of the League's collective security machinery, it was a safe and respectable organisation which incurred few, if any, of the criticisms directed at the largely unilateralist and isolationist Peace Movement of today. (It is sobering to note the insignificant role played in today's Peace Movement by the United Nations

Association compared with that of its counterpart of the inter-war period, the LNU.) The way the LNU's journal, *Headway,* in 1937 described its opponents as a ' "triple alliance" of isolationists, defeatists, and pacifists'[24] has a very familiar ring today – except that this time the accusation is made of, rather than by, the main Peace Movement organisation. 'Communists, Neutralists, Defeatists' – that is the nature of the unholy alliance which critics accuse CND of being (and in their view this is also a more accurate explanation of the acronym).[25]

The 1935 Peace Ballot, in which eleven and a half million people voted, almost forty per cent of the electorate, provides an even clearer indication that the mood of the interested British public at this time was not one of pacifism or appeasement, and – contrary to later opinion – 'peace at any price' was not its preferred course of action. Almost six out of ten voters were prepared to back collective security with military force, and nearly nine out of ten were prepared to back it with sanctions short of war. The Peace Ballot, instead of strengthening appeasement or being a manifestation of it, forced the Government into a policy of sanctions and to abandon its opposition to the idea of collective security. The authoritative *Survey of International Affairs* for 1935 noted 'the almost ludicrously frank precipitancy with which the leading members of the U.K. government now changed their tune' by purporting to support sanctions.[26] That the Peace Ballot was an appeal for militant resistance to aggression, not a manifesto of appeasement, was widely recognised at the time (not least by Churchill) but has since been forgotten or denied. Three years later (1938) Neville Chamberlain lamented that his job was made more difficult by 'the LNU and other warlike pacifists'.[27] Unlike today, the 1930s Peace Movement, as represented by the LNU, advocated decisive military action (and the procurement of the necessary weapons) under League auspices, whereas the Government adopted an indulgent and appeasing attitude. This episode illustrates the danger of referring glibly to 'the' Peace Movement and employing distorting stereotypes.[28]

Norman Podhoretz, a vigorous transatlantic critic of the West European peace movements, has written that unlike 'pacifist thought proper', which has historically been confined to a minority and whose impact on politics has been marginal, its present derivative in its 'bowdlerised form of illusions about and pressures for disarmament'[29] is politically significant. Referring to the Washington Naval

Armaments Treaty of 1922 and the London Naval Agreement of 1930, Podhoretz argues that the best that can be said for these efforts is that they failed (since they did not succeed in preventing war by the reduction of armaments), and the worst, that if they had any effect at all it was to increase rather than decrease the chances of war. The latter assessment he finds to be nearer the truth, quoting in support the views of Barbara Tuchman, shared by other historians,[30] that the 1922 agreement 'fueled the rising Japanese militarism that led eventually to Pearl Harbor', and of Eugene V. Rostow that both agreements 'helped to bring on World War II, by reinforcing the blind and wilful optimism of the West, thus inhibiting the possibility of military preparedness and diplomatic actions through which Britain and France could easily have deterred the war'. Podhoretz believes that the contemporary nuclear arms negotiations between the superpowers display 'almost exactly the same characteristics' as the arms control agreements of the inter-war period; they have resulted in cutbacks by the democratic side and increases by the totalitarian ones. Then as now, the former is eager to cut back its armaments whereas the latter wishes to consolidate and enhance its advantages. Disarmament negotiations can again offer only a fraudulent hope because, as in the 1930s, there is an absence of common agreement on fundamentals between the opposing sides since one of them aims to overturn the existing international order (preferably through intimidation rather than war).

Another area of fundamental disagreement between an important section of the Peace Movement and its critics concerns the nature of peace. As conceived by the former, it frequently implies not only a disarmed world but also one in which war and other manifestations of violent conflict have disappeared. What is envisaged at the extreme is not simply a world without war but a community without conflict, a polity without politics, a world in which the struggle for power, its control and use, is superseded.[31] An agenda which is as ambitious as this is bound to fail because it is inherently Utopian; by aiming so high – and, in consequence, by often despising the lesser but more realistic goals – the end result is likely to be counterproductive. The basic datum ignored or denied by the peace Utopian is the pervasiveness of conflict and power. In this context, the 'realist' argues that the realm of the political has its own rules and regulations and also that it is as difficult to root out power and conflict from the international system as from the life of the individual. In this view, the elusiveness of world peace is a reflection of the way inner peace escapes us. The Christian realist, when confronted with the Christian pacifist, is likely to draw on Reinhold Niebuhr's critique of pacifism to justify his position as Christian. Niebuhr criticises the pacifist's over-optimistic view of human nature, his failure to take the presence of evil seriously or to admit his inclination towards injustice (as well as justice), his inability to realise that morally right action does not guarantee a happy outcome or that without coercion no community can exist. In Niebuhr's words, 'it is not possible to disavow war absolutely without disavowing the task of establishing justice' and 'the political order must be satisfied with relative peace and relative justice'.[32]

Such relative peace is unlikely to be attained without a willingness to engage in power politics. The Peace Movement has often assumed, on the basis of a harmony of interest doctrine, that peace is the natural state of affairs between men as between societies, but this happy situation has been vitiated by vested interests and erroneous beliefs which education and social reform should overcome. By contrast, the realist maintains that there is nothing natural or inevitable about peace, and stresses that peace is no accident but the result of careful and constant effort. Critics of the Peace Movement sometimes point out that its very own history and current activities demonstrate the fallacy of its fundamental assumption. The belief that conflict and power struggle are not inherent in human society but merely the result of misunderstanding or the expression of aberrant behaviour (of certain individuals, groups, social systems or ideologies) and that peace and harmony are the essential characteristics of reality, is belied not only by events in the realm of 'high politics' but also in the microcosm which the Peace Movement represents. Keith Robbins concludes his study of the British Peace Movement during the First World War by drawing attention to this fact:

> Perhaps the greatest testimony to the inadequacy of its ideology lay in the Peace Movement itself. The peace societies preached the possibility of permanent unity and concord on a universal scale, yet on their own small scale exhibited few signs of co-operation between themselves. . . . Pacifists constantly condemned 'power politics', yet, within the Peace Movement the struggle for mastery constantly showed itself both between individuals and groups. They ostracised their opponents as fiercely as they were themselves ostracised.[33]

Just as critics of the Peace Movement reject the identification of disarmament with peace, so they dispute the equation of armament and war. Disarmament does not necessarily result in peace, nor armament in war. The major premiss of the Peace Movement's campaign is that armaments are one of the main causes of war. The invention, manufacture and deployment of weapons is regarded as a fundamental disease, both an affliction and an addiction, which will inevitably erupt in war. The massive and volatile arsenals, together with the instruments and strategy pertaining to an age of ballistic missile warfare (with notions of pre-emptive and first strike, launch on warning, use or lose weapons), have attracted even more adherents to this view. It asserts that the arms race has spiralled out of control and has developed a momentum of its own. A military–industrial complex, driven by a technological–scientific imperative, is fuelling this seemingly unstoppable race into a cataclysmic catastrophe. Images of impending doom abound and are deliberately evoked by the Peace Movement to increase awareness and anxiety among the population and thereby elicit protest.[34]

We have already referred to the view, shared by many theorists as well as practitioners of international politics, that war and weapons are the inevitable consequences of an international system which lacks the properties of government and which forces states to take charge of their own security for their survival. It follows that critics of the Peace Movement do not seriously entertain the notion that the existence and proliferation of arms is largely the outcome of the machinations of a malign, secretive and self-serving military–industrial complex, or that the acquisition and development of arms increasingly resembles an autistic process (i.e. one without reference to the international environment). The accuracy or aptness of the 'arms race' metaphor, which is accepted as self-evident not only in the Peace Movement but far beyond, is similarly disputed. The notion of a 'race' is not always substantiated by statistical data and is often wrongly applied to the replacement of obsolete weapons. Furthermore, when the metaphor is meant to imply a mad drive for new military technology, 'we should not uncritically accept that innovation is bad' according to Laurence Martin. He observes: 'It is difficult to think of any other area of modern life in which so many people assume that today's technology is the best imaginable. In reality much military innovation is devoted to making weapons safer to handle and more amenable to control.'[35]

The main burden of the argument against the British Peace

Movement resides not primarily, however, in an objection to disarmament *per se* – the overriding instrumental goal of that movement – but in the nature of this objective and in the manner in which it is being pursued, i.e. unilateral nuclear disarmament. This proposed disarmament measure, at least in the first instance, is being confined to both one country and one category of weapon. Many in the Peace Movement recognise that general, multilateral disarmament is the ideal strategy but find that in practice this strategy has proved to be sterile. Therefore, the deadlock should be broken and an example set by this country, and since nuclear weapons are deemed to be the most dangerous and evil of the existing instruments of war, they have to be removed first. Unilateralism and anti-nuclearism, the main features of the post-Second World War British Peace Movement, are in the opinion of the critics dangerous and deficient strategies when such factors as the military balance and the international context, in particular the nature of Britain's main opponent, are taken into account.

The single most powerful attraction of unilateralism is the belief that it will enhance the prospects not only of peace but of sheer survival: *Protest and Survive* is the categorical imperative of the British Peace Movement of today.[36] The dangerousness of this belief has been mockingly expressed in the title of another publication, *Protest and Perish*.[37] Critics of unilateralism reject the arguments deployed in its cause (and draw out the dangers inherent in acting on it) – e.g. that weapons cause war, that nuclear weapons have not kept the peace, that multilateral disarmament has not worked, that unilateralism is the start of a process of multilateral disarmament, that the danger of war comes from the USA and NATO rather than from the Soviet Union, that a neutral and non-aligned Britain would be more secure than it is at present. This last view is held by a significant section of the Peace Movement, which often draws an analogy with the security of non-aligned Sweden or Switzerland. The validity of this analogy is disputed, since an examination of the relative security of these countries must take into account the degree to which the existence of a strong Western alliance is a precondition of and guarantee for their neutrality. Isolationism and the breaking-up of NATO would endanger peace and stimulate a nuclear and conventional arms build-up. The cause of nuclear non-proliferation in the West (and elsewhere) has been greatly assisted by the guarantees now provided by the US through NATO (and other alliances). One prominent critic of unilateralism argues that, rather than being responsible for arms proliferation, 'alliances have been incomparably the most effective arms control measures since World War II';[38] 'Conversely those unilateralists . . . who are dedicated to "destabilising" military alliances are in fact, though not in intention, furthering the arms race' (elsewhere Towle deploys the same argument not so much against those on the Left but against the neo-Gaullists who, being more influential, constitute a greater long-term threat to the survival of the Atlantic Alliance).[39]

It is also pointed out that if unilateral disarmament is meant to be exemplary neither the historical record nor contemporary events offer encouragement for this belief. The lament of Prime Minister Ramsay MacDonald in 1934 is held up as a warning: 'We have gone further in disarmament than any other country in the world . . . no-one thinks of following our example. Disarmament by example has completely broken down and we alone are not in a position to lift effectively a little finger in the event of trouble.'[40] The unilateral abandonment of Britain's nuclear weapons has to be argued on different grounds than those of inspiring others to follow suit (or to refrain from initiating a nuclear weapons programme). Advocates of British unilateralism tend to exaggerate the extent to which its implementation would influence the strategic calculations of others on these matters; it is likely that 'it would be seen more as a symptom of Britain's decline than an impressive gesture'.[41] When confronted with an adversary like the Soviet Union, one-sided disarmament conveys the wrong message: what is meant to be a moral gesture will be interpreted as a confirmation of the view that the West is decadent and has lost its will to resist. What was true of the 1930s is also true of today: unilateral disarmament by the West will make war less likely only on condition that the West is prepared to accede to the political demands of the Soviet Union. In other words, 'military weakness must be accompanied by appeasement if it is not to be a recipe for war and defeat'.[42] Any comparison of the present situation with that of the 1930s is anathema to the Peace Movement of today if only because the comparison of Nazi Germany with the Soviet Union is regarded as odious. But, like many other critics of the Peace Movement, Michael Howard has argued that, although the two states are not totally comparable, essential similarities do exist.[43] The Soviet Union, as a global power, is revisionist (even if as a European power she is not) and her regime is characterised by a ruthlessly totalitarian ideology which shows utter contempt for Western bourgeois liberal morality and which displays an attitude of cold and implacable enmity towards it.

The exclusive concern of CND and END with nuclear weapons, and the concomitant proposals for a declaration of a policy of no first use of nuclear weapons, the establishment of nuclear-free zones and a nuclear freeze, are often criticised as an unwitting manifestation of unilateralism. Since the end of the Second World War, the West has relied on nuclear weapons (of which initially it had a monopoly and later a superiority) in order to offset the superiority in conventional forces of the Soviet Union and its allies. The maintenance of security at lower cost and with fewer risks – the traditional objective of arms control and disarmament policies – requires equitable reductions in *all* categories of weapons. For essentially the same reason, namely the preponderance of Soviet conventional forces, the West has been unwilling to commit itself, unlike its adversary, to a policy of no first use of nuclear weapons. Such a declaration is held to weaken, even if only marginally, the nuclear-induced constraint on the Soviet Union's temptation to exploit its conventional advantage. It is further argued that such a declaration is redundant anyway since it is already subsumed in a more basic doctrine according to which NATO, as a defensive alliance, is committed to a policy of no first use of force *tout court*. However, given the steady erosion of the credibility of nuclear first use to deter a conventional attack, there is increasingly common ground on this issue between the Peace Movement and its critics. The change to 'no early use' of nuclear weapons which some analysts propose is perhaps the first step on the way to a no first use doctrine (which would require a strengthening of conventional forces).

The common objection to a nuclear-free zone policy is that it provides no guarantees that such a zone will also be nuclear-safe. To many critics nothing better illustrates the naïve ideas and illusions of the Peace Movement than the popularity of this policy. In the vivid phrase coined by Dean Inge in a previous era of disarmament agitation: 'It is useless for the sheep to pass resolutions in favour of vegetarianism while the wolf remains of a different opinion.'[44] They also point out, here as elsewhere, the unilateralist nature of policy declarations of this kind: they are cost-free for a country like the Soviet Union, where public opinion or popular pressure has no bearing on matters of this kind and where governmental inhibitions against infringing agreements are consequently far weaker than in the democracies (where such agreements have more than a paper existence). Moreover, the slogan of a nuclear-free zone from 'Poland to Portugal' is deceptive since it bears no relation to any existing political reality. As Lawrence Freedman has noted, 'It assumes a natural break in Europe at the Polish–Soviet border and ignores the very real break that runs through the middle of Europe.' A basic reality overlooked in this and similar Peace Movement proposals is that 'the American involvement in Europe is by invitation [whereas] the Soviet involvement is by geography'.[45]

Lastly, a nuclear freeze cannot be simply declared, but has to be negotiated in order to contribute to international security, and this involves the question of verification. One of the reasons why a freeze has to be agreed is because it would otherwise perpetuate existing imbalances which presently affect particularly the European theatre forces (where the West has a disadvantage that would be unacceptable to it).[46] The common denominator of most criticisms of specific proposals such as the above is that they carry their own dangers, which are ignored or dismissed by those who argue for radical change. Lawrence Freedman has admonished the disarmers: 'unexploded bombs need to be dismantled with caution and respect . . . lest the attempt to render them safe causes an explosion . . . Simple-minded schemes for disarmament might be cures more dangerous than the disease.'[47]

Apart from taking issue with the specific proposals for nuclear disarmament put forward by the Peace Movement (some of which were touched upon above), many of its opponents believe that the real threat to peace resides not in nuclear but in conventional weapons. As Morton Kaplan has argued, 'if one wishes significantly to reduce or eliminate the threat of nuclear war in Europe, the first step is to reduce or eliminate the threat of war in Europe; and this threat lies in conventional confrontation'.[48] He believes that the leaders of East or West will only resort to the use of nuclear weapons over a European issue when a conventional European war would be in progress or about to take place. Such resort he thinks unlikely if only modest forces (insufficient for the conquest of other nations) were present in Europe. In the absence of a threat to the survival of the nation, 'it is only in a disordered fantasy that one imagines leaders in Moscow or Washington pressing the red button'. More recently, Evan Luard has similarly argued that nuclear weapons have been accorded 'an altogether inflated importance'[49] and that the main danger of war today comes from conventional rather than nuclear arms. He advocates, on the one hand, a departure from current NATO strategy which relies on the threat of a nuclear response to deter a conventional attack (which he terms a 'transparent hoax') and a strengthening of conventional forces in order to ensure that they are adequate to deter a conventional attack;[50] and, on the other hand, a disarmament strategy which focuses on conventional weapons. The fact that 'nearly 95% of military expenditure today is devoted to conventional weapons [and] 100% of warfare is conducted with such weapons' suggests that this strategy should be our priority.

The inadequacy – indeed, many would argue, inanity – of the various measures proposed by the British Peace Movement can be explained by its belief that the only threat to peace is the existence of (selected) instruments of war. It either ignores that military means serve political ends or it frequently maintains that the dangers of war arise from the policies and intentions of the West rather than from those of its Communist adversary. Many in the Peace Movement who disagree with the latter view believe that the Soviet threat is less significant, however, than that posed by the nuclear armouries themselves. They fail to see that the unique predicament of our age is that it faces the double challenge of nuclear devastation and totalitarian encroachment. As Richard Falk has noted, 'The risks of the age burden us with the moral necessity to meet both challenges, although meeting one too ardently leads to an increased vulnerability to the other.'[51] The Peace Movement stands accused of being blind to the reality of this dilemma by either denying the totalitarian threat to the West or by proffering a false solution, popularly known as 'Better red than dead'.[52]

Among the most persuasive critics of the British Peace Movement (as of the Western Peace Movement generally), are citizens of totalitarian states who have the considerable courage to speak their minds (and as a result frequently are expelled or incarcerated). It is therefore not surprising that Western opponents of the Peace Movement regularly call upon those with first-hand experience of totalitarianism in order to reinforce their argument. One of the most prominent, Milovan Djilas, echoes Falk when he asserts: 'The devil is even blacker than one imagines him to be . . . The danger of nuclear war is a brutal reality, but so is the Soviet Union.'[53] But, as he indicates, the differences between East and West seem to be rendered irrelevant and insignificant by the nuclear threat which greatly contributes to the misunderstanding of the Soviet system. However, it is this system which constitutes the major obstacle to disarmament. At its centre is the Communist Party, which considers the whole outside 'capitalist' world as an enemy and regards as the duty of proletarian internationalism the undermining of the Western political and social order. Although the ideological fervour of the early Bolshevists has gone and few, if any, still wholeheartedly believe in this Soviet mission, the Soviet ruling elite, for the sake of its own legitimacy and survival, has no option but to keep the myth intact and act accordingly. Vladimir Bukovsky likewise believes that 'one of the most serious mistakes of the Western peace movement and of its ideologists is the obdurate refusal to understand the nature of the Soviet regime';[54] i.e. it fails to recognise that there is internal oppression and external aggression and that both are inseparably linked. The Soviet rulers 'need international tension as a thief needs the darkness of the night. In the political climate of latent civil war . . . the only hope for stability lies in the need to cope with an external threat: "hostile encirclement" and the subversive activity of "world imperialism".'[55] If they are frightened to the point of aggressiveness, Bukovsky suggests, it is not because of the military hardware of the West but because of its freedom and prosperity.

Whereas those in the Western Peace Movement frequently argue that the goals of peace and disarmament have a greater urgency than human rights, and that Western insistence on the latter is provocative and likely to increase Soviet hostility and to jeopardise *détente,* dissidents invariably equate peace with freedom and point out that respect for human rights, far from being a luxury (which can wait until significant disarmament has been achieved and the danger of war has subsided) is a vital ingredient of peace. While the Western Peace Movement is overwhelmingly a disarmament movement, the independent Peace Movement in Communist societies is overwhelmingly a human rights movement. Critics of the Western Peace Movement argue that it would be more effective if its strength was put in the service of the independent peace movements in the Communist world instead of, as is now commonly the case, the former aiding and abetting (whether willingly or not) the oppressor of the latter. As Bukovsky admonishes the peace movements of the West: 'There are 400 million people in the East whose freedom was stolen from them and whose existence is miserable. It so happens that peace is impossible while they remain enslaved, and only with them (not with their executioners) should you work to secure real peace in our world.'[56] This fundamental divergence regarding the meaning of peace and the suggested ways towards it accounts for the reticence which the Western Peace Movement experiences in its dealings with its East European counterpart. Václav Havel has recently provided an eloquent and sobering 'anatomy' of this reticence for the benefit of participants in END's second congress, held in Amsterdam in July 1985. He makes clear the compelling logic of the significance of human rights for the achievement of peace when he writes:

> Without internal peace, that is, peace among citizens and between the citizens and the state, there can be no guarantee of external peace: a state that ignores the will and the rights of its citizens can offer no guarantee that it will respect the will and the rights of other peoples, nations and states. A state that refuses its citizens right of public supervision of the exercise of power cannot be susceptible to international supervision . . . A state that does not hesitate to lie to its own people will not hesitate to lie to other states. All of that leads to the conclusion that a respect for human rights is the fundamental condition and the sole genuine guarantee of true peace.[57]

This interpretation of peace differs not only from the meaning which the Western Peace Movement attributes to this concept but even more so from the one underlying the official Communist 'struggle for peace'. The ubiquity of this slogan throughout the Communist world (in both geographical and historical terms) is a reflection of the importance which Communist ideology attaches to this appealing notion in its propaganda battles. Because of the equation of Communism with peace, and 'capitalism' with imperialism, militarism and war, the Communist meaning of peace is radically and perversely different from the non-Communist one. If the Soviets are talking about a peace policy, an expert on the Soviet military observes, 'the one thing . . . of which one can be quite certain is that they are *not* using it in the sense of "peace and goodwill towards the bourgeois world" '.[58] As a result of this Orwellian inversion of meaning (which is, of course, not confined to this word alone),[59] for the ordinary citizen of the Communist world 'the word "peace" has been drained of all content . . . this word awakens distrust, scepticism, ridicule and revulsion'.[60]

In view of the above it may cause little surprise that the Western Peace Movement – which is normally quick to criticise its own democratic government but not its totalitarian opponents, advocates unilateral disarmament, condones Soviet aggression, and denies that dissidents represent genuine public opinion – is regarded with scepticism and cynicism, and even outright hostility, by the informed and independent public opinion of the Communist world. As Havel points out, the reticence is mutual, and East European dissidents tend to appear to the West European Peace Movement 'as a fifth column of Western establishments east of the Yalta line'.[61] Philip Towle finds that his criticism of British unilateralism coincides with that of the independent peace movements in the Eastern bloc – CND's counterparts. Referring to one of them, the East German Peace Movement, he notes that its policy 'most closely resembles the serious multilateralism of NATO . . . while CND's is rather like that of the militarist and totalitarian East German government'.[62] His conclusion that this should lead CND to examine its conscience is likely to meet considerable resistance, since many in the Western Peace Movement believe (if they do not altogether reject the view that there is a Soviet threat and substitute an American and NATO threat) that both superpowers are equally dangerous and that the dissolution of both the alliances promises the best hope for peace. This kind of even-handedness is apparent when E. P. Thompson writes, without any qualification, 'the foreign forces in Europe today are not forces of occupation';[63] or when a Finnish supporter of the West European peace movements says that they are directed 'against the anti-democratic and totalitarian nature of advanced capitalist societies in Europe'.[64] Decisions to deploy weapons in Western Europe are also frequently depicted by its Peace Movement as enforced by the US on reluctant client states, whereas the opposite is normally nearer the truth.

Opponents of the Peace Movement find this attitude which assumes equidistance between the two superpowers morally repugnant, intellectually dishonest and politically dangerous. As the main purveyor of neutralist, anti-American and anti-NATO views, the Peace Movement is in danger of breaking up the Western alliance and jeopardising the peace it has brought. Against these views one American commentator has argued that:

> the free world is a reality and not a counterfeit construct, to be referred to sardonically in inverted commas; that its institutions represent an immense human achievement not easily duplicated; that its survival is threatened by an imperialism fully comparable in political, moral and military terms to Nazi Germany in the late 1930s; and that the future of liberty and democracy depends on the power and resolve of the U.S., not in Europe alone but in such other vital areas as the Middle East and Central America.[65]

These truths, which are appreciated by a silent majority in Europe, have been obscured, he finds, by the antics of a 'raucous minority . . . the coalition of neutralists, pacifists and Soviet apologists known by verbal usurpation as the "peace" movement'.[66] Likewise Havel, who admits to having no great illusions about the American establishment and American foreign policy, writes that 'to consider the current situation simply symmetrical, in the sense that both . . . powers are equally dangerous, appears to be a monstrous oversimplification'.[67] In view of the benevolent, generous and (in the history of international politics) untypical behaviour of the US towards its European allies since (and during) the Second World War, the Peace Movement, in its neutralist and anti-American stance, is accused by many of its critics, here and in the US, of adding insult to injury.

The attitude of moral equivalence assumes particular importance when voiced by that non inconsiderable part of the Peace Movement which is church-based. An important document in the current debate, *The Church and the Bomb* (the report of a working party of the Church of England), has been criticised, among other reasons, for affecting an even-handed objectivity between the Communist and the free worlds. Lord Chalfont, for instance, regards this 'an especially unpleasant aspect' of the report, and Ray Whitney finds it 'both wrong and deeply offensive. . . . The reality of the Soviet Union is something that the Church working party does not seem to come to grips with.'[68] Another critic writes that 'a credibility problem is presented by a report that extols exemplary disarmament but spares not so much as a couple of paragraphs on what to make of developments in Afghanistan and Poland or the blatant Soviet flouting of the non-territorial aspects of the Helsinki accords'.[69] More generally, another commentator has drawn attention to the 'general softening' of Christian political thought and to the selectivity of moral indignation as a characteristic of left–liberal Christian thinking. Whilst excepting some ecclesiastical commentators, David Martin finds that there are plenty of others who assume 'that the moral score is at best even between representatives of the Western and Soviet worlds'. He reveals the lack of political insight of certain clergy who assert that we have to accept, possibly as an instance of Christian charity, different ways of political life and imply that each political system is roughly on a moral parity. 'This liberal presupposition', Martin writes, 'is in total opposition to the view held by those who wield power in the Eastern bloc, who are armed with an ideology in which both liberalism and Christianity are part of the world that is passing away, and must inevitably give place to their system.'[70]

A persistent objection of Christian critics of the Peace Movement (in its main manifestation of unilateral nuclear disarmament) is that the vocal Christian element in this movement frequently presents its stance as the only legitimate one for Christians. It is difficult, however, to sustain the moral argument for nuclear pacifism since its presupposes the possibility of making a valid moral distinction between different kinds of weapons. In this respect the nuclear pacifist faces problems which do not arise for the outright pacifist, who believes that all war is evil and all armaments wicked. Thirty years ago, when Canon John Collins, the chairman of CND, took the moral high ground in the debate on British nuclear disarmament, other Christians accused him of making *ex cathedra* pronouncements which were not backed by reasoned argument and of committing 'a monstrous abuse of his clerical authority' by suggesting that anyone who did not accept the moral obligation of British nuclear disarmament was guilty of the height of wickedness.[71] The same absolutist claim is being made by some Christians today, and fellow Christians again are provoked to refute it by arguing that the case for deterrence and multilateral disarmament is no less moral.[72]

Lastly, a popular criticism of the British Peace Movement which must be referred to briefly is the political nature of its most important organisation, CND. It is no secret that Communists and others belonging to the far Left have always played a significant role in the organisation, and that in various ways it has been associated with Soviet or Soviet-inspired peace organisations.[73] Since CND's programme in many ways corresponds to the main objectives and goals of Soviet foreign policy, some are tempted to conclude that CND is virtually run from Moscow. This view is rejected by informed critics as paranoid; they accept that the vast majority of CND members are bona fide and that there is no reason to impugn their motives. The concern and fear of the disarmers, and the desire to bring about change through their involvement in CND, are entirely respectable. The critique of CND rests in the first place on an examination and refutation of its policies; however, given the importance which the Soviet Union attaches to the 'struggle for peace' in its political warfare, it is inevitable that CND, like the rest of the Western Peace Movement, is subjected to close scrutiny for evidence of Soviet influence.[74]

Lawrence Freedman expresses the view of most critics when he writes: 'The suggestion that the protestors are merely dupes of Kremlin propaganda is unhelpful, inaccurate and does slight justice to the real concerns that animate the protest.'[75] His own estimate of the Peace Movement goes beyond this since he acknowledges its searching questions and probing of traditional formulas that have benefited 'a tired and somewhat exclusive discussion'. Furthermore, 'few who engaged the protest groups in serious discussion could say that their views were not sharpened or altered in any way through the experience'.[76] Michael Howard, who played, albeit unintentionally, an important role in the reawakening of the recent Peace Movement, likewise credits his critics with furnishing our societies 'not only with a conscience but also with a critical intelligence' and with saving us 'from the cynical *immobilisme*'[77] that characterises bureaucratic establishments. In a 'peace setting' (cf. Beales, above) of some sort, the function of the Peace Movement is not the same as it was in the past. But as the comments of Freedman and Howard illustrate, it is unlikely that in the perennial attempt to establish peace the Peace Movement will ever become superfluous.

References

1 For an overview and criticism of such theories see Warren E. Steinkraus, 'War and the Philosopher's Duty', in Robert Ginsberg (ed.), *The Critique of War: Contemporary Philosophical Explorations*, Chicago, 1969, pp. 3–29, and the section 'Bellicist Theories' in James E. Dougherty and Robert L. Pfaltzgraff, Jr., *Contending Theories of International Relations*, Philadelphia, 1971, pp. 159–64.

2 Michael Howard, 'The causes of war', *Encounter*, March 1982, p. 23 (reprinted in his *The Causes of Wars and other Essays*, London, 1983).

3 Pitirim A. Sorokin, *Contemporary Sociological Theories* (1928), New York, 1964, esp. Ch. VI, 'Sociological Interpretation of the "Struggle for Existence" and the Sociology of War', pp. 309–56.

4 See the thought-provoking 'Reflections on the debate about nuclear weapons' by F. H. Hinsley in *The Cambridge Review*, 7 February 1981, pp. 71–4 (reprinted in David Martin and Peter Mullen (eds.), *Unholy Warfare: The Church and the Bomb*, Oxford, 1983).

5 Alun Chalfont, 'The great unilateralist illusion', *Encounter*, April 1983, p. 19. Or, as the editor of the same journal put the same idea in more graphic terms: 'What is continually distressing in the manifestos for the Peace Movement' is the offensive simple-mindedness which allows it to say, '*We* are for the survival of the smiling children, *you* are for their charcoal corpses'. Melvin J. Lasky, 'Footnotes to war and peace', *Encounter*, November 1983, p. 91.

6 F. J. Strauss, 'Peace and Pacifism', in Joseph Godson (ed.), *Challenges to the Western*

Alliance, London, 1984, p. 34.

7 He went on to indicate, however, that the word should be reserved for a more precise meaning. Cf. Martin Ceadel, *Pacifism in Britain 1914–1945: The Defining of a Faith*, Oxford, 1980, p. 146.

8 'The way of peace: a discussion', *The Listener*, 16 February 1938, as reprinted in 'King and country: that ill-starred resolution', *The Listener*, 16 February 1978, p. 196.

9 A. C. F. Beales, *The History of Peace: A Short Account of the Organised Movements for International Peace*, London, 1931, p. 317.

10 The question of whether there is a single Peace Movement is addressed by Nigel Young, *The Peace Movement in Britain: Tradition and Innovation*, Oslo, 1985 (PRIO Paper 6/85), esp. pp. 8–14.

11 Philip Towle, 'Between the Bomb and the Kremlin: strategies for peace', *Encounter*, March 1983, p. 79.

12 See, for example, Rip Bulkeley, 'The Great Wall of China: Notes on the Ideology of Nuclear Deterrence', in Nigel Blake and Kay Pole (eds.), *Objections to Nuclear Deterrence: Philosophers on Deterrence*, London, 1984, pp. 144–67.

13 Michael Howard, 'Problems of a disarmed world', in Herbert Butterfield and Martin Wight (eds.), *Diplomatic Investigations: Essays in the Theory of International Politics*, London, 1966, p. 214.

14 Hedley Bull, 'Disarmament and the International System', in John Garnett (ed.), *Theories of Peace and Security: A Reader in Contemporary Strategic Thought*, London, 1970, pp. 136–8.

15 On this kind of unilateralism (which is radically different from that advocated by the Peace Movement) see also Laurence Martin, who writes that 'it is as an organic element of [unilateral] restraint within defence policy rather than as the subject of international treaties that arms control can probably contribute most to international security'. *The Two-Edged Sword: Armed Force in the Modern World*, London, 1982, pp. 66–7.

16 Michael Howard, 'The causes of war', *Encounter*, p. 30.

17 One contemporary critic of the Peace Movement seems to believe that this is still the case today. In a chapter entitled 'Pacifist Illusions' he writes: 'Though there seems nothing to justify hopes of peace in our time, not to mention universal and perpetual peace, pacifists continue to believe . . . that the superpowers dare not use their ultimate weapons and the world will at least be spared nuclear war.' N. A. Smith, *The New Enlightenment: An Essay in Political and Social Realism*, London, 1976, p. 211. Given the anti-nuclear orientation of the British (and other Western) peace movements and their despondent attitude, the realism of this assertion is to be doubted.

18 Bull, *Theories of Peace and Security*, p. 148.

19 Hans J. Morgenthau, 'Does Disarmament Mean Peace?', in Milton L. Rakove (ed.), *Arms and Foreign Policy in the Nuclear Age*, New York, 1972, pp. 417–23.

20 Important in this context is the following assertion: 'It cannot be repeated too often that Chamberlain did appease not because he could not resist, but because he wanted to appease, as a matter of systematic policy.' University Group on Defence Policy, *The Role of the Peace Movements in the 1930s*, London, 1959 (Pamphlet no. 1), p. 11.

21 Arthur Salter, 'Neville Chamberlain: Appeasement', in his *Personality in Politics: Studies in Contemporary Statesmen*, London, 1947, p. 85.

22 Donald S. Birn, *The League of Nations Union 1918–1945*, Oxford, 1981, p. 1.

23 Ceadel, *Pacifism in Britain*, pp. 317–18.

24 Birn, *League of Nations Union*, p. 180.

25 *CND – Communists, Neutralists, Defeatists* is the title of a leaflet of the Coalition for Peace Through Security (London, 1982).

26 Quoted in *The Role of the Peace Movements*, p. 15.

27 Birn, *League of Nations Union*, p. 26.

28 This danger has recently been demonstrated again in Paul Mercer's *'Peace' of the Dead: The Truth Behind the Nuclear Disarmers*, London, 1986. In his eagerness to demonstrate the wrongheadedness of past as well as present peace movements the author commits errors of fact and interpretation. His only reference to the League of Nations Union is that it was among 'a number of smaller groups' than the Peace Pledge Union which were also involved in 'pacifist activity' (p. 49). Elsewhere he writes: 'In the 1930s Churchill and the percipient few who might have prevented the Second World War were dubbed "war-mongers" by the "peace" movement' (p. 6). This ignores the (admittedly, uneasy) alliance which existed between Churchill and the leading Peace Movement of the period (cf. Birn, *League of Nations Union, passim*).

29 Norman Podhoretz, 'Appeasement by any other name', *Commentary*, July 1983, p. 28.

30 Christopher Bartlett, for example, concludes his balanced article, 'Naval Limitation Treaties between the World Wars', by saying that 'American restraint in the early 1930s may well have been one of the contributory causes of Pearl Harbor.' Ervin Laszlo and Jong Youl Yoo (eds.), *World Encyclopedia of Peace*, 2, Oxford, 1986, p. 21.

31 See, for example, the chapter 'The Repudiation of Politics' in Hans J. Morgenthau, *Scientific Man vs. Power Politics*, Chicago, 1946.

32 Richard Harries, 'Reinhold Niebuhr's Critique of Pacifism and his Pacifist Critics' and esp. James F. Childress, 'Niebuhr's Realistic-Pragmatic Approach to War and "the Nuclear Dilemma" ', in Richard Harries (ed.), *Reinhold Niebuhr and the Issues of our Time*, London, 1986.

33 Keith Robbins, *The Abolition of War: The 'Peace Movement' in Britain, 1914–1919*, Cardiff, 1976, p. 217.

34 On the intellectual attraction of apocalypse, and the view that the Peace Movement is the principal home of apocalypticism today (and that it is a false and therefore dangerous one) see John R. Silber, 'Apocalypses then and now: the peace movement and the antinuclear crusade', *Public Opinion*, August/September 1982, pp. 42–6.

35 Laurence Martin, *The Two-Edged Sword*, pp. 11, 72.

36 E. P. Thompson, *Protest and Survive*, London and Nottingham, 1980. See also the reply by Michael Howard (the initial butt of Thompson's protest): 'Surviving a Protest', in his *The Causes of Wars*.

37 Philip Towle, Iain Elliot and Gerald Frost, *Protest and Perish: A Critique of Unilateralism*, London, 1982. A criticism commonly made of the Peace Movement is its reduction of complex issues to appealing catch-phrases (sufficiently concise and arresting for displaying on badges, banners and T-shirts). An anxious and impressionable public is easily persuaded by such appealing but deceptive slogans.

38 Philip Towle *et al.*, *Protest and Perish*, p. 52.

39 Philip Towle, 'Nationalism, the threat to NATO', *The Times*, 15 August 1983.

40 Quoted in Philip Towle *et al.*, *Protest and Perish*, p. 6.

41 Lawrence Freedman, *Britain and Nuclear Weapons,* London, 1980, p. 140. David Martin regards this and similar lofty proposals as instances of 'the old imperial *folie de grandeur* transferred to morality'. Cf. his 'The Christian Ethic and the Spirit of Security and Deterrence' in his and Peter Mullen (eds.), *Unholy Warfare,* p. 104.

42 Philip Towle *et al., Protest and Perish,* p. 85.

43 Michael Howard, 'They were wrong in the 1930s . . . and they are wrong today!', *Sunday Times,* 20 February 1983 (reprinted in *Encounter,* December 1983, pp. 22–3).

44 Quoted by Alun Chalfont, *Encounter,* p. 33. It is puzzling to see him attribute this phrase elsewhere to Ray Whitney, MP (see his contribution in David Martin and Peter Mullen (eds.), *Unholy Warfare,* p. 19. Moreover, contrary to what he writes, Whitney does not use the phrase in his contribution to the same volume).

45 Gerald Segal, Edwina Moreton, Lawrence Freedman, John Baylis, *Nuclear War and Nuclear Peace,* London, 1983, pp. 114–15.

46 *Ibid.,* pp. 55–7.

47 Lawrence Freedman, 'A criticism of the European Nuclear Disarmament Movement', *ADIU Report,* October/November 1980, p. 1.

48 Morton Kaplan, 'A Proposal to End the Danger of War in Europe', in Peter van den Dungen (ed.), *West European Pacifism and the Strategy for Peace,* London, 1985, p. 195.

49 Evan Luard, 'Exploding conventional wisdom about the Bomb', the *Independent,* 7 January 1987.

50 This point is also emphatically made by Andrei Sakharov, for example in his 'The Danger of Thermonuclear War: An Open Letter to Dr. Sidney Drell', in Sidney D. Drell, *Facing the Threat of Nuclear Weapons,* Seattle, 1983, pp. 102–3 (reprinted in Edward D. Lozansky (ed.), *Andrei Sakharov and Peace,* New York, 1985).

51 Richard A. Falk, *Law, Morality and War in the Contemporary World,* New York, 1963, p. 45.

52 A thesis argued, for instance, by Anthony Kelly, who starts his analysis, as the title of his essay indicates, from the opposite belief: 'Better Dead than Red', in Nigel Blake and Kay Pole (eds.), *Objections to Nuclear Defence,* pp. 12–27. His analysis, like most others which come to a similar conclusion (i.e. 'better Red than dead'), proceeds without any discussion of the factors which make the dilemma 'entirely illusory and the very formula . . . fatuous'. This is the view of Alexander Shtromas, who elaborates this thesis in 'Pacifism and the Contemporary International Situation' in Peter van den Dungen (ed.), *West European Pacifism,* pp. 34–50.

53 Milovan Djilas, 'Why the West must not lower its guard', *The Times,* 28 June 1983.

54 Vladimir Bukovsky, *The Peace Movement and the Soviet Union,* London, 1982, p. 41 (first published in *Commentary,* May 1982, pp. 25–41).

55 *Ibid.,* p. 51.

56 *Ibid.,* p. 57.

57 Václav Havel, *The Anatomy of a Reticence: East European Dissidents and the Peace Movements in the West,* Stockholm, 1985, p. 25.

58 In fact, he demonstrates that in Soviet diplomacy the word 'peace' is often regarded as being synonymous with 'peace and *ill*-will'. P. H. Vigor, *The Soviet View of War, Peace and Neutrality,* London, 1975, p. 169. See also the chapter 'The "Struggle for Peace" ' in Jean-François Revel's *How Democracies Perish,* New York, 1985, pp. 144–59. Some shorter studies of the Soviet concept of peace which are still useful (and

which were published during Communist peace offensives of an earlier period) are W. N. Ewer, *Communists on Peace,* London, 1953, and Leon Dennen, *The Soviet Peace Myth,* New York, 1951.

59 See, for example, R. N. Carew Hunt, *A Guide to Communist Jargon,* London, 1957, and Ilya Zemtsov, *Lexicon of Soviet Political Terms,* Fairfax, Virginia, 1984.

60 Havel, *Anatomy of a Reticence,* pp. 6–7.

61 *Ibid.,* p. 5.

62 Philip Towle *et al., Protest and Perish,* p. 94.

63 E. P. Thompson, 'The "Normalisation" of Europe', in David Martin and Peter Mullen (eds.), *Unholy Warfare,* p. 51.

64 Esko Antola, *Campaigns Against the New European Peace Movements,* Helsinki and Geneva, 1984, p. 12. 'Smearing' is an over-used word in this unimpressive document. The fact that it was commissioned and published by the International Peace Bureau will do little to restore the image of this once respected and respectable organisation which played an important role in the pre-1914 Peace Movement.

65 Norman Podhoretz, 'NATO and American Public Opinion', in Joseph Godson (ed.), *Challenges to the Western Alliance,* p. 108.

66 *Ibid.*

67 Havel, *Anatomy of a Reticence,* p. 28.

68 Lord Chalfont, 'Unilateralism, Neutralism and Pacifism', p. 17, and Ray Whitney, 'Peace through Arms Control', pp. 24–5 in David Martin and Peter Mullen (eds.), *Unholy Warfare.*

69 Neville Brown, 'The Church and the Bomb: a critical review', *ADIU Report,* November/December 1982, p. 7.

70 David Martin, 'The Christian Ethic and the Spirit of Security and Deterrence', in his and Peter Mullen (eds.), *Unholy Warfare,* pp. 101–4.

71 See, for example, the debate in the letter columns of *The Times,* reprinted in *The Nuclear Dilemma: Letters to the Editor,* London, 1958, esp. pp. 38–45. The reading of a history of the Peace Movement leaves a strong impression of 'plus ça change, plus c'est la même chose', as Nicholas Sims discovered. Cf. Lorna Lloyd and Nicholas Sims, *British Writing on Disarmament from 1914 to 1978: A Bibliography,* London, 1979, pp. 11–12.

72 The latter case is presented in Francis Bridger (ed.), *The Cross and the Bomb: Christian Ethics and the Nuclear Debate,* London, 1983, and in several contributions in John Gladwin (ed.), *Dropping the Bomb: The Church and the Bomb Debate,* London, 1985. That the churches have failed to influence substantially the terms of the moral debate about nuclear weapons, owing to the general secularisation of Christian values in the West, is argued by T. E. Utley and Edward Norman, *Ethics and Nuclear Arms: British Churches and the Peace Movement,* London, 1983, which is severely critical of both.

73 See Paul Mercer, *'Peace' of the Dead,* and Clive Rose, *Campaigns Against Western Defence: NATO's Adversaries and Critics,* London, 1985. The latter book, by a former UK Ambassador to NATO, is both more general in its coverage of the Peace Movement and more generous in its treatment of it.

74 See, for example, Alexander Shtromas, 'The Soviet Union and the Politics of Peace', pp. 129–57, and Claude Harmel, 'The Soviet Union and the Uses of Pacifism', pp. 158–70, in Peter van den Dungen (ed.), *West European Pacifism;* Wynfred Joshua,

'Soviet manipulation of the European peace movement', *Strategic Review*, Winter 1983, pp. 9–18; Gerhard Wettig, 'The Western peace movement in Moscow's longer view', in *ibid.*, Spring 1984, pp. 44–54.

75 Lawrence Freedman, 'Tell and Trust the People', in Godson (ed.), *Challenges to the Western Alliance*, p. 111.

76 Lawrence Freedman, *The Price of Peace: Living with the Nuclear Dilemma*, London, 1986, p. 7.

77 Michael Howard, *The Causes of Wars*, p. 72.

Britain and the International Peace Movement in the 1980s

RICHARD TAYLOR
AND NIGEL YOUNG

The British Peace Movement in the 1980s

After a period of quiescence,[1] the British Peace Movement, in common with similar movements throughout Western, and to an extent Eastern, Europe, erupted into mass activism in the early 1980s. Mass demonstrations in 1981, for example, took place in London and eleven other major European cities, involving between two and three million people.[2] By the mid-1980s, national membership of CND – Britain's largest peace organisation – exceeded 100,000, and its annual budget was over £1 million. This compares with CND's small pressure-group existence of the 1970s when its membership was a few thousand, its budget minimal, and its public impact virtually nil. The renewed growth of the International Peace Movement was thus rapid and dramatic, and captured public (and media) attention.

The Peace Movement of the 1980s fanned out from the Netherlands to Germany and Britain, to Belgium and Italy; it elicited the first signs of an independent peace mood in Eastern Europe; it steadily expanded through Scandinavia and the Mediterranean; it reached the United States; and, last of all, France. These campaigns had their decisive catalyst in the December 1979 NATO decisions to deploy a new generation of missiles in the context of what appeared to many as a new Cold War, and of the abandoning of serious disarmament negotiation after SALT 2 was left unratified.

The arms race seemed to be accelerating; there was a feeling that neither the superpowers nor the independent nuclear powers in Europe had any will to initiate serious efforts at disarmament or nuclear disengagement. A number of things contributed in Britain at least to a new sense of international tension and potential escalation of the kind experienced in the years from 1960 to 1963: the debate over the Moscow Olympic boycott, the propaganda use of the Afghan occupation, fears over American adventures in Iran and tensions in the Middle East, the war-fighting rhetoric of some Western leaders, and governmental civil defence preparations.[3] The brash assertiveness of Thatcher and Reagan merely confirmed existing fears, as did the nuclear alerts and accidents of 1980–81,[4] and the horrific Chernobyl disaster of 1986, and lent impetus to the groundswell of public opinion throughout Europe.

This was a more transnational and massive protest than anything in the sixties, and it also involved a broader political coalition with new elements contributed during the period of the Vietnam War and by the women's, environmental and anti-nuclear power movements. These gave a transnational as well as international dimension to the protest, together with new forms of political organisation, less reliance on formal structure and leadership, and a greater political awareness.[5]

The churches were also more centrally involved than they had been in the nuclear disarmament campaigns twenty years earlier. Following the example of the Dutch churches, the Church of England, often in the past called the Tory Party at prayer, produced a commission report advocating a non-nuclear Britain.[6] Yet a further new dimension, particularly apparent in Britain, was a grass-roots movement for peace education in and out of schools, organised from below by parents, pupils, teachers, local councillors and churches. This was of such strength that the British Secretary of State attacked it publicly as 'appeasement' education, and the Government widely circulated its own counter-propaganda. In response, in 1981 the Labour Party Shadow Education Secretary called for peace studies in every school.[7]

Probably the key factor in salvaging CND, and 'resurrecting' it as the major organisational focus of the British Peace Movement in the 1980s, was the astute and sensitive leadership of Mgr Bruce Kent as Secretary, and Joan Ruddock as Chairperson of the Campaign. However, and unlike the fifties and sixties, a multitude of other local peace groups, women's groups, peace programmes, peace action groups, peace camps, anti-Cruise missile campaigns, European disarmament (END), and other groups arose in each locality. Sometimes they paralleled CND groups, and sometimes they took the place of CND groups, but were often affiliated to CND.

Also, in 1978, the World Disarmament Campaign (WDC) was created, as a consequence of the first United Nations Special Session on Disarmament (SSDI), by the late Philip Noel-Baker and Fenner Brockway, in order to campaign for non-governmental, and largely multilateralist, initiatives through the UN Special Session on Disarmament II in New York in June 1982. Despite setbacks owing to lack of progress at the UN, the WDC continued its campaigning through the 1980s and many local peace groups used its propaganda material.

The Freeze movement, a similarly broad-based, eclectic initiative, was launched in 1984, largely as a result of the growing importance of its American counterpart.

Whilst both organisations attracted support from a wide constituency, their role was somewhat superficial and tangential to the main core of Peace Movement activism because they lacked both political focus and political dynamism. As with the 'Steps to Peace' initiative of the 1960s, it was not the content of their programmes but their generalised, politically unexciting and morally ambivalent positions which explained their relative lack of impact.

The policy objectives of CND, and to a large extent of the wider Peace Movement, incorporated most of the central demands that were put by the Movement in the 1960s, but less emphasis was placed upon unilateral nuclear disarmament *per se* and rather more on the immediate issues of Cruise and Trident. Although CND policy is fixed at annual conference, and therefore varies over time, the Campaign's aims and priorities can be seen in the following extracts from its constitution and its broadsheet *Steps to Survival*:

Aims
The aim of the Campaign for Nuclear Disarmament is the unilateral abandonment by Britain of nuclear weapons, nuclear bases and nuclear alliances as a pre-requisite for a British foreign policy which has the world-wide abolition of nuclear, chemical and biological weapons leading to general and complete disarmament as its prime objective.

The Campaign for Nuclear Disarmament is opposed to the manufacture, stockpiling, testing, use and threatened use of nuclear, chemical and biological weapons by any country, and the policies of any country or group of countries which make nuclear war more likely, or which hinder progress towards a world without weapons of mass destruction. Steps to survival:

1. Stop the Trident nuclear submarine.
2. Refuse all Cruise missiles.

3. Get rid of all other nuclear weapons and bases from Britain.
4. Introduce less aggressive forms of conventional defence.
5. Put our weight behind the creation of a nuclear-free zone in Europe.
6. Put pressure on both the USA and USSR for a freeze on the development, production and deployment of new nuclear weapons. Call for the dismantling of existing weapons on both sides.
7. If the USA or other NATO countries refuse to follow this path, consider Britain's position in NATO and if necessary withdraw.
8. Promote the implementation of the Non-proliferation Treaty to stop the spread of nuclear weapons to other countries.
9. Call for and contribute to the redirecting of resources from arms production to socially useful production both here and in the Third World.
10. Start to find ways of cutting back on all weapons of mass destruction in every country so that the world's peoples can live without violence and fear.

The major debates in the British Peace Movement remained as in the sixties, the issue of alignment, NATO membership, the role of British peace activity *vis-à-vis* Europe, and the relationship with the Labour Party. Civil disobedience has been a much less divisive issue than in the 1960s. The overwhelming consensus accepted mass NVDA, and training for it, as necessary to obstruct deployment. This shift in opinion was partly due to the civil disobedience campaigns of 1959–63 and the direct actions against Polaris and US bases, and partly, in the seventies, due to those against nuclear power plants. Not least, civil disobedience gained new respect due to admiration for the symbolic witness of the strongly feminist camps at Greenham Common (with Comiso in Sicily, one of the first sites for Cruise missiles) and Molesworth: these were among at least ten peace camps in the 1980s in Britain, and there were others in Germany, Italy, and Holland. In addition there has been a marked *increase* in extra-parliamentary politics, and emphasis upon individuals and groups taking their own decisions on the whole range of social and poltical matters – from children's pelican crossings to the abolition of nuclear weapons. Moreover, there has been a similarly marked *decrease* in the centrality afforded to parliamentary politics, and a growth in society at large of scepticism of all politicians and political parties. (These issues are discussed in more detail below, in the context of the movement's political strategies for advance.)

New strands in the Movement

There are four factors of particular importance in the Movement of the 1980s, all of which have had a major impact: the European dimension; the 'Greens'; the Women's Movement; and the changes in the Labour Party. The latter two aspects have been discussed in some detail in Chapters 6 and 10 (and are returned to briefly in the concluding section of this chapter). Here, attention is concentrated on the other two areas.

The European Nuclear Disarmament movement (END) stemmed from Britain, and represented a significant new strategic ingredient in Europe. An appeal drafted by E. P. Thompson and edited by Ken Coates was circulated in 1980 by the Bertrand Russell Peace Foundation in Nottingham with support from other Europeans. From the appeal sprang an inchoate END organisation of signatories and subscribers with a shadow organisation in London which produced a newsletter and organised collateral groups. By the early 1980s END or similar groups existed all over Western and Northern Europe and to some extent in Eastern Europe too. END played a major role in organising the European Peace Conventions, which brought together large numbers of activists from all Western European peace movements (at various locations: Brussels, Berlin, Perugia, Amsterdam, etc.), and involved also activists from both the official and dissident peace movements of Eastern Europe.

END added a new emphasis on transnational linkage and non-alignment to the Peace Movement. Its campaigns were for a nuclear-free Europe or a nuclear-free zone or zones in Europe (e.g. Nordic, Balkan, Central European). Based on these demands, it tried to link the national unilateralist and multilateralist groups into a common third force crossing national boundaries and bridging East and West.[8] Its slogans, 'No Cruise, no SS20s' or 'An end to NATO and the Warsaw Pact', a nuclear-free zone 'from Poland to Portugal' (or 'Atlantic to the Urals') were accused of being a crude attempt at evenhandedness, naïve about the possibilities of unfreezing the Cold War or generating an independent peace movement in the East.[9]

In response, END argued that such a political shake-up was an essential part of any strategy to disarm Europe: forcing both the superpowers back into their national fortresses of mutual assured destruction was Utopianism with a strong dash of strategic realism.

END recognised that greater Europe was a key sector if theatre nuclear weapons were to be deployed alongside the battlefield ones already in place.[10] The paralysis of Europe represented by Communist Party government in the East, and even the Social Democratic governments in the West, could be alleviated only by a cross-national and non-governmental campaign built from within the regions and communities, which challenged the hegemony of the nuclear monoliths and the lesser 'independent' nuclear powers of France and Britain.

One effect of END in Britain was to create pressure on CND to be clearly non-aligned between East and West, to broaden to an internationalist and European approach, and also to open up dialogue between unilateralists and multilateralists around the ideas of reciprocal initiatives and regional nuclear-free zones.[11]

In this debate, movements like CND questioned whether 'multilateral' approaches or calls for 'general and complete disarmament' by negotiation, or bilateral arms control or limitation, were either sincere or effective campaigning platforms.

Thus 'unilateralism' was seen as essential, but it had to be accompanied by the building of a network of such unilateral, graduated steps across Europe – East and West – as a programme and strategy that would become multilateral at the level of the Movement *as well as* in talks between political leaders.

END also gave to the local grass-roots movements the idea that they could create their own local nuclear-free zones by winning 130 British local authorities (including the whole of Wales) over to the idea, creating community nuclear-free zones, and then pairing them with nuclear-free municipalities on the European continent. Through END many British peace activists were also brought into contact with the grass-roots activism and ideas of the European movement. This has been a critical factor in internationalising movements like the British, which were narrowly insular and inward-looking in the 1960s, as was discussed in Chapter 6.

Overall, then, END has inherited much of the politics of the New Left of the 1957 to 1962–63 period (see Chapter 8): it has maintained that strand within the Peace Movement that holds to 'positive neutralism', and to the need for the Movement to be linked clearly into a radical, 'Third Way' foreign policy perspective, which argues not only for *détente* between the superpowers but for the forging of a new socialist but also democratic and humanistic ideology. Indeed, the foremost figures in END are themselves from this broad tradition, and the most notable campaigner of all, E. P. Thompson, was himself among the most prominent and creative activists in the New Left of the 1950s and 1960s. The major difference in the 1980s is thus not over ideology – the underlying positions of the New Left and of END are very similar – but over specific policy demands (such as those mentioned earlier), and over the international nature of the Movement. In both these respects END's politics in the 1980s is in a far stronger and more positive position than was the case with the New Left in the earlier period.

Such strengths were enhanced considerably in the 1970s and 1980s by the development and prominence of the ecological, or Green movement. The Green movement became an international phenomenon of considerable political importance in the 1970s and 1980s, and was especially prominent in North America and West Germany. Its perspective went far beyond orthodox politics and cannot be classified within conventional ideological categories. Thus, whilst the Greens were certainly radical, they were neither fully 'socialist' nor fully 'anarchist', though they had strong tendencies towards certain tenets of both socialism and anarchism (their belief in greater equality, and their distrust of centralisation and the modern state, for example). Central to Green politics was a concern both with the protection of the natural environment, and with a radical re-ordering of values, relationships and political structures.[12] They emphasised the importance – and legitimacy – of linking local community initiatives to globalism and environmentalism.

The result of industrial civilisation for the Greens has been the stark immorality of resource misallocation, so that, for example, 'what is spent in just *two* weeks (on armaments) could house, clothe and feed *everyone* in need for a year'.[13] The Greens stressed the need for a radical change in patterns of consumption and in individual and social attitudes. Their concentration was upon neither class nor gender but upon ecological and defence issues (though they supported both greater social equality and feminist objectives). Thus the Green Party (formerly the Ecology Party), Friends of the Earth (the primary non-electoral campaigning organisation) and Greenpeace were linked closely to peace movement activities and concerns, and in the latter case especially, had a considerable international impact.

Nuclear weapons were seen by the Greens as the culmination of a whole social structure fundamentally out of touch with both human needs and environmental reality. In this sense, nuclear disarmament was seen not as a single, autonomous issue, but as part of the wider struggle to reorientate and restructure human society. Similarly, opposition to nuclear power has been central to the Greens' concerns (as it has to those of the Peace Movement generally, in marked contrast to the 1950s and 1960s). In part, this was because of the mounting evidence of very serious environmental damage resulting from radioactive waste emanating from nuclear power stations (viz. the beaches of the Cumbrian coast polluted by the leaks from Windscale/Sellafield); and, of course, there was in the background the very real possibility of a major nuclear power disaster. Opposition to nuclear power has also been based in part, however, upon the now proven connection between nuclear power and nuclear weapons. 'The plutonium connection between nuclear power and nuclear weapons is so inextricable that lasting nuclear disarmament remains an improbable dream until such time as the last nuclear reactor is finally decommissioned.'[14]

In various contexts the Greens have thus been active in the Peace Movement: at Torness in their NVDA opposition to nuclear power installations; at Greenham and Molesworth peace camps; and in the organisation of 'Green gatherings' (held near Glastonbury, and attracting several thousand participants to a large number of events and workshops 'on every Green subject under the sun').[15] Even more important than such examples of direct activism, however, has been the Greens' role in broadening out the Peace Movement's constituency. No longer, by the mid-1980s, was the Movement seen as concerned exclusively with defence and strategic issues (and still less with the complex 'number-crunching' technicalities of the hardware specialists). The Movement was recognised as having direct, and exciting, *political* aspects, as illustrated by the discussion of END earlier, *and* as linking in directly to the pervasive concern of large sections of society with conservation, ecological and related issues.

In these senses then – and especially given the influence of the Women's Movement and the positive changes in the Labour Movement discussed in earlier chapters – the Peace Movement, by the mid-1980s, was deep-rooted, prominent and well-established as a major social and political force. Perhaps more than ever before, there were real prospects for success on both immediate policy issues (Cruise, Trident, Civil Defence, etc.), and on longer-term political and cultural changes.[16]

The problems facing the Movement

This is not to say, of course, that the Movement faces no problems in the remaining years of the twentieth century! As has been pointed out on numerous occasions, despite the huge and international growth of the Peace Movement since 1979, not one single new missile in Britain or the rest of Europe has been dismantled, and the arms race escalates relentlessly. Although the 'Gorbachev initiatives' of the later 1980s offer real hope of significant arms reductions, the fact remains that, despite their campaigning, the Peace Movements in Britain and elsewhere have not yet achieved any of their central objectives.

The crucial problems for the Movement remain as they have been for many years – and as they have applied, generally, to most political movements seeking radical, 'Left-oriented' change. These problems centre on two related areas: the appropriate agency or agencies for change, and the appropriate strategies to achieve those changes.

The Peace Movement in the 1980s, as in the 1960s, has all the advantages and disadvantages which apply to mass issue movements: it has the ability to mobilise vast numbers of people, and attracts a very wide and disparate measure of support for its policies in the community as a whole. (With the notable exception of the period of the general election campaign in 1983,[17] public opinion polls have showed consistently that there are clear majorities against the siting of Cruise missiles and the development of Trident.) But such 'umbrella' support is fragile in two crucial respects. Much of the support is at a superficial level, and is liable to be swayed fairly easily by concentrated propaganda or by a change in political 'fashions': the remarkable changes in public opinion during the 1983 general election campaign are one indication of this; others include the relatively low percentage of the population supporting unilateral nuclear disarmament (usually around thirty per cent) and the even lower number favouring withdrawal from NATO. Secondly, whilst there is a measure of agreement over the objectives of the Movement in specific policy terms – although such agreement is by no means total – there is a wide disparity of ideological stance amongst the different strands of the Movement. Thus there are enormous potential problems and conflicts between Labour Party supporters, Trotskyists, anarchists, Greens, feminists, Liberals, radical secular pacifists, Quakers and other Christian Pacifists, Communists, the 'apolitical' moral protesters, and other groupings in the

Movement.[18] Such problems are, of course, much more likely to arise, usually in terms of mutual recrimination, when the Movement is in crisis and decline; and this is indeed what happened in the early 1960s, with the resultant internecine feuding, fragmentation, and reversion of each tendency to its own, more uncompromising, ideological stance.

Even were they able to avoid such pitfalls – which is unlikely[19] – issue movements cannot of themselves attain their objectives. Some other, political, agency is required: and it is in this sense that such movements are to be seen as 'pressure groups' rather than autonomous political forces or embryonic political *parties*.[20] Thus the question of agency becomes crucial: if such movements cannot of themselves achieve their objectives, which agencies should they work through and with? In Britain, in the post-1945 period at least, several solutions to this problem have been posited: the Labour Party path of parliamentary reformism; one or other of the Marxist scenarios; the mobilising of mass public opinion, on a 'moral' basis, so that governments will be *compelled* to change their policies; NVDA, merging into anarchistic, or 'alternativist' scenarios of various types, centring on the Gandhian concepts of mass, radical, coercive but non-violent direct action;[21] or the Green scenarios of greater local control over major decision-making.

None of these strategies is viable in exclusivity. And all have severe, and often fundamental, weaknesses at both the theoretical, conceptual and practical, political levels, as has been argued in earlier chapters of this book, and as we have argued elsewhere.[22] The history of the Movement in the 1960s demonstrated both the difficulties of bringing together the disparate groupings within the Movement, and the necessity for overcoming such fragmentation if progress were to be achieved.

There were, and are, moreover, longer-term, structural and ideological barriers to radical progressive change in Britain. In brief, these can be summarised as: the overwhelmingly conservative (and nationalist) culture which has prevailed in Britain not for decades but for centuries, and shows every sign of persisting through the twentieth century: and the bureaucratic, militaristic impetus underlying the arms race and the powerful technological institutions whose vested interests are so influential in supporting armaments development. This latter factor has resulted, so it is argued,[23] in the arms race moving beyond rational, political control: the world is dominated by an insane, inhuman 'exterminist' impulse.

Given these problems at both the specific and the general levels, can the Movement succeed in its aims, or will it be subject to the cyclical process which has characterised the history of such Movements internationally in the twentieth century, and which has resulted in a world far *more* violent and conflict-ridden?[24] It is to a consideration of this question that attention is finally turned.

Conclusion: the future of the British Peace Movement

The success of the Peace Movement internationally – in the sense of, first, the avoidance of nuclear war, and, second, the creation of a positively peaceful international social and political order – is without question the most important issue confronting humankind. All other issues are, after all, predicated upon human existence.

Our concerns here, however, are necessarily somewhat narrower and more parochial, though it must always be remembered that the British Peace Movement, as other such movements, has its ultimate meaning only within this international, long-term context. Internationally, as has been noted earlier, the Movement is stronger, more widespread, and more prominent than ever before. But it has become so, of course, in part because of the escalation of the Cold War and the arms race, the collapse of *détente,* and the belligerent stances of the superpowers and their acolytes.

In the British and European context any significant advance by the Peace Movement must include a broad internationalist stance with alternative foreign and defence policies clearly articulated – and subsequently adopted – as a part of the programme.[25] In Britain in the 1980s the prospects for the Peace Movement attaining such a breakthrough are better than at any time since the onset of the nuclear Cold War in the 1940s.

Despite the strength of the forces ranged against it, and despite the bureaucratic inertia of military and state institutions (as argued in the 'exterminist' thesis), there is now a greater unity and strength, and, equally important, a stronger and more firmly based non-aligned Left, within the Peace Movement. The non-aligned Left – the heirs to the New Left of the earlier period and espousing very similar political perspectives – has had a crucial catalytic role to play in bringing together the disparate elements of the peace coalition, and has developed within a more favourable context than was the case in the

1960s.[26] There are three aspects to this. First, the socio-economic, and cultural, instability of the social order in the 1980s has led to a greater degree of alienation and questioning of the status quo throughout society, thereby providing, *inter alia,* greater opportunities for the growth of a radical neo-socialist stratum. (Although it should be noted that this has not resulted in any growth of support for the 'orthodox', established groups on the Left, whether the Labour Party, the Communist Party or the Trotskyist groups.)[27] Second, the radical 'disaffected' middle-class stratum has grown considerably in the 1970s as a result of the expansion of tertiary education and the onset of the recession. Within this context the growth of the Women's Movement has been of key importance – particularly in relation to the Peace Movement (see Chapter 10). And, of course, the Women's Peace Movement has been a major *international* phenomenon. For example, the women's marches from Scandinavia, first to Paris and then to Moscow, have played a key part in spreading the Movement symbolically and in establishing cross-border links. They helped to give the Women's Movement a major role in the Peace Movement and, like the human arm-chain linking the US and Russian embassies in Stockholm, made this *transnationalism* more real, inspiring groups elsewhere, as at Greenham.

Finally, the Labour Party, as analysed in Chapter 6 (and some sections of the Marxist Left, as analysed in Chapter 8), have become more genuinely and fundamentally committed to Peace Movement policies and more tolerant and eclectic in their approach. Thus, not only has the Labour Party committed itself specifically to Peace Movement policies on Cruise, Trident, US bases and unilateral nuclear disarmament, but it has also moved its overall politics, to a significant extent, into the arena of co-operation and empathy with the predominantly extra-parliamentary radicalism of the Peace Movement.

Problems of a frightening magnitude of course remain, and many of these are beyond the *direct* influence of the British – or any other – Peace Movement initiatives. But, if the problems of the 'exterminist' drift are to be overcome, it is surely through the creative interaction of orthodox, party-centred initiatives and electoral propagandising, *and* the extra-parliamentary movements of popular mobilisation and transnational character that have been created in the 1980s.

Both aspects of the Movement have local as well as national dimensions, and one of the key strengths of the Movement in the 1980s has been the building of deep-rooted, grass-roots support, located securely, in ideological as well as institutional terms. In that sense, the Movement of the 1980s is significantly stronger than at any time in the recent past, and is a central part of a genuinely 'alternative culture'.

The British Peace Movement has a long and varied history, as this study has illustrated, but the tasks that lie ahead are of greater magnitude and greater importance than at any time in the past. It has the potential to achieve its objectives but, as always, the end result of its activism will depend upon the complex interaction of human endeavour and external circumstances.

References

1 For discussion of the decline of the Peace Movement in Britain from the mid-1960s onwards, see Nigel Young, *An Infantile Disorder? The Crisis and Decline of the New Left*, Routledge and Kegan Paul, 1977; John Minnion and Philip Bolsover (eds.), *The CND Story*, Allison and Busby, 1983; and Richard Taylor and Colin Pritchard, *The Protest Makers, the British Nuclear Disarmament Movement of 1958 to 1965, Twenty Years on*, Pergamon Press, 1980.

2 Among the cities where major demonstrations were held in 1981 were: London, Bonn, Brussels, Paris, Athens, Bucharest, Rome, Madrid, Amsterdam, Helsinki, Oslo, Berlin, Stockholm and Copenhagen.

3 One of the key moments in Britain was when Edward Thompson responded in style to the Government's Civil Defence brochure, *Protect and Survive*, with his own pamphlet which was also a riposte to a military strategic thinker, Michael Howard of the Institute of Strategic Studies. (*Protect and Survive*, Nottingham, Spokesman, 1981.) This latter sold tens of thousands of copies in 1980. For a more theoretical critique see Thompson's 'Notes on exterminism', *New Left Review*, 121, May/June 1981, reprinted in Thompson's *Exterminism and Cold War*, Verso and New Left Books, 1982.

4 One must include in this the Three Mile Island disaster, when confidence in the safety of civil nuclear power programmes was severely shaken, fuelling public suspicion of official nuclear weapons policy.

5 In the Netherlands, Germany, and Britain there were mass anti-nuclear protests between 1958 and 1963: so that the 1980s movements in those countries, their symbols and tactical slogans represented a revived, rather than an entirely new, movement. In these and many other countries, lateral groups (or 'affinity' or 'like-minded' groups), have emerged, especially among church people, peace teachers, trade unionists, anti-war feminists, ecologists, conscientious objectors, and councillors in nuclear-free municipalities: the list is a long one.

6 *The Church and the Bomb*, Church Commissioners, 1982, reviewed in the *Guardian*, 18 December 1982. Rejected by the Synod in February 1983. See Ch. 9.

7 The Shadow Minister was Neil Kinnock, interviewed in *World Studies Journal*, 3 June 1981. For a more extensive account of this debate in Britain and beyond, see Nigel Young, 'The new Peace Education Movement', *Perspectives*, 1, February 1983.

8 END has been accused of 'unilateralism' by the UN-oriented WDC (World Disarmament Campaign) and 'multilateralism' by some in CND. What it really does is to try to bridge the gap by linking unilateral initiatives into some overall multilateral (or regional, or bilateral) scheme, and not only at the state level. Obviously reciprocity is desirable, indeed essential, and without it the END strategy ultimately will fail, and with it any hope for the success of the European nuclear-free zone idea.

9 Through END and similar groups and movements the ideas of socialist internationalism have been revived with a concern both for anti-militarism and human rights. This synthesis has been missing from the Peace Movement for a very long time (although it was implicit in the early Vietnam War protests).

10 It is the fear of escalation from first use of battlefield nuclear weapons (e.g. in Germany) that has led to proposals like the Palme Commission Report, advocating a battlefield nuclear weapons-free zone (strip) in Central Europe, although this is much less than END is demanding.

11 CND's internationalist work in the 1960s consisted of exchanges of marchers and speakers with other anti-nuclear movements; the formation of the International Confederation for Disarmament and Peace (ICDP) in 1963 as a non-aligned alternative to the World Peace Council; and public support for the non-aligned movement (of mainly Third World powers). In this respect it was both slower and more limited in building its cross-border ties and more governmental in orientation.

12 See, for example, *Embrace the Earth: A Green View of Peace,* CND publication, 1983.

13 *Ibid.,* p. 10.

14 *Ibid.,* p. 18.

15 Letter from Peter Cadogan to Richard Taylor, 22 August 1983.

16 On the policy issues much valuable work has been undertaken by the Alternative Defence Commission in its various reports, most notably *Defence without the Bomb,* Taylor and Francis, 1983; *Without the Bomb,* Granada, 1985; and *The Politics of Alternative Defence,* London, Paladin, 1987. The emergence of a large number of authoritative professional groups (e.g. doctors, engineers, etc.) has also been of a great benefit to the Movement in the 1980s.

17 See Richard Taylor, 'CND and the 1983 Election', in Ivor Crewe and Martin Harrop (eds.), *Political Communication: the General Election Campaign of 1983,* Cambridge University Press, 1986, pp. 207–16.

18 For a discussion of these differences in the context of the Movement in the 1958 to 1965 period, see Taylor and Pritchard, *The Protest Makers.*

19 See Richard Taylor and Kevin Ward, 'Community Politics and direct action: the non-aligned Left', in D. Coates and G. Johnston (eds.), *Socialist Strategies,* Martin Robertson, Oxford, 1983, for further discussion of single-issue movements.

20 For discussion of this distinction see, for example, W. N. Coxall, *Parties and Pressure Groups,* Longman, Harlow, 1980, and R. M. Punnett, *British Government and Politics,* (4th edn), Heinemann, London, 1980.

21 Richard Taylor would like to take this opportunity of acknowledging that in one specific instance he has misrepresented, inadvertently, Michael Randle's views of direct action politics. The issue in question relates to the strategy of the direct action movement in the early 1960s and specifically to the decision, after the 17 September sit-down in 1960, to organise demonstrations at the bases in December.

Randle's view was, and is, that if there was going to be an insurrectionary stage then the Movement was clearly far from it. However, if tens of thousands of people could have been persuaded to take NVDA at the bases, this would have had an enormous impact just as later demonstrations at nuclear power plants have done.

The use of a quotation from an interview with Michael Randle gives the false impression that he judged the success of the campaign on the basis of how far it could *physically* impede the Government's nuclear war preparations. This was not, clearly, his position.

Both on this specific point, and in the more general context, therefore, Richard Taylor would like to make it quite clear that any impression given in his various writings that Randle is in agreement with his analysis is quite erroneous, and to apologise if that impression has been given inadvertently.

22 For further discussion of these strategic and political questions, see Young, *An Infantile Disorder?*; Taylor and Pritchard, *The Protest Makers*; Richard Taylor, 'The British Peace Movement and Socialist Change', in Ralph Miliband and John Saville (eds.), *Socialist Register 1983*, Merlin Press, London, 1983.

23 See E. P. Thompson, 'Notes on Exterminism', in Thompson *et al.*, *Exterminism and Cold War*, Verso and New Left Books, London, 1982.

24 On the cyclical nature of peace movements, see Nigel Young, 'Why peace movements fail', *Social Alternatives*, Vol. 4, No. 1, March 1984.

25 The work of the Alternative Defence Commission in Britain has been of central importance in this context, as has the research and analysis of central aspects of defence and foreign policy by CND.

26 For discussion of this, see Richard Taylor, 'The British Peace Movement and Socialist Change'.

27 Indeed, membership of all three has declined since 1980.

Index

'exterminism' 2, 4, 193

Fairbairns, Zoë 121
Falk, Richard 275
Families Against the Bomb 241
Fascism, Fascists and the Peace Movement 73, 84–97, 266
Fawcett, Millicent 222–4
Federal Union 96
Fellowship of Reconciliation (FOR) 12, 19, 38, 76, 78, 94, 191, 205, 214, 227
Feminist Peace Movement see Women's Peace Movement
First World War see world wars
Fishwick, Gertrude 199, 236
Foot, Michael 101, 106, 113, 124
Fox, George 24
Franco, General 89
Frankau, Pamela 207
Freedman, Lawrence 274, 281
Freeze movement 289
Friedan, Betty 239
Friends of the Earth 293
Friends' Peace Committee 207
Fryer, Peter 173
(East) Fulham by-election, 1933, 85

Gaitskell, Hugh 102, 103, 105, 107, 110, 111–19, 125–6, 146
Gale, Jack 175
Gamble, Mary 234
Gandhi, Mohandas, K. 2, 7, 14, 20, 94, 132, 233
Gbedemah, Mr 133
general elections:
    1951 102
    1959 102, 105, 109, 126, 167
    1970 121
    1974 121
    1983 101–2
Gibbs, Olive 106, 236–7
GMWU 108–9, 116
Gollan, John 166–7
Gollancz, Victor 207
Gorbachev 295
Gore-Booth, Eva 229
Goss, Arthur 106
Gray, Revd Herbert 83
'Greenham women', Greenham Common 13, 20, 131, 221, 241–6, 250–3, 290, 298
Greenpeace 294

'Greens', Green Party, the 3, 170, 172, 184, 214, 288, 291, 293–5
Gregg, R. 234
Groom, A. J. R. 199
Guild Socialism 147

Haldane 56–7
Hall, Stuart 115, 177, 182
Hardie, Frank 262
Hardie, Keir 15, 27–8, 32, 43, 52, 78
Harries, Richard, Bishop of Oxford 212–13
Harrington, protest at 1, 35
Hart, Judith 104
Hattersley, Roy 179
Havel, Václav 277–9
Hawkes, Jacquetta 100, 106–7, 237
Hayek, F. A. 96
H-Bomb National Campaign 107, 206
Healey, Denis 123, 179
Healy, Gerry 175
Henderson, Arthur 57
Heseltine, Michael 123
Hinkes, Revd Sidney 209
Hinton, James 67
Hiroshima (and Nagasaki), bombing of 66–7, 193–4, 197–8, 205–6
Hirst, Francis 30
Hitler 84–7, 92, 96, 205–6, 234
Hoare–Laval agreement 88
Holtom, Gerald 134
Holy Loch, protests at 131, 135, 137, 138, 149, 157
Horner, John 107
Howard, Michael 264, 272, 281
Hoyland, Francis 136
Huddleston, Trevor, C. R. 106, 207
Hughes, Father Gerard 213
Hungarian uprising, 1956 133, 273
Huxley, Aldous 24, 91

Independent Labour Party (ILP) 14–16, 27, 34, 41, 52, 56–8, 60, 62–3, 65, 68, 84, 93, 124, 147, 222, 227
Independent Nuclear Disarmament Election Committee (INDEC) 119, 146, 153
industrial conscription 40
Inge, Dean 273
International Committee of Women for Permanent Peace (ICWPP) see also WILPF 224